JHN E. WILLIAMS

EDERICK E. TRINKLEIN

CLARK METCALFE

modern physics
EXERCISES and EXPERIMENTS
in PHYSICS

Holt, Rinehart and Winston, Publishers
New York • London • Toronto • Sydney

JOHN E. WILLIAMS, 2947 Java Road, Costa Mesa, Californ 92626; formerly physics and chemistry teacher at Newport H bor High School, Newport Beach, California; and Head of Science Department, Broad Ripple High School, Indianapo Indiana.

FREDERICK E. TRINKLEIN, 131 Brookville Road, G Head, New York 11545; Dean of Faculty and physics teach Long Island Lutheran High School, Brookville, New York; a Adjunct Professor, Physical Science Department, Nassau Co munity College, Garden City, New York.

H. CLARK METCALFE, P.O. Box V2, Wickenburg, Ariz 85358; formerly chemistry teacher at Winchester-Thurst School, Pittsburgh, Pennsylvania; and Head of the Scier Department, Wilkinsburg Senior High School, Wilkinsbu Pennsylvania.

Editorial Development   William N. Moore, Roland J. Cormier, Pamela Hirschfeld
Editorial Processing   Margaret M. Byrne, Richard D. Sime, Sharon Moyer
Art, Production, and Photo Resources   Frank P. Lamacchia, Vivian Fenster,
Fred C. Pusterla, Robin Swenson, Beverly Silver
Product Manager   John W.M. Cooke
Advisory Board   John Taggart, Maurice E. Fey, Norman Hughes, David J. Miller
John W. Griffiths, William L. Paul
Consultant   John Matejowsky
Researchers   Eileen Kelly, Pamela Floch, Gerard La Van

The cover design of Modern Physics 1980 is a photograph of a fully operational magnetic bubble lattice device, courtesy of the International Business Machines Corporation, Research Division.

Preface

Exercises and Experiments in Physics is designed primarily as a supplement to the 1980 edition of MODERN PHYSICS by Williams, Trinklein, and Metcalfe, but may be used with any standard text for secondary schools. Exercises, each dealing with a major topic of physics according to the order of presentation in MODERN PHYSICS, are grouped together at the front of the book; experiments, in similar order, are found in the latter part of the book.

The exercises, as well as the experiments, are in semi-looseleaf form and may be detached or left intact at the option of the instructor. The authors recommend that the exercises be left in this book. It is easy to locate and check the exercise after it has been completed, and the completed exercises then become a source of readily available review material for the student. Each exercise begins on a right-hand page, and the spaces for answers are on the right side of each page. This makes for easy and rapid checking. Many types of questioning techniques have been used, including multiple choice, matching, direct questions, completion, and diagram types. The exercises have been designed to promote good study habits. Many require clear thinking before writing in complete statement answers. Others promote understanding of basic physical principles by means of a sequential development of related items within the exercise. The problem work in the exercises has been designed to check the student's understanding of the mathematical principles involved. The exercises can be used either as study assignments or as reviews to precede tests.

The experiments have meaningful laboratory activities and a great variety of experimental procedures. We have included sufficient experiments to permit the teacher to make selection of ones that will best fit in with the local plan of work. Physics students should have as much laboratory experience as can be provided. The experiments have been chosen as basic and desirable for an adequate program of physics experimentation. They are adjusted for successful use in one 50-minute laboratory period. Many experiments have been extensively rewritten for the 1980 edition. New experiments on power, relative humidity, the mechanical equivalent of heat, and transistors have been added. In experiments 1–18, which deal with mechanics, a new section entitled Analyzing the Data replaces Questions, which appeared in the previous editions. Analyzing the Data directs the student to use the measurements in equations and graphs, to integrate and evaluate observations in order to achieve the purposes of the experiment, and to consider group data in determination of results where appropriate. Students and teachers are encouraged to submit their reactions to this 1980-edition innovation.

The Introduction contains many helpful suggestions for working out both the exercises and experiments. Careful attention has been given to providing clear and detailed instructions for basic laboratory procedures. A discussion of problem-solving techniques, including the methods of performing calculations with significant figures, has been included.

The Appendix contains specific instructions for the use of electric instruments, a Mathematics Refresher, and tables of physical quantities that are useful not only in working out the experiments, but also in verifying the results.

On pages xii and xiii is included a table that correlates the Exercises and the Experiments with the sections and chapters of the MODERN PHYSICS textbook.

John E. Williams
Frederick E. Trinklein
H. Clark Metcalfe

Introduction

Exercises and Experiments in Physics is intended to serve as a guide for study and as a laboratory manual. It is designed to make your study time more profitable and to give you a better understanding of physics. Some general directions are given here for both exercises and experiments. You should study these procedures before you start to use this book. As necessary, you will be referred back to various sections of this Introduction throughout the course of your work. Other special instructions for some of the exercises and experiments are included within the exercises and experiments themselves.

EXERCISES

The exercises are based on the fundamental principles of physics found in any good textbook written for secondary school students. There are several ways in which the exercises may be used. For example:

(1) The student studies the textbook assignment thoroughly. Then, from memory, as much of the exercise as possible is worked out. These responses are checked against the textbook. Imperfectly learned and omitted items are reviewed, corrected, and completed after further textbook study.

(2) The student reads fairly rapidly the assignment in the textbook. Then, referring to the textbook as frequently as necessary, the exercise is worked out. If any questions are answered from memory, their correctness is verified by checking against the textbook when the exercise is completed.

(3) The student begins work with the exercise itself, and looks up each answer in the textbook as the question is encountered. When the exercise is finished, the entire section being studied is read through in sequence for a more complete understanding of the topic.

Unless directed by your instructor to make omissions, you should answer all the exercise items. Some exercises have blank spaces to be filled in or questions to be answered by complete statements. Other exercise items are of the multiple choice or matching type. Still others consist of diagrams that you are to draw or complete, and problems that you are to solve.

PROBLEMS

It is absolutely necessary to follow an orderly procedure when solving problems. Such a procedure is discussed in Section 2.7 of MODERN PHYSICS and is repeated below for your convenience. You should refer to this procedure frequently to solve the problems in this book.

1. Read the problem carefully and make sure that you know what is being asked and that you understand all the terms and symbols that are used in the problem. Write down all given data.

2. Write down the symbol for the physical quantity or quantities called for in the problem, together with the appropriate units.

3. Write down the equation relating the known and unknown quantities of the problem. This is called the *basic equation*. In this step, you will have to draw upon your understanding of the physical principles involved in the problem. It is helpful to draw a sketch of the problem and to label it with the given data.

4. Solve the basic equation for the unknown quantity in the problem, expressing this quantity in terms of those given in the problem. This is called the *working equation*.

5. Substitute the given data into the working equation. In this step, be sure to use the proper units and carefully check the significant figures.

6. Perform the indicated mathematical operations with the units alone to make sure that the answer will be in the units called for in the problem. This process is called *dimensional analysis*.

7. Estimate the order of magnitude of the answer.

8. Perform the indicated mathematical operations with the numbers. Be sure to observe the rules of significant figures.

9. Review the entire solution and compare the answer with your estimate.

Solving a problem in physics is not merely a matter of "plugging" a set of numbers into the appropriate equations. Understanding the basic principles of the problem is much more important than "getting the right answer." Carefully study the following example to see how the steps of problem solving are applied in an actual example.

Example

The volume of the moon has been calculated at $2.20 \times 10^{19}\,m^3$. A rectangular specimen of rock on the earth has the following dimensions: $1.52\ cm \times 2.63\ cm \times 2.15\ cm$. The rock has a mass of 28.8 g. Assuming that the rock has the same mass density as the moon, find the moon's mass.

Solution

We are given the volume of the moon and information about the mass and volume of the earth rock. We are asked to determine the mass of the moon.

This is basically a density problem, and we have a known mass density relationship as our *basic equation*. Since the density of the moon is the same as the density of the rock, we can derive a *working equation* into which the information given in the problem can be substituted.

Basic equation: $D = \dfrac{m}{V}$

For the moon: $m_m = D_m V_m$

$D_m = D_r$

$m_m = D_r V_m$

$D_r = \dfrac{m_r}{V_r} = \dfrac{m_r}{(l \times w \times h)_r}$

Working equation: $m_m = \dfrac{m_r V_m}{(l \times w \times h)_r}$

We now have an equation that gives the mass of the moon in terms of the volume of the moon, the mass of the rock, and the dimensions of the rock—the information given in the problem. In order to give the answer in kilograms rather than grams and to reconcile the different volume units, two conversion factors are inserted in the substitution step that follows. Such conversion factors are not a part of the working equation.

$$m_m = \frac{(28.8\ g)(2.20 \times 10^{19}\,m^3)}{(2.63\ cm)(1.52\ cm)(2.15\ cm)} \left(\frac{10^6\ cm^3}{m^3}\right)\left(\frac{kg}{10^3\ g}\right)$$

By dimensional analysis, we recognize that our answer will be in kilograms.

$$\frac{g \times m^3}{cm \times cm \times cm} \times \frac{cm^3}{m^3} \times \frac{kg}{g} = kg$$

By estimating the order of magnitude of the answer, we would expect to arrive at a numerical answer of the order of 10^{23}. Solving for m_m,

$$m_m = 7.35 \times 10^{22}\ kg$$

You will notice that the rules of significant figures have been observed in this solution so that the answer has the same precision as the data in the problem. Orders of magnitude were used to check on the reasonableness of the answer. In addition, dimensional analysis was used to check the unit of the answer.

EXPERIMENTS

You will be more successful in your laboratory work and work more efficiently if you read each experiment through before coming to the laboratory. The *Purpose* of the experiment tells you what you are expected to learn, to do, and to observe. The *Apparatus, Introduction,* and *Suggestions* are intended to explain the apparatus used, to describe the problem presented, and to show a practical application of the experiment.

When you enter the laboratory, you should procure the necessary apparatus, set it up according to the directions given in the experiment or furnished by your instructor, have your setup checked by the instructor if necessary, and proceed to obtain the necessary data. Make sure the apparatus is working properly during the course of the experiment. You should strive for as high a degree of accuracy as possible, but a less accurate result honestly obtained is always better than the worthless perfect results obtained by "doctoring" readings and other data. High school students with high school apparatus are not expected to obtain results that are as accurate as those obtained by experienced physicists with highly refined apparatus.

During the course of the experiment, the printed sheet should be used only for the directions it contains. No data should be entered on this sheet during the laboratory period. All original data should be recorded on tablet paper or in a special notebook. Only after you have completed your calculations and have had them checked by the instructor should you enter them on the printed report sheet.

MEASUREMENTS

Obtaining data in most physics experiments consists of making measurements. For making measurements we use such instruments as metersticks, spring balances, platform balances, thermometers, watches, and electric meters. Generally the smallest divisions on the scale of any of these instruments are not numbered. With a Celsius thermometer, for example, there are no numbers between the 0° C mark and the 10° C mark. Since the space between these divisions is subdivided into ten equal parts, each subdivision must represent 1° C.

In reading thermometers, voltmeter and ammeter scales, etc., you should count the number of divisions between consecutive numbers and then divide the difference between such numbers by the number of divisions. The quotient equals the value of the smallest scale division. The reading should then be made by estimating to the nearest tenth of this smallest subdivision.

The numbers that represent the value of a measurement are *significant figures*. *The numbers obtained directly from the scale graduations and one number (the rightmost) obtained as an estimate between two successive scale graduations are significant figures.* For example, with a meterstick, which is graduated in tenths of a centimeter, we can measure the length of a block with certainty to the nearest tenth of a centimeter and estimate the length to the nearest hundredth of a centimeter. The figures that represent the value of this measurement are significant figures. The measurements in the experiments in this book are to be made in significant figures.

CALCULATIONS

In making calculations with measured quantities, we must follow certain precautions to ensure that the calculated values obtained from the measurements are not expressed with greater precision than the precision of the original measurements warrants. Detailed directions for performing calculations with significant figures are given in MODERN PHYSICS, Section 2.3. A brief summary is given here.

(1) Addition or subtraction. When adding or subtracting similar measurements, each measurement should be rounded off so that the rightmost column of digits is the only one containing uncertain digits.

Example

The lengths of three wooden blocks are 5.3 cm, 4.57 cm, and 1.385 cm. What is their combined length?

Solution

The combined length of the three blocks cannot be expressed more precisely than the least precisely measured block. In the addition set up below, the final digit of each of the numbers is uncertain. Hence the first column containing an uncertain digit is the tenths column.

$$
\begin{array}{l}
5.3 \quad \text{cm} \\
4.57 \quad \text{cm} \\
\underline{1.385 \text{ cm}}
\end{array}
$$

The values are rounded off to tenths, as shown below, and the addition is performed. The combined length of the three blocks is 11.3 cm.

$$
\begin{array}{l}
5.3 \text{ cm} \\
4.6 \text{ cm} \\
\underline{1.4 \text{ cm}} \\
11.3 \text{ cm}
\end{array}
$$

(2) Multiplication or division. When multiplying or dividing measurements, the product or quotient should not usually contain more significant figures than are found in the term with the least number of significant figures used in the multiplication or division. In a series of multiplications or divisions, round off after each separate calculation.

Example

What is the area of the surface of a rectangular block that is 7.64 cm long and 5.45 cm wide?

Solution

The calculation of the surface area is shown at the right; the product is 41.6 cm². There is no justification in keeping more than three digits because an area cannot be determined precisely to the nearest ten thousandth of a square centimeter if the length and width are measured only to the nearest hundredth of a centimeter.

$$\begin{array}{r} 7.64 \text{ cm} \\ 5.45 \text{ cm} \\ \hline 3820 \\ 3056 \\ 3820 \\ \hline 41.6380 \text{ cm}^2 \end{array}$$

Example

Multiply 64.7 cm × 89.3 cm.

Solution

64.7 cm × 89.3 cm = 5777.71 cm². But since there are only three significant figures in each of the numbers multiplied, we are permitted to keep only three digits in the product. 5777.71 cm² expressed to three significant figures becomes 5780 cm² or 5.78×10^3 cm². See Section 2.4 of the textbook for the method of writing numbers in scientific notation.

ERRORS AND DEVIATIONS

In most of the experiments you will be asked to compare your results with certain accepted values or to compare two or more of your findings with each other. The difference between your experimental or calculated results and an accepted value is called "absolute error." When expressed as a percentage of the accepted value, the difference is called "relative error." In other words,

$$E_a = \left| O - A \right|$$

where E_a is the absolute error, O is the observed or calculated value, and A is the accepted value. Also,

$$E_r = \frac{E_a}{A} \times 100\%$$

where E_r is the relative error, E_a the absolute error, and A the accepted value.

When you compare two or more findings with each other (and do not compare them with any accepted values), then the differences are called "deviations." The equations for finding the absolute and relative deviations of your data are

$$D_a = \left| O - M \right|$$

where D_a is the absolute deviation, O is an observed or calculated value, and M is the mean or average of several readings. Also,

$$D_r = \frac{D_a \text{ (ave)}}{M} \times 100\%$$

where D_r is the relative deviation, D_a is the absolute deviation, and M is the mean or average of the set of readings.

Be sure to record the kind of error or deviation called for in an experiment and then calculate it with the help of the equations given above.

ANALYZING THE DATA

In Experiments 1–18, the procedure is followed by directions that tell you how to use the data you have recorded in order to carry out the purpose(s) of the experiment. This will usually involve the solving of equations that apply to the quantities being measured. You will frequently be asked to plot graphs of your data. Carefully read the instructions on Graphs that are given below.

OBSERVATIONS

In certain experiments our primary concern is not with making measurements but with performing certain operations and observing the results. In such experiments you are called upon to record your observations. These are to be concise statements that clearly indicate what you observed when the experimental procedure was carried out. Record your observations in the form of complete sentences insofar as possible.

CONCLUSIONS

At the end of certain experiments you will be called upon to state your conclusions. Faulty conclusions often arise from incorrect observations or from failure to understand some part of the experiment. Read all the instruments with the greatest possible precision, and then compare the purpose of the experiment with your observations and data before you attempt to draw conclusions.

QUESTIONS

The questions that appear at the end of the experiments after No. 18 are designed to help you check your understanding of the experiment, to help you draw the proper conclusions from your experimental data, and to point out other possible applications of the experiment. Answers should be complete statements.

GRAPHS

One of the most useful methods of discovering the relationship between two variable quantities is graphing the results of an experiment in which one quantity is varied, the resultant variation in the second quantity is noted, and all other factors are held constant. The Boyle's law experiment is an experiment of this type. Boyle's law states that if the temperature is held constant, the volume of a gas varies inversely with the pressure to which it is subjected. An inverse relation of this sort means that if we start with 1 liter of gas at 1 atmosphere pressure, an increase in the pressure to 2 atmospheres causes the volume to be reduced to 1/2 liter; if the pressure is increased to 3 atmospheres, the volume is reduced to 1/3 liter, and so on. If the pressure is reduced to 1/2 atmosphere, the volume becomes 2 liters. A complete summary of the results of such an ideal experiment is shown in the table at the right.

In constructing a graph to illustrate such data, the values of the controlled variable are usually plotted on the horizontal X axis as abscissas, and the values of the dependent variable are plotted on the vertical Y axis as ordinates. The ratio between the width and height of the grid, or rulings, should be about 1.5 to 1 for best results. In order to obtain this ratio, proper adjustment of the size of scale values must be made.

In the graph in Figure A, each unit on the X axis represents 1 atmosphere pressure; to maintain the proper ratio of width to height, each unit on the Y axis represents 1.50 liters. The scale should be so planned that the plotted data will require the use of almost all the scale with some space on the grid above and below the plotted values. While the scale values in the lower left-hand corner of the graph should both be zero, it is permissible to "break" the scale both horizontally and vertically so as to center the curve and use as large a portion of the grid as possible.

The location of the plotted points is made in the customary algebraic manner. If the relationship is direct and should produce a straight line graph, a ruler is used and the graph is drawn to give an average location of the points, as if they did fall along a straight line. If the relationship is nonlinear, a French curve is used to guide the plotting of the graph.

PRESSURE-VOLUME RELATIONSHIP OF A GAS (Temperature Constant)	
Pressure in Atmospheres	Volume in Liters
0.20	5.00
0.25	4.00
0.33	3.00
0.50	2.00
1.00	1.00
1.50	0.67
2.00	0.50
3.00	0.33
4.00	0.25

Scale captions are placed on both axes to clearly identify the scale values. Both the subject of the scale and the units used must be indicated. The caption for the horizontal scale is generally placed under the horizontal axis at the center. The caption for the vertical axis is placed vertically to the left and center of the vertical axis.

The title of the graph must give the what, where, and when of the data. The position of the title is determined by the use of the graph. In general the title is centered at the top. It should be printed in large letters.

It is usual practice to include the table that gives the data from which the graph was constructed. The graph and the data table should always be included in the laboratory report.

When several variables are included on the same graph, it is necessary to identify each by using a key or legend. A sample of each type of line, color, shading, or cross hatching used for distinguishing purposes is indicated and identified. This identifying key or legend is generally enclosed within a box, and where possible, is placed within the grid itself.

The proper placing of the elements of a graph is shown in Figure A.
The following characteristics of the model graph should be noted:
1. The completeness of the title.
2. The relative size of the lettering in the title, scale captions, etc.
3. The location of the scale captions.
4. The "round" values on the scale.
5. The emphasized curve line.
6. The order of the plotted data, from the smallest to the largest.

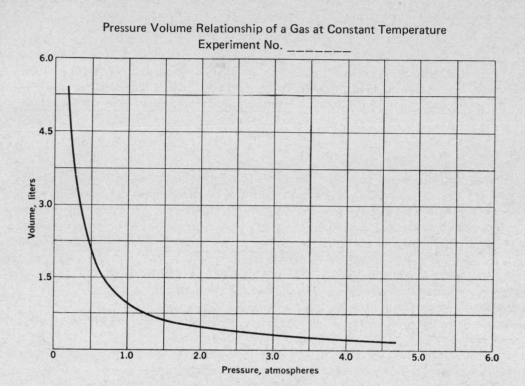

Figure A

Contents

EXERCISES

EXPERIMENTS

Correlation Table of Exercises and Experiments in Physics with Modern Physics 1980

exercise **3b**

Acceleration

Sections 3.5–3.7

1. Complete the table at the bottom of the page by obtaining velocity data from Fig. 3B-1 and calculating the average acceleration and displacement for each time interval. Then calculate the total displacement.

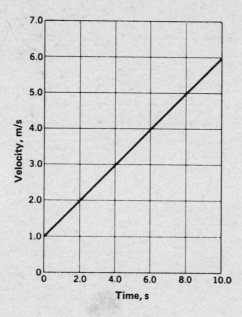

Figure 3B-1

Time (s)	Velocity (m/s)	Acceleration (m/s²)	Displacement (m)
0.0			
2.0			
5.0			
10.0		Total displacement (m)	

15

2. Complete the table below by obtaining velocity data from Fig. 3B-2 and calculating the average acceleration and displacement for each time interval. Then calculate the total displacement.

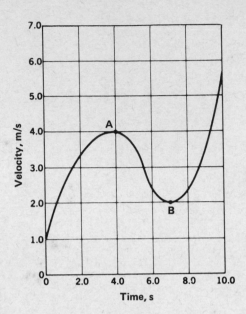

Figure 3B-2

Time (s)	Velocity (m/s)	Acceleration (m/s²)	Displacement (m)
0.0			
1.0			
2.0			
3.0			
4.0			
5.0			
6.0			
7.0			
8.0			
9.0			
10.0		Total displacement (m)	

DIRECTIONS: In the blank space at the right of each statement, write the word or expression that BEST completes the meaning.

3. The rate of change of velocity is called ..(3)...   _____ 3

4. If the velocity of a body is constant, its acceleration is ..(4)...   _____ 4

5. When the velocity of a body increases or decreases the same amount in successive units of time, the acceleration is ..(5)...   _____ 5

6. Motion of this kind is described as ..(6).. accelerated motion.   _____ 6

7. An object that moves linearly 2.0 m during the first second, 6.0 m during the second second, and 10.0 m during the third second has an acceleration of ..(7)...

_____ 7

8. In terms of Δd and Δt, acceleration is expressed as ..(8)

_____ 8

9. The acceleration due to gravity (is constant, varies) ..(9).. over the earth's surface.

_____ 9

10. In air, dense objects fall (slower than, at the same speed as, faster than) ..(10).. objects of lower density.

_____ 10

DIRECTIONS: Write the answers to the following questions in the spaces provided. Where appropriate, make complete statements.

11. What algebraic relationship expresses the displacement of an object in terms of its average velocity and elapsed time of travel?

_____ 11

12. In cases of uniformly accelerated motion, how may the final velocity be expressed in terms of initial velocity, acceleration, and elapsed time?

_____ 12

13. During any interval of time in which the initial and final velocities are known, how is the average velocity expressed algebraically?

_____ 13

14. When we substitute the expression for final velocity from No. 12 in the equation of No. 13, what does the expression for average velocity become?

_____ 14

15. Substituting the expression for average velocity from No. 14 in the equation of No. 11, what does the displacement of the object now equal?

_____ 15

16. Solve the equation of No. 12 for Δt.

_____ 16

17. If the equations of No. 15 and No. 16 relate to the same observation of the same system, Δt in No. 16 may be substituted for Δt in No. 15. Make this substitution and solve for v_f.

_____ 17

18. Do the equations developed above apply to cases of uniformly decelerated motion? _____

_____

_____

19. Do the equations for accelerated motion apply to freely falling bodies? _____

_____

20. What is the effect of the force of gravity on an object thrown upward?_____

_____

exercise **3c**

Newton's Laws of Motion—Gravitation

Sections 3.8-3.14

DIRECTIONS: In the blank space at the right of each statement, write the word or expression that BEST completes the meaning.

1. A push or a pull is a(n) ..(1)...

             _____ 1

2. Quantities that require magnitude, direction, and point of origin for their descriptions are ..(2).. quantities.

             _____ 2

3. A physical quantity that can affect the motion of an object is a(n) ..(3)...

             _____ 3

4. When no net force acts on a body, either ..(4a).. force acts on the body or the ..(4b).. of all forces acting on the body is ..(4c)...

             _____ 4a

             _____ 4b

             _____ 4c

5. If there is no net force acting on a body, it will continue in its state of ..(5a).. or will continue moving along a(n) ..(5b).. line with ..(5c).. speed.

             _____ 5a

             _____ 5b

             _____ 5c

6. A common unbalanced force that makes it difficult to prove Newton's first law of motion experimentally is ..(6)...

             _____ 6

7. The property of matter that is the concern of the first law of motion is ..(7)...

             _____ 7

8. If an object is stationary, its inertia tends to keep it ..(8a)..; if an object is in motion, its inertia tends to keep it ..(8b)...

             _____ 8a

             _____ 8b

9. Uniform motion in a straight line is the only motion possible for an object ..(9).. other objects.

             _____ 9

10. Nonuniform motion of an object is always caused by the ..(10).. of some other object.

             _____ 10

DIRECTIONS: In the space at the right, place the letter or letters indicating EACH choice that forms a correct statement.

11. The acceleration of a body is (a) directly proportional to the force exerted, (b) inversely proportional to the mass of the body, (c) in the same direction as the applied force, (d) dependent on its initial velocity.

             _____ 11

12. If a body is moving in a straight line and a force is applied in the direction of its motion, (a) the velocity is constant, (b) the acceleration is constant, (c) the body will increase in speed as long as the force continues, (d) the body will decrease in speed.

             _____ 12

13. If a body is moving in a straight line and a force is applied in the direction opposite to its motion, (a) the velocity is changing, (b) the acceleration is changing, (c) the body may stop, (d) the body may move in the opposite direction.

             _____ 13

14. The *newton* (a) is a unit of force in the MKS system, (b) is the force required to accelerate 1 kg of mass at the rate of 1 m/s^2, (c) is a derived unit, (d) is 1 kg m/s^2. _____ 14

15. The force required to accelerate an object of known weight is (a) directly proportional to the weight of the object, (b) directly proportional to the acceleration desired, (c) directly proportional to the acceleration due to gravitation, (d) not related in any way to the acceleration due to gravitation. _____ 15

16. The relationship between the mass of a body and its weight is (a) weight = mass $\times$ 9.80 m/s^2, (b) weight $\div$ mass = acceleration due to gravitation, (c) $F_w = mg$, (d) $F = ma$. _____ 16

17. Newton's third law of motion deals with (a) one object and two forces, (b) two objects and one force, (c) two objects and two forces, (d) action and reaction. _____ 17

18. When an automobile is accelerated forward, (a) the tires exert a forward action force on the road, (b) the road exerts a forward reaction force on the tires, (c) the tires exert a rearward action force on the road, (d) the road exerts a rearward reaction force on the tires. _____ 18

DIRECTIONS: Write the answers to the following questions in the spaces provided. Where appropriate, make complete statements.

19. Write the equation for the law of universal gravitation and explain each of the terms. _____

_____

_____

_____

20. If the masses of both objects are doubled, how is the force of gravitation affected? _____

_____

21. If the distance between their centers of mass is doubled, how is the force of gravitation affected?

_____

_____

22. If a person's mass remains constant, what variation, if any, is there in weight as the person descends from a mountain into an adjacent valley? _____

23. What is a gravitational field? _____

_____

24. In which areas of physics is the study of force fields useful? _____

_____

25. What force, in newtons, is required to accelerate a body having a mass of 40.0 kg at the rate of 2.0 m/s^2 in a westward direction? _____

26. What is the mass of a person whose weight on the earth's surface is $81\overline{0}$ n? _____

27. Calculate the acceleration due to gravity on the surface of Jupiter. _____

28. What would be the mass and the weight of the person of No. 26 on the surface of Jupiter?

_____

exercise **7a**

Molecules and Atoms—Solids

Sections 7.1–7.11

DIRECTIONS: Write the answers to the following questions in the spaces provided. Where appropriate, make complete statements.

1. Give two conclusions that can be drawn from a sequence of experiments in which a rock salt crystal is crushed and the properties of the powder are examined; the powder is dissolved in water and the properties of the solution are examined; the water is subsequently evaporated and the residue is examined.

   a. _____

   b. _____

2. What kinds of information are included in the modern atomic theory? _____

   _____

   _____

3. What is a molecule? _____

   _____

4. What is an atom? _____

   _____

5. What is the meaning of the term *phase* in describing matter? _____

   _____

6. Name the three phases of matter and describe the particle spacing in each.

   a. _____

   b. _____

   c. _____

7. What are two basic aspects of the kinetic theory of matter?

   a. _____

   b. _____

8. Compare the magnitudes of the molecular forces in the three phases of matter. _____

   _____

9. How does the force between like molecules vary with the distance between them? _____

   _____

   _____

   _____

   _____

   _____

   _____

   _____

45

10. Describe the motion of molecules of solids, liquids, and gases.

a. _____

b. _____

c. _____

DIRECTIONS: In the space at the right, place the letter or letters indicating EACH choice that forms a correct answer.

11. The particles of a solid **(a)** do not move, **(b)** are held in relatively fixed positions, **(c)** have a smaller amplitude of vibration at lower temperatures, **(d)** lose kinetic energy as the temperature is raised.   _____ 11

12. *Diffusion* **(a)** occurs rapidly in solids, **(b)** is evidence of the vibratory motion of the particles of solids, **(c)** proceeds slowly in solids because the particles are closely packed, **(d)** does not occur in solids because of the orderly particle arrangement.   _____ 12

13. *Cohesion* is the force of attraction between molecules **(a)** of the same material, **(b)** that can be shown with polished metal blocks, **(c)** of unlike materials, **(d)** that acts as a binding force.   _____ 13

14. *Adhesion* is the force of attraction between molecules **(a)** of the same material, **(b)** of unlike materials, **(c)** that causes one material to stick to another, **(d)** that acts at a distance.   _____ 14

15. *Tensile strength* **(a)** is a property of solids, **(b)** of copper is greater than that of steel, **(c)** depends on the cohesive forces between molecules, **(d)** is the force per unit cross-sectional area applied perpendicularly to the cross section that is required to break a rod or wire of that material.   _____ 15

16. *Ductility* **(a)** is a property of metals, **(b)** is dependent on the force of adhesion between molecules, **(c)** enables a metal to be drawn into a wire, **(d)** is determined by the cohesive force existing between the atoms of a metal.   _____ 16

17. *Malleability* **(a)** is dependent on cohesion, **(b)** is the property of metals enabling them to be pounded out into thin sheets, **(c)** of gold is not very pronounced, **(d)** depends on the ability of atoms to hold together while being shifted from one position in the crystal pattern to another.   _____ 17

18. *Elasticity* **(a)** of solids depends on molecular forces, **(b)** cannot restore a wire to its original length after an applied force has stretched it, **(c)** measurements may involve stress and shear, **(d)** is a property of materials that return to their original shape after removal of a distorting force.   _____ 18

19. *Hooke's law* **(a)** states that the ratio of stress to strain is a constant, **(b)** is the principle on which a spring balance operates, **(c)** deals with the inverse relationship between amount of distortion and distorting force, **(d)** applies even though the elastic limit is exceeded.   _____ 19

20. *Young's modulus* **(a)** is the ratio of stress/strain, **(b)** is the ratio of distorting force per unit area to the relative amount of distortion thus produced, **(c)** is reasonably the same for a given solid material regardless of its shape, **(d)** may be expressed in n/m^2.   _____ 20

DIRECTIONS: Place the answers to the following problems in the spaces provided at the right.

21. The atomic mass of a silver atom is 106.90509 u.
    a. What is its mass in kilograms? _____ 21a
    b. What is its mass number? _____ 21b

22. What force is required to break a steel rod 0.50 cm in diameter? The tensile strength of steel is 2.90×10^8 n/m^2. _____ 22

23. A spring balance is stretched 0.010 m by a force of 5.0 n. How far will it be stretched by a force of $10\overline{0}$ n if the elastic limit is not exceeded? _____ 23

24. From a steel beam 5.00 m long, cross-sectional area 8.10 cm^2, hangs a load of 3750 n. How far does the beam stretch if Young's modulus for steel is 20.0×10^{10} n/m^2? _____ 24

exercise **7b**

Liquids and Gases

Sections 7.12–7.23

DIRECTIONS: In the parentheses at the right of each word or expression in the second column, write the letter of the expression in the first column that is MOST CLOSELY related.

a. Conversion of vapor molecules to liquid molecules	Brownian movement	( )	1
b. Conversion of solid molecules to liquid molecules			
c. Indicates that liquid molecules move	capillarity	( )	2
d. Conversion of liquid molecules to solid molecules			
e. Depends on cohesion and surface tension	condensation	( )	3
f. Conversion of solid or liquid molecules to vapor molecules	evaporation	( )	4
g. Depends on adhesion and cohesion			
h. Conversion of solid molecules to vapor molecules	freezing	( )	5
i. Conversion of liquid molecules to vapor molecules			
j. Indicates that solid molecules move	melting	( )	6
k. Depends on adhesion and surface tension			
l. Conversion of solid molecules to liquid molecules by increased pressure and subsequent reconversion to solid molecules when pressure is decreased	meniscus	( )	7
	regelation	( )	8
	sublimation	( )	9
	vaporization	( )	10

DIRECTIONS: In the space at the right, place the letter or letters indicating EACH choice that forms a correct statement.

11. In a *liquid,* (a) the particles are close together, (b) the kinetic energy of the particles completely overcomes the attractive forces between them, (c) the particles are in motion, (d) the motion of the particles is slow. _____ 11

12. *Diffusion* in liquids (a) is faster than in solids, (b) occurs counter to the force of gravity, (c) is never complete, (d) is possible because liquid particles have both mobility and an open arrangement. _____ 12

13. *Surface tension* (a) causes a liquid to behave as if it has a thin surface film, (b) is the result of attractive forces between the molecules of a liquid, (c) causes liquid films to be flexible, (d) causes a free liquid to assume a spherical shape. _____ 13

14. *Capillarity* is (a) the depression of a liquid in a small-diameter tube that the liquid wets, (b) the elevation of a liquid in a small-diameter tube that the liquid does not wet, (c) directly proportional to the tube diameter, (d) reduced by an increase in temperature. _____ 14

15. During *melting* (a) the potential energy of the particles increases, (b) the kinetic energy of the particles increases, (c) the energy supplied overcomes the forces holding the particles in fixed positions, (d) the temperature of a crystalline solid rises. _____ 15

16. During *melting* (a) most substances contract, (b) most substances expand, (c) the separation of particles changes because of a change in their potential energy, (d) water molecules move closer together.   _____ 16

17. In a *gas*, (a) the particles are close together, (b) the kinetic energy of the particles completely overcomes the attractive forces between them, (c) the particles are in motion, (d) the motion of the particles is rapid.   _____ 17

18. During *vaporization* (a) the identity of the particles remains the same, (b) the energy of the particles remains the same, (c) the separation of the particles remains the same, (d) the temperature of the particles remains the same.   _____ 18

19. *Equilibrium vapor pressure* (a) is added pressure exerted by vapor molecules in equilibrium with liquid, (b) is independent of the identity of the molecules, (c) increases with a decrease in the temperature of the molecules, (d) is independent of the kinetic energy of the vapor molecules.   _____ 19

20. *Boiling* (a) occurs when the vapor pressure of a liquid equals the pressure on its surface, (b) is rapid vaporization that disturbs the liquid, (c) is a constant-temperature process, (d) is a constant-energy process.   _____ 20

DIRECTIONS: In the blank space at the right of each statement, write the word or expression that BEST completes the meaning.

21. Since water clings to a clean glass rod, the adhesion of water molecules to glass is (less than, equal to, greater than) ..(21).. the cohesion of water molecules.   _____ 21

22. Since mercury does not cling to a clean glass rod, the adhesion of mercury molecules to glass is (less than, equal to, greater than) ..(22).. the cohesion of mercury molecules.   _____ 22

23. The cleaning action of a detergent is partly due to its ability to lower the ..(23).. of water.   _____ 23

24. When viewed from above, the surface of water in a glass container is slightly ..(24)...   _____ 24

25. When viewed from above, the surface of mercury in a glass container is slightly ..(25)...   _____ 25

26. Water in a glass capillary tube creeps up the walls because of ..(26a).. and produces a curved liquid surface; this surface tends to be flattened by ..(26b)... These two forces raise the water above its surrounding level until they are counterbalanced by the ..(26c).. of the elevated liquid.   _____ 26a
    _____ 26b
    _____ 26c

27. The melting point and freezing point of pure crystalline solids are (the same, different) ..(27).. temperature(s) for a given pressure.   _____ 27

28. For most substances, an increase in pressure (lowers, raises) ..(28a).. the freezing point because it (aids, hinders) ..(28b).. the movement of the particles into a more compact regular pattern.   _____ 28a
    _____ 28b

29. The freezing point of a liquid is (lowered, raised) ..(29a).. by the addition of a dissolved substance because its presence (aids, hinders) ..(29b).. crystal formation.   _____ 29a
    _____ 29b

50

30. A gas completely fills its container because it has the property of
..(30)...

_____ 30

31. When a rubber balloon is inflated, the walls stretch because of increased ..(31).. exerted by the gas molecules.

_____ 31

32. At a given temperature, the rates of diffusion of gases and their densities are (directly, inversely) ..(32a).. related because heavier molecules move more ..(32b)...

_____ 32a

_____ 32b

33. The molecules that evaporate from a liquid obtain their energy from the ..(33a).. or from the ..(33b)... Thus, evaporation has a(n) ..(33c).. effect on the environment.

_____ 33a

_____ 33b

_____ 33c

34. In a closed bottle containing a liquid, evaporation and condensation (continue, cease) ..(34).. to occur.

_____ 34

35. The water vapor pressure in the atmosphere divided by the equilibrium vapor pressure at that temperature equals the ..(35)...

_____ 35

36. If the water vapor pressure is 6.6 mm of mercury when the air temperature is $22^{\circ}C$, the relative humidity is ..(36)...

_____ 36

37. The temperature at which a given amount of water vapor exerts equilibrium vapor pressure is the ..(37)...

_____ 37

38. At one atmosphere pressure, boiling occurs at the ..(38a).. boiling point. If the pressure is increased, the boiling temperature is ..(38b)..; if the pressure is lowered, the boiling temperature is ..(38c)...

_____ 38a

_____ 38b

_____ 38c

39. Solids dissolved in liquids generally ..(39).. the boiling temperature of the liquid.

_____ 39

40. Gases dissolved in liquids generally ..(40).. the boiling temperature of the liquid.

_____ 40

exercise **8a**

Thermal Units and Thermal Expansion

Sections 8.1–8.10

DIRECTIONS: In the parentheses at the right of each word or expression in the second column, write the letter of the expression in the first column that is MOST CLOSELY related.

a. 0°C	calorie	( ) 1
b. 273.16°K		
c. 273°K, 1 atm	coefficient of linear expansion	( ) 2
d. 760 mm mercury		
e. 4.18065 j	coefficient of volume expansion	( ) 3
f. $\Delta l / l \Delta T$		
g. $V' = Vp/p'$	Charles' law	( ) 4
h. $V' = Vp'/p$		
i. $\Delta V / V \Delta T$	standard temperature	( ) 5
j. $V' = VT_K/T_K'$		
k. $V' = VT_K'/T_K$	triple-point temperature	( ) 6
l. $V' = V(p/p')(T_K'/T_K)$		
m. $V' = V(p'/p)(T_K/T_K')$	Boyle's law	( ) 7
	standard pressure	( ) 8
	STP	( ) 9
	general gas law	( ) 10

DIRECTIONS: In the space at the right, place the letter or letters indicating EACH choice that forms a correct statement.

11. The thermal energy of a material is related to **(a)** its potential energy, **(b)** its kinetic energy, **(c)** the motion of its particles, **(d)** the arrangement of its particles. _____ 11

12. Heat **(a)** is thermal energy absorbed by a body at lower temperature from a body at higher temperature, **(b)** is thermal energy given up by a body at higher temperature to a body at lower temperature, **(c)** is thermal energy transferred between two bodies having the same temperature, **(d)** may be measured in work units. _____ 12

13. The temperature of a material **(a)** is its "hotness" or "coldness," **(b)** is related to its thermal energy content, **(c)** is proportional to the average kinetic energy of translation of its particles, **(d)** determines whether it transfers heat to or from a nearby body. _____ 13

14. When the temperature of a typical solid is raised, **(a)** it will increase in length, **(b)** its thickness will be unchanged, **(c)** the amplitude of vibration of its atoms and molecules is increased, **(d)** the average distance between its atoms and molecules is unaffected. _____ 14

15. The change in length of a typical solid with a change in temperature **(a)** is directly proportional to its length, **(b)** depends on the nature of the solid, **(c)** is inversely proportional to the coefficient of linear expansion, **(d)** is directly proportional to the temperature change. _____ 15

53

16. When the temperature of a typical liquid is raised, **(a)** it will increase in volume, **(b)** the thermal energy of its molecules remains the same, **(c)** the amplitude of vibration of its molecules is unchanged, **(d)** the average distance between its molecules is decreased.   _____ 16

17. The change in volume of a typical liquid with a change in temperature **(a)** is directly proportional to its volume, **(b)** depends on the nature of the liquid, **(c)** is directly proportional to the coefficient of volume expansion, **(d)** is inversely proportional to the temperature change.   _____ 17

18. Water **(a)** expands when its temperature is raised from $0°C$ to $4°C$, **(b)** expands when its temperature is raised from $4°C$ to $100°C$, **(c)** has a point of maximum density at $4°C$, **(d)** has a point of minimum density at $100°C$.   _____ 18

19. As the temperature of water is raised from $0°C$ to $4°C$, **(a)** the distance between the molecules increases, **(b)** the open crystal fragments begin to collapse, **(c)** the speed of the molecules increases, **(d)** the effect of the collapsing crystal structure is more significant than the change in speed of the molecules.   _____ 19

20. The change in volume of a typical gas with a change in temperature at constant pressure **(a)** is directly proportional to its volume, **(b)** depends on the nature of the gas, **(c)** is inversely proportional to the kinetic energy of its molecules, **(d)** is directly proportional to the Kelvin temperature change.   _____ 20

DIRECTIONS: In the blank space at the right of each statement, write the word or expression that BEST completes the meaning.

21. The unit of temperature difference is the ..(21)...   _____ 21

22. The temperature at which a constant-temperature process occurs can be used as a(n) ..(22).. in establishing a temperature scale.   _____ 22

23. The Kelvin temperature of the triple point of water is ..(23)...   _____ 23

24. On the Celsius scale the temperature at which alcohol freezes is −115 ..(24a).., the temperature at which alcohol boils is 78 ..(24b).., and the interval between these temperatures is ..(24c)...   _____ 24a

    _____ 24b

    _____ 24c

25. The difference between the melting point and boiling point of mercury is $395.5C°$. This temperature interval is ..(25).. $K°$.   _____ 25

26. At $0°K$ the kinetic energy of the particles of matter is ..(26)...   _____ 26

27. In assigning numbers on the Kelvin temperature scale, both a fixed point, the ..(27a).. of water, and a measurable physical property of a substance that is ..(27b).. to the Kelvin temperature are required.   _____ 27a

    _____ 27b

28. The most consistent results in temperature measurement are obtained with a constant ..(28).. thermometer.   _____ 28

29. Mercury-in-glass thermometers are in practical use because the expansions of mercury and glass are fairly ..(29).. over the useful temperature range of such instruments.   _____ 29

30. A quantity of heat is measured by the ..(30).. it produces.   _____ 30

31. The coefficient of linear expansion of most solids (does not vary, varies slightly, varies greatly) ..(31a).. with temperature. This effect (may be, is never) ..(31b).. neglected.   _____ 31a

    _____ 31b

54

32. The magnitude of the coefficient of linear expansion (depends, does not depend) ..(32).. on whether length is measured in meters or centimeters.

_____ 32

33. In designing and building devices that will undergo temperature changes, allowances must be made not only for changes in ..(33a).. due to expansion and contraction but for different ..(33b).. of expansion and contraction of different materials.

_____ 33a

_____ 33b

34. Mercury rises in the tube of a glass thermometer when the temperature rises because the coefficient of volume expansion of mercury is (lower than, the same as, higher than) ..(34).. the coefficient of volume expansion of glass.

_____ 34

35. When the temperature of a mass of water is raised above 4°C, the effect of collapsing crystal structure is (less than, equal to, more than) ..(35a).. the effect of increasing molecular speed, and the volume of the water (decreases, remains the same, increases) ..(35b)...

_____ 35a

_____ 35b

36. No ice forms on the surface of a fresh-water pond until the temperature of the entire pond is ..(36).. or below.

_____ 36

37. The coefficient of volume expansion for gases is ..(37).. the volume at 0°C.

_____ 37

38. If two quantities are in direct proportion, their ..(38a).. is a constant and their graph is a(n) ..(38b)...

_____ 38a

_____ 38b

39. At constant volume, the pressure of a given mass of gas varies ..(39).. with the Kelvin temperature.

_____ 39

40. If two quantities are in inverse proportion, their ..(40a).. is a constant and their graph is a(n) ..(40b)...

_____ 40a

_____ 40b

41. At constant temperature, the density of a given mass of gas varies ..(41).. with the pressure.

_____ 41

42. At constant pressure, the density of a given mass of gas varies ..(42).. with the Kelvin temperature.

_____ 42

43. Under usual temperature and pressure conditions, real gases approximate the behavior of the ideal gas because the molecules are so far apart that the effects of their ..(43a).. and the ..(43b).. between them are negligible.

_____ 43a

_____ 43b

44. The amount of a molecular substance containing the Avogadro number of molecules of that substance is one ..(44a)... If the mass of such a substance is divided by its gram-molecular weight, the quotient represents the number of ..(44b).. of the substance.

_____ 44a

_____ 44b

45. From the ideal gas equation, any one of these five quantities may be calculated if the other four are known: ..(45a).., ..(45b).., ..(45c).., ..(45d).., and ..(45e)...

_____ 45a

_____ 45b

_____ 45c

_____ 45d

_____ 45e

55

DIRECTIONS: Place the answers to the following problems in the spaces provided at the right.

46. Convert to Kelvin scale temperatures:

    a. $58°C$ _____ 46a

    b. $-142°C$ _____ 46b

47. Convert to Celsius scale temperatures:

    a. $298°K$ _____ 47a

    b. $218°K$ _____ 47b

48. A copper wire is $30\overline{0}$ m long at $20.0°C$. If the temperature rises to $45.0°C$, what is its increase in length?   _____ 48

49. An aluminum rod is 10.0 cm long at $15.0°C$. How much longer is the rod at $100.0°C$?   _____ 49

50. What is the increase in volume of $25\overline{0}$ mL of mercury at $0.0°C$ when it is heated to $30.0°C$?   _____ 50

51. A quantity of air occupies $80\overline{0}$ mL at $50.0°C$. What will be its volume at $150.0°C$ if its pressure remains unchanged?   _____ 51

52. A mass of gas occupies 25.0 L at a pressure of $75\overline{0}$ mm of mercury. With the temperature constant, calculate the volume the gas will occupy when subjected to a pressure of $80\overline{0}$ mm.   _____ 52

53. A $50\overline{0}$-mL sample of gas is collected at a temperature of $25.0°C$ and a pressure of $76\overline{0}$ mm. What will be the volume of the gas at $-25.0°C$ and a pressure of $80\overline{0}$ mm?   _____ 53

54. A sample of gas occupies $20\overline{0}$ mL at STP. At what Celsius temperature and 735 mm pressure will its volume be $30\overline{0}$ mL?   _____ 54

55. What volume will 4.00 kg of helium (He) occupy at STP?   _____ 55

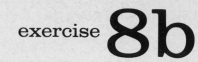

exercise **8b**

Measuring Heat—Change of Phase

Sections 8.11–8.24

DIRECTIONS: In the blank space at the right of each statement, write the word or expression that BEST completes the meaning.

1. A mass of aluminum cools more (slowly, rapidly) ..(1a).. than an equal mass of zinc because the heat capacity of aluminum is (lower, higher) ..(1b).. than that of zinc.

_____ 1a

_____ 1b

2. In the equation $Q = mc\,\Delta T$, Q will be given in calories if m is in ..(2a).., c is in ..(2b).., and ΔT is in ..(2c)...

_____ 2a

_____ 2b

_____ 2c

3. The specific heat of most substances is (less than, the same as, more than) ..(3).. the specific heat of water.

_____ 3

4. An important source of error in high school-laboratory heat experiments is the ..(4).. to the surroundings.

_____ 4

5. When the temperature and pressure conditions of a pure substance are established, its ..(5a).. and ..(5b).. are determined.

_____ 5a

_____ 5b

6. The discontinuity between phases of a substance in equilibrium is known as a(n) ..(16)...

_____ 6

7. In the triple-point diagram for a typical crystalline substance, the solid-liquid curve has a(n) ..(7).. slope.

_____ 7

8. At ordinary temperatures the vapor pressure of solids is (less than, equal to, greater than) ..(8a).. that of liquids. Consequently, solids evaporate (slower than, at the same rate as, faster than) ..(8b).. liquids.

_____ 8a

_____ 8b

9. A mixture of two liquids having different boiling points usually has a boiling temperature (the same as, different from) ..(9).. that of the lower boiling liquid.

_____ 9

10. When water boils below 100°C under reduced pressure, the heat of vaporization is (less than, equal to, more than) ..(10).. 539 cal/g.

_____ 10

11. When a given mass of ice becomes water at 0°C, the volume ..(11a)..; when a given mass of water becomes steam at 100°C at constant pressure, the volume ..(11b)...

_____ 11a

_____ 11b

12. Above its critical temperature, a substance can exist only in the ..(12).. phase.

_____ 12

13. At the critical point, the density of the liquid phase is (less than, equal to, greater than) ..(13a).. the density of the vapor phase, and the heat of vaporization is ..(13b)...

_____ 13a

_____ 13b

14. At temperatures above the critical temperature, the vapor phase of a substance is usually called a(n) ..(14a)..; at temperatures below the critical temperature, it is called a(n) ..(14b)...

_____ 14a

_____ 14b

57

15. For a gas to be a useful refrigerant, it must ..(15).. readily by
pressure alone at room temperature.

_____ 15

DIRECTIONS: Write the answers to the following in the spaces provided. Where appropriate, make complete statements.

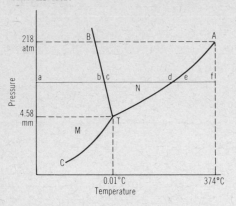

Figure 8B-1 Temperature-pressure
curves for pure water

Figure 8B-2 **Temperature vs time of heating
for a constant heat input of 10$\overline{0}$ cal/min,
starting with 10$\overline{0}$ g of ice at −20.0°C**

16. On Fig. 8B-1, label appropriate areas: **solid, liquid, vapor**; label appropriate points: **triple point, critical point.**

17. Where on Fig. 8B-1 do the following conditions prevail?

   a. Water vapor and water are in equilibrium. _____

   b. Water vapor and ice are in equilibrium. _____

   c. Ice and water are in equilibrium. _____

   d. Ice, water, and water vapor are in equilibrium. _____

18. In Fig. 8B-1, which curve is the equilibrium vapor pressure curve for water? _____

19. a. Can a solid at the temperature and pressure conditions represented by **M**, Fig. 8B-1, sublime? _____

   _____

   _____

   b. Can a liquid at the temperature and pressure conditions represented by **N**, Fig. 8B-1, vaporize? _____

   _____

   _____

20. On Fig. 8B-1, points **b** and **c** are the same point, as are points **d** and **e**. On Fig. 8B-2, points **a, b, c, d, e, f** have the same characteristics as the similarly designated points on Fig. 8B-1. Label appropriate portions of the graph in Fig. 8B-2: **solid (ice), liquid (water), vapor (steam).**

21. On Fig. 8B-2, label appropriate portions of the graph: **melting of ice, boiling of water.**

22. In Fig. 8B-2, what kind of potential and/or kinetic energy change is represented by segments **ab, cd,** and **ef**?

   _____

   _____

23. In Fig. 8B-2, what kind of potential and/or kinetic energy change is represented by segments **bc** and **de**?

   _____

24. What constant-temperature processes are shown in Fig. 8B-2? _____

   _____

25. What quantity of heat is required for each segment of the graph in Fig. 8B-2? Show the smooth form computation.

    a. Segment ab _____ 25a

    b. Segment bc _____ 25b

    c. Segment cd _____ 25c

    d. Segment de _____ 25d

    e. Segment ef _____ 25e

DIRECTIONS: In the parentheses at the right of each word or expression in the second column, write the letter of the expression in the first column that is MOST CLOSELY related.

a. −119°C for oxygen	critical point	( )	26
b. Amount of heat needed to vaporize a unit mass of liquid at its boiling point	critical pressure	( )	27
c. Separation of liquids having different boiling points	critical temperature	( )	28
d. Lowering the temperature of a substance below the normal freezing point without solidification	distillation	( )	29
	fractional distillation	( )	30
e. Amount of heat needed to melt a unit mass of a substance at its melting point	heat of fusion	( )	31
f. Lower limit of the liquid-gas evaporation curve	heat of vaporization	( )	32
g. Pressure at the critical point	heat pump operation	( )	33
h. Evaporation, then condensation in a separate vessel	normal boiling point	( )	34
i. Pressure at the triple point	supercooling	( )	35
j. Upper limit of the liquid-gas evaporation curve			
k. Point on liquid-gas evaporation curve at one atmosphere pressure			
l. Portion of the liquid-gas evaporation curve characterized by varying pressures and temperatures near room temperature			

DIRECTIONS: Continue the following definitions in the spaces provided, forming accurate and complete sentences.

36. The *heat capacity* of a body is _____

_____

37. The *specific heat* of a material is _____

38. The *law of heat exchange* states that _____

_____

_____

39. The *method of mixtures* is _____

_____

40. A *calorimeter* is _____

59

DIRECTIONS: Place the answers to the following problems in the spaces provided at the right.

41. What is the specific heat of silver if 112 cal is required to raise the temperature of 80.0 g of silver from 25.0°C to 50.0°C?

_____ 41

42. What is the final temperature of the mixture of 60.0 g of water at 70.0°C and 30.0 g of water at 0.0°C?

_____ 42

43. Calculate the mass of water at 20.0°C to which 10$\overline{0}$ g of zinc (specific heat = 0.092 cal/g C°) at a temperature of 150.0°C can be added in order to produce a final temperature of 40.0°C.

_____ 43

44. A calorimeter (specific heat = 0.090 cal/g C°) has a mass of 145 g. It contains 14$\overline{0}$ g of water at 20.0°C. The final temperature that results when a 15$\overline{0}$-g mass of tungsten at 330.0°C is added to the water in the calorimeter is 30.0°C. Calculate the specific heat of tungsten.

_____ 44

45. Calculate the mass of ice at 0.0°C that must be added to 40$\overline{0}$ g of water at 80.0°C so that the final water temperature is 15.0°C.

_____ 45

46. How many calories of heat are needed to change 25.0 g of ice at −10.0°C to water at 100.0°C?

_____ 46

47. How many grams of alcohol can be vaporized at 78.5°C by 9.18 $\times 10^3$ calories?

_____ 47

48. 10.0 g of steam at 100.0°C is passed into cool water at 20.0°C. The resulting final water temperature is 60.0°C. What is the mass of the cool water?

_____ 48

49. What final temperature results from mixing 30.0 g of ice at 0.0°C, 20.0 g of water at 0.0°C, and 10.0 g of steam at 100.0°C?

_____ 49

50. A calorimeter, mass 15$\overline{0}$ g, specific heat 0.090 cal/g C°, contains 125 g of water at 60.0°C. Ice, 70.0 g at −20.0°C, is added to the water. The resulting water temperature is 10.0°C. Calculate the heat of fusion of ice.

_____ 50

exercise **9**

Heat and Work

Sections 9.1–9.7

DIRECTIONS: Write the answers to the following questions in the spaces provided. Where appropriate, make complete statements.

1. What is *thermodynamics*? _____

_____

_____

2. What is *internal energy*? _____

_____

3. State the *first law of thermodynamics.* _____

_____

_____

4. What is an *adiabatic process*? _____

_____

5. In what two ways may *heat be converted to useful work*?

   a. _____

   b. _____

6. What is an *isothermal process*? _____

_____

7. What is an *ideal heat engine*? _____

_____

_____

8. What change in operating conditions increases the efficiency of an ideal heat engine? _____

_____

_____

_____

9. State the *second law of thermodynamics.* _____

_____

_____

_____

10. State the *law of entropy.* _____

_____

_____

_____

DIRECTIONS: In the blank space at the right of each statement, write the word or expression that BEST completes the meaning.

11. The mechanical equivalent of heat in the MKS system is ..(11)...

_____ 11

12. The first law of thermodynamics is a special case of the law of ..(12)...

_____ 12

13. When heat is converted to another form of energy, or vice versa, there is (great, some, no) ..(13).. loss of energy.

_____ 13

14. In the Joule experiment, no heat enters or leaves the insulating jar. The water-churning process is, therefore, a(n) ..(14).. one.

_____ 14

15. Work done by a gas is considered positive when the gas ..(15a).. and negative when the gas ..(15b)...

_____ 15a

_____ 15b

16. When the volume of a gas increases isothermally, its pressure ..(16a).. and its temperature ..(16b)...

_____ 16a

_____ 16b

17. During an isothermal expansion, the internal energy ..(17a).. and the potential energy ..(17b)...

_____ 17a

_____ 17b

18. When the volume of a gas increases adiabatically, its pressure ..(18a).. and its temperature ..(18b)...

_____ 18a

_____ 18b

19. During an adiabatic expansion, the internal energy ..(19a).. and the potential energy ..(19b)...

_____ 19a

_____ 19b

20. The source of the heat equivalent of the work done by an ideal gas during isothermal expansion is its ..(20a).., while the source of the heat equivalent of the work done by an ideal gas during adiabatic expansion is its ..(20b)...

_____ 20a

_____ 20b

21. The c_p of a gas is always ..(21).. the c_v.

_____ 21

22. The reason for No. 21 is that ..(22a).. must include work done on the movable part of the gas container, while ..(22b).. does not.

_____ 22a

_____ 22b

23. The second law of thermodynamics makes it impossible to attain a temperature of ..(23)...

_____ 23

24. Entropy is the amount of energy that cannot be converted into mechanical ..(24)...

_____ 24

25. Natural processes tend to increase ..(25).. in the universe.

_____ 25

DIRECTIONS: Place the answers to the following problems in the spaces provided at the right.

26. In the Joule experiment, a paddle wheel was rotated in a calorimeter cup containing water. The total water equivalent was $20\overline{0}$ g. The rotation was produced by a falling 20.0-kg mass coupled by pulleys to the paddle wheel. If the mass dropped 5.00 m and the resulting temperature rise in the water was 1.15 C°, find the mechanical equivalent of heat. Assume that the mass has no kinetic energy at the bottom of its fall.

_____ 26

27. A gas expands from a volume of 2.00 m^3 to 6.00 m^3 and does 6912 joules of work against a constant outside pressure. Find the outside pressure. _____ 27

28. A gas that has a volume of 24$\overline{0}$ m^3 at 0.0°C is heated to 182°C at a constant pressure of 9.25 n/m^2. What is the external work done? _____ 28

29. Find the efficiency of an ideal heat engine operating between temperatures of $-10\overline{0}$°C and 50$\overline{0}$°C. _____ 29

30. How much would the efficiency of an ideal heat engine be improved if its lower temperature were changed from 80.0°C to 40.0°C while the upper temperature remained at 30$\overline{0}$°C? _____ 30

exercise 10

The Nature of Waves

Sections 10.1–10.16

DIRECTIONS: In the space at the right, place the letter or letters indicating EACH choice that forms a correct statement.

1. Energy can be transferred **(a)** by the movement of materials, **(b)** by the movement of heated gas, **(c)** through matter by mechanical waves, **(d)** through space by electromagnetic waves.

      _____ 1

2. A wave **(a)** is a disturbance that moves only through solids, liquids, and gases, **(b)** produces a transfer of energy without the transport of matter, **(c)** involves a quantity that changes in magnitude with respect to time at a given location, **(d)** involves a disturbance that changes in magnitude from place to place at a given time.

      _____ 2

3. To produce a mechanical wave we need **(a)** an energy source, **(b)** a medium that behaves like an array of spring-connected particles,, **(c)** to produce a displacement of some sort in matter, **(d)** a form of matter in which the displacement of one particle has no effect on adjacent particles.

      _____ 3

4. A pulse moving along a spiral spring **(a)** carries particles of matter along with it, **(b)** is a method of energy transfer, **(c)** can be a crest or trough in longitudinal wave motion, **(d)** can be a compression or a rarefaction in transverse wave motion.

      _____ 4

5. A periodic wave **(a)** is related to the simple harmonic motion of the wave source, **(b)** that is transverse may be generated in a horizontal spring attached to a weight which vibrates vertically, **(c)** requires no continuing supply of energy, **(d)** that is longitudinal may be generated in a horizontal spring attached to a weight which vibrates horizontally.

      _____ 5

6. When a transverse pulse is reflected at the fixed termination of a medium, **(a)** the shape of the pulse is changed, **(b)** action and reaction forces are involved, **(c)** a crest is reflected as a crest, **(d)** a crest is reflected as a trough.

      _____ 6

7. The impedance **(a)** of a medium is the ratio of the applied wave-producing force to the resulting displacement velocity, **(b)** of a terminating medium is infinite in cases of total in-phase reflection, **(c)** of a terminating medium exactly matches that of the transmitting medium in cases of zero energy transfer between the media, **(d)** mismatch of two wave-propagation media may be reduced by an impedance transformer.

      _____ 7

8. Superposition **(a)** involves two or more waves moving simultaneously through the same medium, **(b)** allows complex waves to be analyzed in terms of simple wave combinations, **(c)** produces constructive interference when the crest of one wave coincides with the trough of a second wave, **(d)** produces destructive interference when the compression of one wave coincides with the rarefaction of a second wave.

      _____ 8

65

9. A standing wave is generated by two wave trains (a) of different wavelength but of the same frequency and amplitude traveling in the same direction, (b) of different frequency but of the same wavelength and amplitude traveling in the same direction, (c) of different amplitude but of the same wavelength and frequency traveling in the same direction, (d) of the same wavelength, frequency, and amplitude traveling in opposite directions. _____ 9

10. In a standing wave pattern (a) the particles vibrate in simple harmonic motion, (b) the amplitude of motion for all vibrating points is the same, (c) energy is transferred along the vibrating string, (d) there are alternate loops and nodes. _____ 10

DIRECTIONS: Write the answers to the following questions in the spaces provided. Where appropriate, make complete statements.

11. Describe the particle vibration that occurs in *transverse waves.* _____
_____

12. Describe the particle vibration that occurs in *longitudinal waves.* _____
_____

13. What is a *crest*? _____
_____

14. What is a *trough*? _____
_____

15. What is a *compression*? _____
_____
_____

16. What is a *rarefaction*? _____
_____
_____

17. What are the characteristics of particles of a vibrating medium that are *in phase*? _____
_____
_____

18. What is the *frequency* of a wave? _____
_____

19. What is the MKS unit of *frequency* and what is its dimension? _____
_____

20. How is the *period* of a wave related to its frequency? _____
_____

21. What is the *wavelength* of a wave? _____
_____
_____

22. What is the *speed* of a wave? _____

_____

23. What is a *dispersive* transmitting medium?_____

_____

_____

24. How is the power transmitted by a wave system related to the amplitude and frequency of the waves?_____

_____

_____

25. State the *law of reflection.* _____

_____

_____

DIRECTIONS: In the parentheses at the right of each word or expression in the second column, write the letter of the expression in the first column that is MOST CLOSELY related.

a. Movement through a uniform medium in a straight line	v	( )	26
b. hertz	λ	( )	27
c. $f\lambda$	f	( )	28
d. Periodic transverse straight waves	T	( )	29
e. Change in wave speed on passage from one medium to another	damping	( )	30
f. $1/f$	rectilinear propagation	( )	31
g. vT	reflection	( )	32
h. Periodic transverse circular waves	refraction	( )	33
i. Spreading of a wave disturbance beyond the edge of a barrier	diffraction	( )	34
j. Occurs at the boundary of the transmitting medium	interference	( )	35
k. Mutual effect of two waves in the same medium			
l. Reduction in wave amplitude due to dissipation of wave energy			

exercise **11**

Sound Waves

Sections 11.1–11.16

DIRECTIONS: In the space at the right, place the letter or letters indicating EACH choice that forms a correct statement.

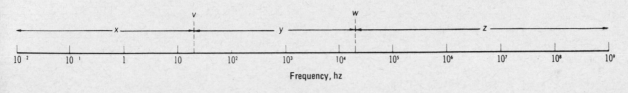

Frequency, hz

Figure 11-1

1. On the sonic spectrum frequency scale shown in Fig. 11-1, (a) y represents the audio range, (b) x represents the region of infrasonic waves, (c) z represents the region of ultrasonic waves, (d) $x + y + z$ represents the region of sound. _____ 1

2. Sounds are produced by (a) matter at rest, (b) matter in vibration, (c) solids only, (d) solids, liquids, or gases. _____ 2

3. As a steel strip vibrates from left to right, it is (a) doing work on the gas molecules to the right, (b) removing energy from the gas molecules to the right, (c) producing a maximum compression in the molecules to the right at its equilibrium position, (d) producing no change in the molecules to the right at its point of minimum displacement. _____ 3

4. Sound waves are (a) longitudinal waves in space, (b) longitudinal waves in matter, (c) transverse waves in space, (d) transverse waves in matter. _____ 4

5. The most common transmitting medium for sound vibrations is (a) metal wires, (b) earth, (c) water, (d) air. _____ 5

6. Sound waves are transmitted better through (a) rarefied gases than dense gases, (b) gases than through liquids, (c) gases than through solids, (d) solids and liquids than through gases. _____ 6

7. Sound travels (a) with the same speed as light, (b) faster than light, (c) slower than light, (d) at a rate of approximately 331.5 m/s in air at 0°C. _____ 7

8. The speed of sound in air (a) decreases with a rise in temperature, (b) is not affected by temperature change, (c) increases approximately (0.6 m/s)/C°, (d) is approximately 346 m/s at 25°C. _____ 8

DIRECTIONS: In the blank space at the right of each statement, write the word or expression that BEST completes the meaning.

9. The time rate at which sound energy flows through a unit area normal to the direction of propagation is its ..(9)... _____ 9

69

10. The physiological effect of the sound characteristic of No. 9 is
..(10)...

_____ 10

11. The intensity of a sound in a uniform medium at 1.5 km from
a point source is ..(11).. as great as at 0.5 km.

_____ 11

12. The intensity level of sound during conversation is ..(12)...

_____ 12

13. On the sonic spectrum frequency scale, Fig. 11-1, the lower limit
of audibility for most people is represented by point ..(13a)..
with a value of ..(13b).. hertz, while the upper limit of audibility
is represented by point ..(13c).. with a value of ..(13d).. hertz.

_____ 13a

_____ 13b

_____ 13c

_____ 13d

14. The minimum intensity level for audible sounds is the threshold of
..(14a).., while the upper intensity level for audible sounds is the
threshold of ..(14b)...

_____ 14a

_____ 14b

15. The number of hertz of a sound wave is its ..(15)...

_____ 15

16. The physiological effect of the sound characteristic of No. 15 is
..(16)...

_____ 16

17. The Doppler effect is associated with the variation in ..(17).. heard
when a source of sound and the ear are moving relative to each other.

_____ 17

18. As a locomotive approaches a crossing, the pitch of its horn heard by
the engineer is ..(18).. than the pitch of the horn heard by the crossing guard.

_____ 18

19. As the locomotive passes the crossing, the pitch of the horn heard by
the engineer (becomes higher, remains the same, becomes lower)
..(19a).., while the pitch of the horn heard by the crossing guard
(becomes higher, remains the same, becomes lower) ..(19b)...

_____ 19a

_____ 19b

20. The Doppler effect observation of light from many distant stars
which suggests that the universe is expanding is called the ..(20)...

_____ 20

DIRECTIONS: Write the answers to the following in the spaces provided. Where appropriate, make complete
statements.

21. When a guitar string vibrates as a whole,

a. what is characteristic of the frequency of the tone produced?_____

_____

b. what name is given to this tone? _____

_____

22. If a fundamental tone has a frequency of $44\overline{0}$ hz, its first harmonic has a frequency of _____

_____

23. The fourth harmonic of the fundamental of No. 22 has a frequency of _____

_____

24. What are *forced vibrations*? _____

_____

_____

25. What are *sympathetic vibrations*? _____

_____

_____

26. What is the approximate wavelength of the fundamental resonant frequency of a closed tube 35 cm long?

_____

27. What is the wavelength of the fundamental resonant frequency of an open tube 68 cm long and 4.0 cm in

diameter? _____

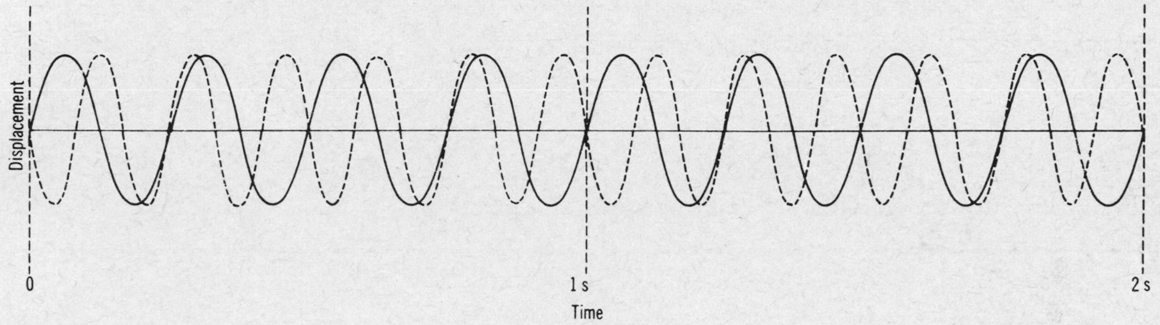

Figure 11-2

28. Figure 11-2 shows the superposition of two waves, one having a frequency of 4 hz, the other of 6 hz. Draw the resultant wave on Fig. 11-2.

29. How many beats per second result from the wave superposition of
No. 28?   _____ 29

30. What is the average frequency of the wave superposition of No. 28?   _____ 30

DIRECTIONS: In the space at the right, place the letter or letters indicating EACH choice that forms a correct statement.

31. The vibration of a string (a) is a longitudinal wave motion, (b) will decrease in amplitude unless energy is continually supplied to it, (c) sets up a transverse wave of the same frequency as that of the string in the surrounding air, (d) transfers energy to molecules of gases in the air.   _____ 31

32. A string that vibrates in four segments produces (a) its fundamental, (b) its first four harmonics, (c) its fundamental and fourth harmonic, (d) its fourth harmonic.   _____ 32

33. The *quality* of a sound depends on (a) the intensity of the fundamental, (b) the number and prominence of the harmonics present, (c) the frequency of the fundamental, (d) the characteristics of the instrument producing it.   _____ 33

34. The vibrating frequency of a string may be increased by (a) decreasing its length, (b) decreasing its tension, (c) plucking it more rapidly, (d) lowering its temperature.   _____ 34

35. The vibrating frequency of a string is inversely proportional to its (a) length, (b) diameter, (c) density, (d) tension.   _____ 35

71

exercise $12a$

The Nature of Light

Sections 12.1–12.14

DIRECTIONS: In the space at the right, place the letter or letters indicating EACH choice that forms a correct statement.

1. Rectilinear propagation, reflection, refraction, interference, and diffraction are all properties of **(a)** sound waves but not water waves, **(b)** water waves but not sound waves, **(c)** light waves only, **(d)** waves in general. _____ 1

2. The corpuscular theory assumes that **(a)** light consists of streams of tiny particles coming from a luminous source, **(b)** particles of light travel at such high speeds that their paths are straight lines, **(c)** particles of light are perfectly elastic and rebound in regular fashion from a reflecting surface, **(d)** particles of light move faster through air than through water. _____ 2

3. The corpuscular theory failed during the nineteenth century because **(a)** it could not explain rectilinear propagation satisfactorily, **(b)** the speed of light was shown to be slower in water than in air, **(c)** interference and diffraction cannot be explained very well by the behavior of particles, **(d)** particles of light were found to undergo inelastic collisions. _____ 3

4. The wave theory assumes that **(a)** light is a train of waves having wave fronts in the same direction as the paths of the light rays, **(b)** each point on a wave front may be regarded as a new source of disturbance, **(c)** the speed of light in optically dense media is less than that in air, **(d)** a ray of light is the line of direction of waves sent out from a luminous source. _____ 4

5. The electromagnetic theory **(a)** was developed by James Clerk Maxwell, **(b)** describes the manner in which radiated energy is propagated in free space, **(c)** predicts that heat radiations travel in space with the speed of light, **(d)** states that the energy of electromagnetic radiations is equally divided between an electric field and a magnetic field. _____ 5

6. The electromagnetic spectrum consists of a range of radiation frequencies extending from **(a)** 10^{-1} to 10^{-25} hz, **(b)** 3×10^{7} to 3×10^{-17} hz, **(c)** 10^{1} to 10^{25} hz, **(d)** 3×10^{17} to 3×10^{-7} hz. _____ 6

7. The photoelectric effect demonstrates that **(a)** the rate of emission of photoelectrons is directly proportional to the intensity of the light falling on the emitting surface, **(b)** the rate of emission of photoelectrons is inversely proportional to the frequency of the light falling on the emitting surface, **(c)** an increase in light intensity results in an increase in the velocities of emitted photoelectrons, **(d)** an increase in light intensity results in an increase in the number of photoelectrons emitted per second, these electrons having the same group of discrete velocities. _____ 7

73

8. Following the discovery of the photoelectric effect, the wave theory became inadequate because it could not explain why (a) the magnitude of the photoelectric current is proportional to the incident light intensity, (b) all substances have characteristic cut-off frequencies above which emission does not occur no matter how intense the illumination, (c) there is a time lag between the illumination of a surface and the ejection of a photoelectron, (d) a very feeble light containing frequencies above a minimum value causes the ejection of photoelectrons.

_____ 8

9. The quantum theory assumes that a transfer of energy between light and matter occurs only in discrete quantities proportional to (a) the intensity of the light, (b) the frequency of the radiation, (c) the quantity of the matter, (d) the temperature of the matter.

_____ 9

10. The modern view of the nature of light assumes that (a) light behaves in some circumstances like waves, (b) light behaves in some circumstances like particles, (c) light energy is transported in photons, (d) photons are guided along their path by a wave field.

_____ 10

DIRECTIONS: In the blank space at the right of each statement, write the word or expression that BEST completes the meaning.

11. The transmission of light does not require the presence of ..(11)...

_____ 11

12. The main person supporting the corpuscular theory of light was ..(12a).., while the wave theory of light was upheld chiefly by ..(12b)...

_____ 12a

_____ 12b

13. An electromagnetic wave is a(n) ..(13a).. disturbance involving ..(13b).. and ..(13c).. forces.

_____ 13a

_____ 13b

_____ 13c

14. Light is ..(14a).. that a human observer can ..(14b)..

_____ 14a

_____ 14b

15. The emission of electrons by a substance when illuminated by electromagnetic radiation is known as the ..(15)...

_____ 15

16. The fact that photoelectric emission consists of ejected electrons was first established by measuring the ..(16).. of the negative electricity.

_____ 16

17. Energy required to overcome the forces binding an electron within the surface of a material is known as the ..(17).. of that surface.

_____ 17

18. In any photoelectric situation the electrons ejected with maximum energy have their origin in the ..(18).. of atoms.

_____ 18

19. The negative potential on the collector of a photoelectric cell at which photoelectric current drops to zero is called the ..(19).. potential.

_____ 19

20. The cut-off potential for a given photoelectric system measures the kinetic energy of the ..(20).. photoelectrons ejected from the emitting surface.

_____ 20

21. The velocity of photoelectrons expelled from an emitting surface is independent of the ..(21).. of the light source.

_____ 21

74

22. The cut-off potential for a given photoelectric system is independent of the ..(22).. of the incident radiation.

_____ 22

23. The cut-off potential for a given photoelectric system depends only on the ..(23).. of the incident radiation.

_____ 23

24. For any emitting surface there is a characteristic frequency of illumination ..(24a).. which no photoelectrons are ejected; this is known as the ..(24b).. frequency of the emitter.

_____ 24a

_____ 24b

25. To increase the maximum kinetic energy of photoelectrons, one must ..(25).. the frequency of the radiation illuminating the emitting surface.

_____ 25

26. The wave theory of light assumes that the light energy is distributed uniformly over the advancing ..(26)...

_____ 26

27. According to the wave theory, radiation of any frequency should produce photoelectric emission provided its ..(27).. is high enough.

_____ 27

28. The beginning of the quantum theory is closely associated with the work of ..(28a).. and ..(28b)...

_____ 28a

_____ 28b

29. Light quanta are known as ..(29)...

_____ 29

30. In the expression $E = hf$, if E is expressed in joules and f in hertz, h will have the dimensions ..(30)...

_____ 30

31. The energy of photons is directly proportional to the ..(31).. of the light.

_____ 31

32. According to the electromagnetic theory, electrons moving about the nucleus of an atom experience an acceleration and must ..(32).. energy.

_____ 32

33. The unique assumption of the Bohr model of the atom is that an electron cannot experience a(n) ..(33).. while occupying a discrete orbit.

_____ 33

34. The photon behaves as if it has a(n) ..(34).. equal to h/λ.

_____ 34

35. Any matter particle having a mass m and a velocity v may be considered to have a(n) ..(35).. equal to h/mv.

_____ 35

36. Waves having different frequencies and random phase relationships are said to be ..(36a).., while waves with identical frequencies and a constant phase relationship are said to be ..(36b)...

_____ 36a

_____ 36b

37. The device that produces monochromatic light having in-phase parallel waves is a(n) ..(37)...

_____ 37

38. The standing ..(38a).. wave in a ruby laser is similar to the standing ..(38b).. wave in an organ pipe.

_____ 38a

_____ 38b

39. A practical application of the inverse photoelectric effect is the production of ..(39)...

_____ 39

40. A beam of light shines first on a totally reflecting surface and then on a totally absorbing surface. The pressure of the light on the first surface is ..(40).. that on the second.

_____ 40

exercise **12b**

Illumination

DIRECTIONS: In the parentheses at the right of each word or expression in the second column, write the letter of the expression in the first column that is MOST CLOSELY related.

a. Several rays of light coming from a point	luminous	( )	1
b. Transmits light but diffuses it			
c. Seen because of reflected light	illuminated	( )	2
d. A group of closely spaced rays	transparent substance	( )	3
e. Emits light because of energy of its	opaque substance	( )	4
accelerated particles			
f. Some rays of light are excluded	ray	( )	5
g. A single line of light			
h. Several rays of light proceeding toward	beam	( )	6
a point	diverging pencil	( )	7
i. Transmits light readily			
j. Point at which light rays converge	converging pencil	( )	8
k. Does not transmit light	umbra	( )	9
l. All rays of light are excluded			
	penumbra	( )	10

DIRECTIONS: In the space at the right, place the letter or letters indicating EACH choice that forms a complete statement.

11. In the practical study of light, all of the following are measured except (a) luminous intensity, (b) luminous flux, (c) luminous velocity, (d) illumination.   _____ 11

12. The luminous intensity of a 40-watt incandescent lamp is approximately (a) 35 candles, (b) 40 candles, (c) 80 candles, (d) 20 candles.   _____ 12

13. The efficiency of incandescent lamps in terms of the ratio of light output to wattage rating (a) increases with wattage increase, (b) decreases with wattage increase, (c) is constant for a given filament metal, (d) appears to be independent of the wattage.   _____ 13

14. The photometric quantity most closely related to power in mechanical systems is (a) luminous intensity, (b) luminous flux, (c) illumination, (d) candle power.   _____ 14

15. A 100-watt incandescent lamp emits luminous flux at the rate of approximately (a) 100 lm, (b) 130 lm, (c) 1600 lm, (d) 314 lm.   _____ 15

16. A 16.0-candle source at the center of a sphere of 1.00-meter radius provides illumination on the spherical surface of (a) 16.0 lm/m^2, (b) 4π lm/m^2, (c) 4.00 lm/m^2, (d) 201 lm/m^2.   _____ 16

17. If the spherical radius in No. 16 is increased to 4.00 meters, the illumination on the spherical surface becomes (a) 64.0 lm/m^2, (b) 4.00 lm/m^2, (c) 50.2 lm/m^2, (d) 1.00 lm/m^2.   _____ 17

77

18. The maximum illumination obtained from a 40.0-candle source 3.00 meters away is (a) 4.44 cd, (b) 13.3 lm/m^2, (c) 4.44 lm/m^2, (d) 120 cd.

_____ 18

19. If the luminous intensity of the source in No. 18 is tripled, the maximum illumination 3.00 meters away is (a) 13.3 cd, (b) 13.3 lm/m^2, (c) 40.0 lm/m^2, (d) 120 cd.

_____ 19

20. The Joly photometer (a) measures directly the intensity of a light source, (b) is more sensitive than the grease-spot photometer, (c) uses two blocks of paraffin separated by a metal plate, (d) compares the illumination from an unknown source to that from a standard source.

_____ 20

DIRECTIONS: In the blank space at the right of each statement, write the word or expression that BEST completes the meaning.

21. The energy of the thermal radiation given off by hot bodies depends upon the ..(21a).. of the body and the ..(21b).. of its surface.

_____ 21a

_____ 21b

22. As the temperature of a hot body increases, the amount of visible radiation emitted ..(22)...

_____ 22

23. A substance that transmits light but diffuses it so that objects cannot be seen clearly through it is said to be ..(23)...

_____ 23

24. Light travels (faster, slower) ..(24).. in air than in a vacuum.

_____ 24

25. Expressed in scientific notation and one significant figure, the speed of light in a vacuum in m/s is approximately ..(25)...

_____ 25

26. The quantitative study of light is called ..(26)...

_____ 26

27. The unit of luminous intensity of a source of light is the ..(27)...

_____ 27

28. The portion of the total energy radiated per unit of time from a luminous source that can produce the sensation of sight is known as ..(28a)..; the unit of measurement is the ..(28b)...

_____ 28a

_____ 28b

29. A sphere with radius r has a surface area expressed by the formula ..(29)...

_____ 29

30. A luminous source having an intensity of 1 candle radiates luminous flux at the rate of ..(30)...

_____ 30

31. The illumination on a surface pertains to the ..(31).. of the luminous flux on the surface.

_____ 31

32. The MKS unit of illumination is the ..(32)...

_____ 32

33. The inverse square law applies to calculations of illuminations from a point source on surfaces ..(33).. to the beam.

_____ 33

34. In the general case, the illumination on a surface varies ..(34a).. with the square of the distance from the luminous source and ..(34b).. with the ..(34c).. of the angle between the luminous flux and the normal to the surface.

_____ 34a

_____ 34b

_____ 34c

35. The instrument used to measure the candle power of a light source by comparing its intensity with that of a standard source is called a(n) ..(35)...

_____ 35

36. Laboratory comparison measurements of the intensities of light sources make use of the fact that when the comparing apparatus is correctly positioned, the intensities of the two light sources are ..(36a).. proportional to the ..(36b).. of their ..(36c).. from the screen.

_____ 36a

_____ 36b

_____ 36c

37. A(n) ..(37).. photometer is used commercially to measure the luminous intensity of electric lamps.

_____ 37

DIRECTIONS: **Place the answers to the following problems in the spaces provided at the right.**

38. A table is located 1.50 m directly below a 13$\overline{0}$-candle lamp. What is the illumination on the surface of the table?

_____ 38

39. A Bunsen photometer is equally illuminated when it is 35 cm from a standard lamp of 18 candles and 55 cm from a lamp of unknown intensity. What is the intensity of the unknown lamp?

_____ 39

40. A screen located 2 m from a luminous source has 9 times the illumination of a second screen illuminated by the same source. How far is the second screen from the luminous source?

_____ 40

exercise **13**

Reflection

Sections 13.1–13.12

DIRECTIONS: (A) In the blank space at the right of each statement, write the word or expression that BEST completes the meaning. (B) Use a well-sharpened pencil and straightedge in all constructions.

1. The returning of light to the first medium from the boundary between two media is called ..(1)... _____ 1

2. In Fig. 13-1, the reflecting surface is represented by the line segment ..(2)... _____ 2

3. The ray of light incident on the reflecting surface is shown as ..(3)... _____ 3

4. The *normal* drawn from the point of incidence is ..(4)... _____ 4

5. The *angle of incidence* is ..(5)... _____ 5

6. The *angle of reflection* is ..(6)... _____ 6

7. The angle of reflection is equal to the ..(7)... _____ 7

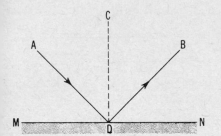

Figure 13-1

8. In Fig. 13-2, label the *center of curvature* as **C**, the *vertex* as **V**, and the *principal focus* as **F**.

9. Construct the *principal axis* as a line segment **PV** and a secondary axis as **SS**'.

10. A *normal* to the surface of a spherical mirror is a(n) ..(10a).. _____ 10a
    drawn from a point of ..(10b)... _____ 10b

11. The *focal length* of the mirror is the distance from the ..(11a).. _____ 11a
    to the ..(11b)... _____ 11b

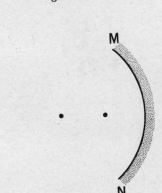

Figure 13-2

12. In Fig. 13-3, construct the two line segments representing rays that will locate the image of point **A**. Label the image as point **A**'.

13. Using the point of incidence of the ray already drawn that is not perpendicular to the point of incidence, construct the normal as a dashed line.

14. A ray parallel to the principal axis of a spherical mirror will be reflected through the ..(14)... _____ 14

15. A ray that follows the path of a ..(15).. will be reflected back upon itself. _____ 15

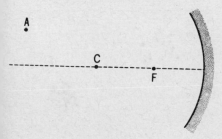

Figure 13-3

DIRECTIONS: (A) Write the answers to the following questions in the spaces provided. Where appropriate, make complete statements. (B) Use a well-sharpened pencil and straightedge in all constructions.

16. Describe the image formed by a concave mirror of an object located between the center of curvature and the principal focus. _____

_____

17. How does the size of the image formed by a concave mirror compare with that of an object located at the center of curvature? _____

_____

18. What are two distinct differences between virtual images and real images, as formed by curved mirrors?

a. _____

b. _____

_____

19. In Fig. 13-4, complete the construction to locate the image **A'B'** of the object **AB**.

20. Describe the image formed in Fig. 13-4. _____

_____

_____

21. In Fig. 13-5, complete the construction to locate the image **A'B'** of the object **AB**.

22. Describe the image formed in Fig. 13-5. _____

_____

_____

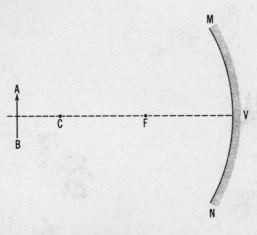

Figure 13-4

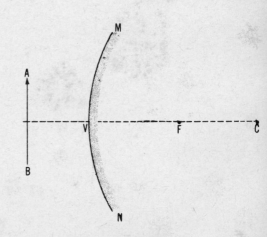

Figure 13-5

23. An object 7.0 cm high is $3\overline{0}$ cm in front of a concave mirror that has a focal length of $1\overline{0}$ cm. How far from the mirror is the image formed and how high is it? _____

_____

24. A 4.0-cm high object is placed $1\overline{0}$ cm in front of a concave mirror. The mirror has a focal length of 25 cm. Where, with respect to the mirror, is the image formed; how far from the mirror is it; how high is it?

_____

exercise **14a**

Optical Refraction

Sections 14.1–14.14

DIRECTIONS: In the blank space at the right of each statement, write the word or expression that BEST completes the meaning.

1. The speed of light in glass or water is (faster than, the same as, slower than) ..(1).. the speed of light in air.

    _____ 1

2. A property of a transparent material that is an inverse measure of the speed of light through the material is called ..(2)...

    _____ 2

3. The bending of light rays as they pass obliquely from one medium into another of different optical density is called ..(3)...

    _____ 3

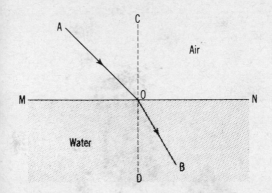

Figure 14A-1

4. In Fig. 14A-1, which illustrates the path of a light ray from air into water, **AO** is known as the ..(4).. ray.

    _____ 4

5. Ray **OB** is known as the ..(5).. ray.

    _____ 5

6. The line **CO** is the ..(6a).. drawn to the point of refraction, and **OD** is the ..(6b)...

    _____ 6a

    _____ 6b

7. Angle ..(7).. is the *angle of incidence.*

    _____ 7

8. The *angle of refraction* is ..(8)...

    _____ 8

9. A ray of light passing from one medium into another along the normal (is, is not) ..(9).. refracted.

    _____ 9

10. The ratio of the speed of light in a vacuum to its speed in a substance is known as the ..(10).. of that substance.

    _____ 10

DIRECTIONS: In the parentheses at the right of each word or expression in the second column, write the letter of the expression in the first column that is MOST CLOSELY related.

a. Transparent object having two nonparallel curved surfaces

b. Distance between optical center and principal focus

c. Formed on the same side of the lens as the real focus

d. Thicker at the edge than in the middle

e. Principal focus through which light rays actually pass

f. Passes through the center of the lens and is perpendicular to the lens plane

g. Formed on the same side of the lens as the virtual focus

h. Point of convergence of parallel rays parallel to the principal axis

i. Thicker in the middle than at the edge

j. Passes through the center of the lens not perpendicular to the lens plane

k. Principal focus from which light rays appear to originate

l. Contains the principal focus and is perpendicular to the principal axis

converging lens ( ) 11

diverging lens ( ) 12

focal length ( ) 13

principal axis ( ) 14

principal focus ( ) 15

real image ( ) 16

real focus ( ) 17

secondary axis ( ) 18

vitual focus ( ) 19

virtual image ( ) 20

DIRECTIONS: (A) Write the answers to the following questions in the spaces provided. Where appropriate, make complete statements. (B) Use a well-sharpened pencil and a straightedge in all constructions.

21. What are the three laws of refraction?

a. _____

_____

b. _____

_____

c. _____

_____

_____

_____

_____

_____

22. How did Snell define the index of refraction? _____

_____

_____

_____

23. What is a *refractometer* and for what is it used? _____

_____

_____

24. Why is the atmospheric refraction of light from the sun gradual rather than distinct? _____

_____

_____

_____

25. What is the size of the angle of refraction when the critical angle of incidence is reached? _____
   _____

26. Calculate the critical angle for ethyl alcohol, which has an index of refraction of 1.36. _____

27. Given a right-angle crown-glass prism with two sides equal, what path will a ray of light follow if it is incident
   perpendicular to one of the equal surfaces? _____
   _____
   _____
   _____
   _____

28. How are the focal length of a lens and the near point used to determine the magnification of a simple magnifier? _____
   _____

29. What position relationship does the objective lens of a compound microscope have to the object and the
   image formed? _____
   _____
   _____

30. List one similarity and one difference between prism binoculars and a refracting telescope. _____
   _____
   _____
   _____
   _____

31. Complete the construction in Fig. 14A-2, locating the image of the object shown.

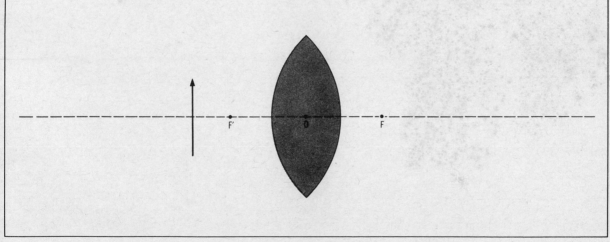

Figure 14A-2

32. Using a centimeter rule, measure the focal length of the lens and the object distance in Fig. 14A-2. Calculate
   the image distance and compare with your construction. _____

33. Measure the object height in Fig. 14A-2. Calculate the image height and compare with your construction.
   _____

34. Complete the construction in Fig. 14A-3, locating the image of the object shown.

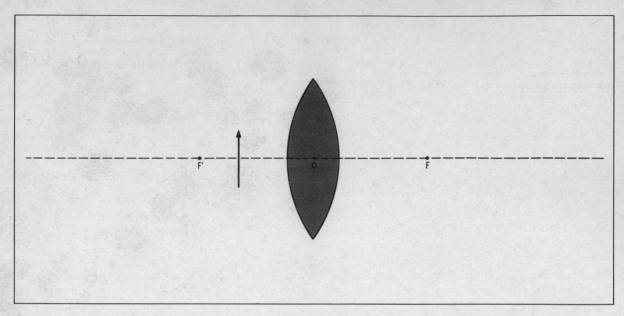

Figure 14A-3

exercise **14b**

Dispersion

Sections 14.15–14.21

DIRECTIONS: In the parentheses at the right of each word or expression in the second column, write the letter of the expression in the first column that is MOST CLOSELY related.

a. Two colors that combine to form white

b. Combining primary colors

c. Continuous band of colors

d. Lower limit of visibility

e. Light composed of several colors

f. Nonfocusing of light of different colors

g. Red, green, blue

h. Light consisting of a single color

i. Upper limit of visibility

j. Cyan, magenta, yellow

k. Combining primary pigments

l. Property of light reaching the eyes

solar spectrum	( )	1
monochromatic light	( )	2
polychromatic light	( )	3
color	( )	4
complementary colors	( )	5
primary colors	( )	6
primary pigments	( )	7
additive process	( )	8
subtractive process	( )	9
chromatic aberration	( )	10

DIRECTIONS: In the blank space at the right of each statement, write the word or expression that BEST completes the meaning. Numbers 11–15 refer to Fig. 14B-1, which shows the distribution of radiant energy from an ideal radiator.

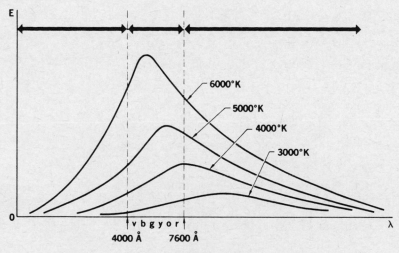

Figure 14B-1

11. Label appropriate regions: *visible, infrared, ultraviolet.*

12. The wavelength of light at the lower limit of visibility is ..(12a).., while that at the upper limit of visibility is ..(12b)... This repre-sents a range of frequencies of about a(n) ..(12c)...

_____ 12a

_____ 12b

_____ 12c

87

13. An increase in the temperature of the radiating body (increases, decreases, does not affect) ..(13).. the amount of visible radiation.

_____ 13

14. The temperature of the tungsten filament in a lamp is about $3000°K$. At this temperature most of its radiation is in the ..(14).. region.

_____ 14

15. Approximately how many times greater is the amount of energy detected as yellow light from a $6000°K$ source compared with that from a $3000°K$ source?

_____ 15

16. The dispersion of sunlight into several colors was described by ..(16)...

_____ 16

17. When white light is dispersed by a prism, ..(17a).. light is refracted least while ..(17b).. light is refracted most.

_____ 17a

_____ 17b

18. In precise measurements of the index of refraction of a substance, ..(18a).. light must be used and the ..(18b).. must be indicated.

_____ 18a

_____ 18b

19. Color bears the same relationship to light as ..(19).. does to sound.

_____ 19

20. An opaque object described as *blue* reflects the ..(20).. portion of the solar spectrum.

_____ 20

21. If examined under a red light in a darkened room, the object of No. 20 will appear to be ..(21)...

_____ 21

22. An opaque object described as *white* ..(22).. all colors of the sunlight incident upon its surface.

_____ 22

23. An opaque object described as *black* ..(23).. all colors of the sunlight incident upon its surface.

_____ 23

24. The color of an opaque object depends upon the ..(24a).. of the light incident upon it and upon the ..(24b).. of the light it reflects.

_____ 24a

_____ 24b

25. A ..(25).. transparent object transmits all colors.

_____ 25

26. The color of a transparent object depends upon the color of the light that it ..(26)...

_____ 26

27. If the red light is subtracted from dispersed white light, the remaining colors will combine to form ..(27).. light.

_____ 27

28. If the blue light is subtracted from dispersed white light, the remaining colors will combine to form ..(28).. light.

_____ 28

29. If the green light is subtracted from dispersed white light, the remaining colors will combine to form ..(29).. light.

_____ 29

30. The complement of an elementary color (can be, cannot be) ..(30).. another elementary color.

_____ 30

31. The primary pigments are the ..(31).. of the primary colors.

_____ 31

32. If white light is incident on a pigment, the light subtracted is the ..(32).. of the light reflected.

_____ 32

33. A pigment that subtracts blue light from white light appears ..(33a).. due to the reflection of both ..(33b)...

_____ 33a

_____ 33b

34. A pigment that subtracts red light from white light appears ..(34a).. due to the reflection of both ..(34b)...

_____ 34a

_____ 34b

35. If the two pigments of Nos. 33 and 34 are mixed, the only color not absorbed is ..(35)...

_____ 35

exercise **15**

Interference, Diffraction, and Polarization

Sections 15.1–15.12

DIRECTIONS: In the space at the right, place the letter or letters indicating EACH choice that forms a correct statement.

1. Constructive interference between two light rays results in **(a)** a loss of energy, **(b)** destruction of the wave front, **(c)** energy reinforcement, **(d)** bright areas of light.

                              _____ **1**

2. Interference phenomena **(a)** provided Newton with his strongest arguments in favor of the corpuscular theory, **(b)** are observed in soap films and oil slicks, **(c)** require a wave model of light, **(d)** are difficult to observe without special apparatus.

  _____ **2**

3. Thin-film interference results from the **(a)** refraction of some of the incident light at both the upper and lower surfaces of the film, **(b)** reflection of some light at the upper surface and the refraction of some light at the lower surface, **(c)** reflection of some light at both the upper and lower surfaces, **(d)** transmission of light through the film.

  _____ **3**

4. A thin film observed by reflected monochromatic light appears **(a)** bright where the thickness is one-quarter wavelength, **(b)** dark where the thickness is one-quarter wavelength, **(c)** bright where the thickness is one-half wavelength, **(d)** dark where the thickness is one-half wavelength.

  _____ **4**

5. The spreading of light into the region behind an obstruction **(a)** is made evident by interference effects, **(b)** is most pronounced when the obstruction is large with respect to the wavelength of the light, **(c)** is known as diffraction, **(d)** was first explained by Fresnel.

  _____ **5**

6. In the case of a transmission grating situated in a light beam, **(a)** the ruled lines act as transmission slits, **(b)** new wavelets are generated at the narrow spaces between the ruled lines, **(c)** no diffraction effects are produced if the ruled lines are very close together, **(d)** spectra are produced that are generally less intense than those formed by prisms.

  _____ **6**

7. Light radiated from luminous bodies is unpolarized because **(a)** the radiation occurs in all directions, **(b)** the primary radiators oscillate independently, **(c)** the oscillation planes of the wave trains are randomly oriented, **(d)** the magnitudes of the vertical and horizontal components of the light vectors are equal to zero.

  _____ **7**

8. Light can become plane-polarized **(a)** through interactions with matter, **(b)** by reflection from a surface, **(c)** by refraction through some crystals, **(d)** by selective absorption of light in some crystals.

  _____ **8**

9. The two plane-polarized beams of light that emerge from an illuminated calcite crystal cannot interfere with each other because **(a)** they are transmitted through the crystal at different speeds, **(b)** they have a common source, **(c)** their planes of polarization are perpendicular to each other, **(d)** their separate intensities are below the interference threshold.

  _____ **9**

10. The scattering phenomenon is an example of (a) diffraction, (b) interference, (c) polarization, (d) none of the above. _____ 10

DIRECTIONS: In the blank space at the right of each statement, write the word or expression that BEST completes the meaning.

11. The mutual effect of two beams of light that results in the loss of energy in certain areas and reinforcement of energy in others is known as ..(11)... _____ 11

12. The phenomenon of No. 11 was first demonstrated with light by ..(12a).. in the year ..(12b)... _____ 12a

_____ 12b

13. Light waves reflected from the upper surface of a thin soap film (do, do not) ..(13).. undergo a phase inversion. _____ 13

14. Light waves that pass into a thin soap film and are reflected from its lower surface (do, do not) ..(14).. undergo a phase inversion. _____ 14

15. A thin film appears bright by reflected monochromatic light where its thickness is a(n) ..(15).. number of quarter wavelengths. _____ 15

16. A thin film appears dark by reflected monochromatic light where its thickness is a(n) ..(16).. number of quarter wavelengths. _____ 16

17. A thin wedge of air between two glass plates yields a regular interference pattern. The glass plates are said to be ..(17)... _____ 17

18. Light that spreads into a region behind an obstruction is said to be ..(18)... _____ 18

19. The distance between adjacent ruled lines on a diffraction grating is called the ..(19)... _____ 19

20. The light waves that pass through a diffraction grating and constructively interfere and produce a first-order image are out of phase by ..(20).. wavelength(s). _____ 20

21. Interference and diffraction phenomena provide the best evidence of the ..(21).. characteristics of light. _____ 21

22. When light is polarized, the oscillations are confined to a(n) ..(22).. perpendicular to the line of propagation. _____ 22

23. Since light can be polarized, the wave-like character is considered to be ..(23)... _____ 23

24. Sound is a(n) ..(24).. disturbance and cannot be polarized. _____ 24

25. Tourmaline, which transmits light in one plane of polarization and absorbs light in other polarization planes, is said to have the property of ..(25)... _____ 25

26. *Polaroid* film polarizes light passing through it by the method of ..(26)... _____ 26

27. The polarization of reflected light is complete when the incident light strikes the reflecting surface at the particular angle of incidence known as the ..(27).. angle. _____ 27

28. A calcite crystal placed on a line of print differs from a glass plate in that ..(28).. refracted image(s) of the print can be seen. _____ 28

92

29. A doubly refracting crystal transmits ..(29a).. beam(s) of polarized light, ..(29b).. of which conform(s) to Snell's law.

    _____ 29a

    _____ 29b

30. When a beam of light passes through a calcite crystal, it is separated into two beams incapable of ..(30).. with each other.

    _____ 30

31. If two light waves cannot be made to interfere with each other, their oscillations must lie in ..(31)...

    _____ 31

32. Materials that become doubly refracting when under stress are said to be ..(32)...

    _____ 32

33. When scattering occurs, the light sent off to the side consists mainly of the ..(33).. wavelengths.

    _____ 33

34. As a consequence of the phenomenon of No. 33, the setting sun has a(n) ..(34).. appearance.

    _____ 34

35. Cane sugar may be described as a(n) ..(35).. substance because it rotates the plane of polarized light transmitted through it.

    _____ 35

exercise **16**

Electrostatics

Sections 16.1–16.17

DIRECTIONS: In the parentheses at the right of each word or expression in the second column, write the letter of the expression in the first column that is MOST CLOSELY related.

a. A material through which an electric charge is not readily transferred

b. Change in potential per unit of distance

c. Used to observe the presence of an electro-static charge

d. Acquires a charge opposite in sign to that of the body producing it

e. Force per unit positive charge at a point in an electric field

f. Acquires a charge of the same sign as that of the body producing it

g. Process that produces electric charges on an object

h. Exists in a region of space if an electric charge placed in that region is subject to an electric force

i. Quantity of charge per unit area

j. Commonly produced by friction between two surfaces in close contact

k. Work done per unit charge

l. Has a number of easily moved free electrons

electrification	( )	1
static electricity	( )	2
conductor	( )	3
insulator	( )	4
charged by conduction	( )	5
charged by induction	( )	6
electric field	( )	7
electric field intensity	( )	8
potential difference	( )	9
potential gradient	( )	10

DIRECTIONS: Complete the diagrams below to show the sequence of events when a negatively charged rod is brought toward an uncharged pith ball. Add the pith ball and silk thread in appropriate positions to (B), (C), and (D), and use + and − signs to show the location and nature of the charges on the pith ball in all four diagrams.

11.

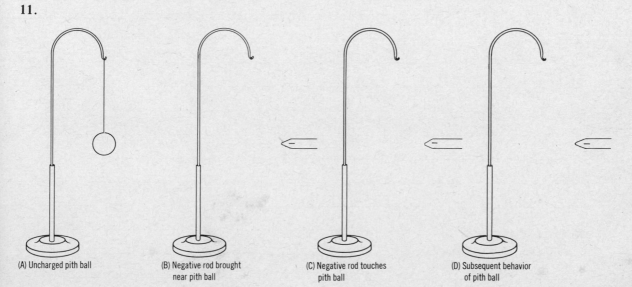

(A) Uncharged pith ball

(B) Negative rod brought near pith ball

(C) Negative rod touches pith ball

(D) Subsequent behavior of pith ball

DIRECTIONS: Complete the diagrams below to show the steps in charging an electroscope negatively by induction. Add the two leaves to each electroscope and use + and – signs to show the location and nature of the charges.

12.

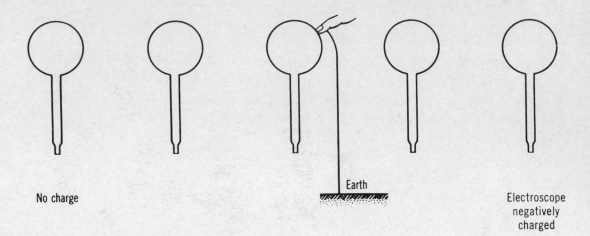

No charge

Earth

Electroscope negatively charged

DIRECTIONS: Complete the following review table for metric prefixes.

13.

Letter prefix	k	m	M	p	µ
Name prefix					
Power of ten					

DIRECTIONS: Write statements or definitions of each of the following in the spaces provided. Make complete statements.

14. Basic law of electrostatics. _____

_____

_____

15. Coulomb's law of electrostatics. _____

_____

_____

_____

16. Coulomb. _____

17. Volt. _____

_____

_____

_____

18. Farad. _____

_____

_____

DIRECTIONS: In the blank space at the right of each statement, write the word or expression that BEST completes the meaning.

19. An electric line of force is a line so drawn that a(n) ..(19a).. to it at any point indicates the orientation of the ..(19b).. at that point.

_____ 19a

_____ 19b

20. The electric field intensity is proportional to the number of ..(20a).. per ..(20b).. normal to the field.

_____ 20a

_____ 20b

21. The resultant force acting on a test charge placed at the midpoint between two equal charges is ..(21)...

_____ 21

22. If a charge located in an electric field moves in response to the electric force, work is done by the ..(22a).. and ..(22b).. is removed from the system.

_____ 22a

_____ 22b

23. If a charge located in an electric field is moved against the electric force, work is done on it and ..(23).. is stored in the system.

_____ 23

24. If work is done as a charge moves from one point to another in an electric field, these two points differ in ..(24)...

_____ 24

25. If work is required to move a charge from one point to another in an electric field, these two points differ in ..(25)...

_____ 25

26. The magnitude of this work is a measure of the ..(26)...

_____ 26

27. The earth may be considered to be an inexhaustible ..(27a).. of electrons or a limitless ..(27b).. for electrons; for practical purposes the potential of the earth is arbitrarily taken as ..(27c)...

_____ 27a

_____ 27b

_____ 27c

28. The potential at any point in an electric field is the ..(28a).. between the point and the ..(28b).. taken as the zero reference potential.

_____ 28a

_____ 28b

29. All the electrostatic charge on an isolated conductor resides ..(29)...

_____ 29

30. There can be no ..(30).. between two points on the surface of a charged isolated conductor.

_____ 30

31. If points that have the same potential in an electric field near a charged object are joined, a(n) ..(31).. line or surface within the field becomes apparent.

_____ 31

32. An electric field has (a, no) ..(32).. force component along an equipotential surface.

_____ 32

33. A sharply pointed charged conductor may be discharged rapidly due to ..(33).. of the air.

_____ 33

34. The slow leakage of charge from sharp projections of charged bodies is known as a brush or ..(34).. discharge.

_____ 34

35. A combination of conducting plates separated by an insulator and used to store an electric charge is called a(n) ..(35)...

_____ 35

36. The ..(36).. of a capacitor is the ratio of the charge on either plate to the potential difference between the plates.

_____ 36

37. In practice, the dielectric constant of dry air at one atmosphere pressure is taken as ..(37)...

_____ 37

38. If a substance having a dielectric constant of 2 is substituted for air as the insulator separating the plates of a certain capacitor, the capacitance will be ..(38)...

_____ 38

39. The capacitances of two capacitors connected in parallel are ..(39).. to give the total capacitance of the combination.

_____ 39

40. For two capacitors connected in series, the total capacitance equals the ..(40a).. of the two capacitances divided by their ..(40b)...

_____ 40a

_____ 40b

exercise 17a

Direct-Current Circuits

Sections 17.1–17.5

DIRECTIONS: In the parentheses at the right of each word or expression in the second column, write the letter of the expression in the first column that is MOST CLOSELY related.

a. Flow of electrons continuously in one direction through a conductor

b. Conversion of mechanical energy into electric energy

c. One path for current

d. Measures difference of potential

e. Two or more electrochemical cells connected together

f. Measuring resistance

g. Average rate of motion of free electrons in the direction of the accelerating force

h. Two or more paths for current

i. Substance whose solution conducts electricity

j. Flow of electrons through a conductor

k. Measures rate of flow of electricity

l. One electrochemical cell

ammeter	( )	1
voltmeter	( )	2
electric current	( )	3
direct current	( )	4
drift velocity	( )	5
electromagnetic induction	( )	6
battery	( )	7
electrolyte	( )	8
series circuit	( )	9
parallel circuit	( )	10

DIRECTIONS: In the space at the right, indicate the meaning of each electric symbol shown below.

11. _____ 11

12. _____ 12

13. _____ 13

14. _____ 14

15. _____ 15

16. _____ 16

17. _____ 17

18. _____ 18

19. _____ 19

20. _____ 20

DIRECTIONS: In the blank space at the right of each statement, write the word or expression that BEST completes the meaning.

21. During the time a capacitor is discharging, a(n) ..(21).. exists in the conducting circuit.

_____ 21

22. An electric current in a conductor is the ..(22).. of charge through a cross section of the conductor.

_____ 22

23. The MKS unit of current is the ..(23a).., which is defined as a current of ..(23b).. per second.

_____ 23a

_____ 23b

24. The direction in which electrons flow through an electric field in a metallic conductor is from ..(24a).. to ..(24b)...

_____ 24a

_____ 24b

25. Resistance is defined as the opposition to the ..(25)...

_____ 25

26. The MKS unit of resistance is the ..(26)...

_____ 26

27. In a closed-loop conducting path that includes a suitable source of electric current, ..(27a).. from the source is utilized in some device called the ..(27b)...

_____ 27a

_____ 27b

28. In the photoelectric cell, ..(28).. energy is transformed into electric energy.

_____ 28

29. In the thermocouple, ..(29a).. energy is transformed directly into electric energy. This is an example of the ..(29b).. effect.

_____ 29a

_____ 29b

30. If a direct current flows from copper to nickel through a junction, the junction (warms, cools) ..(30a)... This is an example of the ..(30b).. effect.

_____ 30a

_____ 30b

31. In the piezoelectric cell, ..(31).. energy is transformed into electric energy.

_____ 31

32. Spontaneous ..(32a).. reactions are a source of continuous current in which ..(32b).. energy is transformed into ..(32c).. energy.

_____ 32a

_____ 32b

_____ 32c

33. An electrochemical cell, such as a flashlight cell, that is replaced when its reactants are used up is a(n) ..(33).. cell.

_____ 33

34. Electrochemical cells, such as those in an automobile battery, that can be repeatedly recharged, are known as ..(34).. cells.

_____ 34

35. The cell in which the chemical energy of the reaction between hydrogen and oxygen to form water is converted directly into electric energy is a(n) ..(35).. cell.

_____ 35

36. The electron-rich electrode of a dry cell is called the ..(36a).., while the electron-poor electrode is called the ..(36b)...

_____ 36a

_____ 36b

37. The open-circuit potential difference across a dry cell is known as the ..(37a).. of the cell and is defined as the ..(37b).. per unit charge supplied by the cell.

_____ 37a

_____ 37b

38. The *emf* of a battery composed of cells connected in ..(38).. is equal to the sum of the emfs of the individual cells.

_____ 38

39. If three identical cells are connected in parallel, the current supplied by each cell is ..(39).. the total current in the circuit.

_____ 39

40. A certain resistance load is designed to operate across a 4.5-volt d-c circuit and when in continuous operation draws 1.00 ampere of current. Draw the circuit diagram in the block below using an appropriate arrangement of No. 6 dry cells to supply 1.00 ampere of continuous current at 4.5 volts.

exercise **17b**

Series and Parallel Circuits

Sections 17.6–17.13

DIRECTIONS: (A) Place the answers to the following problems in the spaces provided at the right. (B) Use a well-sharpened pencil and a straightedge in all diagrams.

1. What is the total resistance of a network of three resistors connected in *series* if each has a resistance of 6 ohms? _____ 1

2. What is the equivalent resistance of a network of three resistors connected in *parallel* if each has a resistance of 6 ohms? _____ 2

3. Given a *series* circuit with resistors $R_1, R_2,$ and R_3 of 3 ohms, 4 ohms, and 5 ohms respectively, **a.** what is the combined resistance of R_1 and R_2? **b.** What is the total resistance of the circuit? _____ 3a
_____ 3b

4. If R_1, of $6\overline{0}$ ohms, is connected in *parallel* with R_2, of $3\overline{0}$ ohms, what equivalent resistance do they present to the circuit? _____ 4

5. A *series* circuit contains two resistances, R_1 and R_2. Two cells connected in *series* serve as the source of emf. An ammeter is connected in the circuit to read the current through the external circuit, and a voltmeter is connected across the external circuit. In block **A**, draw the circuit diagram.

A

6. An electric circuit consists of two cells connected in *parallel* as a source of emf, resistors R_1 and R_2 in *parallel*, an ammeter to read total current, and a voltmeter to read the potential difference across the external circuit. In block **B**, draw the circuit diagram.

B

7. A circuit consists of a battery of four cells in *series*, a resistor R_1 connected in *series* with a *parallel* combination of R_2 and R_3. In block C, draw the circuit diagram.

C

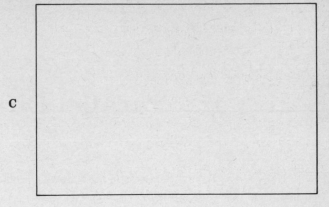

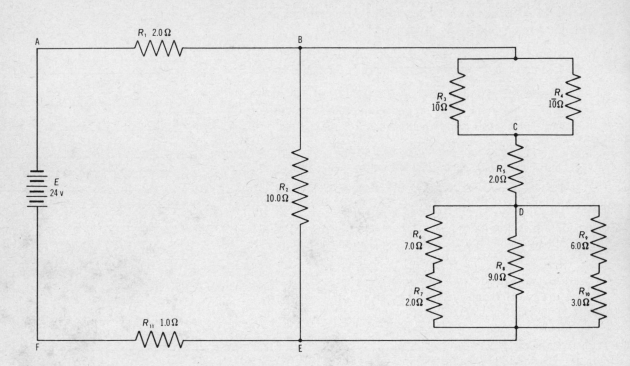

DIRECTIONS: Place the answers to the following problems, which refer to the circuit above, in the spaces provided at the right. Do the computations mentally, if possible.

8. What is the equivalent resistance of R_3 and R_4? _____ 8

9. What is the combined resistance of R_6 and R_7? _____ 9

10. What is the combined resistance of R_9 and R_{10}? _____ 10

11. What is the equivalent resistance from D to E? _____ 11

12. What is the equivalent resistance from B to E? _____ 12

13. What is the total resistance of the external circuit (from A to F)? _____ 13

14. What is the total current in the external circuit? _____ 14

15. What potential drop occurs across R_1? _____ 15

16. What is the drop in potential from B to E? _____ 16

17. How much current is in R_2? _____ 17

18. How much current is in R_5? _____ 18

19. What is the potential drop from B to C? _____ 19

20. What is the current in R_3? _____ 20

21. What is the voltage drop across R_5? _____ 21

22. What is the current in each branch of the circuit from D to E? _____ 22

23. What is the potential drop across R_6? _____ 23

24. What potential drop occurs across R_7? _____ 24

25. What is the potential drop across R_8? _____ 25

26. What is the sum of the potential drops across R_9 and R_{10}? _____ 26

27. Find the sum of the potential drops from A to B, B to E, and E to F. _____ 27

28. What resistance is in parallel with R_2? _____ 28

29. What is the sum of all currents between B and E? _____ 29

30. Does Ohm's law apply to each part of the circuit as well as to the circuit as a whole? _____ 30

DIRECTIONS: In the space at the right, place the letter or letters indicating EACH choice that forms a correct statement.

31. Materials whose resistance may usually be neglected in electric circuit calculations include (a) silver, (b) copper, (c) nichrome, (d) carbon granules molded with clay. _____ 31

32. Ohm's law (a) relates emf, current, and resistance, (b) states that E/I is constant, (c) indicates that current is inversely proportional to emf, (d) indicates that emf is directly proportional to resistance. _____ 32

33. The ohm (a) equals amperes/volts, (b) equals kg m^2/c^2 s, (c) is the MKS unit of resistance, (d) is the unit for measuring internal resistance and load resistance. _____ 33

34. In a series circuit (a) there is a drop in current around the circuit, (b) there is a drop in potential around the circuit, (c) the current around the circuit is constant, (d) the potential around the circuit is constant. _____ 34

35. Kirchhoff's (a) first law states that the algebraic sum of the currents at any circuit junction equals zero, (b) second law states that the algebraic sum of all the changes in potential around a circuit equals zero, (c) first law is a law of conservation of charge, (d) second law is a law of conservation of energy. _____ 35

36. In a parallel circuit (a) the current in each branch is equal, (b) the total resistance is the sum of the separate resistances, (c) the potential difference across all branches is the same, (d) the total current equals the sum of the currents in the separate branches. _____ 36

37. The resistance of (a) pure metals decreases with a rise in temperature, (b) semiconductors does not vary with temperature changes, (c) constantan increases with a rise in temperature, (d) a metal is related to the thermal agitation of its particles. _____ 37

38. The resistance of a uniform conductor (a) is directly proportional to its length, (b) is directly proportional to its cross-sectional area, (d) depends on the material of which it is made, (d) equals its resistivity multiplied by the ratio of its length to its cross-sectional area. _____ 38

105

39. Superconductivity is related to **(a)** cryogenics, **(b)** transition temperature, **(c)** zero resistance, **(d)** ultra-low temperature research. _____ 39

40. Resistance measurement **(a)** involves application of Ohm's law, **(b)** by the voltmeter-ammeter method is convenient but not very precise, **(c)** by the Wheatstone bridge method involves a proportion of four resistances, **(d)** by the Wheatstone bridge method involves using lengths of two segments of a uniform conductor in place of their resistances. _____ 40

exercise 18a

Heating Effects

Sections 18.1–18.6

DIRECTIONS: Write the answers to the following questions in the spaces provided. Where appropriate, make complete statements.

1. What is the source of the electric energy expended in the external circuit as the electric charge moves through the circuit in response to a potential difference placed across it? _____

_____

_____

_____

_____

_____

_____

_____

_____

2. In what form is the electric energy expended in an external circuit that consists of an ordinary resistor?

_____

_____

3. State Joule's law. _____

_____

_____

_____

4. In the expression for Joule's law, $Q = \dfrac{I^2 R t}{J}$, show how Q may be expressed in kilocalories.

5. What is the relationship of the watt, joule, and second? _____

_____

6. What is the relationship between electric power expended by a current in a resistance and the current in the resistance? _____

_____

_____

107

7. Is electric power dissipated within the source of emf in an electric circuit? Explain. _____
_____
_____
_____

8. What is the relationship between the total power consumed in an electric circuit, the power dissipated within the source, and the power expended in the load? _____
_____
_____
_____

9. Under what conditions is maximum power transferred to the load connected across a source of emf?
_____
_____
_____

10. In what unit is commercially sold electric energy measured? _____
_____

DIRECTIONS: In the blank space at the right of each statement, write the word or expression that BEST completes the meaning.

11. When one coulomb of electric charge is moved through a potential difference of one volt, one ..(11).. of work is done.   _____ 11

12. The equation for No. 11 is ..(12)...   _____ 12

13. One coulomb of electric charge transferred in one second constitutes a current of one ..(13)...   _____ 13

14. The equation for No. 13 is ..(14)...   _____ 14

15. Combining the equations of Nos. 12 and 14, the equation for the energy expended in the resistance of an external circuit in terms of the potential difference across the resistance, the current through the resistance, and the time the current flows is ..(15)...   _____ 15

16. The equation for the potential difference across the resistance of an external circuit in terms of the current in the circuit and the resistance of the circuit is ..(16)...   _____ 16

17. Substituting the equation of No. 16 in the equation of No. 15, the equation for the energy expended in the resistance of an external circuit in terms of the current in the resistance, the magnitude of the resistance, and the time the current flows is ..(17)...   _____ 17

18. In all cases when work is being done by an electric current, part of the work appears as ..(18).. because of the inherent resistance of the circuit.   _____ 18

19. Electric power is the ..(19).. at which electric energy is delivered to the circuit.   _____ 19

20. When the load resistance connected across a source of emf is equal to the internal resistance of the source, the source and the load are said to be ..(20)...   _____ 20

108

DIRECTIONS: Place the answers to the following problems in the spaces provided at the right.

21. How much heat is produced by a current of 6.0 amperes in a load resistance of $3\overline{0}$ ohms for 5.0 minutes?

_____ 21

22. The heating element of an electric stove draws 12.0 amperes when connected across a $12\overline{0}$-volt circuit. What is the resistance of the element?

_____ 22

23. How much heat will be produced by the heating element in No. 22 in 8.00 minutes?

_____ 23

24. How many kilograms of water can be heated from 20.0°C to 100.0°C by 165 kcal of heat?

_____ 24

25. What is the cost of the electricity used by the heating element in No. 22 at 5.0 cents per kilowatt hour?

_____ 25

exercise **18b**

Electrolysis

Sections 18.7–18.9

DIRECTIONS: In the parentheses at the right of each word or expression in the second column, write the letter of the expression in the first column that is MOST CLOSELY related.

a. Chemical energy to electric energy	anode	( ) 1
b. Grams per coulomb	cathode	( ) 2
c. $Cu^{++} + 2e^- \rightarrow Cu^0$		
d. Electric energy to chemical energy	chemical equivalent	( ) 3
e. Charged particle of matter	electrochemical cell	( ) 4
f. Negative terminal of an electrolytic cell		
g. Coulombs	electrochemical equivalent	( ) 5
h. Positive terminal of an electrolytic cell	electrolyte	( ) 6
i. $Cu^0 \rightarrow Cu^{++} + 2e^-$		
j. Ratio of gram-atomic weight to ionic charge	electrolytic cell	( ) 7
	Faraday	( ) 8
k. Laws of electrolysis		
l. Conducting solution of a cell	faraday	( ) 9
	ion	( ) 10

DIRECTIONS: In the blank space at the right of each statement, write the word or expression that BEST completes the meaning.

11. Electron-transfer reactions that are spontaneous can be sources of ..(11)...

_____ 11

12. An arrangement in which a spontaneous electron-transfer reaction occurs is known as a(n) ..(12).. cell.

_____ 12

13. The products of a spontaneous electron-transfer reaction have (more, less) ..(13).. energy than the reactants.

_____ 13

14. Electron-transfer reactions that are not spontaneous can be forced to occur by supplying ..(14).. from an external source.

_____ 14

15. An arrangement in which a forced electron-transfer reaction occurs is known as a(n) ..(15).. cell.

_____ 15

16. The products of a forced electron-transfer reaction have (more, less) ..(16).. energy than the reactants.

_____ 16

17. When an electrolytic cell is in operation, the anode is given a(n) ..(17a).. charge and the cathode is given a(n) ..(17b).. charge.

_____ 17a

_____ 17b

18. When the electrodes are charged, ..(18a).. ions migrate to the cathode, acquire ..(18b).. of high potential energy, and are discharged.

_____ 18a

_____ 18b

111

19. Ions having a(n) ..(19a).. charge migrate to the anode, give up ..(19b).. of low potential energy, and are discharged.

_____ 19a

_____ 19b

20. The conducting solution of an electrochemical or electrolytic cell contains a(n) ..(20a).. that furnishes positively and negatively charged ..(20b)...

_____ 20a

_____ 20b

21. The ..(21a).. of electrons by the cathode and the ..(21b).. of an equal number of electrons by the anode is, in effect, the ..(21c).. of electric charge through an electrolytic cell.

_____ 21a

_____ 21b

_____ 21c

22. The ..(22a).. of electric charge through a solution of a(n) ..(22b).., together with the resulting ..(22c).. changes is called ..(22d)...

_____ 22a

_____ 22b

_____ 22c

_____ 22d

23. The products of an electrolysis depend on the kinds of ..(23a).., on the nature of the ..(23b).., and to some degree on the ..(23c).. of the source.

_____ 23a

_____ 23b

_____ 23c

24. Electrolytic cells are used in ..(24a).. compounds and in refining and plating ..(24b)...

_____ 24a

_____ 24b

25. In an electroplating cell, the object to be plated is connected in the circuit as the ..(25)...

_____ 25

26. In an electroplating cell, the ..(26).. is made of the plating metal.

_____ 26

27. In an electroplating cell, the conducting solution contains a(n) ..(27).. of the metal to be plated.

_____ 27

28. The action at the cathode results in electrons being (acquired by, removed from) ..(28).. that electrode.

_____ 28

29. The action at the anode results in electrons being (acquired by, removed from) ..(29).. that electrode.

_____ 29

30. The metallic ions are removed from the plating solution at the ..(30a).., plating out as ..(30b).. of the metal.

_____ 30a

_____ 30b

31. In effect, atoms of the metal are transferred from ..(31a).. to ..(31b).. during the electroplating process.

_____ 31a

_____ 31b

32. In effect, electrons from the external circuit are transferred from ..(32a).. to ..(32b).. during the electroplating process.

_____ 32a

_____ 32b

33. Very small amounts of impurities in copper cause a marked increase in its electric ..(33)...

_____ 33

34. In purifying copper by electrolysis, the equation for the anode reaction is ..(34a).., while the equation for the cathode reaction is ..(34b)...

_____ 34a

_____ 34b

35. The important relationship between the quantity of electric charge passing through an electrolytic cell and the quantity of a substance liberated by the chemical action was discovered by ..(35)...

_____ 35

36. The mass of an element deposited during electrolysis is proportional to the quantity of ..(36).. that passes through the cell.

_____ 36

37. The quantity of electric charge that will liberate 1 gram of hydrogen will also deposit ..(37a).. of silver and ..(37b).. of aluminum.

_____ 37a

_____ 37b

38. From the atomic weights of these elements, it is apparent that each ion of silver gains ..(38a).. and each ion of aluminum gains ..(38b).. when discharged by electrolytic action.

_____ 38a

_____ 38b

39. The quantity of electric charge required to deposit the chemical equivalent of an element is approximately ..(39).. coulombs.

_____ 39

40. This quantity of electric charge is called a(n) ..(40)...

_____ 40

exercise **19a**

Magnetism

Sections 19.1–19.7

DIRECTIONS: In the blank space at the right of each definition, write the term that is defined.

1. The property of materials that are strongly attracted by magnets. _____ 1

2. The property of materials that are slightly attracted by very strong magnets. _____ 2

3. The property of materials that are feebly repelled by very strong magnets. _____ 3

4. An atom possessing the characteristics of a permanent magnet. _____ 4

5. A group of atoms that form a microscopic magnetic region in a ferromagnetic material. _____ 5

6. The group of ferromagnetic substances used in a new magnet technology. _____ 6

7. A theoretical N pole that repels with a force of 1 dyne an exactly similar pole placed 1 centimeter away. _____ 7

8. A region in which a magnetic force can be detected. _____ 8

9. A line in a magnetic field drawn so that a tangent to it at any point indicates the direction of the magnetic field. _____ 9

10. The number of flux lines per unit area permeating a magnetic field. _____ 10

DIRECTIONS: In the blank space at the right of each statement, write the word or expression that BEST completes the meaning.

11. Natural magnets consist of an iron ore called ..(11)... _____ 11

12. Three common metallic elements that have ferromagnetic properties are ..(12)... _____ 12

13. Magnetism is a property of an electric charge that is ..(13)... _____ 13

14. An electron has two kinds of motion: it ..(14a).. about the nucleus of an atom and it ..(14b).. on its own axis. _____ 14a

_____ 14b

15. If only the planetary motions of electrons were involved in the magnetic character of substances, all would be ..(15)... _____ 15

16. Electrons spinning in opposite directions may form ..(16a).. and neutralize their ..(16b).. character. _____ 16a

_____ 16b

17. The strong ferromagnetic properties of iron are explained by the four ..(17a).. electrons having ..(17b).. oriented spins in its atom. _____ 17a

_____ 17b

115

18. When a ferromagnetic material is subject to an external magnetic field, favorably oriented domains may ..(18a).. and other domains may become ..(18b)...

_____ 18a

_____ 18b

19. The temperature above which the domain regions of a ferromagnetic material disappear is called the ..(19)...

_____ 19

20. _Like_ magnetic poles ..(20a)..; _unlike_ poles ..(20b)...

_____ 20a

_____ 20b

21. The force between two magnetic poles is ..(21a).. proportional to the product of the strengths of the poles and ..(21b).. proportional to the square of their distance apart.

_____ 21a

_____ 21b

22. The lines of flux perpendicular to a specified area in a magnetic field are referred to collectively as the ..(22)...

_____ 22

23. The MKS unit of magnetic flux is the ..(23)...

_____ 23

24. Flux density in the MKS system is expressed in ..(24)...

_____ 24

25. Flux lines that are drawn to show how small magnets behave at various points in a magnetic field produce a(n) ..(25).. of the field.

_____ 25

DIRECTIONS: Write the answers to the following questions in the spaces provided. Where appropriate, make complete statements.

26. Arrange the following materials in order of increasing permeability: iron, air, aluminum, zinc. _____

_____

27. What physical change occurs when a bar of soft iron is placed in a magnetic field? _____

_____

28. Describe the polarity of a nail, the head of which is attracted to and in contact with the S pole of a strong bar magnet. _____

_____

29. What is _magnetic declination_? _____

_____

30. What is _magnetic inclination_? _____

_____

31. What is the magnetic inclination at the North Magnetic Pole? _____

_____

32. What do physicists believe is the cause of the earth's magnetic field? _____

_____

_____

33. What is the _magnetosphere_? _____

_____

_____

34. What is the _solar wind_? _____

_____

35. What regions of the magnetosphere contain energetic protons and electrons trapped by the earth's magnetic field? _____

116

exercise **19b**

Electromagnetism—d-c Meters

Sections 19.8–19.15

DIRECTIONS: In the space at the right, place the letter or letters indicating EACH choice that forms a correct statement.

1. An electron flow from north to south in a straight conductor supported *above* a compass **(a)** causes a deflection of the N pole of the compass toward the east, **(b)** produces no change in the compass-needle equilibrium, **(c)** causes a deflection of the S pole of the compass toward the east, **(d)** causes a deflection of the N pole of the compass toward the west.

_____ 1

2. An electron flow from south to north in a straight conductor supported *below* a compass **(a)** causes a deflection of the N pole of the compass toward the east, **(b)** produces no change in the compass-needle equilibrium, **(c)** causes a deflection of the S pole of the compass toward the east, **(d)** causes a deflection of the N pole of the compass toward the west.

_____ 2

3. The strength of a magnetic field around a conductor varies **(a)** directly with the distance from the conductor, **(b)** directly with the magnitude of the current, **(c)** inversely with the distance from the conductor, **(d)** inversely with the square of the distance from the conductor.

_____ 3

4. Ampère's rule for a straight conductor **(a)** requires that the direction of the current be known, **(b)** stipulates that the right thumb is to be extended in the direction of the electron flow, **(c)** enables one to predict the direction of the magnetic flux encircling a conductor, **(d)** can be used to show whether the forces acting on two parallel conductors are attractive or repulsive.

_____ 4

5. When a current is in a solenoid, **(a)** the two faces of the solenoid show magnetic polarity, **(b)** the core of each turn becomes a magnet, **(c)** the core of the solenoid becomes a magnetic tube through which nearly all of the flux passes, **(d)** the solenoid acts as a bar magnet.

_____ 5

6. Ampère's rule for a solenoid **(a)** requires that the direction of the current be known, **(b)** stipulates that the fingers of the right hand encircle the coil in the direction of the electron flow, **(c)** is not valid for a single turn, **(d)** indicates the end of the core that acts as the N pole.

_____ 6

7. When a soft iron rod is used as the core of a solenoid, **(a)** the flux density is not changed appreciably, **(b)** the solenoid becomes a strong electromagnet, **(c)** the permeability of the core is increased over that for air, **(d)** either the current must be reduced or some turns must be removed.

_____ 7

8. An electromagnet for lifting large quantities of scrap iron should have a core made of **(a)** air, **(b)** soft iron, **(c)** hardened steel, **(d)** wood.

_____ 8

117

DIRECTIONS: In the blank space at the right of each statement, write the word or expression that BEST completes the meaning.

9. The sensitivity of a galvanoscope can be increased by ..(9).. the number of turns of the conductor.

_____ 9

10. A galvanometer can consist of a(n) ..(10a).. wound on a(n) ..(10b).. core and pivoted on jeweled bearings between the poles of a(n) ..(10c).. horseshoe magnet.

_____ 10a

_____ 10b

_____ 10c

11. When a current is in the galvanometer coil, the coil becomes a(n) ..(11).. free to turn on its own axis.

_____ 11

12. When a current is in the coil of a galvanometer situated between the poles of a permanent magnet, a(n) ..(12a).. acts on the coil which rotates in an attempt to align its plane ..(12b).. to the direction of the field of the permanent magnet.

_____ 12a

_____ 12b

13. The final position of the galvanometer coil is reached when the torque acting on it is ..(13).. by the reaction of the control springs.

_____ 13

14. When the galvanometer coil reaches its equilibrium position, the opposing torques are ..(14a).. and the deflection angle of the coil is ..(14b).. to the current in it.

_____ 14a

_____ 14b

15. In order to convert a galvanometer movement for service as a d-c voltmeter, a high resistance must be added in ..(15).. with the moving coil.

_____ 15

16. To convert a galvanometer movement for service as a d-c ammeter, a very low resistance must be added in ..(16).. with the moving coil.

_____ 16

17. Because the total resistance of the ..(17a).. is very low, it is connected in ..(17b).. with the load; because the total resistance of the ..(17c).. is very high, it is connected in ..(17d).. with the load.

_____ 17a

_____ 17b

_____ 17c

_____ 17d

18. The use of an ohmmeter in measuring resistance is actually a modified version of the ..(18).. method.

_____ 18

DIRECTIONS: Write the answers to the following questions in the spaces provided. Where appropriate, make complete statements.

19. For a voltmeter to have negligible effect on the current in a load across which it is connected, how should its resistance compare with that of the load? _____

_____

20. What would be the effect on the total current of incorrectly connecting such a voltmeter in series with the load? _____

_____

21. For an ammeter to have a negligible effect on the magnitude of current in a load when connected in series with it, how should its resistance compare with that of the load? _____

_____

22. What would be the effect on the total current of incorrectly connecting such an ammeter in parallel with the load? _____

_____

23. What would be the effect on the ammeter if such a mistake were made? _____

_____

_____

24. If a voltmeter designed to read from 0 to 150 volts has a sensitivity of 1000 ohms per volt, would it be a suitable meter to use across a load resistance of 8000 ohms?   Explain. _____

_____

_____

25. What would be the result of using the voltmeter of No. 24 to read the voltage across a load resistance of 100,000 ohms? _____

_____

exercise **20a**

Induced Currents—Generators

Sections 20.1–20.13

DIRECTIONS: In the space at the right, place the letter or letters indicating EACH choice that forms a correct statement.

1. Electromagnetic induction was discovered by **(a)** Faraday, **(b)** Henry, **(c)** Lenz, **(d)** Oersted.   _____ 1

2. A current is induced in a conducting loop **(a)** when the loop is poised in a strong magnetic field, **(b)** when the loop is moved in a magnetic field perpendicular to the flux, **(c)** when the loop is moved in a magnetic field parallel to the flux, **(d)** as a result of relative motion producing a change of flux linking the conductor.   _____ 2

3. The magnitude of current induced in a conducting coil in a magnetic field is increased by **(a)** increasing the number of turns comprising the coil, **(b)** increasing the relative motion between the coil and flux, **(c)** increasing the strength of the magnetic field, **(d)** decreasing the rate at which the flux linked by the conductor changes.   _____ 3

4. An emf is induced across a loop cutting through flux lines **(a)** only if the loop is a part of a closed conducting path, **(b)** even if the ends of the loop are open, **(c)** and is proportional to the relative motion between the loop and flux, **(d)** only if the ends of the loop are open.   _____ 4

5. A coil of 10^2 turns moving perpendicular to the flux of a magnetic field for 10^{-2} s experiences a change in flux linkage of 5×10^{-5} weber. The emf induced across it is **(a)** 10^{-5} v, **(b)** –0.5 v, **(c)** 5×10^{-1} v, **(d)** 5×10^3 v.   _____ 5

6. A straight wire held in a north-south direction in a magnetic field in which the flux lines extend from west to east is pushed downward through the field. The north end of the wire **(a)** acquires a negative charge, **(b)** acquires a positive charge, **(c)** remains uncharged, **(d)** is more difficult to move than the south end.   _____ 6

7. A wire 5 cm long moving through a magnetic field of 10^{-2} weber/m² perpendicularly to the flux with a velocity of 1 m/s, has an emf induced across it of **(a)** 0.05 v, **(b)** 0.005 v, **(c)** 5×10^{-4} v, **(d)** 0.5 mv.   _____ 7

8. Lenz's law **(a)** illustrates the conservation of energy principle, **(b)** is true of all induced emfs, **(c)** states that an induced current is in such a direction that it opposes the change that produced it, **(d)** indicates that work must be done to induce a current in a conducting circuit.   _____ 8

9. For electrons to acquire potential energy in a magnetic field, **(a)** they must move parallel to the flux, **(b)** they must move perpendicular to the flux, **(c)** the conductor must be moved in opposition to a magnetic force, **(d)** the region of the field into which the conductor moves must be weaker than the region behind it.   _____ 9

10. Work done by an induced current in an external load expends energy acquired by the electrons **(a)** in the internal circuit, **(b)** resulting from work done in moving the wire in the magnetic field, **(c)** in the external circuit, **(d)** as they fall through the potential difference across the load. _____ 10

DIRECTIONS: In the blank space at the right of each statement, write the word or expression that BEST completes the meaning.

11. An electric generator converts ..(11a).. energy into ..(11b).. energy. _____ 11a

_____ 11b

12. The conducting loops across which an emf is induced form the ..(12).. of a generator. _____ 12

13. As the armature of a simple a-c generator rotates through a complete cycle, there are ..(13).. reversals in direction of the induced current. _____ 13

14. A current that has one direction during part of a generating cycle and the opposite direction during the remainder of the cycle is a(n) ..(14).. current. _____ 14

15. The prefix used to designate direct-current properties is ..(15a).., while the prefix used to designate alternating-current properties is ..(15b)... _____ 15a

_____ 15b

16. The magnitude of a varying voltage at any instant of time is called the ..(16).. voltage. _____ 16

17. An armature loop rotating at a constant rate in a magnetic field of uniform flux density has a voltage induced across it the magnitude of which varies ..(17).. with respect to time. _____ 17

18. In general, the instantaneous voltage across the loop is expressed as ..(18)... _____ 18

19. Instantaneous current is expressed as ..(19)... _____ 19

20. The output of a practical generator is increased by increasing the number of ..(20a).. on the armature, or increasing the ..(20b)... _____ 20a

_____ 20b

21. The number of cycles of current or voltage per second is the ..(21)... _____ 21

22. A commutator is a(n) ..(22a).. ring, each segment of which is connected to a(n) ..(22b).. of a corresponding armature ..(22c)... _____ 22a

_____ 22b

_____ 22c

23. If the armature turns of an a-c generator are connected to a commutator, the generator can supply ..(23).. current. _____ 23

24. A d-c generator in which a portion of the induced power energizes the field magnets is said to be ..(24)... _____ 24

25. The resistance of the armature turns of a generator is analogous to the ..(25).. of a battery. _____ 25

122

DIRECTIONS: Write the answers to the following questions in the spaces provided. Where appropriate, make complete statements.

26. What are the essential components of an electric generator? _____
_____
_____

27. What is the purpose of slip rings and brushes in an electric generator? _____
_____
_____

28. For what is the generator rule commonly used, and what two considerations are taken into account in its application? _____
_____
_____
_____
_____

29. To what does the *displacement angle* of a generator loop refer? _____
_____
_____

30. Why is exciter voltage, rather than armature voltage, transferred by the slip rings and brushes in a large commercial generator? _____
_____
_____

31. How does the nature of the current output of a d-c generator compare with that of an electrochemical source? _____
_____
_____

32. How does an increase in the load affect the induced emf of series-wound and shunt-wound generators?
_____
_____
_____

Motors—Inductance

Sections 20.14–20.22

DIRECTIONS: In the parentheses at the right of each word or expression in the second column, write the letter of the expression in the first column that is MOST CLOSELY related.

a. Squirrel-cage rotor	electric motor	( ) 1
b. Connected to the load	back emf	( ) 2
c. A coil		
d. Emf induced by generator action of a motor	universal motor	( ) 3
e. Converts mechanical energy to electric energy	induction motor	( ) 4
f. Connected to a current source		
g. $L_1 + L_2 + L_3$	synchronous motor	( ) 5
h. Converts electric energy to mechanical energy	primary coil	( ) 6
i. Emf induced by motor action of a generator	secondary coil	( ) 7
j. Operates on either a-c or d-c power		
k. $1/L_1 + 1/L_2 + 1/L_3$	inductor	( ) 8
l. Electric clock	L_T	( ) 9
	$1/L_T$	( ) 10

DIRECTIONS: Complete the following statements forming accurate and complete sentences.

11. The *mutual inductance* of two circuits is _____

_____

12. The mutual inductance of two circuits is *one henry* if _____

_____

_____

13. The self-inductance of a coil is the ratio of _____

coil.

14. The self-inductance of a coil is *one henry* if _____

_____

_____

15. The *turns ratio* of a transformer is the ratio of the number of turns in the _____

_____

DIRECTIONS: In the blank space at the right of each statement, write the word or expression that BEST completes the meaning.

16. A current-carrying conductor poised in a magnetic field experiences
a(n) ..(16).. force.   _____ 16

17. When the plane of a conducting loop is parallel to the magnetic flux, the magnitude of the torque on the loop is ..(17a)..; when the plane of the loop is perpendicular to the magnetic flux, the magnitude of the torque is ..(17b)...

_____ 17a

_____ 17b

18. The motor rule: Extend the thumb, forefinger, and middle finger of the ..(18a).. hand at right angles to each other. Let the forefinger point in the direction of the ..(18b).. and the middle finger in the direction of the ..(18c)..; then the thumb points in the direction of the ..(18d)...

_____ 18a

_____ 18b

_____ 18c

_____ 18d

19. As a motor gains speed, the back emf ..(19a).. and the circuit current ..(19b)...

_____ 19a

_____ 19b

20. In order to decrease the pulsation of the torque in practical d-c motors, the armature and field are composed of ..(20).. coils.

_____ 20

21. In an induction motor, the rotor must ..(21).. behind the field in order for a torque to be developed.

_____ 21

22. The synchronous motor is a constant ..(22).. motor.

_____ 22

23. The magnitude of the induced emf in mutual inductance is increased by ..(23a).. the relative motion between conductors and flux, by increasing the number of turns in the ..(23b).., and by placing a soft-iron core in the ..(23c)...

_____ 23a

_____ 23b

_____ 23c

24. The magnitude of the induced emf in self-inductance is increased by ..(24).. the rate of change of current in the inductor.

_____ 24

25. The inductance of a coil depends on the number of ..(25a).., the ..(25b).. of the coil, the ..(25c).. of the coil, and the nature of the ..(25d)...

_____ 25a

_____ 25b

_____ 25c

_____ 25d

26. Because inductance in electricity is analogous to ..(26a).. in mechanics, inductance imparts a(n) ..(26b).. effect in a circuit having a varying current.

_____ 26a

_____ 26b

27. If the primary of a transformer has a larger number of turns than the secondary, the transformer is called a step- ..(27).. transformer.

_____ 27

28. The resistance of the wires in the primary and secondary coils of a transformer produces the energy loss called ..(28)...

_____ 28

29. Closed loops of induced current circulating in a conducting mass in planes perpendicular to the magnetic flux are called ..(29)...

_____ 29

30. Eddy current losses in transformers are reduced by ..(30).. the cores.

_____ 30

DIRECTIONS: Place the answers to the following problems in the spaces provided at the right.

31. The mutual inductance of two coils is 1.50 henrys. What is the average emf induced in the secondary if the primary current rises to 5.00 amperes in 0.0200 second?

_____ 31

32. The turns ratio of a transformer is 0.125. If the primary voltage is 115 volts, what is the secondary voltage?

_____ 32

exercise $21a$

Alternating Current

Sections 21.1–21.8

DIRECTIONS: In the blank space at the right of each statement, write the word or expression that BEST completes the meaning.

1. The alternating current in a resistance load is ..(1).. with the alternating voltage applied across it.

_____ 1

2. When current and voltage are in phase, the graph of instantaneous power as a function of time varies between ..(2a).. and some ..(2b).. maximum.

_____ 2a

_____ 2b

3. The effective value of current or voltage is the ..(3a).. of the mean of the instantaneous values ..(3b).. and is frequently called the ..(3c).. value.

_____ 3a

_____ 3b

_____ 3c

4. An electrodynamometer is similar to a(n) ..(4a).., except that in place of a permanent magnet the electrodynamometer has a pair of ..(4b)...

_____ 4a

_____ 4b

5. The watt-hour meter is essentially a small single-phase ..(5a).. that turns at a rate proportional to the ..(5b).. used.

_____ 5a

_____ 5b

6. Inductance produces a(n) ..(6).. phase angle in an a-c circuit.

_____ 6

7. The *power factor* in an a-c circuit is equal to the ..(7a).. of the phase angle between current and voltage; it is ..(7b).. when the phase angle is zero and ..(7c).. when the phase angle is 90°.

_____ 7a

_____ 7b

_____ 7c

8. The nonresistive opposition to current in an a-c circuit is called ..(8a).. and is expressed in ..(8b)...

_____ 8a

_____ 8b

9. When the nonresistive opposition to current is due to inductance in the circuit, it is referred to as ..(9)...

_____ 9

10. The reactance in an a-c circuit due to inductance is ..(10a).. proportional to the product of the ..(10b).. and the inductance.

_____ 10a

_____ 10b

11. In a practical a-c circuit containing reactance and resistance, their joint effect is called ..(11)...

_____ 11

12. Impedance has a magnitude equal to ..(12a).. and a direction angle ϕ whose tangent is ..(12b)...

_____ 12a

_____ 12b

13. Capacitance produces a(n) ..(13).. phase angle in an a-c circuit.

_____ 13

14. Reactance due to capacitance in an a-c circuit is called ..(14)...

_____ 14

15. Reactance in an a-c circuit due to capacitance is ..(15a).. proportional to the product of the ..(15b).. and the capacitance.

_____ 15a

_____ 15b

DIRECTIONS: Write the answers to the following questions in the spaces provided. Where appropriate, make complete statements.

16. How is the *effective value* of an alternating current defined? _____

_____

_____

_____

17. What is the basic difference between the power considerations in d-c and a-c circuits? _____

_____

_____

_____

18. Distinguish between *apparent power* and *actual power* in an a-c circuit. _____

_____

_____

_____

19. What is the cause of a difference in phase between current and voltage in an a-c circuit? _____

_____

_____

20. What causes movement of the pointer in an iron-vane meter when current flows through the meter? _____

_____

_____

21. In what respect is a hot-wire meter unique in its principle of operation? _____

_____

_____

22. What is a *phasor*? _____

_____

23. What is the form of the Ohm's law expression for an entire a-c circuit? _____

24. Briefly describe the construction of an impedance diagram. _____

_____

_____

_____

_____

_____

25. Explain the meaning of the expression $Z = 120 \ \Omega \underline{|-27°}$. _____

_____

_____

exercise **21b**

Series a-c Circuits

Section 21.9

DIRECTIONS: Place the answers to the following problems in the spaces provided at the right. For Nos. 9–15 show the essential steps of your solution in computation form in the spaces below each problem.

1. A capacitor of 2.00 microfarads capacitance is placed in a circuit operating at a frequency of 1.00×10^3 hertz. What is the capacitive reactance in the circuit?   _____ 1

2. If the frequency in No. 1 is reduced to 10.0 hertz, what is the capacitive reactance of the circuit?   _____ 2

3. What is the inductive reactance of a coil of 2.00 henrys inductance when placed in a circuit operating at a frequency of 5.00×10^2 hertz?   _____ 3

4. If the frequency in No. 3 is reduced to 5.00 hertz, what is the inductive reactance in the circuit?   _____ 4

A circuit operating at 60.0 hertz has a resistance of 2.0×10^3 ohms, a capacitance of 1.00 microfarad, and an inductance of 10.0 henrys, all connected in series.

5. In block A, draw the circuit diagram for the above circuit.

6. Determine the magnitude of the impedance.   _____ 6

7. Compute the phase angle.   _____ 7

8. In block B, construct the impedance diagram using a scale of 0.3 cm to 100 ohms.

A

B

An a-c generator develops $11\overline{0}$ volts at 60.0 hertz across a load consisting of 8.00 ohms resistance, 53.1 milli-henrys inductance, and 189.7 microfarads capacitance connected in series.

9. What is the magnitude of the circuit impedance? _____ 9

10. Compute the phase angle. _____ 10

11. What is the magnitude of the circuit current? _____ 11

12. What is the magnitude of the potential difference across the capacitor? _____ 12

13. What is the magnitude of the potential difference across the inductor? _____ 13

14. What is the magnitude of the potential difference across the resistance? _____ 14

15. What is the magnitude of the potential difference across the entire load? _____ 15

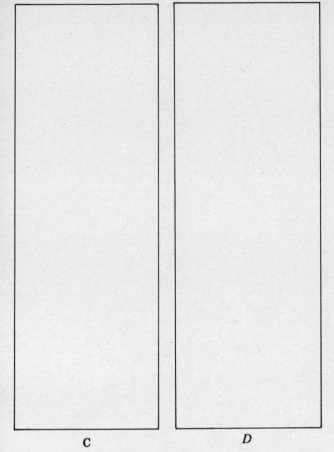

C   D

16. What is the phase relationship between the voltage across the load and the circuit current?

_____

_____

_____ 16

17. In block C, construct the impedance diagram showing X_C, X_L, X, R, Z and Φ. Use a scale of 0.3 cm to 1 ohm.

18. In block D, construct the voltage diagram for the series circuit using a scale of 0.3 cm to 11 volts.

exercise **21c**

Resonance

Sections 21.10–21.13

DIRECTIONS: In the space at the right, place the letter or letters indicating EACH choice that forms a correct statement.

1. The inductive reactance of an inductor in an a-c circuit **(a)** increases with the time rate of change of current, **(b)** decreases with frequency, **(c)** varies inversely with frequency, **(d)** increases as the frequency is raised.   _____ 1

2. A graph of the inductive reactance of a coil as a function of frequency yields **(a)** a hyperbolic curve, **(b)** a linear curve, **(c)** a curve that starts at the origin of the coordinates regardless of the inductance of the coil, **(d)** a curve whose slope is constant.   _____ 2

3. The capacitive reactance of a capacitor in an a-c circuit **(a)** increases with frequency, **(b)** varies inversely with frequency, **(c)** is infinite at a frequency equal to zero, **(d)** is a negligible value at extremely high frequencies.   _____ 3

4. A graph of the capacitive reactance of a capacitor as a function of frequency yields **(a)** a hyperbolic curve, **(b)** a curve of constant slope, **(c)** a curve that starts at the origin of the coordinates regardless of the capacitance of the capacitor, **(d)** a curve that approaches zero at extremely high frequencies.   _____ 4

5. When an inductor and a capacitor are connected in series in an a-c circuit, **(a)** the voltage across one cancels the voltage across the other, **(b)** the voltages across the two are of opposite polarity, **(c)** the same current must be in each, **(d)** at low frequencies the current in the inductor will be larger than that in the capacitor.   _____ 5

6. When an a-c circuit contains inductive reactance and capacitive reactance in series, **(a)** the frequency of the applied signal determines the reactance of the circuit, **(b)** the reactance of the circuit will be equal to zero at some particular frequency, **(c)** the impedance of the circuit is constant regardless of the frequency, **(d)** the circuit current is constant at all frequencies.   _____ 6

7. In a series circuit containing inductance, capacitance, and resistance, **(a)** the impedance equals zero at the resonant frequency, **(b)** the circuit is inductive at frequencies above the resonant frequency, **(c)** the circuit is capacitive at frequencies below the resonant frequency, **(d)** the reactance equals zero at the resonant frequency.   _____ 7

8. At the resonant frequency of an *L-R-C* series circuit **(a)** the phase angle is zero, **(b)** the voltage across the inductance equals zero, **(c)** the voltage across the capacitance is equal to the voltage across the inductance but is opposite in polarity, **(d)** the circuit current is maximum.   _____ 8

9. The property of a resonant circuit that discriminates among signal voltages of different frequencies is known as its **(a)** sensitivity, **(b)** power factor, **(c)** selectivity, **(d)** resonant frequency.   _____ 9

133

10. The characteristics of a series-resonant circuit depend primarily on
    (a) the ratio of the inductive reactance to the circuit resistance,
    (b) the ratio of the capacitive reactance to the circuit resistance,
    (c) the ratio of the resistance to the circuit impedance, (d) the
    magnitude of the signal voltage applied.
    _____ 10

DIRECTIONS: In the blank space at the right of each statement, write the word or expression that BEST completes the meaning.

11. Since a steady, direct current can be thought of as an alternating current having a frequency of ..(11a).. hertz, inductive reactance in a d-c circuit must be ..(11b)...
    _____ 11a
    _____ 11b

12. When a capacitor in a d-c circuit is fully charged, the current in the circuit is ..(12a).. and the capacitor reactance is ..(12b)...
    _____ 12a
    _____ 12b

13. In a capacitor in an a-c circuit, electrons flow in one direction during one half-cycle, charging the capacitor in one sense. During the other half-cycle, electrons flow in the ..(13a).. direction, charging the capacitor in the ..(13b).. sense.
    _____ 13a
    _____ 13b

14. In *series resonance,* the impedance of the *L-R-C* series circuit is equal to the ..(14a).. of the circuit and the voltage and circuit current are ..(14b)...
    _____ 14a
    _____ 14b

15. When a signal voltage of constant magnitude and varying frequency is applied to an *L-R-C* series circuit, a distinct ..(15).. in circuit current occurs as the resonance frequency is approached.
    _____ 15

16. At *resonance,* the phase angle is zero and the power factor is ..(16)...
    _____ 16

17. The lower the resistance of an *L-R-C* series circuit, the ..(17).. is the current at resonance.
    _____ 17

18. The frequency at which a series circuit resonates is determined by the combination of ..(18a).. and ..(18b).. used.
    _____ 18a
    _____ 18b

19. A resonant circuit responds to impressed voltages of different frequencies in a(n) ..(19).. manner.
    _____ 19

20. The ratio X_L/R of a series-resonant circuit is commonly called the ..(20).. of the circuit.
    _____ 20

134

Electronic Devices

Sections 22.1–22.15

DIRECTIONS: In the blank space at the right of each definition, write the term that is defined.

1. Converts alternating current to direct current. _____ 1

2. Separates the useful component from a complex signal. _____ 2

3. Increases the strength of a signal. _____ 3

4. The electrode of a vacuum tube that serves as the source of electrons. _____ 4

5. The electrode of a vacuum tube that attracts electrons. _____ 5

6. An electrode of a vacuum tube that is used to control the flow of electrons. _____ 6

7. A three-electrode vacuum tube. _____ 7

8. The escaping of electrons from a hot surface. _____ 8

9. The negative charge in the interelectrode space of a vacuum tube. _____ 9

10. The smallest negative grid voltage, for a given plate voltage, that causes the tube to cease to conduct. _____ 10

DIRECTIONS: In the blank space at the right of each statement, write the word or expression that BEST completes the meaning.

11. When Edison sealed a metal plate near the filament inside an electric lamp and connected it through a galvanometer to the filament battery, there was a galvanometer deflection when the plate was connected to the ..(11a).. terminal of the battery but no deflection when the plate was connected to the ..(11b).. terminal. _____ 11a

    _____ 11b

12. Thomson's explanation of the Edison effect attributed the galvanometer deflection to the flow of electrons from the ..(12a).. to the ..(12b)... _____ 12a

    _____ 12b

13. The first diode, called the ..(13a).., was used as a(n) ..(13b).. for radio signals. _____ 13a

    _____ 13b

14. The first triode, called the ..(14a).., was used as a(n) ..(14b).. for radio signals. _____ 14a

    _____ 14b

15. The rate at which electrons escape from an emitting surface (increases, decreases) ..(15).. as the temperature of the emitter is raised. _____ 15

16. The number of substances suitable for use as emitters to produce satisfactory thermionic emission is limited by the ..(16).. required. _____ 16

17. Power diodes are used as ..(17a).. while signal diodes are used as ..(17b).. and ..(17c)...

_____ 17a

_____ 17b

_____ 17c

18. A triode contains a cathode, an anode, and a third electrode called a(n) ..(18a).. that is normally maintained at some ..(18b).. potential with respect to the cathode.

_____ 18a

_____ 18b

19. The direction of the plate current inside a vacuum tube is from ..(19a).. to ..(19b)...

_____ 19a

_____ 19b

20. The direction of the plate current outside the tube is from ..(20a).. to ..(20b)...

_____ 20a

_____ 20b

21. When a signal voltage on the grid of a tube is at its positive maximum instantaneous value, the voltage on the plate is at its ..(21).. instantaneous value.

_____ 21

22. A television-picture tube is a special kind of vacuum tube known as a(n) ..(22)...

_____ 22

23. Chemicals that emit visible light when struck by an electron beam have the property of ..(23a)..; their after-glow is called ..(23b)...

_____ 23a

_____ 23b

24. In a cathode-ray tube, the two methods of deflecting the electron beam are ..(24a).. deflection and ..(24b).. deflection.

_____ 24a

_____ 24b

25. A faint light incident on the photoemission cathode of a six-stage photomultiplier tube produces three photoelectrons per millisecond. Each electron impact produces three secondary electrons. The number of electrons arriving at the collector plate per millisecond has an order of magnitude of ..(25)...

_____ 25

26. Semiconductors have a unique property that permits a relatively ..(26a).. flow of electrons in the forward direction with a small applied voltage, and a very ..(26b).. flow of electrons in the reverse direction with a much larger applied voltage.

_____ 26a

_____ 26b

27. The amplifying property of a transistor is a result of changes in ..(27a).. that occur in the different regions of the structure when proper ..(27b).. are applied.

_____ 27a

_____ 27b

28. The ratio of the output power of a P-N-P common-base amplifier circuit to the input power is called the ..(28).. of the circuit.

_____ 28

29. For amplifying an input signal in a situation where high current gain is desired, the common ..(29a).. circuit is preferred; where large power gain is desired, the common ..(29b).. circuit is preferable.

_____ 29a

_____ 29b

30. The direct conversion of radiant energy to electric energy is known as the ..(30).. effect.

_____ 30

DIRECTIONS: Write the answers to the following questions in the spaces provided. Where appropriate, make complete statements.

31. What characteristics of a germanium crystal are significant in its property of semiconduction? _____

_____

_____

_____

_____

32. Why is phosphorus referred to as a *donor* element when minute traces are added to germanium? _____

_____

_____

_____

_____

33. Why is aluminum referred to as an *acceptor* element when minute traces are added to germanium? _____

_____

_____

_____

_____

34. What is the difference between N- and P-types of semiconductors? _____

_____

_____

_____

_____

_____

35. What is the P-N junction? _____

_____

_____

exercise **23**

Atomic Structure

Sections 23.1–23.12

DIRECTIONS: In the space at the right, place the letter or letters indicating EACH choice that forms a correct statement.

1. Experimental evidence shows that a hydrogen atom is composed of **(a)** at least two parts, **(b)** parts with opposite electric charges, **(c)** parts having equal masses, **(d)** positive and negative particles, the negative particles having larger masses. _____ 1

2. The Thomson experiment **(a)** involved a special cathode-ray tube, **(b)** established a value for the charge on an electron, **(c)** established a value for the mass of an electron, **(d)** established a value for the e/m ratio for an electron. _____ 2

3. The Millikan experiment **(a)** involved cathode rays, **(b)** established a value for the charge on an electron, **(c)** made possible the computation of the mass of an electron, **(d)** established a value for the diameter of an electron. _____ 3

4. The *electron* **(a)** is a negatively charged particle, **(b)** has about the same mass as a hydrogen atom, **(c)** was discovered by Millikan, **(d)** has a rest mass of $5.486 \times 10^{-4}\ u$. _____ 4

5. The *proton* **(a)** is a neutral particle, **(b)** has about the same mass as a hydrogen atom, **(c)** was discovered by Thomson, **(d)** has an atomic mass of $1.007276470\ u$. _____ 5

6. The *neutron* **(a)** is a neutral particle, **(b)** has about the same mass as a hydrogen atom, **(c)** was discovered by Chadwick, **(d)** has a mass of $9.109534 \times 10^{-31}\ kg$. _____ 6

7. The *atomic nucleus* **(a)** was discovered by Rutherford, **(b)** is negatively charged, **(c)** is the dense central part of an atom, **(d)** contains an equal number of protons and neutrons. _____ 7

8. The electron *shells* of an atom **(a)** are definite electron paths about a nucleus, **(b)** compose the electron cloud, **(c)** may be designated by the letters K to Q, **(d)** consist of groups of orbitals. _____ 8

9. *Isotopes* **(a)** contain the same number of protons but differ in the number of neutrons, **(b)** contain the same number of neutrons but differ in the number of protons, **(c)** are atoms of the same element, **(d)** are atoms of different elements. _____ 9

10. *Nuclides* **(a)** are varieties of atoms distinguished by their nuclear composition, **(b)** may be atoms of the same element, **(c)** may be atoms of different elements, **(d)** that are isotopes have the same atomic number. _____ 10

DIRECTIONS: In the blank space at the right of each statement, write the word or expression that BEST completes the meaning.

11. An atom is composed of smaller particles that are arranged in (simple, complex) ..(11).. ways.

_____ 11

12. Different atoms are formed when subatomic particles are ..(12).. in different ways.

_____ 12

13. The first subatomic particle to be identified and studied was the ..(13)...

_____ 13

14. The rays that cause the glass walls of an evacuated tube to glow with a greenish fluorescence are called ..(14).. rays.

_____ 14

15. By the use of a magnet, Perrin concluded that cathode rays were streams of ..(15).. coming from the negative electrode in an evacuated tube.

_____ 15

16. Because the nature of cathode-ray particles did not change when Thomson changed the composition of the cathode or the gas in his cathode-ray tubes, he concluded that cathode-ray particles are present in (no, some, all) ..(16).. forms of matter.

_____ 16

17. By studying how an electron beam is influenced by an electric field and a magnetic field, Thomson was able to determine the ..(17).. ratio of the electron.

_____ 17

18. An electron with a positive charge is called a(n) ..(18)...

_____ 18

19. When X rays of known energy produce a pair of electrons, the rest mass of the electrons can be calculated by using the equation, ..(19)...

_____ 19

20. Electrons (do, do not) ..(20).. account for a large share of the mass of substances.

_____ 20

21. Millikan determined the charge on a(n) ..(21a).. by means of the ..(21b).. experiment.

_____ 21a

_____ 21b

22. An electron diffraction pattern indicates that electrons exhibit ..(22).. duality.

_____ 22

23. Rutherford discovered the atomic nucleus by bombarding a thin ..(23a).. with ..(23b)...

_____ 23a

_____ 23b

24. The nucleus of an atom contains most of the mass of the atom, yet is less than ..(24).. the diameter of the atom itself.

_____ 24

25. The number of protons in the nucleus of an atom is the ..(25).. of the atom.

_____ 25

26. An atom containing 13 protons, 14 neutrons, and 13 electrons has ..(26).. nucleons.

_____ 26

27. The average atomic mass of the atoms of an element based on a large number of samples found in nature is the ..(27).. of the element.

_____ 27

28. A mass spectrograph is used to measure the ..(28).. of ionized atoms with great precision.

_____ 28

29. The nuclear binding force is a very short-range force, being effective to a distance about ..(29).. times the radius of a proton.

_____ 29

30. The energy required to move an electron between two points that have a potential difference of one volt is one ..(30)...

_____ 30

DIRECTIONS: Place the answers to the following problems in the spaces provided at the right.

31. A platinum atom consists of 78 protons, 78 electrons, and 116 neutrons. What is its atomic number?   _____ 31

32. What is the mass number of the atom of No. 31?   _____ 32

33. What is the combined mass in atomic mass units of the particles composing the nucleus of the atom of No. 31?   _____ 33

34. If the actual mass of the nucleus in No. 31 is 193.9200 u, what is its nuclear mass defect in atomic mass units?   _____ 34

35. What is the nuclear binding energy of 1.6527 u in Mev?   _____ 35

exercise **24**

Nuclear Reactions

Sections 24.1–24.13

DIRECTIONS: In the parentheses at the right of each word or expression in the second column, write the letter of the expression in the first column that is MOST CLOSELY related.

a. Emission of radiation by a nucleus forming
   a lighter nucleus

b. Formation of a more complex nucleus from
   simple nuclei

c. $^4_2$He

d. Ionized gas molecule

e. Unit of radioactivity

f. Addition of one particle to a nucleus with
   subsequent emission of a second particle

g. $^0_{-1}$e

h. Unit of exposure to gamma rays

i. Break-up of a heavy nucleus into nuclei of
   intermediate masses

j. Half-life

k. High energy photon

l. Unit of measure of absorbed radiation

alpha particle	( )	1
beta particle	( )	2
gamma ray	( )	3
radioactive decay	( )	4
nuclear bombardment	( )	5
fission	( )	6
fusion	( )	7
curie	( )	8
roentgen	( )	9
rad	( )	10

DIRECTIONS: In the blank space at the right of each statement, write the word or expression that BEST completes the meaning.

11. Radioactivity is the spontaneous ..(11a).. of an unstable atomic
    nucleus with the ..(11b).. of particles and rays.

    _____ 11a

    _____ 11b

12. The naturally occurring elements with atomic numbers greater than
    ..(12).. are all radioactive.

    _____ 12

13. The property of radioactive elements that led to their discovery is
    the ability of their radiations to affect the ..(13a).. on a ..(13b)...

    _____ 13a

    _____ 13b

14. The length of time during which half a given number of atoms of a
    radioactive nuclide will decay is called its ..(14)...

    _____ 14

15. The fraction of the original number of atoms of a radioactive nuclide
    remaining after the elapse of four half-lives is ..(15)...

    _____ 15

16. List α particles, β particles, and γ rays in order of increasing speed.

    _____ 16

17. List α particles, β particles, and γ rays in order of increasing penetrating power.

    _____ 17

18. In a(n) ..(18a).. change, the composition of the substance is not
    changed; in a(n) ..(18b).. change, new substances with new properties
    are produced but the nuclei of the interacting atoms are unchanged.

    _____ 18a

    _____ 18b

143

19. All forms of alpha, beta, and gamma emission are examples of ..(19).. change.

_____ 19

20. In symbols like $_1^1H$, which represents a(n) ..(20a).., and $_0^1n$, which represents a(n) ..(20b).., the subscript designates the ..(20c).. of the particle while the superscript indicates the number of ..(20d).. in the particle.

_____ 20a

_____ 20b

_____ 20c

_____ 20d

21. In addition to nuclear binding energy, the neutron-proton ..(21).. affects nuclear stability.

_____ 21

22. The ratio of the number of nuclei decaying per second and the total number of original nuclei is called the ..(22)...

_____ 22

23. The first transformation by nuclear bombardment was produced in 1919 by ..(23)...

_____ 23

24. Cockcroft and Walton verified the equation ..(24).. by bombarding lithium with high-speed protons.

_____ 24

25. Neutrons can penetrate a nucleus more easily than other particles because they have no ..(25)...

_____ 25

26. A material such as graphite that slows down fast neutrons acts as a(n) ..(26)...

_____ 26

27. Elements such as plutonium (at. no. 94), curium (at. no. 96), and fermium (at. no. 100) are known as ..(27).. elements.

_____ 27

28. A thermonuclear reaction is another name for a(n) ..(28).. reaction.

_____ 28

29. The energy of the sun is believed to be released during the fusion of protons to form ..(29a).. and ..(29b)...

_____ 29a

_____ 29b

30. Fusion reactions are more desirable than fission reactions for energy production because ..(30).. is required.

_____ 30

31. A reaction in which the material or energy starting the reaction is also one of the products and can cause similar reactions is a(n) ..(31).. reaction.

_____ 31

32. The amount of radioactive material required to sustain a chain reaction in a reactor is called the ..(32)...

_____ 32

33. A nuclear reactor is a device in which controlled fission produces new ..(33a).. substances and ..(33b)...

_____ 33a

_____ 33b

34. The rate of the fission reaction in a nuclear reactor is regulated by the position of control rods which absorb ..(34)...

_____ 34

35. A reactor in which one fissionable material is produced at a greater rate than another fissionable material is consumed is known as a(n) ..(35).. reactor.

_____ 35

36. When the production of neutrons in a reactor equals the sum of the neutrons that are absorbed and those that escape from the reactor, the reactor is said to be ..(36)...

_____ 36

37. In order to have 100 neutrons produce new fissions in a nuclear reactor, a total of ..(37).. neutrons must be provided.

_____ 37

38. Radioactive isotopes are called ..(38)...   _____ 38

39. Radioactive isotopes are very useful as ..(39).. elements in determining the course of chemical reactions.   _____ 39

40. The age of prehistoric wood samples may be determined by measuring the amount of the radioactive isotope ..(40).. they presently contain.   _____ 40

DIRECTIONS: Complete the following nuclear equations.

41. $^{226}_{88}\text{Ra} \rightarrow \,^{222}_{86}\text{Rn} +$ _____

42. $^{234}_{91}\text{Pa} \rightarrow \,^{234}_{92}\text{U} +$ _____

43. $^{9}_{4}\text{Be} + \,^{4}_{2}\text{He} \rightarrow \,^{12}_{6}\text{C} +$ _____ $+ \text{ energy}$

44. $^{235}_{92}\text{U} + \,^{1}_{0}\text{n} \rightarrow \,^{138}_{56}\text{Ba} + \,^{95}_{36}\text{Kr} +$ _____ $+ \text{ energy}$

45. $4^{1}_{1}\text{H} \rightarrow$ _____ $+ 2^{0}_{+1}\text{e} + \text{ energy}$

exercise **25a**

Quantum Mechanics— Particle Accelerators

Sections 25.1–25.7

DIRECTIONS: Write the answers to the following questions in the spaces provided. Where appropriate, make complete statements.

1. State the *uncertainty principle*. _____

_____

2. What is a *quantum number*? _____

_____

3. What is *quantum mechanics*? _____

_____

_____

4. What is the *first quantum number* and what does it describe? _____

_____

_____

5. What is the *second quantum number* and what does it describe? _____

_____

_____

6. What is the *third quantum number* and what does it describe? _____

_____

_____

_____

7. What is the *fourth quantum number* and what does it describe? _____

_____

_____

8. State the *exclusion principle*. _____

_____

9. Define *ionization energy*. _____

_____

10. What is the equation for the wavelength of a matter wave? Explain each term in the equation. _____

_____

_____

_____

DIRECTIONS: In the blank space at the right of each statement, write the word or expression that BEST completes the meaning.

11. An electron is not free to assume any orbit, but the ..(11a).. and ..(11b)..
    of the electron orbit are governed by the ..(11c)...

    _____ 11a

    _____ 11b

    _____ 11c

12. An electron must remain in its orbit until sufficient ..(12a).. is gained
    or lost so that an abrupt ..(12b).. can occur.

    _____ 12a

    _____ 12b

13. The Bohr theory was too (simple, complex) ..(13).. and was thus un-
    successful in explaining the motions of electrons in atoms with high
    atomic numbers.

    _____ 13

14. If the position of an electron is determined, its ..(14a).. cannot be
    determined; if the velocity of an electron is determined, its ..(14b)..
    cannot be determined.

    _____ 14a

    _____ 14b

15. The experimental evidence for the magnetic quantum number is the
    ..(15).. effect.

    _____ 15

16. An atomic shell that contains its maximum number of electrons is a(n)
    ..(16).. shell.

    _____ 16

DIRECTIONS: In the table below, place the values of n, l, m_l, and m_s for each electron in the neutral sulfur atom.

n	l	m_l	m_s

NOTE: The last two electrons have parallel spins. Students who have had
chemistry could be expected to know this.

17. A complete shell gives ..(17).. to an atom. _____ 17

18. The electrons that are the easiest to remove from an atom are those that are ..(18)... _____ 18

19. The French physicist deBroglie suggested that all matter has ..(19).. characteristics. _____ 19

20. The wavelength of a matter wave varies ..(20).. with the momentum of the particle. _____ 20

DIRECTIONS: Complete the following table.

	Type of Accelerator	Significant Characteristic	Type of Particle Accelerated	Maximum Energy	Advantage	Disadvantage
21.	Van de Graaff generator					
22.	Betatron					
23.	Cyclotron					
24.	Synchro-cyclotron					
25.	Synchrotron					
26.	Intersecting storage accelerator					
27.	Linear accelerator					

exercise **25b**

Detection Instruments— Subatomic Reactions

Sections 25.8–25.16

DIRECTIONS: In the parentheses at the right of each word or expression in the second column, write the letter of the expression in the first column that is MOST CLOSELY related.

a. Makes a permanent record	bubble chamber	( ) 1
b. Contains a hollow copper cylinder	cloud chamber	( ) 2
c. Series of charged metal plates		
d. Particularly suited for study of high-energy particles	electroscope	( ) 3
	Geiger tube	( ) 4
e. Contains photomultiplier tube		
f. Invented by E.O. Lawrence	ionization chamber	( ) 5
g. Movable piece of metal foil	photographic emulsion	( ) 6
h. Contains liquid helium		
i. Zinc sulfide screen	scintillation counter	( ) 7
j. Invented by C.T.R. Wilson	solid-state detector	( ) 8
k. Contains liquid hydrogen		
l. None of the other choices	spark chamber	( ) 9
	spinthariscope	( ) 10

DIRECTIONS: Write the answers to the following questions in the spaces provided. Where appropriate, make complete statements.

11. List three main characteristics of the particles and rays emitted in nuclear reactions.

    a. _____ 11a

    b. _____ 11b

    c. _____ 11c

12. For each of the characteristics of No. 11, identify the detection instruments that are applications of the characteristics by using their item numbers from Nos. 1–10.

                                            a. _____ 12a

                                            b. _____ 12b

                                            c. _____ 12c

13. What determines the rate of discharge of an electroscope? _____

_____

14. What enables current to flow between the cathode and anode of a Geiger tube? _____

_____

_____

15. How are the tracks of alpha particles made visible in a diffusion cloud chamber? _____

_____

_____

16. How are the tracks of protons made visible in a bubble chamber? _____
_____
_____

17. In what way is the bubble chamber superior to the cloud chamber? _____
_____
_____

18. What is the nature of the charged-particle track in a solid-state detector? _____
_____

19. Contrast the spinthariscope with the photomultiplier tube. _____
_____
_____

20. How is the passage of a particle recorded on a photographic film? _____
_____
_____

DIRECTIONS: Complete the following table.

	Category	Name	Symbol	Mass (Mev)	Baryon Number	Lepton Number	Hyper-charge
21.		electron					
22.			n				
23.			Σ^0	1192	+1		0
24.	boson						
25.	baryon			1672			
26.		mu neutrino					
27.	meson			549			
28.			Σ^+				
29.			$\bar{p}$				
30.			Ω^+				

DIRECTIONS: In the blank space at the right of each statement, write the word or expression that BEST completes the meaning.

31. The strong interaction is not effective beyond a distance of ..(31)...   _____ 31

32. The only interaction that can both attract and repel is the ..(32).. interaction.   _____ 32

33. The ratio of the gravitational interaction to the strong interaction is ..(33)...   _____ 33

34. Hypercharge is not conserved in ..(34).. interactions.   _____ 34

35. According to some scientists, all "fundamental" particles may, in turn, be composed of still more elementary bits of matter-energy called ..(35)...   _____ 35

DIRECTIONS: Write the answers to the following questions in the spaces provided. Where appropriate, make complete statements.

36. What happens when a particle and its antiparticle collide? _____
_____
_____

37. What is an *interaction*? _____
_____

38. List the four types of interactions between particles in the order of decreasing strength. _____
_____
_____

39. Name the three conservation laws that are observed in nuclear reactions. _____
_____

40. State the *law of parity*. _____
_____
_____

experiment **1**

Measuring Length

PURPOSE: (1) To learn how to make measurements of length with a meterstick and a vernier caliper. **(2)** To understand the relationship between the construction of a measuring instrument and the precision of the measurements made with it. **(3)** To learn that uncertainty in measurements is unavoidable.

APPARATUS: Meterstick; 15 cm or 30 cm ruler; vernier caliper; rectangular wooden block; numbered metal cylinder of brass or aluminum; numbered rectangular metal blocks; wristwatch.

INTRODUCTION

1. Meterstick

In making measurements with a meterstick, keep the following suggestions in mind:
a. Since the end of the meterstick may be worn, start the measurement at some intermediate mark. See Figure 1-1. Of course, the reading at the mark with which you start the measurement must be subtracted from the final reading.
b. Place the meterstick on edge, as in Figure 1-1. This will avoid errors that are easily made when viewing the stick in the flat position shown in Figure 1-2.
c. Estimate the reading to the nearest 0.5 mm. In other words, the last digit of your measurement, which is an estimate, should be 0 or 5.

2. Vernier caliper

Most vernier calipers consist of two metric and two English scales, as shown in Figure 1-3. The fixed scales have a jaw at one end. The metric fixed scale is subdivided into centimeters and millimeters.

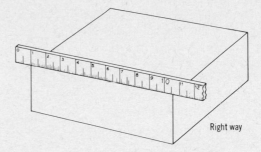

Figure 1-1

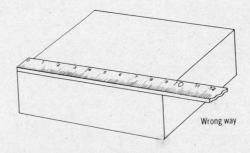

Figure 1-2

The other jaw is attached to the sliding or vernier scales. The metric vernier scale is ruled so that *nine* millimeters is divided into *tenths*. From the enlarged scale of Figure 1-4, it is evident that one division of the metric vernier scale equals 0.9 mm. When the jaws of the caliper are closed, the zero of the fixed scale exactly coincides with the zero of the vernier scale.

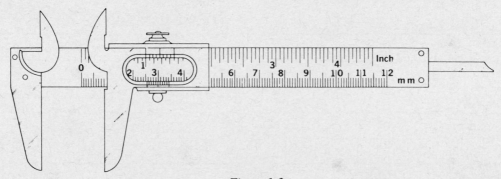

Figure 1-3

155

Figure 1-4

When the vernier scale *B* is moved to the right until its *first* division coincides with the one-millimeter mark on the fixed scale *A*, it has been moved exactly 0.1 mm, or 0.01 cm, and the jaws are separated by that amount. When the vernier scale is moved to the right until its second division coincides with the two-millimeter mark on the fixed scale *A*, it has been moved a total distance of 0.2 mm, or 0.02 cm. Moving the scale to the right 0.03 cm brings its third division opposite the three-millimeter mark on *A*, and so on. The particular division on the vernier scale that coincides with a line or division on the fixed scale reads *hundredths of a centimeter.*

To use the caliper, separate the jaws, place the object to be measured between them, and close the jaws firmly on the object. Then tighten the set screw, if there is one, enough to keep the vernier scale from moving while it is being read. Suppose the vernier scale now occupies the position shown by the dotted lines of Figure 1-4. The zero of the vernier scale shows that the jaws are separated by more than 1.5 cm and less than 1.6 cm. *Centimeters and tenths of centimeters are read on the fixed scale. Hundredths of centimeters are read from the vernier scale by locating the particular division on the vernier scale that coincides with a division on the fixed scale.* As indicated by the arrow, it is the number 6. Therefore, the correct reading is 1.560 cm. If no division on the vernier scale coincides exactly with a division on the fixed scale, then the last digit of the measurement should be a 5. In Figure 1-5, the sixth and seventh

Figure 1-5

divisions on the dotted vernier scale are equally close to a division on the fixed scale. Thus, the correct reading is 1.565 cm.

To measure the inside diameter of a tube or hollow cylinder, the upper parts of the jaws are used. Keep in mind the fact that centimeters and tenths of centimeters are read from the fixed scale, while hundredths of a centimeter are read from the vernier scale.

3. Uncertainty of measurements

Measurements of physical quantities are always uncertain to some degree. These uncertainties are the results of several unavoidable factors: the limitations in the construction of the measuring instruments; the conditions under which the measurements are made; the ability of the person using the measuring instrument. Repeated measurements can help to reduce uncertainties, but the uncertainties can never be completely eliminated.

In the last part of this experiment you will use a watch to determine the time of a specific event. You will then compare your data with those of your classmates and calculate the uncertainty in your measurement data.

PROCEDURE

1. Meterstick

Measure the width of the laboratory table and record this measurement. Repeat the measurement but this time start the measurement at a different mark on the meterstick. For the third trial make a measurement from the opposite end of the table. *All measurements should be made to the nearest 0.5 mm.* The three readings should agree to within 1 mm.

Measure the length, width, and thickness of the rectangular block furnished by the instructor. Make each measurement three times as before. Record your data in the appropriate table.

DATA Part 1

	Trial 1	Trial 2	Trial 3	Average
Width of table				
Length of block				
Width of block				
Thickness of block				
Volume of block				

2. Vernier caliper

Make three measurements of the length and diameter of the numbered cylinder furnished by the instructor. Record your measurements in the appropriate table.

DATA Part 2

TRIAL	CYLINDER NO.		
	Length (cm)	Diameter (cm)	Volume (cm^3)
1			
2			
Average			

3. Comparative precision

Measure the dimensions of the rectangular metal block with both the meterstick and the vernier caliper. Use each instrument to the precision of which it is capable. Record the data in the appropriate table.

DATA Part 3

INSTRUMENT	BLOCK NO.			
	Length (cm)	Width (cm)	Height (cm)	Volume (cm^3)

4. Uncertainty of measurements

Synchronize your watch as closely as possible with the room clock or with the instructor's watch. You will record the reading of your watch the moment you hear the sound of a book that the instructor has dropped on the table. Read the time of the sound to the nearest minute and record in the data table. If your watch has a sweep second hand, record the time to the nearest second. Repeat this procedure for two more trials. Record.

Combine your results with those of your classmates in order to determine the class mean for each trial. Record.

DATA Part 4

TRIAL	Time (s)	Mean (s)	Absolute deviation (s)
1			
2			
3			
Average			s
Relative deviation			%

ANALYZING THE DATA

1. Average the measurements you made of the dimensions of the rectangular wooden block and calculate the volume of the block. *Observe the rules of significant figures in your calculations.* Be sure to write the correct units after the averages and volume.

2. Calculate the volume of the cylinder from the measured length and diameter, using significant figures correctly. Record.

3. Calculate the volume of the rectangular metal block from the measurements made with the meterstick and with the vernier caliper. Record the two volumes separately, using significant figures correctly. How do the precisions of the two answers compare?

_____

_____

4. By using the class mean for each trial, calculate the absolute deviation for each of your time measurements. Then calculate the relative deviation. Observe the rules of significant figures. If the instructor directs, make separate data tables for the measurements made to the nearest minute and those made to the nearest second. How do the relative deviations of the two sets of measurements compare? Are there any measurements that should have been discarded in making the calculations? Why?

_____

_____

experiment 2

Measuring Mass

PURPOSE: **(1)** To learn how to use a platform balance. **(2)** To learn how to use an inertia balance. **(3)** To determine the mass density of an object.

APPARATUS: Single beam platform balance and set of masses, or triple beam platform balance; inertia balance; several identical C-clamps, 100–150 g each; various solid objects with masses below 1 kg; supply of small nails; stopwatch with 10 s sweep, or watch with sweep second hand; rectangular solid and cylinder.

INTRODUCTION

1. Platform balance

The platform balance is a device used to determine the mass of an object by comparison with known masses. Figure 2-1 shows a single beam platform balance. Another type of platform balance is the triple beam, Figure 2-2. Various sliding masses are suspended from the beam so that the use of separate masses is almost unnecessary. The center of the beam and the pans themselves rest upon knife-edged bearings that have little friction. There is a pointer attached to the beam to show when the pans are balanced.

In using a balance, first see that the sliding mass is at the extreme left, or at zero. Then touch one of the pans lightly to start the beam swinging. The pans should move far enough so the pointer swings at least three spaces to either side of the center mark. If it swings farther to one side than it does to the other, the zero adjustment screw may be turned until the pointer moves as many spaces to the left as to the right. The balance is now in equilibrium and is ready for use.

The object whose mass is to be determined with a single beam balance is always placed on the *left* pan of the balance. Select a mass that you judge to be greater than that of the object being measured. Place it on the *right* pan. If it is greater, remove it and add the *next-smaller* mass. If this mass is less than that of the object, continue to add other masses to the right pan. Try masses *successively* from the larger to the smaller, until the last mass added is the ten-gram mass. Then the sliding mass, which is used to indicate mass to the nearest tenth of a gram, should be moved

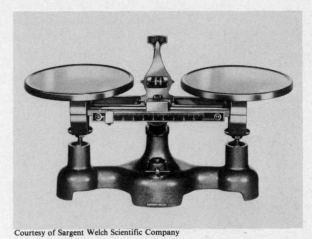

Courtesy of Sargent Welch Scientific Company

Figure 2-1

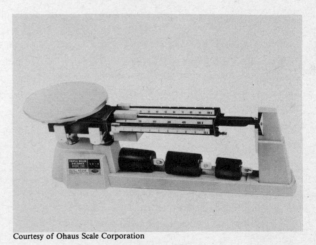

Courtesy of Ohaus Scale Corporation

Figure 2-2

far enough to the right to make the pointer swing as many spaces to the right as to the left. You do not need to wait for the pointer to come to rest. The mass of the object equals the sum of all the masses on the pan plus the mass represented by the sliding mass.

Be careful not to jar the balance when adding or removing the larger masses. Such jarring dulls the knife edges and makes the balance less sensitive. Jarring may be avoided by supporting the pan with one hand while objects are being added to or removed from the pans. The object whose mass is being determined and the large masses should be placed near the center of the balance pan.

When you are finished, see that all the masses are returned to their proper places in the box.

159

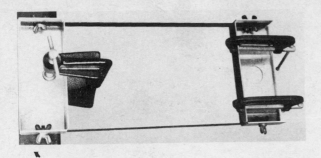

Figure 2-3

2. Inertia balance

The inertia balance is used to compare masses by measuring the period of vibration when a mass is placed on the pan of the balance and the pan is set in horizontal motion. Figure 2-3 is a top view of an inertia balance attached to a laboratory table. On such a balance, masses and periods of vibration are related according to the equation

$$\frac{m_1}{m_2} = \frac{T_1^{\,2}}{T_2^{\,2}}$$

where m_1 and m_2 are different masses and T_1 and T_2 are their respective periods of vibration.

Since m_1 and m_2 include the mass of the balance pan, it is more convenient to measure the periods of several known masses and then to plot a graph of the resulting data. The value of an unknown mass can then be read directly from the graph after the period of the unknown mass is measured. This is the method that will be used in this experiment.

3. Mass density

The mass of a unit volume of a substance is called its *mass density*. To determine the mass density of an object, the mass and volume of the object are measured. The mass density is calculated by dividing the mass by the volume. In this experiment, the volume of a rectangular solid and the volume of a cylinder will be determined from the linear measurements of each.

PROCEDURE

1. Platform balance

Determine the masses of several solid objects, reading the balance to its greatest possible precision.

Find the mass of a group of 20 small, identical nails. Repeat with 40, 60, 80, and 100 nails. In each case, calculate the mass of a single nail. Record all data in the appropriate data table.

DATA   Part 1

Number of nails	Mass (g)	Mass of single nail (g)
Average		

2. Inertia balance

Fasten one of the C-clamps to the pan of the inertia balance. Set the balance in motion, using a small (about 2 cm) vibration amplitude. Get yourself synchronized with the motion of the balance before starting the stopwatch. Start the watch on the count of "zero" and read the time of 20 vibrations to the nearest 0.01 second. Repeat this procedure at least twice more and average your results. Compute the time of a single vibration. This is the period of vibration of the balance. In the same way, find the period of vibration when 2, 3, and 4 clamps are fastened to the pan. Record all data in the appropriate data table.

DATA   Part 2

TRIAL	No. of C-clamps	No. of vibrations	Period (s)
1			
2			
3			
4			
5			

3. Mass density

Measure the length, width, and thickness of the rectangular solid, calculate its volume, and record. Measure the height and diameter of the cylinder, calculate its volume, and record. Use a vernier caliper as required.

Use the balance to find the mass of the block and the cylinder to the precision warranted by the balance. Calculate the mass density of each object, using significant figures. Record.

DATA Part 3

OBJECT	Volume (cm^3)	Mass (g)	Mass density experimental (g/cm^3)	Mass density accepted (g/cm^3)	Absolute error (g/cm^3)	Relative error (%)

ANALYZING THE DATA

1. Plot a graph of the data from Part 1. Use the graph to predict the mass of a random number of nails, for example 29 or 84. Check your prediction with actual measurements made on the platform balance.

2. Find the mass of a single C-clamp on the platform balance. Plot a graph of your data, using the masses as abscissas and the periods of vibration *squared* as ordinates. Connect the points with a smooth line.

3. Place an unknown mass on the pan of the inertia balance and measure its period of vibration. With the help of your graph, estimate the mass of the object. Check this reading against the mass as measured with the platform balance. Use the reading of the platform balance as the accepted value and calculate your relative error. Repeat this procedure with two more unknown masses. Record your data in the appropriate table.

DATA

TRIAL	Period (s)	Mass		Relative error (%)
		Graph (kg)	Platform balance (kg)	
1				
2				
3				
4				

4. If the inertia balance is equipped with a cylindrical mass and a hole in the pan through which the mass fits, measure the period of the balance while the mass is suspended in the hole from a string. Then place the mass in the pan and measure the period again. Compare the results.

5. Find the accepted value of the mass density of the rectangular solid and of the cylinder. Calculate the absolute and relative errors. Record your data in the data table for Part 3.

$$g = 9.8 \, m/s/s \simeq 10 \, m/s/s$$

v (m/s)	t (s)
10 m/s	1
20 m/s	2
30 m/s	3

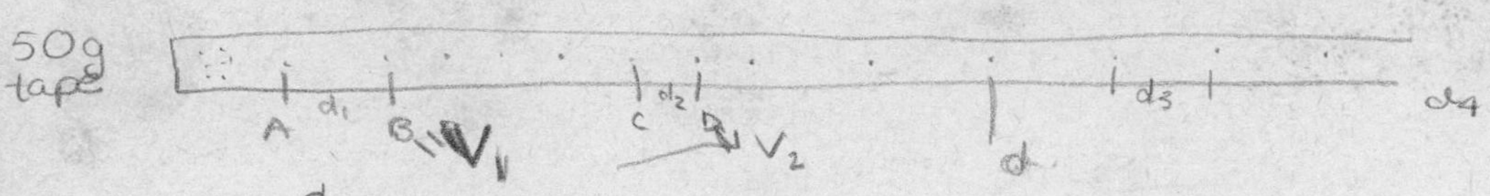

50g
tape

A d_1 B V_1 C d_2 D V_2 d d_3 d_4

$$\frac{d_1}{T} = V_1 \qquad \left.\begin{array}{c} d_1 \\ d_1 \\ d_1 \\ d_1 \end{array}\right\} \bar{d_1} \qquad \frac{\bar{d_1}}{T} = V_1$$

Acceleration — time rate of change of velocity

$$\boxed{a = \frac{v_2 - v_1}{t}} \quad \text{— general formula}$$

↓ total between v's

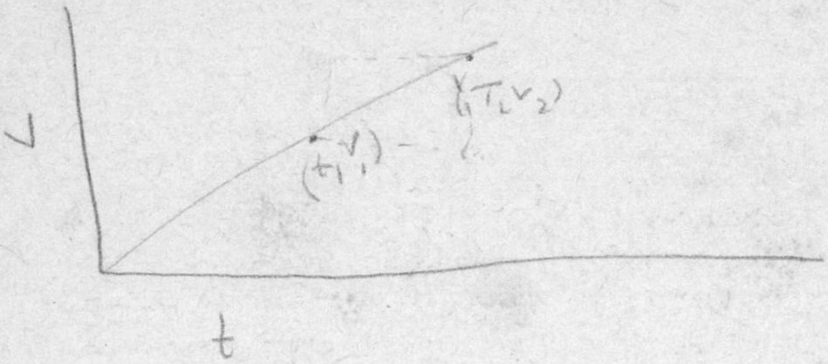

(t_2, v_2)

(t_1, v_1)

v

t

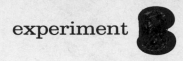

experiment 3

Measuring Time

PURPOSE: **(1)** To learn how to measure short time intervals with a recording timer. **(2)** To measure the speed and acceleration of a falling body. **(3)** To determine whether the acceleration of a falling body is constant.

APPARATUS: Recording timer; timing tape; stopwatch with 10 s sweep, or watch with sweep second hand; dry cell or other dc-power supply; connecting wire; C-clamp; switch; string; set of weights; meterstick.

INTRODUCTION: A recording timer is a device for measuring the time it takes an object to move a short distance. It consists of an electromagnet and a clapper, very much like that in an electric doorbell. See Figure 3-1. A paper tape is inserted under the clapper, and a disk of carbon paper is placed face down between the clapper and the paper tape. Thus, each time the clapper strikes, it makes a dot on the paper tape. Waxed paper tape is used in some timers, thus eliminating the necessity for carbon paper disks. Other timers employ motor-driven chains to produce

the dots. Make sure you know how to use the timer supplied for this experiment.

When the paper tape is pulled through the timer, the distance between two dots on the tape is the distance the tape moved during one back-and-forth vibration of the clapper. The time required for a single vibration is called the *period* of the timer. Once the period is measured, it can be used to determine the time interval for any motion of the paper tape.

In this experiment you will measure the period of a recording timer. This is called calibrating the timer. You will also use the timer to measure the speed and acceleration of a falling object. In later experiments, you will use the timer to study other types of motion.

PROCEDURE

1. Calibrating the timer

Fasten the recording timer to the table with a C-clamp and connect it to the dry cell. Choose a location that will enable you to pull a long section of paper tape through the timer in a straight line without hitting any obstacles. Insert the end of the tape

Figure 3-1

between the clapper and the carbon paper disk as shown in Figure 3-1, making sure that the tape can move freely. One student should hold the roll of tape by passing a pencil through the center as an axis. The other student should hold the end of the tape in one hand and a watch in the other.

Turn on the timer by closing the switch. Then pull the tape steadily through the timer for 3 or 4 seconds, using the stopwatch to measure the time accurately. This is done by walking away from the timer at a steady pace. Turn off the timer and mark the first and last dots on the tape. Count the number of dots. Ignore any variation in the spaces between dots; the spaces between dots represent equal time intervals regardless of variations in the spaces. Repeat this procedure several more times. Record all data and compute the period of the timer. Make sure you have at least three trials that are in good agreement with each other. Find the average of your results and record in the data table.

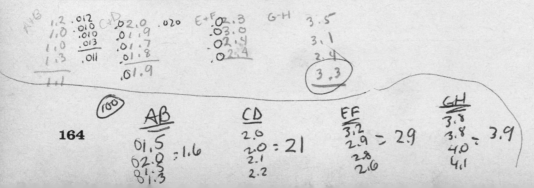

Figure 3-2

DATA Part 1

	TRIAL	Time (s)	No. of dots	Period (s)
Scott	1	1.62	111	.0146
Karen	2	.45	45	.010
Beth	3	.45	57	.008 79
Tony	4	.52	54	.0096
	Average	.76	67	.011

2. Speed and acceleration of a falling object

Set up the timer as shown in Figure 3-2. Cut a piece of paper tape that is at least 20 cm longer than the distance between the table top and the floor. Pass the end of the tape through the timer and fasten a 200-g mass to the end of the tape by using adhesive tape or by hooking the mass through the tape. Hold the mass at a convenient level near the top of the table. Start the timer and let the mass fall to the floor. Stop the timer when the mass hits the floor. Repeat the procedure, using masses of 300 grams and then 400 grams.

Using the tape for the 200-g mass, label the second and third dots A and B, respectively. Count 4 dots from B and label the seventh and eighth dots C and D, respectively. Repeat this procedure for the remainder of the dots that were produced before the mass hit the ground.

Measure the distance between A and B, between C and D, etc. Record in the data table for Part 2. Repeat the procedure for the remaining trials.

DATA Part 2

TRIAL	Mass (g)	Distance (m)					
		A–B	C–D	E–F	G–H	I–J	K–L
1	50	.011	.019	.025	.031		
2	100	.016	.021	.029	.039		
3	200	.014	.023	.030	.034		

1.2 .012   .02.0 .020   E+F .02.3   G-H 3.5
1.0 .010   .01.9   .03.0   3.1
1.0 .013   .01.7   .02.4   2.4
1.3 .011   .01.8   .02.4   (3.3)
       .01.9

(100)   AB   CD   EF   GH
        01.5   2.0   3.2   3.8
        02.8 = 1.6 2.0 = 21   2.9 = 29   3.8 = 3.9
        81.3   2.1   2.8   4.0
                    2.2   2.6   4.1

ANALYZING THE DATA

1. Divide the distance A-B by the period of the timer as determined in Part 1. This is the speed of fall over the distance A-B. Record it as v_1 in the appropriate data table. Repeat the calculation for the other distances and record as v_2, v_3, etc.

2. Calculate and record the acceleration for each change in speed. Use the equation $a_1 = \dfrac{v_2 - v_1}{t}$, where t is 5 times the period of the timer. Why?

_____

_____

3. Determine the average acceleration and the relative deviation. Record. Is the acceleration constant?

_____

_____

4. Repeat Steps 1-3 for the other trials.

5. Does a change in mass result in a change in acceleration?

_____

_____

6. Assume the acceleration due to gravity to be 9.8 m/s² Determine the relative error of your results. Record. Account for possible sources of error.

DATA

$\dfrac{1.\overline{33}}{11} \times 100 = 12\%$

TRIAL	Speed				Acceleration			a_{ave} (m/s²)	Relative deviation (m/s²)	Relative error (%)
	v_1 (m/s)	v_2 (m/s)	v_3 (m/s)	v_4 (m/s)	a_1 (m/s²)	a_2 (m/s²)	a_3 (m/s²)			
1	1	1.7	2.3	2.8	13	11	9	11	12%	
2	1.5	1.9	2.6	3.5	7	13	16	12	28%	
3	1.3	2.1	2.7	3.1	15	11	7	11	24%	
4										

$\dfrac{33}{11} \times 100 = 2$

$\dfrac{1}{6} \times 100 = 3$

$\bar{a} = 11$

Relative deviation between tapes

$11 + 12 + 11 = \bar{a} = 11$

Relative deviation between 2.7%

Da

$|11 - 11| = 0$

$|12| - |11| = 1$

$|11| - |11| = 0$

Dr $\dfrac{0.3}{11} \times 100 = 2.7\%$ error

conclusion
gravity
acceleration due
to gravity

experiment 4

Acceleration - I

PURPOSE: **(1)** To study the change in acceleration of a moving mass when the applied force changes. **(2)** To study the change in acceleration produced by a given force when the mass changes.

APPARATUS: Recording timer; timing tape; connecting wire; dry cell or other dc-power source; set of masses; pulley with table clamp; string; platform balance; dynamics cart; spring balance, 5-n capacity.

INTRODUCTION: Newton's law of acceleration states that an unbalanced force applied to a mass produces acceleration according to the equation

$$F = ma$$

Because of friction, this law seems to contradict common experience. In driving a car, for example, a constant force is required to keep the car moving with a constant velocity. If the force is removed, the force of friction brings the car to a stop. In the absence of friction, however, the car would continue to move with constant velocity after the force is removed. The continued application of force would then result in acceleration.

In this experiment you will study the law of acceleration, first by measuring the change in acceleration when a constant mass is subjected to a varying force, and then by observing the change in acceleration when the force remains constant and the mass varies. Friction will be minimized by using a rolling cart and a small counterweight.

PROCEDURE

1. Constant mass, but varying force

Set up the apparatus as shown in Figure 4-1. (The operation of the recording timer is explained in Experiment 3.) The timing tape is fastened to one end of the cart and the spring balance fastened to the other end.

Measure the mass of the cart on the platform balance and record this value in the data table. Attach the spring balance to the cart and fasten the string to the balance. Check to see that the balance reads zero with no load. Pass the string over the pulley and fasten a 100-g mass to the end. Hold the cart while placing the tape in the timer and attaching the tape to the cart.

Start the timer and release the cart. *While the cart is moving,* read the accelerating force on the spring balance to the nearest 0.01 n. When the 100-g mass hits the floor, stop the cart and then the timer. Remove the tape and label it "Trial 1." Record the force as measured by the balance.

Repeat this procedure for Trials 2 and 3, using 200-g and 300-g masses, respectively. Keep these tapes separate from those in the next step.

2. Constant force, but varying mass

For the three trials in this part of the experiment, keep a 300-g mass on the string in addition to the counterweight. Without adding any masses to the cart, run the experiment and record the total mass

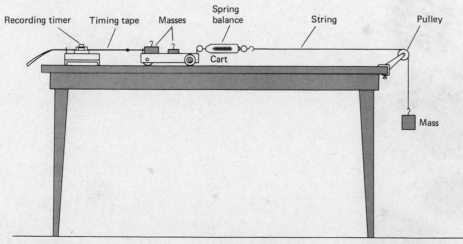

Figure 4-1

and accelerating force under Trial 4 in the data table. For Trial 5 add a 500-g mass to the cart and for Trial 6 add an additional 1000 g.

CALCULATIONS: Place the tape for Trial 1 on a table and tape down both ends. Measure the distance (to the nearest 0.001 m) from the first dot to a dot about one meter away. Make sure you do not measure beyond the point at which the mass hit the floor. Record. Then count the number of dots. Record. Calculate the total time. Record. Repeat these calculations for the other trials.

DATA   Period of timer ＿＿＿ s

TRIAL	Total mass (kg)	Accelerating force (n)	Distance (m)	Time (s)	Acceleration (m/s^2)
1					
2					
3					
4					
5					
6					

ANALYZING THE DATA

1. Since each tape started at $d = 0$ and $t = 0$, you can use the equation $d = 1/2at^2$ to calculate the acceleration, a. Calculate the acceleration for all six trials and record these values in the data table.

2. Using the data for Trials 1–3, plot a graph with the accelerating forces as abscissas and the resulting accelerations as ordinates.

3. Using the data for Trials 4–6, plot a graph with the total masses as abscissas and the corresponding accelerations as ordinates.

4. Using your graphs, describe the relationship between (a) accelerating force and acceleration, (b) mass and acceleration.

   (a) ＿＿＿＿＿＿＿＿＿＿＿＿＿＿＿＿＿＿＿＿＿＿＿＿＿＿＿＿＿＿＿＿＿＿＿＿＿＿

   (b) ＿＿＿＿＿＿＿＿＿＿＿＿＿＿＿＿＿＿＿＿＿＿＿＿＿＿＿＿＿＿＿＿＿＿＿＿＿＿

5. (Optional) Determine whether your data verify the equation $F = ma$.

experiment 5

Acceleration - II

PURPOSE: To study the motion of an object that is under the influence of the accelerating force of gravity.

APPARATUS: Packard's acceleration board; graph paper; carbon paper; level; cellulose tape.

INTRODUCTION: Galileo studied acceleration by rolling a ball down an inclined plane. Such a ball is under the influence of the same accelerating force as is a freely falling object, namely, the force of gravity. The vertical motion of the ball is slowed down by using the inclined plane and is thus easier to measure.

In this experiment, the path of a ball rolling down an inclined plane is recorded on graph paper by using carbon paper. The ball is also given a horizontal velocity. Assuming that this horizontal velocity remains relatively unchanged for each trial, equal horizontal components of the recorded path can be used to measure equal periods of time. The downward component of the path for each time period can then be measured.

PROCEDURE: Set up the acceleration board as shown in Figure 5-1. If special instructions are furnished with the apparatus, study them carefully. The following factors are important to the proper operation of the acceleration board:

(1) The board should be tilted at such an angle that the ball will stay within the width of the graph paper as it rolls down the board. Make several practice runs in order to obtain the necessary tilt angle.

(2) The ball guide and graph paper must be square with the board. Use the level to check this requirement.

(3) The graph paper must be positioned so that the top line is on a horizontal line with the center of the ball as it leaves the ball guide. The Y-axis of the

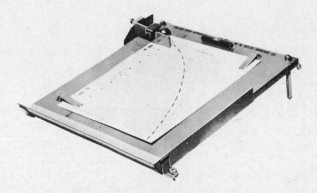

Courtesy of Sargent-Welch Scientific Company

Figure 5-1

graph paper must also coincide with the point where the center of the ball leaves the guide. (This is *not* the point where the ball first strikes the paper. The ball will strike the paper slightly to the right of the Y-axis.)

After the board and graph paper are properly positioned, fasten the graph paper with cellulose tape in addition to using the clips on the board. Place a piece of carbon paper loosely over the graph paper. Let the left edge of the carbon paper extend beyond the left edge of the graph paper.

Release the ball and check its path on the graph paper. If it is a smooth curve and is easily legible, run a second trial with a slightly increased tilt of the board. Then run a third trial on the same graph paper with a still greater tilt angle. In order to make meaningful measurements, the lower portions of the three paths should be separated from each other by about 3 centimeters.

Use the first piece of graph paper for practice runs. After you have learned to position this paper properly and have noted the necessary tilt for each trial, tape a second piece of graph paper over the first for your final runs, using the practice paper as a guide.

ANALYZING THE DATA

1. Divide the horizontal spaces into at least six equal sections. These represent equal intervals of time and correspond to the numbers in the t-column of the data table. d is the distance the ball travels along the Y-axis during increasing time intervals: for $t = 1$, record the number of Y-spaces during the first time interval; for $t = 2$, the number of Y-spaces during the first two time intervals; for $t = 3$, the number of Y-spaces during the first three time intervals; etc.

169

DATA

TRIAL	t X-axis units	d Y-axis units	v_{av} d/t	v_f $2v_{av}$	Acceleration			
					Δv_f	v_f/t	$2d/t^2$	Ave.
1	1							
	2							
	3							
	4							
	5							
	6							
2	1							
	2							
	3							
	4							
	5							
	6							
3	1							
	2							
	3							
	4							
	5							
	6							

2. Compute the average velocities, v_{av}, for each time interval by using the ratio d/t, and enter these values in the table. Then record the final velocities, v_f; v_f is twice the average velocity for a given time interval, or $2v_{av}$.

3. The accelerations are calculated in three different ways: by the change in v_f in each successive time interval, from the equation $v_f = at$, and from the equation $d = \frac{1}{2}at^2$. Calculate the acceleration for each time interval in each of these three ways and enter the results in the data table. Average the results.

4. Is the vertical speed constant?

_____

_____

5. Is the vertical acceleration constant?

_____

_____

6. Would the shape of the curve you obtained in this experiment be changed if you used a more massive ball? Explain.

_____

Resolution of Forces

PURPOSE: To show how a single force may be resolved into two component forces.

APPARATUS: Simple crane boom; 2 spring balances, 20-n capacity; slotted weights; weight hanger; twine; protractor. (If the common form of laboratory apparatus is not available, a meterstick may be used as the boom.)

INTRODUCTION: When a lawn mower is pushed, it does not go in the direction it is pushed. It moves in a direction parallel to the surface of the ground. The force that acts along the handle at an angle with the surface of the ground is resolved into two components. One component acts horizontally and moves the mower along the ground. The other component acts vertically and tends to push the mower into the ground. There are many similar cases where a force that acts on an object in a direction in which it is not free to move is resolved into two component forces.

In Figure 6-1, three forces act on point **P**. The load F_w pulls directly downward. The tensile force measured by the spring balance **S** pulls along the line **PS**. The boom **PR** exerts a thrust force that acts as the equilibrant of the first two forces. Consequently, the resultant of the load force and the tensile force is equal to the thrust force, but acts in the opposite direction.

In this experiment, the thrust force exerted by the boom and the angles at which the three forces act will be measured. Then the equilibrant of the thrust force will be resolved into the load force and the tensile force, and the magnitudes of these two forces will be determined both graphically and mathematically. Finally these values will be compared with those actually used in the experiment.

PROCEDURE: Tie the ring of one spring balance near the top of the upright support rod of the laboratory table. Fasten the crane boom clamp near the bottom of the support rod. Connect the end of the boom to the spring balance hook by means of twine. Add enough weights to the hanger attached to the end of the boom to make the balance **S** read from 12 to 15 n. Then adjust the boom so that it makes a 90° angle with the upright support rod.

Hold a blank sheet of paper against the apparatus so the center of the sheet is behind point **P**. Mark on the paper the position of **P**, and indicate the directions of **P**F_w, **PR**, and **PS**. Measure the angles **SPR** and **RP**F_w. Read the spring balance **S** to determine the force **PS**. Record.

Attach a second spring balance at **P** and pull vertically upward until you just counterbalance the downward force exerted by the weights and the

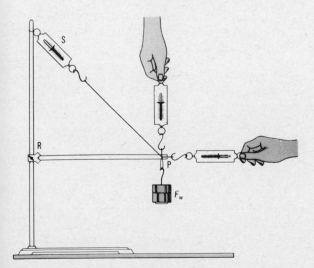

Figure 6-1

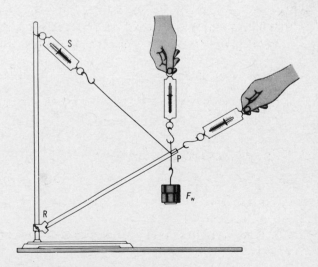

Figure 6-2

171

weight of the boom. This spring balance reading is the equilibrant of force PF_w. Record.

Using the same spring balance at **P**, pull outward in the direction of **PR** extended until the boom just begins to move away from the upright. (The connec-

tion at **R** must allow the boom to move horizontally.) This is the thrust force exerted by the boom and is equal in magnitude but opposite in direction to the resultant of **PS** and PF_w. Mark these actual values in their proper places in the data table.

DATA

TRIAL	PR (n)	∠SPR (°)	∠RPF$_w$ (°)	PS graph (n)	PS calc. (n)	PS actual (n)	PF$_w$ graph (n)	PF$_w$ calc. (n)	PF$_w$ actual (n)
1									
2									

ANALYZING THE DATA

1. On the paper containing the position of **P** and the directions of the three forces, lay off a vector (using a suitable scale) to represent the force **PR**. Using this vector as a diagonal of a parallelogram and the known directions of PF_w and **PS** as the directions of the sides, complete the parallelogram, **PSR**F_w.

2. Measure the length of the vectors **PS** and PF_w in your diagram and, from the scale you have used, determine their graphic values.

3. Determine the values by calculation using the measured values of the vector **PR**, ∠**SPR**, and ∠**RP**F_w.

4. If time permits, repeat the experiment. This time set the boom at a different angle with the upright support rod as shown in Figure 6-2. Record all data and analyze it in the same manner.

5. How does the force along **PS** compare with the total weight supported by the apparatus? Does this help to explain the reason for using a crane boom?

_____

_____

experiment **7**

Composition of Forces

PURPOSE: (1) To find the equilibrant of two forces acting at an angle. (2) To show that the equilibrant of two forces is equal to their resultant, but acts in the opposite direction.

APPARATUS: 3 spring balances, 20-n capacity; wooden block; strong twine; small iron ring, 1.0 cm in diameter; ruler; pencil; pencil compass; protractor; 3 iron table clamps, or force board, or composition-of-forces apparatus.

INTRODUCTION: Two different forces often act simultaneously on a body at the same point. The angle between these two forces may be between 0° and 180°. The resultant of these two forces is the single force that could be substituted for them without altering the effect they produce. If the two forces act at an angle, the resultant is equal to the diagonal of the force parallelogram of which the two forces are the sides. The equilibrant of two or more forces is the single force that can produce equilibrium with them. It is equal in magnitude but opposite in direction to the resultant.

PROCEDURE: Fasten three pieces of twine, each 20–25 cm in length, to the iron ring and to the balance hooks as shown in Figure 7-1. Fasten the

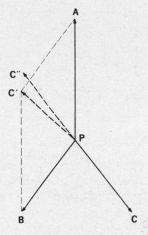

Figure 7-2

balances to the clamps with twine. If a composition-of-forces apparatus is used, follow the manufacturer's directions for attaching the balances. Adjust the length of the twine and the position of the balances so that all balances have a reading within about 3 n of each other. Best results will be obtained if the balances read at least 12 n. The cords must be adjusted so that the pull of each balance is in direct line with the center of the ring.

Place a blank sheet of paper beneath the cords so its center will be directly beneath the center of the ring. Thumb tacks through opposite corners of the paper will keep it from slipping. Three forces are represented by the balances, **A**, **B**, and **C**. Two of them act at an angle on point **P**, represented by the center of the ring. The third force is the equilibrant. Mark the direction of the forces by placing a wooden block on the paper so that its edge just touches the string along the entire length of the block. Be sure it does not displace the string at any point. With a fine-pointed pencil draw a line along the edge of the block just beneath the string. This shows the direction in which the force acts. In a similar manner, locate the direction of the other forces. Read each balance and record its reading along the line that represents the direction of the force.

Remove the paper and extend the lines representing the three forces until they meet. If the work was carefully done, they will meet at point **P**. If they do not meet at a point, consult your instructor to find out whether the error is too great to make your experiment acceptable.

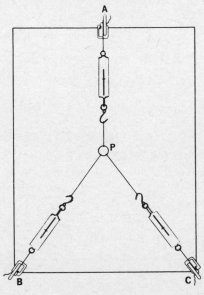

Figure 7-1

DATA

TRIAL		Graphic	Calculated
1	C'P		
	∠APC'		
	Magnitude error (between C'P and C''P)		
	Direction error (∠C'PC'')		
2	A'P		
	∠BPA'		
	Magnitude error (between A'P and A''P)		
	Direction error (∠A'PA'')		
3	B'P		
	∠CPB'		
	Magnitude error (between B'P and B''P)		
	Direction error (∠B'PB'')		

ANALYZING THE DATA

1. Use some convenient unit (1 cm to represent 2.0 or 2.5 n) to measure off on each line from point **P** a distance corresponding to each of the balance readings. Using the two forces **AP** and **BP** as sides, construct a parallelogram and draw the diagonal **C'P**. Use solid lines to represent the forces and dashed lines for the construction lines. See Figure 7-2.

2. Determine the graphic magnitude of **C'P**.

3. Extend the third force line, **CP**, beyond **P** a distance equal to **CP** and label this segment **C''P**.

4. Determine the graphic difference in magnitude between **C'P** and **C''P**. (This is the difference between the theoretical and experimental equilibrants.)

5. Measure the angle between **C'P** and **C''P** and record this as graphic direction error.

6. Using the known values of **AP**, **BP**, and ∠APB, calculate the magnitude of **C'P**. Also calculate the magnitude of ∠APC'.

7. Determine the calculated direction error by obtaining the difference between measured ∠APC'' and calculated ∠APC'.

8. It time permits, run two or more trials using magnitudes and directions for **AP**, **BP**, and **CP** different from the ones used in the first trial. Find the graphic and calculated errors of magnitude and direction as before. Use **AP** as the equilibrant in the second trial and **BP** as the equilibrant in the third trial. Record the errors in the data table.

9. Could the same apparatus be used with more than three concurrent forces? Explain your answer.

_____

_____

_____

174

experiment **8**

Coefficient of Sliding Friction

PURPOSE: **(1)** To resolve the weight of an object into two component forces. **(2)** To find the coefficient of sliding friction.

APPARATUS: Smooth board with hard surface, for use as an inclined plane; wooden block, with hook attached, smooth on one side and with fine sandpaper on other side; meterstick; protractor; spring balance.

INTRODUCTION: When a block rests on an inclined plane, as shown in Figure 8-1, its weight, F_w, concentrated at the center of gravity of the block, acts vertically downward. Since the block cannot move in that direction, the weight of the block is resolved into two component forces. One component, F_P, acts parallel to the plane and tends to slide the block down the plane. The other component, F_N, acts at right angles to the plane and tends to break it or to make the block stick to the plane. If the slope of the plane is great enough to cause the block to slide at uniform speed, the ratio of the parallel force to the perpendicular force is the *coefficient of sliding friction* between the block and the plane.

The coefficient of sliding friction may also be defined as *the ratio of the force required to slide an object at uniform speed over a horizontal surface to the weight of the object itself.* It can be found experimentally by weighing the object and then using a spring balance to measure the force needed to slide the object at slow, uniform speed. For example, if a force of 8 n is required to slide a 20-n block over a horizontal surface at a constant rate, the coefficient of friction is 8 n ÷ 20 n or 0.4. The coefficient of friction depends on the materials and the nature of the surfaces.

PROCEDURE: Place the board in the position shown in Figure 8-1. The slope should be gentle enough so that the wooden block, when placed on the plane, will not slide down. Increase the pitch of the plane gradually until a grade is reached at which the block will slide slowly down the plane with uniform speed when it is given a gentle push. Record this angle as θ.

Place the board down on a horizontal surface. Put the block on the board with the smooth side of the block down. Using the spring balance, pull the block across the board at constant speed. Read the force F_P on the spring scale. Record.

Repeat the above procedure for two more trials, Trial 2 and Trial 3.

Repeat the procedure three times more with the sandpaper side of the block in contact with the board. These shall be Trials 4, 5, and 6.

Use the spring balance to measure the weight, F_w, of the block. Record.

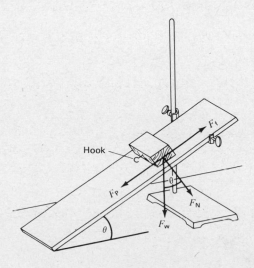

Figure 8-1

DATA

TRIAL	θ (°)	F_P measured (n)	F_W (n)	F_P calc. (n)	Absolute error (n)	F_N (n)	μ
1							
2							
3							
Average							
4							
5							
6							
Average							

ANALYZING THE DATA

1. Using the known value of F_w, draw vector diagrams to find the values of F_P and F_N for both sides of the block.

2. Determine the absolute error between the calculated and measured values of F_P for each side of the block.

3. Calculate the coefficient of sliding friction, μ, for the two sides of the block.

experiment **9**

Center of Gravity and Equilibrium

PURPOSE: **(1)** To observe how the weight of the beam on which the forces act behaves like a force concentrated at the center of gravity of the beam. **(2)** To determine the conditions of equilibrium for several parallel forces.

APPARATUS: Meterstick and knife-edge support; slotted weights; 5 weight hangers; 5 meterstick clamps; platform balance. (Twine and interhooking weights may be used in place of the slotted weights, weight hangers, and meterstick clamps.)

INTRODUCTION: Two conditions must be met in order for equilibrium to be attained with several parallel forces. **(1)** The sum of the forces acting downward must equal the sum of the forces acting upward. **(2)** The sum of the clockwise torques must equal the sum of the counterclockwise torques. If the forces are acting on a rigid beam, the weight of the beam, concentrated at its center of gravity, acts as a force that must be considered when producing equilibrium.

PROCEDURE

1. Weight of meterstick as a force at its center of gravity

Place the meterstick on the platform balance and determine its mass. Compute the weight of the stick in newtons. Record this value.

Locate the center of gravity of the meterstick by balancing it on a pencil or other narrow support. Read this location to three significant figures and record.

Support the meterstick at some location other than its center of gravity and bring it into balance by using a single mass. See Figure 9-1. Record the value of the mass, its weight, and its distance from the

support. Be sure to include the mass of the clamp and hanger when you record the values for the added mass. The positions of the added mass and of the support for the meterstick in Figure 9-1 are meant to be suggestions; different positions may have to be used in order to obtain satisfactory data. The masses and distances should be measured as precisely as possible.

DATA   Part 1

Position of center of gravity	m
Position of meterstick support	m
Mass required for equilibrium	kg
Weight of required mass	n
Position of required mass	m
Length of torque arm for required mass	m
Torque producing equilibrium	mn
Length of torque arm for weight of meterstick	m
Weight of meterstick (experimental)	n
Weight of meterstick (actual)	n
Absolute error	n
Relative error	%

2. Equilibrium of several parallel forces

Support the meterstick at a point other than its center of gravity. As a suggestion, the meterstick in Figure 9-2 is supported at the 0.30-m mark. At the

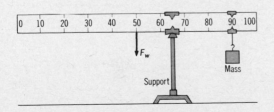

Figure 9-1

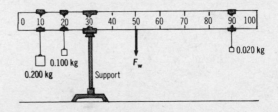

Figure 9-2

177

0.10-m mark hang a 0.200-kg mass; at the 0.20-m mark, a 0.l00-kg mass; and at the 0.90-m mark, a 0.020-kg mass. Locate the position at which a 0.050-kg mass must be hung to produce rotational equilibrium. (This mass and its position are not shown in Figure 9-2.)

After equilibrium has been attained, convert all the masses into force equivalents. Make sure that you include any clamps and weight hangers. Set up a suitable data table and record all torque-producing forces and their respective torque arms. Don't forget the weight of the meterstick and its torque arm in the data. Identify each torque as clockwise or counterclockwise. Draw a diagram of your setup.

ANALYZING THE DATA

1. Calculate the force required at the center of gravity to produce rotational equilibrium in Part 1.

2. Compare the force you have just calculated with the measured weight of the meterstick. Record the difference as the absolute error. Using the measured weight of the meterstick as the accepted value, calculate the relative error.

3. Determine the sum of the clockwise torques and the sum of the counterclockwise torques in Part 2. Find the difference between the two sums and record this value as your experimental deviation.

4. How can the weight of the meterstick be cancelled out in an experiment?

_____

_____

_____

experiment **10**

Parallel Forces

PURPOSE: **(1)** To show that the equilibrant of two parallel forces is equal to their sum. **(2)** To show that the equilibrant of two parallel forces must be between the two forces. **(3)** To show that the two forces are inversely proportional to the length of the arms upon which they act.

APPARATUS: Meterstick; 2 spring balances, 20-n capacity; 3 meterstick clamps; weight hanger and slotted weights, or interhooking weights.

INTRODUCTION: Parallel forces are those that act in the same direction or in opposite directions. The resultant of parallel forces in the same direction is equal to the sum of the separate forces. It acts in the same direction they do. It must be applied between them. The equilibrant force is equal to the sum of the separate parallel forces, but it acts in the opposite direction. When two parallel forces are held in equilibrium by a third force applied at the appro-

priate point, the clockwise and counterclockwise torques are equal. It follows that the two forces are inversely proportional to the lengths of the arms on which they act.

PROCEDURE: Hang the two spring balances from the laboratory table supports so that they are 0.80 m apart. Place three clamps on the meterstick; the one in the middle should be loop downward, the other two loop upward. For your first trial place one clamp at the 0.10-m mark of the meterstick, another at the 0.90-m mark, and the third clamp between them at the 0.50-m mark. (Assume that the center of gravity of the meterstick is at or very near the 0.50-m mark.) Now when the meterstick is hung on the hooks of the balances, the two balances will hang parallel to each other. See Figure 10-1.

Record in your data table the *initial readings* of both balances with the meterstick in position and with the third clamp fastened at **C**.

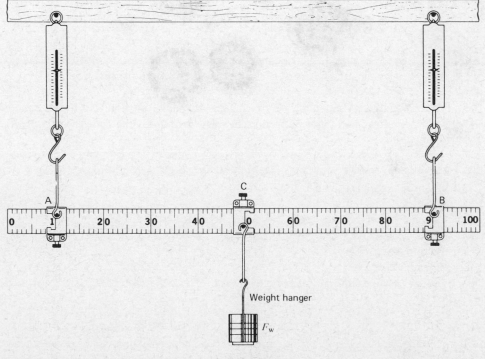

Figure 10-1

Add a weight of 10 n or more to clamp **C** and record the readings of balances **A** and **B** as *final readings*. The *true reading* of each balance is then the difference between its initial and final readings.

In the data table, record the total weight F_w (both weights and hanger, if one is used) as measured by a spring balance, and the distances **AC** and **BC**.

For the second and third trials, move the clamp **C** to different positions—the 0.25-m and 0.60-m marks, for example.

DATA

TRIAL	Balance A			Balance B		
	Initial reading (n)	Final reading (n)	True reading (n)	Initial reading (n)	Final reading (n)	True reading (n)
1						
2						
3						

DATA

Sum of true readings (n)	Total weight F_w (n)	Error (n)	Distance AC (m)	Distance BC (m)	Clockwise torque (mn)	Counter-clockwise torque (mn)	Deviation (mn)

ANALYZING THE DATA

1. Compute the sum of the true readings and record.

2. Find the difference between the sum of the true balance readings and the total weight F_w. This represents the experimental error in determining the values of the upward and downward forces. Record.

3. Consider the point **C** a fixed point at the axis of rotation about which forces tend to turn the meterstick. The true force **A** acts on the arm **AC** and tends to produce *clockwise rotation*. Calculate the product and record it in the proper torque column.

4. The true force **B** acts on the arm **BC** and tends to produce *counterclockwise rotation*. Calculate the product and record it in the proper torque column.

5. The difference between the two torques is the deviation. Record.

6. Repeat 1–5 for the remaining trials.

7. If a single force is to act as an equilibrant of two downward forces, what two conditions must the single upward force fulfill?

_____

_____

Centripetal Force - II

PURPOSE: To measure the relationship between centripetal force, mass, and velocity.

APPARATUS: Air table; plastic or fiberboard puck with small light bulb mounted at center; instant camera and stand; stroboscope; spring scale; spring; meterstick; platform balance; magnifying lens with scale.

INTRODUCTION: In Experiment 11, Centripetal Force-I, the accuracy of the results was affected by friction and by human error in the measurement of time intervals. In this experiment a special apparatus will be used, in which an upward flow of air provides a virtually frictionless surface for the object whose curvilinear motion is to be studied. Human error will be minimized by the use of photographs.

PROCEDURE: Set up the air table, camera stand, and instant camera, as shown in Figure 12-1.

Place a meterstick on the air table. Set the shutter speed of the camera at 3000 and take a picture of the meterstick and air table. *Do not advance the film;* you will need a double exposure for measuring purposes. Remove the meterstick and attach the puck to the center post with the spring. Turn on the air table and move the puck in a circular path. Practice moving the puck in a circular motion several times. Attach the stroboscope. Set the strobe rate at about 20 per second. Set the camera shutter speed at 75. Turn on the light bulb that is mounted on the puck. Darken the room and set the puck in circular motion. Expose the film for approximately three-fourths of a revolution. Do not allow the puck to move more than one complete revolution while the shutter is open. Your photograph should look similar to Figure 12-1.

Weigh the puck on the platform balance. Record. Measure the radius of the puck's path on the photograph. Use the meterstick in the picture to convert to actual meters. Record.

With the spring balance measure the force required to stretch the connecting spring to the length (r) to which it was extended in the picture. Record as F_c.

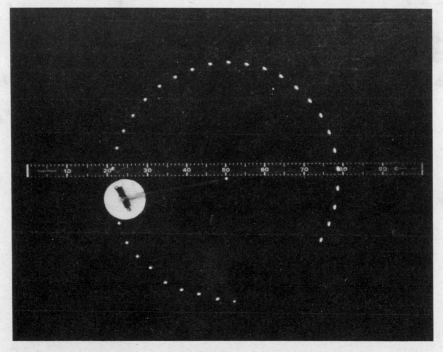

Figure 12-1

DATA

TRIAL	m (kg)	r (m)	F_c measured (n)	v (m/s)	F_c calc. (n)	Absolute error (n)	Relative error (%)

ANALYZING THE DATA

1. Using the magnifying lens, measure the distance between two successive points on the picture. Convert to actual meters and divide by the strobe rate to determine the velocity. Record as v.

2. Determine mv^2/r and record as F_c calculated.

3. Find the difference between F_c measured and F_c calculated and record as your absolute error. Find the relative errror.

4. If a puck with twice the mass were used, what change, if any, would result in the radius?

_____

_____

experiment **13**

The Pendulum

PURPOSE: (1) To determine the factors that affect the period of a pendulum. (2) To use a pendulum to determine the local value of the acceleration of gravity.

APPARATUS: Wooden bob; metal bob; pendulum clamp; meterstick; strong linen thread; stopwatch; protractor; platform balance.

INTRODUCTION: A simple pendulum consists of a small dense weight or bob suspended by a nearly weightless cord from a point about which it can vibrate freely. Such a pendulum is shown in Figure 13-1. The point about which the pendulum swings, **S**, is called the *center of suspension*. As the pendulum swings from **A** to **B** and back again to **A**, it makes a *complete vibration*, or *cycle*. The time required for a cycle is the *period* of the pendulum. The number of cycles a pendulum makes per second is its *frequency*. The *displacement* of the pendulum is its varying distance from **C**. The arc **AC**, representing the maximum displacement of the bob from **C**, is the *amplitude* of vibration. The *length* of a simple pendulum is measured from the center of suspension to the center of gravity of the pendulum bob.

PROCEDURE: Measure the mass of the bob on the platform balance. Measure the time required for 20 cycles of the pendulum bob. Compute and record

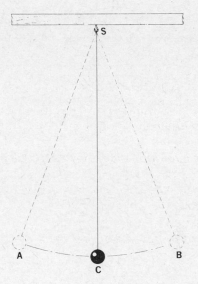

Figure 13-1

the period. Keep the amplitude in all trials between 5° and 10°. Measure the length from the center of suspension to the center of the bob. Record.

Do two more trials using different lengths. Record the periods and lengths.

Keeping the length constant, replace the bob with one having a different mass. Record the mass, period, and length.

Do two more trials with bobs of different mass. Record all data.

DATA

TRIAL	Mass (kg)	Length (m)	Period (s)	g (m/s^2)	Absolute error (m/s^2)	Relative error (%)
1						
2						
3						
4						
5						
6						

185

ANALYZING THE DATA

1. Plot a graph using the periods as abscissas and the lengths as ordinates. Use the data for Trials 1-3 only.

2. Plot a second graph of the periods versus the square roots of the lengths.

3. What is the relationship between the length of a pendulum and its period?

_____

_____

4. What effect, if any, does the mass have on the period of a pendulum?

_____

_____

5. The equation for the period of a pendulum is $T = 2\pi \sqrt{\dfrac{l}{g}}$, where T is the period of the pendulum, l is the length and g is the acceleration of gravity. Solve the equation for g and compute the values of g for each trial. Record.

6. Using an accepted value of 9.8 m/s^2 for g, calculate the absolute and relative errors.

experiment $\mathbf{14}$

Power

PURPOSE: (1) To measure the power output of a person running up a flight of stairs. (2) To learn the meaning of the unit of horsepower.

APPARATUS: Bathroom scale; meterstick; stopwatch.

INTRODUCTION: Power is the time rate of doing work, or

$$P = \frac{F\Delta d}{\Delta t}$$

where P is the power in watts, F is the force in newtons, d is the distance in meters, and t is the elapsed time in seconds.

A simple way to measure the power output of a person is to measure the time it takes the person to run up a flight of stairs of known height. In this experiment, you will compare your power output with that of your classmates (and, perhaps, of your instructor). You will then convert these values into horsepower units.

When James Watt invented his steam engine, he was asked how many horses the engine could replace. To find out, Watt built a rope-and-pulley device with which he could measure the time it took a horse to lift various weights. After many experiments Watt concluded that a horse can produce 760 watts of power for a sustained period of time. (Watt used English units of measurement in his experiments. The metric unit of power was later named in his honor.) Watt's definition of horsepower is still used today, even though the power output of an average horse during the course of a working day is only about two-thirds of a standard horsepower.

An interesting application of human power is the Gossamer Condor airplane. This human-powered airplane made its first successful flight in 1977. The plane now hangs next to the first Wright Brothers airplane in the National Air and Space Museum in Washington, D.C. The builders of the Condor calculated that, even by using very light materials and very long wings, the plane's human engine had to put out between one-fourth and one-third of a horsepower during the flight. This is more than twice the power that a person can produce over a sustained period of time.

PROCEDURE: CAUTION: *Students who have medical conditions that exclude them from participation in sports or physical education classes should not be required to participate in the first part of this experiment.*

Locate a straight staircase at least 1.5 meters in vertical height and preferably with a railing. There should also be a clear area at least 2 meters long at both the top and bottom of the stairs. Measure the height of one step of the staircase and multiply by the number of steps. Record.

Use the bathroom scale to measure the weight of the first participating student. (If necessary, convert the English units on the scale to metric by using the equation 1 pound = 4.45 newtons.)

Set the stopwatch at zero. Ask the student to run up the stairs as fast as possible. The student should grasp the railing for safety as well as added power. Start the watch when *both* feet of the student have left the ground floor and stop the watch when *both* feet are on the top floor. Record the time.

Repeat the procedure for each participating student. Record all data. Some students may wish to repeat their trials in an effort to improve their time.

DATA

NAME	Weight (n)	Height of stairs (m)	Time (s)	Power (w)	Horsepower

ANALYZING THE DATA

1. Use the power equation to calculate the wattage of each student in the data table. Record.

2. Convert the wattage of each participant into horsepower equivalents.

3. Discuss the results in terms of Watt's definition of horsepower, the Gossamer Condor, and sources of error.

_____

_____

_____

_____

experiment 15

Efficiency of Machines

PURPOSE: To measure the efficiency of an inclined plane and a pulley system.

APPARATUS: Inclined plane and car; various pulleys; string; set of weights.

INTRODUCTION: Machines are used to make work more convenient by multiplying force at the expense of speed, or vice versa. A machine does not multiply work, however. The work output of a machine is never greater than the work input; thus the law of conservation of energy is not contradicted. In fact, the useful work output is always less than the work input because of the force of friction. The ratio of the useful work output to the work input is called the *efficiency* of the machine. Efficiency is often expressed as a percentage.

In this experiment the efficiency of two machines will be measured. (It may be necessary to schedule two laboratory periods for the experiment.) In each case, the work output is the product of the weight of the object being raised, F_w, and the height through which it is raised, h. The work input is the product of the force exerted on the machine, F_a, and the distance through which it acts, d. The efficiency is the ratio of these products, or

$$\text{Efficiency} = \frac{F_w h}{F_a d}$$

The relative efficiency is the percentage ratio of these products, or

$$\text{Relative Efficiency} = \frac{F_w h}{F_a d} \times 100\%$$

PROCEDURE

1. Inclined plane
Set up the inclined plane as shown in Figure 15-1. The angle of the plane is arbitrary but should be kept constant during this part of the experiment.

Place a 200-g mass in the car and find the mass that will allow the car to move up the plane with constant velocity once it has been started. Compute the weights of the masses and record them in the data table. Also record the distances; h is the *vertical* dis-

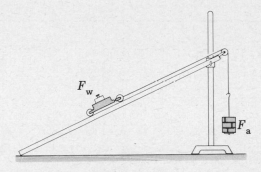

Figure 15-1

tance through which F_w moves while F_a moves through the distance d.

Make several more trials, each time increasing the mass in the car. Record all necessary data.

2. Pulley
Set up a pulley system like the one shown in Figure 15-2. Starting with a 500-g mass, find the

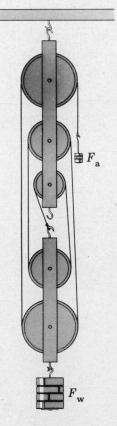

Figure 15-2

mass that will make the 500-g mass move up with constant velocity once it has been started.

Repeat the procedure with different pulley systems (5 pulleys, 6 pulleys, etc.) Record all data.

DATA

TRIAL	MACHINE	F_w (n)	h (m)	F_a (n)	d (m)	Work output (j)	Work input (j)	Relative efficiency (%)
1								
2								
3								
4								
5								
6								

ANALYZING THE DATA

1. Compute the relative efficiency for each trial. Record.

2. For centuries people have tried unsuccessfully to build machines with 100% efficiency. Will such a "perpetual motion" machine ever be invented? Explain.

_____

_____

_____

experiment **16**

Elastic Potential Energy

PURPOSE: To verify the law of conservation of energy in an oscillating spring.

APPARATUS: Hooke's law apparatus; set of masses; several rubber bands.

INTRODUCTION: In the case of a swinging pendulum there is a continuous interchange between potential energy and kinetic energy. The potential energy is at a maximum when the bob is at the highest point in its swing. The kinetic energy is at a maximum when the bob is at its lowest point and is moving with maximum velocity. Except for the effect of friction, the potential energy at the top of the swing is equal to the kinetic energy at the bottom. This is in accordance with the law of conservation of energy.

The apparatus in Figure 16-1 is similar to a pendulum in some respects. An oscillating mass falls under the influence of gravity, as in the pendulum. However, the oscillation is entirely vertical rather than in an arc. Furthermore, the mass oscillates about a midpoint where the tension in the spring is equal to the force of gravitation on the mass. At the top of the oscillation the mass has maximum gravitational potential energy. At the bottom of the oscillation the spring has maximum elastic potential energy. In this experiment, we will compare these two forms of potential energy as a test of the law of conservation of energy.

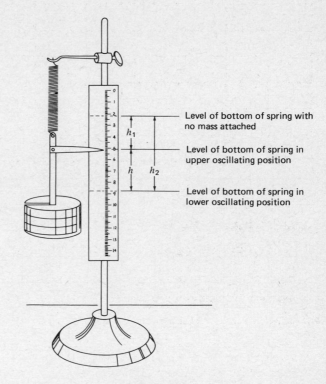

Level of bottom of spring with no mass attached

Level of bottom of spring in upper oscillating position

Level of bottom of spring in lower oscillating position

Figure 16-1

PROCEDURE

1. Elastic constant of the spring

To calculate the potential energy that is stored in a stretched spring, it is necessary to find the force that is required to stretch the spring a given

DATA Part 1

TRIAL	Mass (kg)	Force (n)	Elongation (m)	Elastic constant (n/m)
1				
2				
3				
4				
5				
6				
			Average	

191

amount. This is the *elastic constant*, and it is expressed in units of newtons per meter, n/m.

Place a rubber band at the initial position of the pointer or adjust the scale or pan to read 0.0 cm. Find a mass that will stretch the spring approximately one-quarter full scale. How much mass you add depends on the stiffness of the spring. Convert the mass to force units and record. Also record the elongation of the spring.

Repeat the preceding step until full-scale deflection is obtained. Record all data in the data table for Part 1.

2. Conservation of potential energy

Place a mass on the pan so that the spring is stretched about one-half full scale. Record the mass.

You will need two additional rubber bands on the scale. Use one of the rubber bands to mark a position approximately halfway between the zero reading and the present position of the pointer. Refer to Figure 16-1. Raise the pan until the pointer is at the position where you just placed the rubber band. Let the pan drop. Use the other rubber band to mark the lowest position to which the pan falls, as indicated by the pointer. Record h_1, h_2, and h. See Figure 16-1.

Run several more trials, varying both the mass and the amplitude of oscillation.

DATA Part 2

TRIAL	Mass (kg)	h_2 (m)	h_1 (m)	h (m)	E_p elastic (j)	E_p gravitational (j)	Deviation (j)
1							
2							
3							
4							
5							
6							

ANALYZING THE DATA

1. Calculate the elastic constant k for each trial in Part 1 and determine the average. Record.

2. Using the equation

$$E_p \text{ (elastic)} = 1/2k(h_2^2 - h_1^2)$$

compute the elastic potential energy of the spring for each trial. Record.

3. Compute the gravitational potential energy for each trial by using the equation

$$E_p \text{ (gravitational)} = mgh$$

where $h = h_2 - h_1$.

4. Find the difference between the potential energies and record as your deviation.

5. This experiment is an application of Hooke's law. Does this law apply only to the elasticity of extension? If not, state other forms of elasticity.

experiment 17

Conservation of Momentum—
One Dimension

PURPOSE: To verify the law of the conservation of momentum.

APPARATUS: Recording timer; timing tape; connecting wire; dry cell or other dc-power source; two carts, one with a spring mechanism; platform balance; set of masses; magnifying lens with scale.

INTRODUCTION: The product of the mass of a moving object and its velocity is called its *momentum*. A bullet with a small mass and a high velocity may have the same momentum as a truck with a large mass and a very small velocity.

Newton's law of reaction states that every force is accompanied by an equal and opposite force, or reaction. Thus, when a rifle is fired, the force on the bullet is accompanied by an equal and opposite force on the gun. The momentum of the bullet is equal to the momentum of the gun (and the person holding it).

In this experiment the gun and bullet will be simulated by two carts with unequal masses. One of the

carts contains a spring mechanism to provide the equal and opposite forces for the experiment. The velocities of the carts will be measured with a recording timer. (Experiment 3 contains a more complete description of the timer and its operation.)

The law of the conservation of momentum will also be studied by changing the mass of one of the carts while it is moving. The resulting change in the velocity of the cart will be measured and checked against the equation

$$m_1 \Delta v_1 = m_2 \Delta v_2$$

PROCEDURE: Set up the carts and timer as shown in Figure 17-1. Since both tapes pass through the same timer, place two carbon paper disks back to back between the paper tapes. Study the cart with the spring mechanism so that you will know how to compress and release the spring.

Determine the mass of an unloaded cart and record. Load the second cart with a 1-kg mass. Measure the mass of this loaded cart and record. Com-

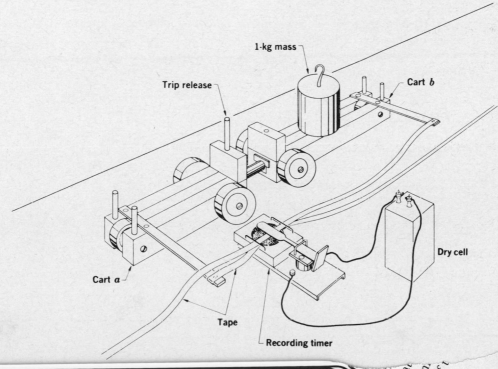

1-kg mass

Trip release

Cart b

Cart a

Dry cell

Tape

Recording timer

fasten
In the da
the circum
glass tube if

press the spring mechanism and position the carts. Make sure there are no obstructions in the paths of the carts.

Turn on the timer and trip the spring mechanism. When the carts have stopped moving, turn off the timer and remove the tapes. Label each tape so that it corresponds to the cart to which it was attached.

Repeat the experiment two more times, using different combinations of masses. Record all data.

Change the mass of a cart en route and measure the resulting change in velocity. A good way to do this is to use an empty cart and place a 1-kg mass on it shortly after the spring is tripped. Measure the velocity of the cart before and after the mass is added and calculate the momentum for each case. Record your data.

Another way to vary the mass of the cart is to remove a 1-kg mass while the cart is in motion. Before the cart starts to move, tie a thread to the mass in order to remove this mass with a minimum of disturbance.

Devise and carry out a method of determining the value of an unknown mass that is placed on one of the carts. Check your results with a platform balance.

DATA

TRIAL	Mass		Velocity		Total velocity	Momentum		Total momentum
	m_a (kg)	m_b (kg)	v_a (mm/dot)	v_b (mm/dot)	$v_a + v_b$ (mm/dot)	$m_a v_a$ (kg mm/dot)	$m_b v_b$ (kg mm/dot)	$m_a v_a + m_b v_b$ (kg mm/dot)
1								
2								
3								
4								

ANALYZING THE DATA

1. Use the magnifying lens with scale to measure three distances between successive dots near the starting point of the tape for each cart. Record the average of the three values for each of the two carts. Since the time interval per dot is constant, the average distances can be recorded as the velocities v_a and v_b in mm/dot. Why?

2. Before the spring was released, the total velocity was zero. Find the total velocity after the spring is released. Remember to include the direction. Record.

3. Is velocity conserved in this experiment?

_____

_____

4. Repeat Steps 1 and 2 for the product of velocity and mass.

5. Define momentum. Is momentum conserved in this experiment?

_____

_____

experiment **18**

Conservation of Momentum—Two Dimensions

PURPOSE: To appy the law of conservation of momentum to elastic, two-dimensional collisions.

APPARATUS: Air table; plastic or fiberboard pucks with small light bulbs mounted at center, mass ratios of pucks approximately 2:1; instant camera and stand; stroboscope; magnifying lens with scale; protractor.

INTRODUCTION: In Experiment 17 the law of conservation of momentum was seen to hold true for objects moving along the same straight line. This is an example of motion in one dimension. In this experiment the same law will be applied to motion in two dimensions. A moving object will be made to collide with a stationary one in such a way that both objects will move away from the collision in different directions. Vector diagrams will then be used to compare the momenta of the objects before and after the collision.

The reduction of friction is an important factor in conservation of momentum experiments, since friction is a dissipative and not a conservative force. In Experiment 17, friction reduction was accomplished by having wheels on the moving objects. In this experiment a special apparatus is used in which an upward flow of air provides a virtually frictionless surface for the moving objects. The round pucks used in the experiment are also designed to make the collisions as elastic as possible.

PROCEDURE: Set up the air table, camera stand, and camera as shown in Figure 18-1. (Tables other than the one shown in the figure may involve different setups, and the instructions for the specific table should be carefully studied.)

Turn on the air flow and place the lighter puck in the center of the table. Propel the heavier puck toward the stationary one from the side of the table. Try to hit the stationary puck slightly off-center so that both pucks will keep moving after the collision. See Figure 18-2. Practice this procedure until you can control the angle between the paths of the two pucks after impact with a fair degree of precision.

Turn on the strobe light and open the shutter of

Courtesy of Eduquip, Inc.

Figure 18-1

pucks reaches the side of the air table. Develop the film to see whether you have obtained a good multiple exposure of the collision. The photo should show the positions of the pucks before and after impact as a series of white dots, as shown in Figure 18-2.

Record the mass of the incident puck, m_i, and the target puck, m_t.

Repeat the procedure for two more trials.

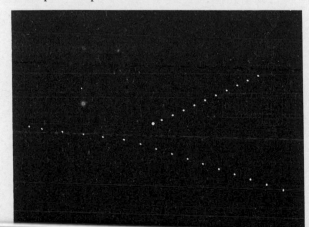

DATA

TRIAL	m_i (kg)	m_t (kg)	v_i (mm/dot)	v_t (mm/dot)	v_i' (mm/dot)	v_t' (mm/dot)	$\angle$ of v_i' (°)	$\angle$ of v_t' (°)
1								
2								
3								

$m_i v_i$ (kg mm/dot)	$m_t v_t$ (kg mm/dot)	$m_i v_i'$ (kg mm/dot)	$m_t v_t'$ (kg mm/dot)

ANALYZING THE DATA

1. Measure the distances between dots before and after the collision. Record these distances as the velocities, in mm/dot, of each puck before and after the collision, v_i, v_i', v_t, and v_t'.

2. Measure the angles made by v_i' and v_t'. Use the path of the incident puck as the base line. Record.

3. Use vectors to determine the sum of the velocities after the collision. Refer to Figure 18-3.

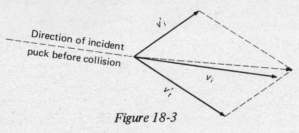

Figure 18-3

4. Find the difference in magnitude between the total velocity before the collision and the total velocity after the collision.

5. Is velocity conserved?

_____

_____

6. Calculate the momentum of the incident and target pucks before and after the collision. Record.

7. Repeat Steps 3 and 4 for momentum instead of velocity.

8. Is momentum conserved?

_____

_____

experiment **19**

The Size of a Molecule

PURPOSE: (1) To determine the order of magnitude of the size of an oleic acid molecule. (2) To determine the number of molecules in one mole of a molecular substance.

APPARATUS: Ripple tank, or other large dish; 1-mL pipette; meterstick; oleic acid in alcohol solution, 1:500; lycopodium powder or fine talcum powder; concentrated hydrochloric acid.

INTRODUCTION: Molecules are much too small to be observed directly. However, because some molecules will form layers that are one molecule thick on water, it is possible to determine the order of magnitude of the size of such molecules with ordinary laboratory equipment.

A mole of a molecular substance is the quantity of the substance that is equal to its molecular weight expressed in grams. The number of molecules in a mole of a molecular substance is an important physical constant known as the Avogadro number. Its value is 6.0219×10^{23} molecules per mole. In this experiment we shall also attempt to verify the Avogadro number.

SUGGESTION: Before the laboratory period, the instructor should prepare a 1:500 solution of oleic acid in denatured alcohol.

PROCEDURE: Pour water into a ripple tank to a depth of about one centimeter and dust the water surface very lightly with lycopodium powder or talcum powder. Using a 1-mL pipette, place one drop of oleic acid solution on the water surface as in Figure 19-1. The oleic acid pushes the powder outward so that the area of the oleic acid layer is visible. Measure the diameter of the layer and calculate its area. Record.

Experimentally determine the number of drops of oleic acid solution per cubic centimeter. Calculate the volume of one drop of solution. Record. Using the dilution ratio of the solution, 1:500, compute the volume of oleic acid in the drop of solution used. This is the volume of the surface layer. Using this

Steve Koch

Figure 19-1A

Steve Koch

Figure 19-1B

of concentrated hydrochloric acid to the water before dusting it with lycopodium or talcum. Measure the diameter of the oleic acid layer as before, and calculate its area, volume, and thickness. Record all data.

The diameter of the oleic acid layer will be considerably larger in the acid solution than it is in plain

Repeat the experiment, but this time add 20 mL   slight attraction between one end of the oleic acid molecule and water. Hydrochloric acid destroys this attraction, however, and in the acid solution the oleic acid molecule floats on its side. Hence a cylinder is a good approximation of the shape of the molecule.

Use the thickness of the oleic acid layer on water as the height of the cylindrical molecule and the thickness on the acid solution as the diameter. Calculate the volume of a single oleic acid molecule using the equation

$$V = \tfrac{1}{4}\,\pi\,d^2\,h$$

The mass density of oleic acid is 0.895 g/cm^3 and one mole has a mass of 282 g. Calculate the volume occupied by one mole of oleic acid. From this value and the volume of an oleic acid molecule, calculate the number of molecules in a mole of oleic acid. Compare your results with the accepted value for the Avogadro number and calculate your relative error. Record all data and show your calculations in your report.

DATA

TRIAL	Diameter of layer (cm)	Area of layer (cm²)	Number of drops of oleic acid solution (per cm³)	Volume of one drop of oleic acid solution (cm³)
in water				
in acid solution				

Volume of oleic acid in one drop of solution (cm³)	Thickness of layer (cm)	Volume of an oleic acid molecule (cm³)	Volume of one mole of oleic acid (cm³)	Avogadro Number experimental (per mole)	accepted (per mole)	Relative error (%)
		⨯	⨯	⨯	⨯	⨯

QUESTIONS (Your answers should be complete statements.)

1. What is the ratio of the height of the oleic acid molecule to its diameter?

2. How could you make sure that the oleic acid, and not the alcohol, is pushing the powder aside?

3. What factors determine the precision of this experiment?

4. What properties of oleic acid make it desirable for this experiment?

5. How does the surface tension of water help in this experiment? How does it hinder the experiment?

experiment 20

Dew Point and Relative Humidity

PURPOSE: To determine the dew point and relative humidity of the air in the laboratory.

APPARATUS: Small, shiny metal can, such as a calorimeter cup; thermometer; ice chips; dew point apparatus, if available.

INTRODUCTION: The amount of water vapor in the atmosphere is an important aspect of the weather. We all know that a warm and "humid" day is more uncomfortable that a "dry" day at the same temperature. That is why many weather forecasts include the moisture content of the atmosphere in a so-called "temperature-humidity index." We also know that a rapid drop in air temperature can result in the condensation of atmospheric moisture in the form of dew or fog.

In this experiment you will determine the temperature at which moisture condenses out of the atmosphere in the laboratory. This is called the *dew point.* You will then use the dew point to calculate the *relative humidity,* which is the ratio of the amount of water vapor in the atmosphere to the amount the air can hold at the same temperature. Relative humidity is usually expressed as a percentage that can be calculated from the dew point and from a vapor pressure table by using the equation

Relative humidity = $p/P \times 100\%$

where p is the equilibrium vapor pressure at the dew point and P is the equilibrium vapor pressure at the temperature of the room.

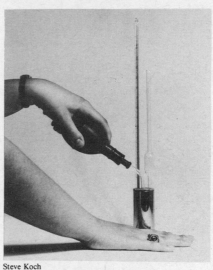

Steve Koch

Figure 20-1

PROCEDURE: If a dew point apparatus such as the one shown in Figure 20-1 is available, carefully follow the instructions for its use. Otherwise, use the procedure given below.

Fill the metal can about half full with tap water. Carefully dry the outside of the can with a cloth or paper towel. Place a thermometer in the can.

Put the can in a part of the room that is free from air currents. *Do not breathe on the can during the experiment.* Put some ice chips in the water in the can and stir the water with the thermometer. Carefully watch the thermometer and the outside surface of the can. As soon as moisture forms on the outside of the can, read the thermometer. Record this temperature as T_1.

DATA   Room temperature _____ °C

TRIAL	T_1 (°C)	T_2 (°C)	Dew point (°C)	Dew-point vapor pressure (mm)	Room-temp. vapor pressure (mm)	Relative humidity (%)
1						
2						

Average

Remove any unmelted ice chips from the water. Add a small amount of tap water to the can while stirring the water in the can with the thermometer. Again watch both the thermometer and the outside of the can carefully. As soon as all the moisture disappears from the outside of the can, read the thermometer. Record this temperature as T_2. Find the average of T_1 and T_2 and record this temperature as the dew point.

Repeat the procedure for two more trials.

Find the equilibrium vapor pressure of water at the dew point in Appendix B, Table 12. Record. Find and record the equilibrium vapor pressure of water at the temperature of the room. Calculate the relative humidity. Repeat this procedure for all three trials. Find the average relative humidity.

If there is a relative humidity gauge in the room, compare your results with the reading on the gauge.

QUESTIONS (Your answers should be complete statements.)

1. Why is it important to avoid air currents while measuring the dew point? Why is it important to avoid breathing on the metal can while measuring the dew point?

_____

_____

2. Why is it necessary to take the average of T_1 and T_2 in finding the dew point?

_____

_____

3. If the dew point and room temperature are equal, what is the relative humidity?

_____

_____

4. Under what conditions does fog form in the air?

_____

_____

5. Why is it more uncomfortable when the relative humidity is high than when it is low, even though the air temperature is the same?

_____

_____

6. How can the relative humidity of the air in a room be decreased without removing water vapor?

_____

_____

experiment **21**

Coefficient of Linear Expansion

PURPOSE: To measure the coefficient of linear expansion of one or more metals.

APPARATUS: Coefficient of linear expansion apparatus; meterstick; steam boiler; tripod, for steam boiler; rubber tubing, for steam delivery; thermometer; burner and rubber tubing; 100-mL beaker, for catching condensate; rods or tubes of aluminum, brass, copper, and steel.

INTRODUCTION: Nearly all substances expand when heated and contract when cooled. The increase in length of a unit length of a solid when heated through a temperature change of one degree is called the *coefficient of linear expansion.* Such an increase is difficult to measure directly. Generally, a rod about 1.0 m long is heated through a temperature change of about 80 C° and the expansion is measured by a device that multiplies the small amount of expansion actually occurring.

With the type of apparatus shown in Figure 21-1, the rod, with one end fixed, is placed in a steam jacket. When steam passes through the jacket, the rod expands and the movable end pushes against the short arm of a bent lever. This pushes the long arm of the lever along a graduated scale.

In other types of coefficient of linear expansion apparatus, the amount of expansion is measured directly by means of a micrometer screw or by an axle that rotates through a measurable angle as the expanding rod or tube moves over it.

PROCEDURE: The general method for this experiment (regardless of the type of apparatus used) is to cause a metal rod or tube of known initial length and known initial temperature to undergo a known increase in temperature and to measure the resulting amount of expansion. One end of the metal rod or tube is kept stationary. The other end is free to expand under the heating effect of the steam used. Its movement is measured by some suitable device.

Inspect the apparatus to determine how the amount of expansion is to be measured. In the bent lever type, the amount of expansion is the product of the change in scale reading (usually in millimeters) and the ratio of the length of the short lever arm to the length of the long lever arm. In the micrometer type, the expansion is the difference between two micrometer readings—one taken with the rod at room temperature, the other taken with the rod at steam temperature. (Make sure you "back off" the micrometer screw during the expansion.) In the rotation method, the expansion is the product of the number of degrees of rotation and the circumference of the axle divided by exactly 360°.

Make determinations with as many different metals as your instructor directs.

Record all necessary data in an appropriate table in the space provided. Compare the experimental coefficient of linear expansion with the accepted value for the metals used. (Appendix B, Table 14.) Compute the relative error for each trial.

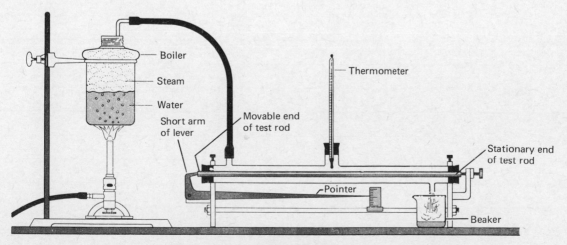

Figure 21-1

DATA

\
\
\
\
\
\
\
\
\
\
\
\
\
\
\

QUESTIONS (Your answers should be complete statements.)

1. On the basis of this experiment, do you think that the linear expansion of the metal rods was the same for each degree rise in temperature? Justify your answer.

\
\
\
\
\

2. A metal sheet has a round hole in it. When the sheet is heated, does the hole get bigger or smaller? Justify your answer on the basis of this experiment. Verify the answer by experimentation, if possible.

\
\
\
\
\
\
\
\
\
\

3. Can you think of a way to modify this experiment so that you could see linear expansion directly?

_____

_____

_____

_____

_____

4. List three factors that determine the precision of the experiment.

_____

_____

_____

_____

_____

_____

_____

_____

_____

_____

_____

experiment **22**

Charles' Law

PURPOSE: **(1)** To learn how the volume of a gas is affected by a change in temperature. **(2)** To verify Charles' law.

APPARATUS: Glass cylinder, 30 cm high; steam boiler with chimney; tripod for boiler; burner and rubber tubing; thermometer; magnifier; glass tube, globule of mercury, and meterstick or Charles' law tube; ice.

INTRODUCTION: Charles' law states that the volume of a dry gas is directly proportional to the Kelvin temperature, provided the pressure remains constant. In this experiment, the volume occupied by a gas at the ice point and at the steam point will be measured. Using the volume of gas measured at the ice point, the Kelvin temperatures at the ice point and at the steam point, and the Charles' law equation, $V/V' = T_K/T_K{}'$, the volume the gas should occupy at the steam point will be calculated. This calculated value will then be compared with the actual volume of the gas at the steam point to verify Charles' law. During the course of the experiment it is assumed that the atmospheric pressure remains constant.

In this experiment, rather than measuring a volume of gas directly, you will measure the length of a column of gas trapped in a glass tube. The length of a column of gas of uniform cross-sectional area is directly proportional to the volume of the gas and can be substituted for the volume in a gas law equation.

The apparatus used in this experiment consists of a glass tube not more than 1.5 mm in diameter and about 350 mm in length. A tiny globule of mercury is introduced into the tube (not more than enough to make a column 5 mm in length), and one end of the tube is sealed so that the enclosed air column is about 250 mm long. (Before inserting the mercury, heat the tube so that any moisture will be expelled. Otherwise, water vapor will push the mercury out of the tube during the experiment.) The glass tube should then be fastened with rubber bands to a section of meterstick. See Figure 22-1. When the tube is heated, the air expands and pushes the mercury globule up the tube. The volume of air trapped in the tube is proportional to the length of the column of air as read from the meterstick.

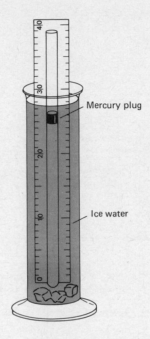

Figure 22-1

Mercury plug

Ice water

PROCEDURE: Record in the data table the meterstick reading of the sealed end of the air column to the nearest tenth of a centimeter. Fill the cylinder with ice and water and support the glass tube and metric scale in the ice-water mixture so it stands vertically. The surface of the water should be at about the same level as the globule of mercury in the glass tube. Find the temperature of the ice-water mixture to the nearest tenth of a degree. It should be approximately 0°C. After the glass tube has stood in the ice-water mixture for about three minutes, read the position of the top of the air column to the nearest tenth of a centimeter. Allow the glass tube to remain in the ice-water mixture for one additional minute. Reread the position of the top of the air column to the nearest tenth of a centimeter. If there is no change in the length of the air column, record the reading in the data table.

Remove the glass tube and meterstick from the ice-water mixture and suspend them in the chimney of the steam boiler so they will be surrounded by the steam from the boiling water. After being suspended in the steam for about three minutes, read the position of the top of the air column to the nearest tenth of a centimeter. Also read the temperature of the steam surrounding the tube to the nearest tenth of a degree. After one additional minute make confirmatory readings using the same procedure as was used at the ice point.

Make two more trials in which you determine the position of the top of the air column and the temperature in both the ice-water mixture and in the steam for each trial. Record the data.

CALCULATIONS: For each trial, determine the length of the air column at the temperature of the ice-water mixture and at the temperature of the steam. Determine the average length of the air column at the temperature of the ice-water mixture and the average length of the air column at the temperature of the steam. Also determine the average temperature of the ice-water mixture and the average temperature of the steam in degrees Celsius.

Convert the average Celsius temperatures of the ice-water mixture and the steam to Kelvin temperatures. Using the average length of the column of air in the ice-water mixture as V, the average Kelvin temperature of the ice-water mixture as T_K, and the average Kelvin temperature of the steam as T_K', calculate the theoretical length of the air column at the temperature of the steam V' by means of the equation $V/V' = T_K/T_K'$. Find the error between your experimental value and this calculated value. Assuming the calculated value to be correct, find the percentage error.

DATA Bottom of air column _____ cm

TRIAL	Top of air column in ice-water mixture (cm)	Top of air column in steam (cm)	Length of air column in ice-water mixture (cm)	Length of air column in steam (cm)	Temperature of ice-water mixture (°C)	Temperature of steam (°C)
1						
2						
3						
Average						

	Temperature of ice-water mixture (°K)	Temperature of steam (°K)	Length of air column in steam (calculated) (cm)	Absolute error (cm)	Relative error (%)
Average					

QUESTIONS (Your answers should be complete statements.)

1. (a) How could this experiment be modified to determine whether air expands uniformly when it is heated?
   (b) How could this experiment be modified to determine whether other gases obey Charles' law?

_____

_____

_____

_____

2. Does the expansion of the glass tube affect the accuracy of this experiment? Explain.

_____

_____

_____

_____

_____

_____

3. Devise a method of determining the length of the air column at an intermediate temperature such as 50°C and verify Charles' law for expansion from the ice point to this temperature.

_____

_____

_____

_____

_____

_____

_____

_____

_____

_____

_____

experiment **23**

Boyle's Law

PURPOSE: (1) To learn how the volume of a given mass of gas varies with the pressure exerted on it. (2) To verify Boyle's law.

APPARATUS: Boyle's law states that if the temperature remains constant, the volume of a dry gas varies inversely with the pressure exerted on it. This means that as the pressure on a gas is increased, the volume of the gas will become smaller at the same rate. Or, as the pressure on the gas is decreased, the volume will increase. If we use p to represent the pressure and V to represent the volume, Boyle's law can be stated algebraically as $pV =$ a constant.

In this experiment we shall use a modification of the method actually used by Robert Boyle in deriving this pressure-volume relationship of gases that now bears his name.

PRECAUTION: In this experiment you will be using mercury. In order to protect any hand jewelry you wear from the action of mercury, remove these articles and place them in your pocket or purse. *Be careful not to spill any mercury and do not handle it.* After the experiment is completed, wash your hands thoroughly with soap and water before replacing your jewelry.

PROCEDURE: Using the medicine dropper, put enough mercury into the J-tube to fill the curved por-

tion and to reach the graduations on the meterstick. Tip the tube sideways so that air flows past the mercury and the mercury columns become the same height in both tubes, as in *A* of Figure 23-1. Record the meterstick reading at the top of the short arm and the height of the mercury in both arms of the tube. The difference between the meterstick reading at the top of the short arm and the height of the mercury in the short arm indicates the *original volume* of air taken. (The volumes of cylinders of the same diameter are directly proportional to their lengths.) The barometer reading is the *original pressure.*

Now add 10 to 15 cm of mercury to the long arm of the tube. Take readings of the height of the mercury level in each arm of the tube. Calculate the new volume of air by subtracting the height of the mercury in the short arm of the tube from the height of the tube itself. Calculate the new pressure by adding the barometer reading to the difference between the height of the mercury levels in the two columns. In the same manner, take three or four more readings and record the results. Calculate the pV product.

When you have obtained all the necessary data, follow your instructor's directions for removing the mercury from the J-tube. Be especially careful when handling a J-tube that contains mercury.

GRAPH: Plot a graph of your data, using the pressures as abscissas and the volumes as ordinates.

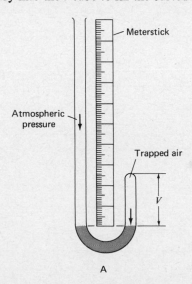

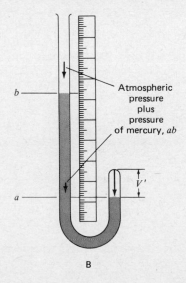

Figure 23-1

DATA

Height of short arm _____ cm   Barometer _____ cm

TRIAL	Mercury level in short arm (cm)	Volume of gas V (cm)	Mercury level in long arm (cm)	Difference in mercury levels (cm)	Pressure on gas p (cm)	pV
1						
2						
3						
4						
5						
6						
7						
8						

QUESTIONS (Your answers should be complete statements.)

1. Describe the relationship between the pressure exerted on a gas and the volume occupied by the gas.

_____

_____

_____

2. (a) How would the presence of air bubbles in the mercury affect the results of this experiment? (b) How would the presence of water in the mercury affect the data?

a. _____

_____

_____

b. _____

_____

_____

3. In what way is a Boyle's law tube like a barometer?

_____

_____

_____

_____

4. What effect does an increase in pressure have on the density of a gas?

_____

_____

5. What determines the upper limit of the pressure that can be exerted in a Boyle's law tube?

_____

experiment **24**

Specific Heat

PURPOSE: To determine the specific heat of one or more metals.

APPARATUS: Calorimeter; thermometer, Celsius –10° to 110°, graduated to 0.2°; stirring rod; steam boiler; tripod, for steam boiler; burner and rubber tubing; platform balance; set of masses; ice cubes; metal block (lead, aluminum, brass, and copper are satisfactory); magnifier; strong twine.

INTRODUCTION: The method of mixtures is used to determine the specific heat of a metal. A certain mass of water in a calorimeter is warmed a measured number of degrees by a solid of known mass as it cools through a measured number of degrees.

The heat gained or lost by a substance when it undergoes a change in temperature is calculated as the product of the mass of the substance, its change in temperature, and its specific heat. According to

DATA

	TRIAL 1	TRIAL 2
1. Kind of metal	_____	_____
2. Mass of metal	_____ g	_____ g
3. Mass of calorimeter cup and stirrer	_____ g	_____ g
4. Mass of calorimeter cup, stirrer, and water	_____ g	_____ g
5. Mass of water	_____ g	_____ g
6. Specific heat of calorimeter	_____ cal/gC°	_____ cal/gC°
7. Temperature of solid, initial (temperature of boiling water)	_____ °C	_____ °C
8. Temperature of water and calorimeter, initial	_____ °C	_____ °C
9. Temperature of solid, water, and calorimeter, final	_____ °C	_____ °C
10. Temperature change of water and calorimeter	_____ C°	_____ C°
11. Calories gained by calorimeter cup and stirrer	_____ cal	_____ cal
12. Calories gained by water	_____ cal	_____ cal
13. Total calories gained	_____ cal	_____ cal
14. Calories lost by solid	_____ cal	_____ cal
15. Temperature change of solid	_____ C°	_____ C°
16. Specific heat of solid	_____ cal/gC°	_____ cal/gC°
17. Accepted value for specific heat of solid	_____ cal/gC°	_____ cal/gC°
18. Absolute error	_____ cal/gC°	_____ cal/gC°
19. Relative error	_____ %	_____ %

the law of heat exchange, the total amount of heat lost by a hot object equals the total amount of heat gained by the cold object with which it comes in contact. Consequently, in this experiment, the total heat lost by the solid on cooling equals the heat gained by the water and calorimeter as they are warmed.

PROCEDURE: Find the mass of the metal block. Attach a piece of twine about 30 cm long to the metal block and lower it into the steam boiler. The boiler should be about half-filled with water. While the water is heating to boiling, find the mass of the inner cup of the empty calorimeter. Then fill the calorimeter about two-thirds full with water that is several degrees colder than room temperature. For best results, it is desirable to have the water approximately as many degrees below room temperature when starting the experiment as the mixture will be above room temperature at the end. (It may be necessary to use ice cubes to get the initial temperature low enough.) The temperature change of the water should be at least 10 C°. Find the mass of the calorimeter cup and water. Replace the cup in its insulating shell.

Take the temperature of the boiling water with the thermometer. Since the solid is being heated in the boiling water, its original temperature is the temperature of the boiling water. Then stir the water in the calorimeter and take its temperature. When making these temperature readings, you should estimate to the nearest 0.1° by using a hand magnifier. Make sure the thermometer bulb is completely immersed in the liquid, and keep your line of sight at right angles to the stem of the thermometer. Considerable error may result from poorly taken temperature readings.

Lift the solid by means of the twine and hold it just above the water, *in the steam,* long enough to let the water that adheres to the solid evaporate. Then quickly transfer the solid to the calorimeter of cold water, as shown in Figure 24-1, and replace the cover. Agitate the solid in the calorimeter and stir the water. The temperature of the mixture should be carefully read to the nearest 0.1° when it has risen to its highest point.

If time permits, make additional trials with other metals.

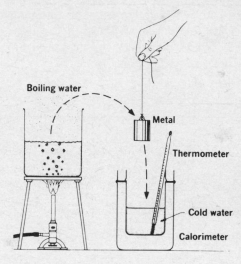

Figure 24-1

QUESTIONS (Your answers should be complete statements.)

1. Why is it desirable to have the water a few degrees colder than room temperature when the initial temperature is taken?

_____

_____

_____

_____

2. Why is the mass of the outer shell of the calorimeter and the insulating ring not incuded in the data for this experiment?

_____

_____

_____

_____

3. What does this experiment show about the specific heat of water?

_____

_____

4. How does the heat conductivity of the metals used in this experiment affect the accuracy of the results?

_____

_____

_____

_____

5. Why should the hot metal be dry before it is introduced into cold water?

_____

_____

_____

_____

experiment **25**

Heat of Fusion

PURPOSE: To determine the heat of fusion of ice.

APPARATUS: Calorimeter; platform balance; set of masses; thermometer, Celsius $-10°$ to $110°$, graduated to $0.2°$; stirring rod; pan for ice; ice cubes; towel; magnifier.

INTRODUCTION: The number of calories needed to melt one gram of any substance at its normal melting point without any temperature change is called its *heat of fusion*. In this experiment, the heat of fusion of ice will be determined by using the method of mixtures. The temperature drop of a given amount of hot water in a calorimeter when a certain quantity of ice is added will be measured. The heat lost by the water does two things: (1) it melts the ice; (2) it warms the water formed by the melting ice from zero up to the final temperature.

PROCEDURE: Find the mass of the empty inner cup of the calorimeter. Fill it about half full of water that has a temperature of about $35°$ C, and find the mass of the calorimeter cup and water. Replace the cup in its insulating shell. Now stir the water in the calorimeter and read its temperature to the nearest

DATA

	TRIAL 1	TRIAL 2
1. Mass of calorimeter cup and stirrer	_____ g	_____ g
2. Mass of calorimeter cup, stirrer, and water	_____ g	_____ g
3. Mass of water	_____ g	_____ g
4. Mass of calorimeter cup, stirrer, and water (after ice is melted)	_____ g	_____ g
5. Mass of ice	_____ g	_____ g
6. Specific heat of calorimeter	_____ cal/gC°	_____ cal/gC°
7. Temperature of water and calorimeter, initial	_____ °C	_____ °C
8. Temperature of water and calorimeter, final	_____ °C	_____ °C
9. Temperature change of water and calorimeter	_____ C°	_____ C°
10. Calories lost by calorimeter	_____ cal	_____ cal
11. Calories lost by water	_____ cal	_____ cal
12. Total calories lost	_____ cal	_____ cal
13. Calories used to warm water formed by melted ice	_____ cal	_____ cal
14. Calories used to melt ice	_____ cal	_____ cal
15. Heat of fusion of ice	_____ cal/g	_____ cal/g
16. Accepted value for heat of fusion of ice	_____ cal/g	_____ cal/g
17. Absolute error	_____ cal/g	_____ cal/g
18. Relative error	_____ %	_____ %

0.1°, using the magnifier. Wipe two ice cubes with a towel to remove adhering water. Put the ice cubes in the calorimeter carefully so that there is no splashing. Stir rather rapidly until all the ice is melted and read the temperature to the nearest 0.1°. Remove the calorimeter cup from its shell and find the combined mass of the cup and its contents. Record all necessary data in the data table and calculate the heat of fusion of ice. Compare your result with the accepted value (Appendix B, Table 13). Calculate your absolute and relative errors. If time permits, make a second trial.

QUESTIONS (Your answers should be complete statements.)

1. Since heat of fusion does not result in a temperature change, where does the energy go?

_____

_____

_____

2. How can heat of fusion be used to guard against frost damage?

_____

_____

_____

_____

_____

3. What source of error is present in this experiment that was not present in previous heat experiments?

_____

_____

_____

_____

_____

experiment 26

Heat of Vaporization

PURPOSE: To determine the heat of vaporization of water.

APPARATUS: Steam boiler, fitted with rubber tubing, a water trap, and a piece of glass tubing about 20 cm long; tripod, for steam boiler; calorimeter; platform balance; set of masses; thermometer, Celsius $-10°$ to $110°$, graduated to $0.2°$; stirring rod; a few chunks of ice are desirable but not essential; burner and rubber tubing; asbestos paper; magnifier; asbestos board; wooden dip stick; barometer.

INTRODUCTION: The heat of vaporization is the amount of heat required to vaporize one gram of a liquid substance at its normal boiling point without any change in its temperature. In this experiment, the heat of vaporization of water will be determined by using the method of mixtures. A known mass of steam at a measured temperature will be passed into a known mass of cold water at a measured temperature. The number of calories that the steam yields as it condenses can be calculated from the rise in temperature of the water. Two things happen when the steam loses heat: (1) the steam condenses; (2) the hot water formed from the condensed steam heats up the cold water in the calorimeter.

PROCEDURE: Set up a steam boiler and partly fill it with water as in Figure 26-1. Connect the water trap and tubing as shown, and light the burner. While the water is heating, find the mass of the inner cup of the calorimeter. Fill it about two-thirds full of water at about $5°$ C and determine the combined mass of the cup and water. Replace the cup in its insulating shell. Stir the water thoroughly. Take its temperature, estimating to the nearest $0.1°$, *just before* the glass tube is placed in the calorimeter and steam flows in. Place the asbestos board between the boiler and the calorimeter as a heat shield.

Pass a steady current of steam into the water, stirring continuously, until the temperature rises to about $35°$ C. Then remove the glass tube from the calorimeter and stir the water thoroughly. Read the thermometer to the nearest $0.1°$ and record the temperature of the stirred water when it reaches its highest point. Remove the calorimeter cup from its outer shell. Find the mass of the cup and contents. The increase in mass equals the mass of steam introduced.

For best results, about 15 g of steam should be introduced into the cold water. This can be determined by using a wooden dip stick and marking it at the height to which 15 more mL of water will raise the surface of the water in the calorimeter cup.

The temperature of the steam may be read directly from the steam boiler or computed from the barometer reading. In making your calculations, you must

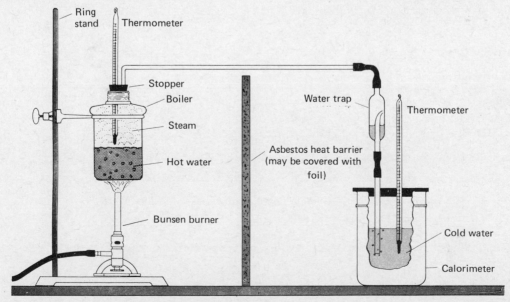

Figure 26-1

217

remember that the steam furnished heat upon condensing, and that it formed an equal mass of water at about 100° C. The water thus formed also furnished heat as it cooled from the boiling point down to the final temperature.

Record all necessary data in the data table and calculate the heat of vaporization of water. Compare your result with the accepted value (Appendix B, Table 13). Calculate your absolute and relative errors. If time permits, make a second trial.

DATA

	TRIAL 1	TRIAL 2
1. Mass of calorimeter cup and stirrer	_____ g	_____ g
2. Mass of calorimeter cup, stirrer, and water	_____ g	_____ g
3. Mass of water	_____ g	_____ g
4. Specific heat of calorimeter	_____ cal/gC°	_____ cal/gC°
5. Temperature of water and calorimeter, inital	_____ °C	_____ °C
6. Temperature of steam	_____ °C	_____ °C
7. Temperature of water and calorimeter, final	_____ °C	_____ °C
8. Mass of water, calorimeter cup, stirrer, and added steam	_____ g	_____ g
9. Mass of steam	_____ g	_____ g
10. Temperature change of water and calorimeter	_____ C°	_____ C°
11. Temperature change of water from condensed steam	_____ C°	_____ C°
12. Calories gained by calorimeter	_____ cal	_____ cal
13. Calories gained by water	_____ cal	_____ cal
14. Total calories gained	_____ cal	_____ cal
15. Calories lost by water formed from steam in cooling to final temperature	_____ cal	_____ cal
16. Calories lost by steam in condensing	_____ cal	_____ cal
17. Heat of vaporization of water	_____ cal/g	_____ cal/g
18. Accepted value for heat of vaporization of water	_____ cal/g	_____ cal/g
19. Absolute error	_____ cal/g	_____ cal/g
20. Relative error	_____ %	_____ %

QUESTIONS (Your answers should be complete statements.)

1. Since heat of vaporization does not result in a temperature change, where does the energy go?

_____

2. Why does steam burn a person more severely than an equal mass of boiling water?

_____

3. Why should the number of calories gained by the water and calorimeter equal those lost by the steam in condensing and cooling to final temperature?

_____

experiment **27**

Mechanical Equivalent of Heat

PURPOSE: To make an approximate measurement of the mechanical equivalent of heat.

APPARATUS: Heavy cardboard tube about 1.0 m long and about 4.0 cm in diameter; 2 cork stoppers to fit ends of tube; 1 kg of buckshot; asbestos-lined box; large metal pan; ice cubes; thermometer; meterstick; platform balance.

INTRODUCTION: The relationship between heat energy and mechanical energy is expressed by the equation

$$J = \frac{W}{Q}$$

where W is the mechanical energy in joules, Q is the heat energy in calories, and J is the mechanical equivalent of heat. The unit abbreviation of the equivalent, J, honors the English physicist James Prescott Joule who measured the relationship between heat energy and mechanical energy in a series of experiments that extended over a period of almost thirty years.

The apparatus used by Joule is too complex to be used in this experiment. But an approximation of J can be obtained by using rather simple materials. You will drop a specific mass of buckshot inside a cardboard tube and measure the resultant increase in temperature. When the buckshot falls the length of the tube and hits the cork stopper at the other end, virtually all the kinetic energy of the buckshot will be converted into heat energy. Because of the insulating properties of the cork and the cardboard walls of the tube, this heat energy will be confined mostly to the buckshot and consequently raise its temperature.

PROCEDURE: Measure the mass of the buckshot, place it in the metal pan, and cool it by setting the pan outside the window for a few minutes (provided it is cool outside) or by setting it on ice cubes. *Be sure to keep the buckshot dry during the entire experiment.*

Pour the buckshot into the asbestos-lined box and carefully measure the temperature of the buckshot 3 times. Shake up the buckshot between readings. Take the average of the 3 readings and record it in the data table.

DATA

	TRIAL 1	TRIAL 2	TRIAL 3
1. Mass of buckshot	_____ g	_____ g	_____ g
2. Average distance of single fall	_____ m	_____ m	_____ m
3. Number of falls	_____	_____	_____
4. Total potential energy of buckshot	_____ j	_____ j	_____ j
5. Average initial temperature	_____ °C	_____ °C	_____ °C
6. Average final temperature	_____ °C	_____ °C	_____ °C
7. Temperature change	_____ °C	_____ °C	_____ °C
8. Specific heat of buckshot	_____ cal/gC°	_____ cal/gC°	_____ cal/gC°
9. Calories gained by buckshot	_____ cal	_____ cal	_____ cal
10. Mechanical equivalent of heat, experimental	_____ j/cal	_____ j/cal	_____ j/cal
11. Mechanical equivalent of heat, accepted	_____ j/cal	_____ j/cal	_____ j/cal
12. Relative error	_____ %	_____ %	_____ %

Close one end of the cardboard tube with a cork stopper and pour the buckshot into the tube. Close the other end of the tube with the other stopper. Then invert the tube 100 times or more in quick succession. Do not raise or lower the tube as you invert it. You must invert the tube fast enough to make the buckshot fall through the entire length of the tube. This can best be done by holding the tube at its center. After each inversion, the end of the tube should rest on the floor or on the top of the lab table as the buckshot hits the bottom of the tube.

After the last inversion of the tube, quickly pour the buckshot back into the asbestos-lined box and make 3 temperature measurements as before. Record the average.

To obtain the average distance that the buckshot falls during each inversion, pour it back into the tube and measure from the top of the pile of buckshot to the bottom of the cork stopper when it is in place in the other end of the tube.

Repeat the entire procedure for 2 more trials and record all necessary data.

QUESTIONS (Your answers should be complete statements.)

1. Could this experiment be completed without measuring the mass of the buckshot? Explain.

_____

_____

2. Why should the buckshot be cooled below room temperature before starting the experiment?

_____

_____

3. What are the main sources of error in this experiment?

_____

_____

_____

_____

4. How does this experiment help to explain errors in other heat experiments?

_____

_____

5. Taking into account only the mechanical equivalent of heat, how much warmer does the water in a waterfall become by dropping 40 m?

6. How is the mechanical equivalent of heat used in the operation of a heat engine?

_____

_____

experiment **28**

Pulses on a Coil Spring

PURPOSE: (1) To observe the behavior of transverse and longitudinal pulses on a stretched coil spring. (2) To verify the effects of free-end and fixed-end terminations of a medium on the traveling pulse.

APPARATUS: Two long coil springs, a Slinky and a heavy metal coil matched to give approximately equal amplitudes of reflected and transmitted pulses; light string; meterstick or metric tape; stopwatch; chalk.

INTRODUCTION: The Slinky is a large "soft" spring, edge wound of flat wire, that transmits a pulse slowly enough to be observed with relative ease. When a heavy metal spring is attached to the end of the Slinky, the energy of a traveling pulse is partly reflected at the junction and partly transmitted across the junction. The inertia of the heavy spring is greater than that of the Slinky. Thus, at the junction of the two springs, the Slinky has a relatively fixed-end termination while the heavy spring has a relatively free-end termination.

SUGGESTION: At least four students should work as a group with one set of apparatus as there are several assignments to be carried out during each experiment. These assignments should be rotated frequently within the group to provide all members with a full measure of participation.

PROCEDURE

1. Transverse pulse

Place a large, light spring (a Slinky) on a smooth floor and stretch it to a length of approximately 8 m. (*Suggestion:* Mark one end position on the floor with chalk and mark other positions 6 m, 8 m, 10 m, and 12 m away. Determine the best stretch distance for your coil by experiment, being careful not to exceed the stretch limit of the spring being used.) Station group partners at each end of the Slinky to hold it securely in position while stretched.

CAUTION: *Avoid releasing an end of the stretched spring; the untangling process can be very difficult.*

With the ends of the stretched Slinky held rigidly in place, form a pulse by grasping a loop near one end of the spring and displacing it to one side by a quick back-and-forth motion of the hand. Practice this motion until a pulse can be formed that travels down only one side of the spring. Why is the pulse called a *transverse pulse*? Make a statement about a transverse pulse relating the motion of the separate coils of the spring to the path traversed by the pulse.

Observation: _____

_____

_____

_____

_____

The coil spring is the medium through which the pulse travels. Send a short pulse down the spring. Observe the shape of the pulse as it moves along the spring. How does the shape change? Can you suggest a reason? Upon what does the initial amplitude of the pulse depend? Does the speed of the pulse appear to change with its shape? Generate single pulses of different amplitudes. Does the pulse speed appear to depend on the size of the pulse?

Observation: _____

_____

_____

_____

_____

Measure the length of the stretched Slinky and the travel time of a pulse generated at one end. Assuming that the pulse speed remains unchanged after reflection, the time required for the pulse to make a few excursions back and forth along the spring could be measured. Can you devise a way to check this assumption? Compute the speed of the traveling pulse.

Change the tension in the Slinky and determine the pulse speed as before. Is the speed of propagation through the spring affected by the tension? Does the stretched Slinky, under different tensions, represent the same or different transmitting media?

221

Observation: _____

_____

_____

_____

Generate single pulses simultaneously from opposite ends of the stretched Slinky. Observe the way they meet and pass through each other. The superposing of the two pulses is called *interference*. Send two pulses of approximately equal amplitudes toward each other on the same side of the spring. Describe the interference as they pass through each other. How does the pulse amplitude during interference compare with the individual amplitudes before and after superposition?

Repeat the experiment, but with the two pulses traveling on opposite sides of the spring. Compare the interference with that of the previous trial. Observe the region of interference closely to see if there is a point on the spring that does not move appreciably during interference. What conclusions can you draw about the displacement of the medium at a point where two pulses interfere?

Observation: _____

_____

_____

_____

With the far end of the Slinky held firmly in place (fixed-end termination), send a single pulse down one side of the spring. Observe the *reflected* pulse. Compare its amplitude with that of the transmitted pulse just before reflection. What is its phase relative to the transmitted pulse?

Attach a light string about 2 m long to the far end of the Slinky and maintain the tension on the spring by holding the end of the string. This approximates a *free-end* termination for the Slinky. Send a pulse down one side of the spring as before and observe the pulse reflected from the "free" end. Compare reflection from the "free" end of the spring with reflection from the fixed end.

Observation: _____

_____

_____

_____

_____

Investigate the transfer of a pulse from one medium to another by attaching a heavy metal spring of about 2 cm diameter to the end of the Slinky. Would you expect the pulse speed to remain the same in both sections of the stretched combination? To the extent that the second spring produces an impedance mismatch at its junction with the Slinky, the pulse energy arriving at the junction will be partly reflected and partly transmitted.

Send a single pulse down the stretched combination, first from one end and then the other. Observe what happens when each pulse reaches the junction of the two springs. How does the speed of propagation in the heavy spring compare with that in the Slinky?

Send a pulse down one side of the Slinky toward the junction and observe the relative phase of the pulse reflected at the junction. Similarly determine the relative phase of the pulse transferred across the junction to the heavy spring. Repeat these phase observations for a pulse sent down the heavy spring toward the junction. If the difference in pulse speeds in the two springs was greater, how would you expect the relative portions of the pulse energy reflected and transmitted at the junction to be affected? Summarize your observations of the reflection of pulses from the junction of two media in which they have different speeds.

Observation: _____

_____

_____

_____

_____

2. Longitudinal pulse

With the heavy metal spring removed, stretch the Slinky as before and ensure that the far end is held firmly against the floor by a partner. While holding your end of the spring securely, pull about 0.5 m of stretched spring together toward the end with your free hand and release it. **CAUTION**: *Do not let go of the end of the Slinky.* Observe the pulse that travels back and forth through the spring. Why is it called a *longitudinal pulse*? Make a statement about a longitudinal pulse relating the motion of the separate coils of the spring to the path traversed by the pulse.

Observation: _____

_____

_____

_____

experiment **29**

Wave Properties

PURPOSE: **(1)** To learn how to produce and project water waves with a ripple tank. **(2)** To study reflection, refraction, diffraction, and interference of water waves.

APPARATUS: Ripple tank, similar to the one shown in Figure 29-1; tank attachments to produce straight and circular waves; hand stroboscope; cork; stopwatch or watch with second hand; straight barrier; rubber hose, at least 2 cm in diameter; glass plate; protractor; paraffin blocks.

INTRODUCTION: A disturbed water surface provides a familiar example of wave motion. When a stone is dropped into a body of calm water, the disturbance spreads out from the point of impact in a rhythmic, circular pattern. Energy is transmitted through the water in a two-dimensional wave pattern.

Wave systems such as those of sound and light are three-dimensional, but many of their properties can be simulated and studied by means of two-dimensional water waves. The ripple tank has been designed for this purpose. It consists essentially of a thin layer of water supported by a sheet of clear glass. Waves are produced in the water by a vibrating bar or by one or more vibrating prongs. A light source above the water is used to project images of the water waves on a white screen below the ripple tank. The waves act as lenses that reproduce the crests and troughs of the surface waves as light and dark images on the screen.

SUGGESTION: At least two sessions should be provided for this experiment.

PROCEDURE

1. Producing straight and circular waves

Fill the ripple tank to a depth of about 0.5 cm. Check the depth of all four corners of the tank to make sure that it is level. Dip the edge of a ruler into the tank and observe the wave that is produced. Turn on the projection light and adjust it until sharp images are produced on the screen. Dip the end of a pencil into the tank and study the resulting wave. Compare it with the wave produced by the ruler. Draw a sketch of the results in Block A.

Attach the device for producing straight waves and start the vibrating motor. Adjust the position of the vibrator and the motor speed until distinct periodic waves are produced that are parallel to the side of the tank toward which they move. Place a cork on the water and observe its motion.

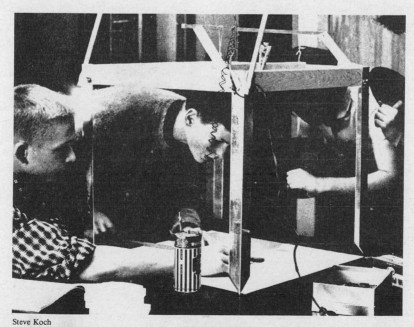

Steve Koch

Figure 29-1

A

Observation: _____

_____

_____

_____

2. Wavelength, frequency, velocity

A ripple tank projects magnified images of water waves. Therefore, in making measurements on the screen, it is necessary to take this magnification into account. To measure the magnification, place an object of known length (such as a pencil) in the tank and measure its length on the screen. Record the magnification factor in the data table.

Set up periodic straight waves in the tank and "stop" them with the hand stroboscope. Your instructor will show you the proper way to use this instrument. With the help of a fellow student, measure the distance between two crests on the screen. Correct this reading with the magnification factor and record the actual wavelength in the data table.

Another way to measure wavelength is to place a straight barrier in the path of the waves, perpendicular to the direction of wave motion. Produce standing waves by adjusting the position of the barrier or the frequency of the generator. Recall the spacing of adjacent nodes or adjacent crests in a standing wave pattern when measuring the wavelength this way.

Measure the frequency of the wave by holding a piece of paper against the vibrating motor counting the number of times the vibrator strikes the paper in a given period of time. (It may be necessary to count the vibrations in groups of three or more.) Record the frequency.

With the stopwatch, measure the time required for a wave to cover a known distance on the screen. Make several trials and record the average. Correct for magnification. Record the speed.

Calculate the speed from the wavelength and frequency. Compare it with the speed as measured directly. Record the difference as your error.

3. Reflection

Place a straight barrier diagonally in the ripple tank. Produce periodic straight waves and observe them as they strike the barrier. Draw a sketch of the resulting wave pattern in Block B.

B

Adjust the barrier so that the waves strike it at an angle of 45°. Measure the angle of the reflected waves. (Angles of incidence and reflection are measured as the angles between the direction of wave motion and a perpendicular to the surface from which they are reflected.) Slowly turn the barrier and study the effect on the angles of incidence and reflection. Record your conclusions in a general statement.

Conclusion: _____

_____

_____

_____

Replace the straight barrier with a parabolic one. A thick rubber hose serves well for this purpose. In Block C sketch the pattern that results. Mark the spot on the screen where the reflected waves are focused. Turn off the vibrator and dip your pencil into the tank at the point in the tank that corresponds to the mark on the screen. Record your observations

DATA Magnification Factor: _____

| TRIAL | Wavelength (m) | Frequency (hz) | Speed | | Absolute error (m/s) |
			measured (m/s)	calculated (m/s)	
1					
2					
3					

and conclusions concerning reflection from a curved surface.

C

Observations and conclusions: _____

_____

_____

_____

4. Refraction

The velocity of water waves depends on the depth of the water. Friction has a greater effect on the propagation of the wave in shallow water than in deep water. Consequently, waves slow up when they pass from deep to shallow water. If the waves strike the boundary between deep and shallow water at an angle, the wavefront will change direction at the boundary. This bending of waves is called *refraction*.

To produce refraction, place a glass plate in the tank and adjust the water level so that the plate is covered with a very thin layer of water. Position the plate so that the forward edge is at an angle to the approaching wavefronts. Turn on the vibrator and sketch the resulting wave pattern in Block D. Measure the angle of incidence, i, and angle of refraction, r, with a protractor. Change the orientation of the glass plate and measure the angles again. Calculate the index of refraction from the ratio of the sines of these angles. Use the equation

$$n = \frac{\sin i}{\sin r}$$

where n is the index of refraction, and i and r are the angles of incidence and refraction, respectively. Record these values.

D

Measure the speed of the incident and refracted waves using the method described in Part 2. Calculate the index of refraction from the ratio of these speeds.

$$n = \frac{\text{speed in deep water}}{\text{speed in shallow water}}$$

Record this value and compare it with the one obtained from the angles. Record the difference as your error.

5. Diffraction

Place a paraffin block on edge in the tank so that it extends about half way across the tank and is parallel to the advancing straight waves. Start the vibrator. Observe the waves as they pass the edge of the paraffin block. Sketch the wave pattern in Block E.

Vary the frequency of the vibrator and describe any changes in the wave pattern.

Place another paraffin block in the tank, leaving an opening between the blocks about 3 cm long. Adjust the frequency of the vibrator to produce waves about 1.5 cm long. Sketch the resulting wave pattern in Block F. Vary the opening between the blocks as

E

DATA

TRIAL	i (°)	r (°)	sin i	sin r	n	Speed			Absolute error (m/s)
						deep (m/s)	shallow (m/s)	n	
1									
2									
3									

well as the frequency of vibration and describe the effect on the wave pattern.

F

Observation: _____

_____

_____

_____

_____

The bending of waves as they pass obstacles or small openings is called *diffraction*.

6. Interference

Arrange two prongs and the vibrator in such a way that circular waves will be produced a short distance apart. Turn on the vibrator and sketch the resulting wave patterns in Block G.

G

When two waves with the same frequency and wavelength interact, it is called *interference*. See how the interference pattern is affected when the *frequency* and distance between wave sources are changed. Sketch the result in Block H.

H

QUESTIONS (Your answers should be complete statements.)

1. What does the motion of the cork show about the transmission of energy in wave motion?

_____

_____

_____

2. Is the magnification factor involved in measuring wave frequency? Elaborate.

_____

_____

3. What is the general relationship between wavelength and diffraction?

_____

4. List similarities and differences between water waves and sound waves.

_____

_____

_____

_____

5. How does this experiment explain the fact that sound travels around corners?

_____

_____

experiment **30**

Resonance; The Speed of Sound

PURPOSE: (1) To determine the best resonant length of a closed tube for sounds of known frequency. (2) To determine the speed of sound from the wavelengths and frequencies of several sounds.

APPARATUS: Tuning forks of known frequency. C-fork, 261.6 hz; E-fork, 329.6 hz; G-fork, 392 hz; and C'-fork, 523.2 hz are all satisfactory. (Physical pitch forks of 256 hz to 512 hz may also be used); glass tube, 2.5 cm to 4.0 cm in diameter and at least 40 cm long; tall cylinder; thermometer; meterstick; tuning fork hammer or large rubber stopper.

INTRODUCTION: Resonance, or sympathetic vibration, occurs when the natural vibration rates of two objects are the same. The air column in a closed glass tube produces its best resonance when it is approximately one-fourth as long as the wavelength of the sound that it reinforces. For example, a tube one meter long produces resonance with a sound wave that is about four meters long. A small correction in wavelength must be made for the internal diameter of the tube. The wavelength of the sound may be calculated from the resonant length of the tube by using the equation $\lambda = 4 \, (l + 0.4d)$, where λ is the wavelength, l is the length of the closed tube, and d is the diameter of the tube.

In this experiment the best resonant length of a closed tube will be determined. From this length and the diameter of the tube, the wavelength of the sound will be calculated. The speed of sound will then be calculated from the equation $v = f\lambda$, where v is the speed of sound, f is the frequency, and λ is the wavelength.

SUGGESTION: This experiment can be performed successfully by pairs of students, providing *they do not talk* while other members of the class are finding the best resonant length of the tube. However, to avoid the confusion that arises when several students in the laboratory are attempting to find the best resonant length, some instructors may prefer to perform this experiment with the class working as a group.

PROCEDURE: Hold the tube vertically in a cylinder nearly full of water, as shown in Figure 30-1.

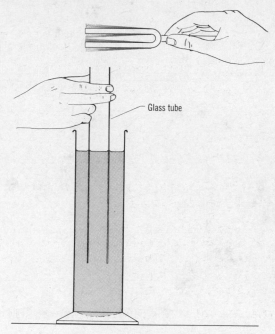

Figure 30-1

Make a tuning fork vibrate by holding it by the shank and striking it with the tuning fork hammer or striking it on a large rubber stopper. *Do not strike the tuning fork on the table top or other hard surface.* As you hold the vibrating tuning fork over the open end of the tube, move the glass tube slowly up and down in the water of the cylinder until you find that position where resonance produces the loudest sound. Then hold the glass tube firmly while another student measures the length of the tube from its top to the water surface inside the tube. This length should be recorded to the nearest thousandth of a meter. Carefully measure the internal diameter of the tube to the nearest thousandth of a meter also. Use the thermometer to determine the temperature of the air inside the tube in degrees Celsius. A second and a third trial should be taken using forks of different frequencies.

For each fork, compute the speed of sound from the resonant length of the tube and the known frequency of the fork. Compare this value with the accepted value for the speed of sound at the temperature inside the tube. Compute the relative error.

DATA

TRIAL	Length of tube (m)	Diameter of tube (m)	Wavelength (m)	Frequency (hz)	Temperature (°C)	Speed of sound		Relative error (%)
						experimental (m/s)	accepted (m/s)	
1								
2								
3								

QUESTIONS (Your answers should be complete statements.)

1. Through what fraction of a vibration has the prong of a tuning fork moved while the sound wave traveled down to the water surface and was reflected back up to the fork again?

   _____

   _____

   _____

2. If a longer glass tube were available, would it be possible to find another position where resonance is produced? Explain.

   _____

   _____

   _____

3. How could you modify this experiment to determine whether the water vapor inside the tube affects the results?

   _____

   _____

4. How does the amplitude of vibration affect the data? Verify your answer by experimentation.

   _____

   _____

   _____

5. How could you modify the experiment to find the resonant length of an open pipe?

   _____

   _____

   _____

228

experiment **31**

Frequency of a Tuning Fork

PURPOSE: To determine the frequency of a tuning fork.

APPARATUS: Pendulum and tuning fork apparatus, or vibrograph; glass plates; stopwatch; whiting suspended in alcohol.

INTRODUCTION: In this experiment, a stylus attached to one prong of a vibrating tuning fork traces a curved path on a coated glass plate that is pulled steadily beneath the stylus. At the same time, a small pendulum to which a needle is attached traces a second curved path. See Figure 31-1. If the length of the pendulum is known, the time required for it to make a complete vibration can be calculated from the pendulum equation $T = 2\pi\sqrt{l/g}$. Or it may be just as simple to count the number of vibrations the pendulum makes per second. Next the number of vibrations the fork makes while the pendulum is making a complete vibration is counted. Then the frequency of the fork can be calculated.

SUGGESTION: One set of apparatus is sufficient for an entire class since it takes only a very short time to trace the vibrations after the glass is prepared. A little practice is necessary to enable the student to draw the glass at the proper speed. There should be one glass plate for each student.

PROCEDURE: Prepare a glass plate with a coating of whiting suspended in alcohol. As the alcohol evaporates, the whiting is left as an even coating on the plate. Lay the plate on the apparatus base and adjust the tuning fork so the stylus will just touch the plate. The stylus of the fork should be rather close to the needle of the pendulum. Adjust the pendulum so that the point of its needle will just touch the glass plate as the pendulum vibrates through an arc of small amplitude.

Start the pendulum swinging and set the fork into vibration by pinching the two prongs together, then releasing them suddenly. Draw the glass plate beneath the fork and pendulum at such a rate that the pendulum will make at least two complete vibrations while the plate is beneath the fork and the pendulum. Make the fine adjustments necessary and enough practice runs to insure getting a successful recording.

After all adjustments have been made, determine the frequency of the pendulum using a stopwatch and the method learned in earlier experiments. Place a

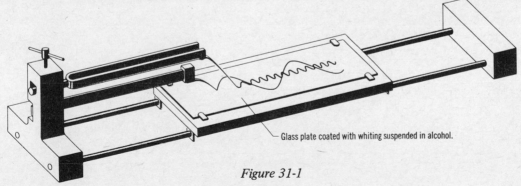

Glass plate coated with whiting suspended in alcohol.

Figure 31-1

DATA

1. Frequency of pendulum	_____	hz
2. Period of pendulum (time required for a complete vibration)	_____	s
3. Number of complete vibrations fork makes while pendulum makes one vibration	_____	
4. Frequency of tuning fork	_____	hz

freshly coated glass plate on the base, set both the pendulum and the fork in motion, and make a record of their tracings.

Count the number of vibrations made by the fork while the pendulum was making a complete vibration. Then calculate the time required for the pendulum to make a complete vibration, and also the number of vibrations the fork makes in one second. Record the results in the appropriate data table.

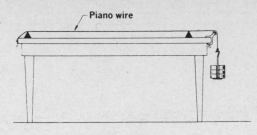

Piano wire

Figure 31-2

ALTERNATE PROCEDURE: Stretch a No. 6 piano wire across two triangular blocks on a table or an inclined plane board, and tune it in unison with a C tuning fork by adding weights to the hanger. Measure the length l of the wire, from one block to the other. Then use another block beneath the wire, and shorten it until it is in unison with a second fork of unknown frequency of higher pitch than the C-fork. Measure the length l' of the wire. Using the appropriate law of strings, determine the frequency of the second fork. Record the results in a suitable data table.

DATA

1. Length (l) of string when tuned in unison with C-fork _____ m

2. Length (l') of string when tuned in unison with unknown fork _____ m

3. Frequency of fork of unknown vibration rate _____ hz

QUESTIONS (Your answers should be complete statements.)

1. How do the following factors affect the frequency of a tuning fork? **(a)** amplitude of vibration; **(b)** mass; **(c)** temperature; **(d)** position.

_____
_____
_____
_____
_____
_____
_____

2. Does the pressure of the stylus affect the results of this experiment? Check your answer by experimentation.

_____
_____
_____

experiment **32**

Photometry

PURPOSE: (1) To measure the intensity of sources of light by photometric means. (2) To determine the efficiency of several light sources.

APPARATUS: Meterstick; meterstick supports; Joly, Bunsen, or photoelectric photometer; galvanometer and hook-up wire (for use with photoelectric photometer only); lamp sockets with cord and plug; calibrated (standard) 40-w lamp, or new 40-w lamp; 25-w, 40-w, 60-w, and other incandescent lamps as indicated by the instructor.

INTRODUCTION: The candle is the unit in which the intensity of a source of light is measured. While today the candle is defined in terms of the intensity of the light emitted from a source at the temperature of solidifying platinum, originally the candle was defined as the amount of light emitted by a standard sperm candle.

In order to determine the intensity of a light source, we compare it with a standard light source. This is usually done by means of a photometer. The photometer is placed with respect to the light sources so that the two sides of the photometer screen are equally illuminated. Under this condition of equal illumination, the intensities of the sources are directly proportional to the squares of their respective distances from the photometer. If the intensity of the unknown lamp is I_2, the intensity of the standard is I_1, the distance of the unknown lamp from the photometer is r_2, and the distance of the standard from the photometer is r_1, then $I_2 = I_1 \times r_2{}^2/r_1{}^2$.

In this experiment we shall determine the intensity of several incandescent lamps by comparison with a standard lamp, or a new 40-watt lamp that is assumed to have an intensity of 32 candles. The efficiency of the lamps in candles/watt will then be found.

SUGGESTION: A good way to isolate each setup in the laboratory is to make portable hoods out of cardboard or plywood that are large enough to cover the meterstick and accessory apparatus. The hoods should be painted black on the inside. A hole should be cut in the front of the hood so that photometer observations can be made without lifting the hood. In the absence of such hoods, the laboratory should be darkened and the instruments positioned in such a way as to keep the errors due to extraneous light as low as possible.

PROCEDURE

Bunsen or Joly photometer
Make a preliminary examination of your photometer head under varying conditions of illumination. If a grease-spot type is used, observe effects by transmission and by reflection of light. Arrange the meterstick, photometer, standard light source, and unknown light source as illustrated in Figure 32-1. Place the two light sources at opposite ends of the meterstick and adjust the position of the photometer until it is equally illuminated from both sides. With a Bunsen photometer, this condition is reached when the grease spot is made as nearly invisible as possible. With a Joly photometer, the translucent blocks must appear equally illuminated to the same depth. Knowing the positions of the photometer and both lamps, record the distance of each lamp from the photometer head.

Repeat this procedure with the other light sources specified by your instructor.

ALTERNATE PROCEDURE

Photoelectric photometer
Connect the galvanometer to the photoelectric photometer terminals and place the photometer on the meterstick facing a standard lamp mounted on

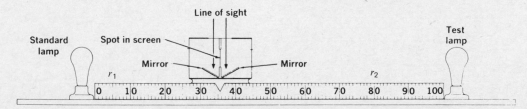

Figure 32-1

one end of the meterstick. Move the photometer as necessary to give an approximately midscale deflection on the galvanometer, then adjust this position for a precisely known output reading on the galvanometer scale. *Remember this scale reading.* Knowing the positions of the photometer and standard lamp, record the distance r_1 of the standard source (from the photometer head).

Substitute an unknown lamp for the standard lamp, keeping the same socket position, and move the photometer head to a position that gives precisely the same output reading on the galvanometer as for the standard lamp. Record the distance r_2 of the unknown source (from the photometer head).

Repeat this procedure with the other light sources specified by your instructor.

NOTE: Because of variations in galvanometer sensitivities and photometer output currents, the instructor may wish to modify the "midscale deflection" standard suggested above.

CALCULATIONS: For each trial the distances of the unknown source and standard source from the photometer are known. Assuming that your photometer functions according to the inverse square law, calculate the intensity of the unknown source for each trial. Compute the efficiency of each lamp in cd/watt.

OPTIONAL: Using three or four identical light sources, see if you can get data that show that the squares of the distances from the sources to the photometer are proportional to the intensities of the source. Can you show that the photometer does function according to the inverse square law?

DATA

TRIAL	Power rating of unknown source (w)	Intensity of standard source I_1 (cd)	Distance of standard source r_1 (cm)	Distance of unknown source r_2 (cm)	Intensity of unknown source I_2 (cd)	Efficiency of unknown source (cd/watt)
1						
2						
3						

QUESTIONS (Your answers should be complete statements.)

1. How does the efficiency of an old incandescent lamp compare with that of a new one? Give several possible reasons for the difference. Why is platinum used as a standard of luminous intensity?

_____

_____

_____

_____

2. Could this experiment be used to compare the intensities of light sources having different colors? Justify your answer. Try to verify it experimentally.

_____

_____

_____

_____

_____

3. Is the intensity of an incandescent lamp equal in all directions? Explain and verify.

_____

_____

_____

4. Is the intensity of a lamp changed by placing a mirror behind it? Explain.

_____

_____

5. In terms of efficiency, do you think it is better to use one 100-watt lamp or two 50-watt lamps? Explain.

_____

_____

experiment **33**

Plane Mirrors

PURPOSE: (1) To verify the laws of reflection.
(2) To show how images are formed by plane mirrors.

APPARATUS: Plane mirror; rectangular wooden block; ruler; protractor; pins; drawing paper; rubber bands or cellulose tape.

INTRODUCTION: The laws of reflection state: (1) the incident ray, the reflected ray, and the normal to the reflecting surface lie in the same plane and (2) the angle of incidence is equal to the angle of reflection. This experiment is designed to enable you to verify both of these laws.

The image of an object in a plane mirror is a virtual image. It is the same size as the object, erect, reversed right and left, and as far behind the mirror as the object is in front of the mirror. By a process of construction, we shall see how the image of an object in a plane mirror is formed. From this constructed image, we can verify the characteristics of images formed by plane mirrors.

PROCEDURE

1. Laws of reflection

Draw a line **MN** across the middle of a sheet of unlined paper. Place the mirror on the line **MN** so that the edge of its reflecting surface coincides with **MN**. The mirror must stand vertically and may be fastened to the rectangular wooden block by means of a rubber band or a piece of cellulose tape. Place a pin at some point **P**, as indicated in Figure 33-1, about 3 or 4 cm from the front of the mirror. Lay a straight edge or ruler on the paper, at **A** for example, far enough from the point **P** so the angle **AOD** will be 30° or more. Sight along the edge of the ruler at the *image* of the pin **P** as you see it in the mirror. Then draw a line along the edge of the ruler, using a sharp-pointed pencil. In the same manner locate a second

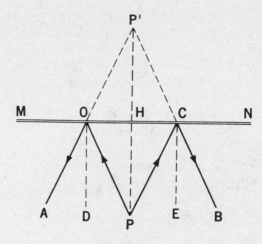

Figure 33-1

sight line for the pin **P**, but from an entirely different angle, from **B** for example. Then remove the mirror and extend the two sight lines until they meet at the point **P**′. *All lines extending behind* **MN** *should be dashed lines.* Draw the lines **PO** and **PC** which *represent incident rays of light from the pin to the mirror.* Draw the lines **OD** and **CE** perpendicular to the mirror line **MN**. Measure the distances **HP** and **HP**′ to the nearest millimeter. Measure the angle of incidence **POD** and the angle of reflection **AOD**. Also measure the angle of incidence **PCE** and the angle of reflection **BCE**. Record these pairs of measurements in the data table together with the construction error for each pair.

2. Formation of images

As before, draw a line **MN** across the middle of a sheet of unlined paper and place the mirror on the line. In front of the mirror and not less than 4 cm from it, draw a scalene triangle. The sides of the triangle should be between 4 cm and 7 cm long. See Figure 33-2. Place a pin at one of the vertices of the

DATA

Length of line **PH**	_____ mm	Angle **POD**	_____ °	Angle **PCE**	_____ °
Length of line **P′H**	_____ mm	Angle **AOD**	_____ °	Angle **BCE**	_____ °
Error	_____ mm	Error	_____ °	Error	_____ °

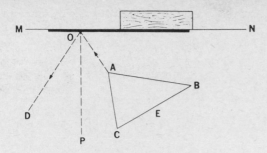

Figure 33-2

triangle, at **A** for example, and locate two sight lines for the image of the pin. Label both of these sight lines **A**. Without moving the mirror, proceed to locate two sight lines for the image of the pin at **B**. Also locate two sight lines for the image of the pin at **C**. If necessary, the mirror may be moved from side to side along the line **MN** to permit a better view, but its reflecting surface must always coincide with the line **MN**.

Remove the mirror and extend the two sight lines for **A** until they intersect behind the mirror, using *dashed lines* behind the mirror line. Label this point of intersection **A'**; it is the image of **A**. Join **A** and **A'**; measure the distance of each from the mirror line and record the distances on the lines themselves. The difference represents the construction error.

In the same manner, extend the sight lines for **B** until they meet at **B'** to form the image of **B**. Join **B** and **B'**, and measure their distance from the mirror line. Extend the sight lines for **C** until they meet at **C'**. Measure the distances of **C** and **C'** from the mirror line. Connect **A'**, **B'**, and **C'** with dashed lines to form the triangle **A'B'C'**. Measure the sides of the triangle **ABC**, and write the measurements along the respective sides. Measure the sides of the image of the triangle **A'B'C'**, and write their lengths along the respective sides. Submit the completed drawing, properly labeled and identified, as part of your laboratory report.

QUESTIONS (Your answers should be complete statements.)

1. Why is it impossible to form real images with a plane mirror?

_____

_____

_____

2. Why are ordinary plane mirrors coated on the back instead of the front? When would such a back coating be undesirable?

_____

_____

_____

_____

_____

3. To take a clear picture of an image in a plane mirror, should the camera be focused on the image or on the surface of the mirror? Try to verify your answer by experimentation.

_____

_____

4. Why must the mirror in this experiment be perpendicular to the table for best results?

_____

_____

_____

5. What error is introduced by the thickness of the mirror?

_____

_____

_____

experiment 34

Curved Mirrors

PURPOSE: (1) To study the images formed by concave mirrors. (2) To study the images formed by convex mirrors.

APPARATUS: Concave and convex mirrors, 4.0-cm diameter, approximately 25-cm focal length; metersticks; image screen of white cardboard, ground glass, or plastic, approximately 25 cm square; candle or clear 25-w aquarium lamp.

INTRODUCTION: Concave mirrors cause parallel rays of light to converge. Different types and sizes of images may be formed by concave mirrors depending upon the distance of the object from the mirror. In this experiment we shall study the formation of these images.

Convex mirrors cause parallel rays of light to diverge. Only one type of image is produced by a convex mirror. Convex mirrors, used as rear view mirrors on buses and trucks, furnish the driver with a wide field of vision, but a misleading impression of distance.

PROCEDURE

1. Concave mirror
a. Determine the focal length, f, of the concave mirror by projecting the image of the sun on a small screen and carefully measuring the image distance from the vertex of the mirror. If a direct view of the sun is not obtainable from the laboratory, the sharply defined image of a distant object outside the laboratory window will give a close approximation of the focal length of the mirror. The laboratory should be darkened as much as possible with one window uncovered sufficiently to permit light from the distant object to reach the mirror. Record the focal length in the data table.

b. Set up the metersticks and concave mirror as shown in Figure 34-1. The apex of the V should be slightly below the center of the mirror. Mount the candle on one meterstick as far away from the mirror as possible. Measure this distance and record it as d_o. Mount the image screen on the other meterstick and move it back and forth until a sharp image of the candle is obtained. (It may be necessary to adjust the

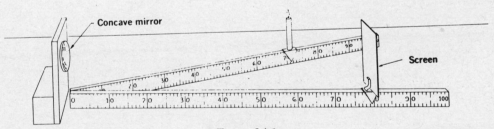

Figure 34-1

DATA Focal length of concave mirror _____ cm, of convex mirror _____ cm

TRIAL	d_o (cm)	d_i (cm)	h_o (cm)	h_i (cm)	$\frac{1}{d_o}$	$\frac{1}{d_i}$	$\frac{1}{d_o}+\frac{1}{d_i}$	$\frac{1}{f}$	Abs. error
1									
2									
3									
4 (Convex)									

position of the mirror and to change the angle between the metersticks in order to locate the image properly on the screen.) Measure the distance between the mirror and image screen and record it as d_i.

Measure the height of the candle flame as accurately as possible. Record it as h_o. Measure the height of the image of the flame and record it as h_i.

c. Interchange the candle and image screen. Make any necessary adjustments in the position of the image screen so as to obtain a sharply defined image. Measure and record d_o, d_i, h_o and h_i.

d. Find the position of the candle and screen for which h_o and h_i are equal.

e. Move the candle so that d_o is equal to the focal length of the mirror. Try to locate the image. Record your observations.

Observation: _____

_____

_____

f. Position the candle between the focal length and the mirror. Try to locate the image. What do you observe when you look into the mirror?

Observation: _____

_____

_____

2. Convex mirror

Replace the concave mirror with a convex mirror. Place the candle at the far end of one meterstick. Describe the image in the mirror. Move the candle closer to the mirror and record the corresponding changes in the image.

Observation: _____

_____

_____

_____

CALCULATIONS: Compute the value of $\frac{1}{d_o}$, $\frac{1}{d_i}$, and $\frac{1}{f}$. Add $\frac{1}{d_o}$ and $\frac{1}{d_i}$ and compare it with $\frac{1}{f}$.

Record the difference as your absolute error.

QUESTIONS (Your answers should be complete statements.)

1. What is the relationship between the data for Parts b and c of Part 1?

_____

_____

2. What is the relationship between the focal length of the mirror and the location of the object and image in Part d?

_____

_____

3. What type of image is formed in Part f? Why is it possible to see the image when looking into the mirror, whereas it is not possible to form it on the screen?

_____

_____

_____

4. List a practical application for each part of this experiment.

_____

_____

_____

_____

_____

_____

_____

_____

experiment **35**

Index of Refraction of Glass

PURPOSE: To determine the index of refraction of glass by means of refracted light rays.

APPARATUS: Glass plate, about 7 cm square and 9 mm thick, or a glass cube 5 cm on each side; glass prism, equilateral, with faces about 7.5 cm long and 9 mm thick; ruler; pencil; compass; pins; protractor; drawing paper.

INTRODUCTION: The index of refraction of a substance is defined as the ratio of the speed of light in a vacuum to its speed in that substance. Since the speed of light in air is only slightly different from the speed in a vacuum, a negligible error is introduced when we measure the index of refraction by permitting light to travel from air into another medium.

Willebrord Snell provided a simple, direct method of measuring the index of refraction by defining it in terms of functions of the angle of incidence and the angle of refraction. The mathematical relationship, known as Snell's law, is

$$n = \frac{\sin i}{\sin r}$$

where n is the index of refraction, i the angle of incidence, and r the angle of refraction. In Figure 35-1,

$$\sin i = \frac{AC}{AO} \quad \text{and} \quad \sin r = \frac{DB}{OB}$$

Since **AO** and **OB** are radii of the same circle, they are equal. Therefore,

$$n = \frac{\sin i}{\sin r} = \frac{AC}{DB}$$

The index of refraction of glass varies with its composition and with the wavelength of the light incident on the glass. Ordinary crown glass, when illuminated by white light, has a refractive index of 1.52; medium flint glass has an index of 1.63. Your experimental results should be precise enough to enable you to identify the glass specimens used in this experiment.

PROCEDURE

1. Index of refraction of glass plate

Place the glass plate or cube on the center of a sheet of unlined paper and outline it with a sharp-pointed pencil. About 1 cm from the lower left-hand corner of the plate place a pin **A** as close to the glass as possible, as in Figure 35-2. At **B**, about 1 cm from the upper right-hand corner of the glass plate, place a

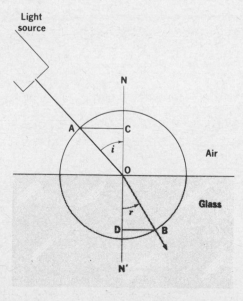

Figure 35-1

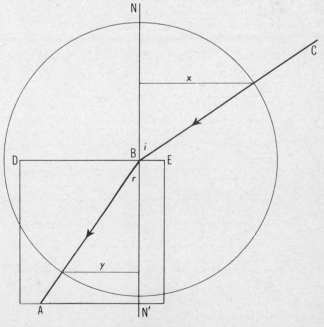

Figure 35-2

second pin, as close to the plate as possible. At a point C not less than 7 cm from B, place a third pin *so that A is in line with B and C as seen through the glass plate.* Keep the eye you sight with near the level of the table top. *(Do not align the pins as seen above the glass plate.)*

Remove the glass plate and join the points A, B, and C to represent the path of the light traveling *from* the pin C through the air to B and through the glass to A. Identify the *incident ray* and the *refracted ray.*

From B construct the normals, NB and BN′, to the line DE. Using as large a radius as possible, describe a circle with point B as the center that intersects BA, BN′, BC, and BN.

From the point of intersection of the circle with the incident ray BC, draw a line *x* perpendicular to BN. Measure the length of *x* to the nearest 0.01 cm and record it in your data table. From the point of intersection of the circle with the refracted ray BA, draw a line *y* perpendicular to the normal BO. Measure the length of *y* to the nearest 0.01 cm and record its value. Compute the index of refraction and record it in the data table.

By means of a protractor, measure the angle of incidence *i* and the angle of refraction *r*. From these data, find the index of refraction of the glass plate.

2. *Index of refraction of glass prism*
Arrange the glass prism on a separate sheet of unlined paper and, using information gained in the previous trial, proceed to determine the index of refraction of the prism. Record all necessary data.

DATA

TRIAL	x (cm)	y (cm)	Index of refraction $\frac{x}{y}$	$\angle i$ (°)	$\angle r$ (°)	Index of refraction $\frac{\sin i}{\sin r}$	Kind of glass
■							
▲							

QUESTIONS (Your answers should be complete statements.)

1. What is the size of the angle of refraction if the angle of incidence is 0°?

_____

_____

2. What is meant by the critical angle?

_____

_____

_____

3. From the values of the index of refraction, calculate the critical angle for the glass prism.

_____

_____

_____

4. How could you verify the critical angles of the plate and prism experimentally?

_____

_____

_____

_____

_____

experiment **36**

Index of Refraction by a Microscope

PURPOSE: To measure the index of refraction of glass and water using a compound microscope.

APPARATUS: Microscope with 16 mm (10x) and 32 mm (4x) objectives (single 16 mm divisible objective will do); vernier calipers, metric; white paper; white index cards; rubber cement; glass plate, 6-10 mm thick; evaporating dish; magnifier; distilled water; china-marking pencil.

INTRODUCTION: The index of refraction of a substance is defined as the ratio of the speed of light in a vacuum to its speed in that substance. Since the speed of light in air is only slightly different from its speed in a vacuum, a negligible error is introduced if the index of refraction is measured by comparing the speed in air with the speed in the second medium.

Because of refraction, objects appear to be closer when viewed through a dense medium, such as glass or water, than when viewed through air. This phenomenon can be used to find the index of refraction n of the medium by means of the equation

$$n = \frac{t}{t - d}$$

where t is the thickness of a transparent medium and d is the apparent shortening of the perpendicular line of sight through the medium.

PROCEDURE

1. Index of refraction of glass

The microscope may be used to measure distances normal to the stage by attaching a vernier scale to the side of the rack as shown in Figure 36-1. Using a very sharp pencil, *carefully* construct a centimeter scale about 6 cm long with 1 mm subdivisions on the edge of a piece of white paper, and a vernier scale on another piece of white paper. The vernier should consist of 10 equal divisions in a space of 9 mm. Figure 36-1 provides a suitable pattern for making these scales. Mount the scales on the microscope as shown in Figure 36-1 so that the zero index of the fixed vernier scale is at or below the zero index of the centimeter scale when the body tube is fully lowered.

Determine whether the 16 mm objective provides the *working distance* required for the thickness of the glass plate. This may be done by making a pencil

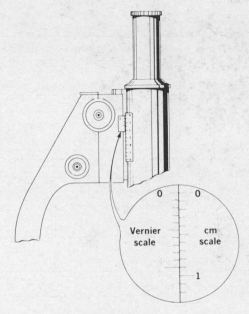

Figure 36-1

mark on a white index card, mounting the card on the stage, and focusing on it with the 16 mm objective in place. Without shifting the position of the card, place the glass plate over the mark and *cautiously* lower the body tube. If the mark can again be brought into sharp focus, the working distance of the lens is adequate and it may be used in this part of the experiment. **CAUTION:** *The objective must not be forced down in contact with the glass plate.*

If this second focus is not achieved, the 32 mm objective must be used; or if the 16 mm objective is divisible, the front lens section may be removed to provide the equivalent lens.

With an adequate working distance assured, again mount the card and bring the pencil mark into sharp focus. Record the body-tube position as the *focus in air* in Part 1 of the data table, using a magnifier to estimate the vernier reading to the nearest 0.001 cm. With the glass plate over the card, again bring the mark into sharp focus. Read the body-tube position as before and record as the *focus in glass*. The distance the objective has been raised is the distance d. Now focus the microscope on the top surface of the glass plate. Read the body-tube position on the vernier scale as before and record as the *surface position*. The total distance the objective has been raised is the thickness of the glass plate, t.

Make two additional marks on the card and determine d and t for each mark, recording the vernier-scale readings as before. Make three trials and compute the average value of n.

2. Index of refraction of water

Make a mark in the bottom of a clean evaporating dish (a sharpened china-marking pencil may be used) and bring it into focus under the microscope using the 32-mm objective. Record the body-tube position as the *focus in air* in your data table. Add distilled water to the dish until it is approximately two-thirds full, focus on the mark and then on the surface, and record the required data for each operation. If difficulty is experienced in focusing on the water surface, a little chalk dust sprinkled on the surface by tapping a blackboard eraser over the dish may help. Repeat these measurements for two other depths of water and record the required data. Make three trials and compute the average value of n.

DATA Part 1

TRIAL	FOCUS POSITION			d	t	n
	In air (cm)	In glass (cm)	Surface (cm)	(cm)	(cm)	
1						
2						
3						
Average value of n for the glass plate						

DATA Part 2

TRIAL	FOCUS POSITION			d	t	n
	In air (cm)	In water (cm)	Surface (cm)	(cm)	(cm)	
1						
2						
3						
Average value of n for water						

QUESTIONS (Your answers should be complete statements. Problem solutions should be set down in the space provided below.)

1. Show that the expression for the index of refraction employed in this experiment can be derived from Snell's law.

2. A pail 35.0 cm deep is filled with water to within 10.0 cm of the rim. What is the apparent depth of the water?

experiment **37**

Converging Lenses

PURPOSE: **(1)** To find the focal length of a converging lens. **(2)** To study the image-forming characteristics of a converging lens.

APPARATUS: Object screen; electric lamp and object box; meterstick; supports for meterstick; lens holder; screen holder; cardboard screen with metric scale; double convex lens, preferably 10-cm or 15-cm focal length; cobalt-glass filter.

INTRODUCTION: Converging lenses can produce both real and virtual images; diverging lenses can produce only virtual images. In this experiment we shall study image formation by a converging lens. A spherical lens made of crown glass has a focal length very nearly equal to its radius of curvature, a fact commonly used in lens diagrams.

When an object is illuminated, each point on its surface acts as a source of diverging rays. When some of these rays from a point on the object are incident on a converging lens properly placed, they converge at a point on the opposite side of the lens forming an image of the object point. Collectively, these image points form an image of the object. Since the rays of light converge to form the image, it is a *real image* and can be projected on a screen.

If a lens is less than its focal distance from an object, the refracted rays do not converge and no real image is formed; instead a *virtual image* is formed. A virtual image can be seen by the eye looking through the lens in the direction of the object, but the image cannot be formed on a screen.

PROCEDURE

1. Focal length

Case 1. Support a converging lens and a cardboard screen on a meterstick as shown in Figure 37-1. Devise a method for locating (and marking) the point on the mounted screen that intercepts the principal axis of the mounted lens. An image formed at this point insures that the sun's rays approach the lens parallel to the principal axis of the lens. Why is this the desired image location? Avoid further shifting of the screen in its mounting while maneuvering it on the meterstick.

Place the lens at the 50-cm mark and the screen near the 70-cm mark. Point the mounted lens toward the sun (**avoid looking directly at the sun**) and maneuver the meterstick until the sun's image is observed on the screen. The image may be found most satisfactorily by aiming the meterstick over the shoulder with your back to the sun.

Observing the image on the screen through a cobalt-glass filter, move the screen along the meterstick until a position is found where the image of the sun is as small as possible and is on the principal axis of the lens. The distance from the lens to the screen may be taken as the *focal length* of the lens. Record this focal length in the data table to the precision possible with your meterstick scale.

If the sun is not visible from a laboratory window, a house or a tree several hundred meters distant may be used as the object. (The cobalt-glass filter is unnecessary in this case.) A distinct image may be ob-

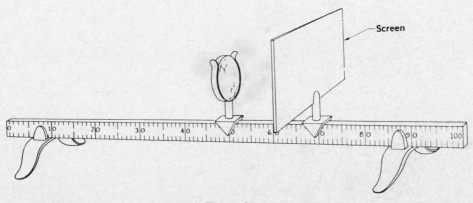

Figure 37-1

served by darkening the laboratory except for the partially open windows required for forming images. Adjust the screen position for maximum image definition. Record the distance between the lens and the image screen in your rough notes.

Move the lens to the 60-cm position and repeat the procedure using a different distant object. Average the two results and record this average image distance in the data table as the focal length of the lens.

2. Formation of images

Case 2. Place the illuminated object screen at one end of the meterstick. Make adjustments to insure that the center of the object screen coincides with the principal axis of the lens. Why? Place the lens far enough from the object screen to give an object distance greater than twice the focal length of the lens. See Figure 37-2. Move the image screen along the meterstick until the image is as well defined as possible. Read and record in the data table the positions of the object, lens, and image. Also record the height of the object, h_o, and the height of the image, h_i.

Case 3. For a second trial, place the lens at a position for an object distance just twice the focal length of the lens. Then adjust the image screen for maximum image definition. Record in the data table the object-screen, lens, and image-screen positions, and the heights of the object and image.

Case 4. For a third trial, locate the lens between one and two focal lengths from the object screen. Adjust the image screen to secure the best-defined image, and record all measurements as in the preceding cases.

Case 5. Place the lens so that it is exactly one focal length away from the object. Try to form an image on the screen.

Observation: _____
_____
_____
_____

Case 6. Place the lens so that it is less than one focal length away from the object. Try to form an image on the screen. Remove the screen, and placing your eye close to the lens, look through the lens at the object. What kind of image may be produced by a converging lens using Case 6?

_____
_____
_____

3. Optional

If you wish to do some additional work with lenses, try to devise a method of locating the virtual images formed by converging and diverging lenses. Investigate the *parallax method* of locating images and see if this suggests a way of determining the image distance of a virtual image.

CALCULATIONS: For each of the three trials recorded, calculate the object distance d_o and the image distance d_i. Next calculate the reciprocals of these distances. Add the values of these reciprocals and compare the sum with the reciprocal of the focal length, $1/f$. In each case also divide the object distance by the image distance and the object size by the image size and compare these two results. Record these values.

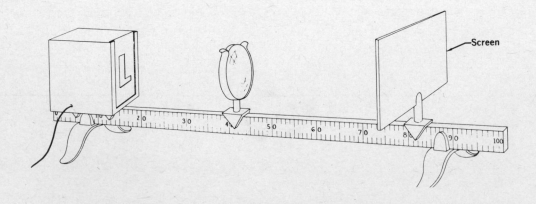

Figure 37-2

DATA Focal length of lens (f) _____cm

Position of object (cm)	Position of lens (cm)	Position of image (cm)	d_o (cm)	d_i (cm)	$\dfrac{1}{d_o}$	$\dfrac{1}{d_i}$	$\dfrac{1}{d_o}+\dfrac{1}{d_i}$	$\dfrac{1}{f}$	h_o (cm)	h_i (cm)	$\dfrac{d_o}{d_i}$	$\dfrac{h_o}{h_i}$

QUESTIONS (Your answers should be complete statements.)

1. Explain the nature of the images in Case 5 and Case 6.

_____

_____

2. Why is it better to use the sun as the distant object than it is to use a house or tree when finding the focal length of the lens?

_____

3. Give a practical application of each of the six cases of image formation by convex lenses.

_____

_____

_____

_____

_____

_____

_____

experiment **38**

Focal Length of a Diverging Lens

PURPOSE: To measure the focal length of diverging lenses.

APPARATUS: Object screen; electric lamp and object box; meterstick and supports; double convex lens, 5-cm focal length; double concave lenses, 10-cm and 15-cm focal lengths; two lens holders; cardboard screen; screen holder.

INTRODUCTION: The relation between the object distance d_o, the image distance d_i, and the focal length f of a lens is given by the fundamental lens equation

$$\frac{1}{d_o} + \frac{1}{d_i} = \frac{1}{f}$$

One standard practice in optics is to use the optical center of the lens as the origin and to measure distances from right to left as negative and distances from left to right as positive, and to let the incident rays travel from left to right. Consequently, d_o is positive for *real* objects and negative for *virtual* objects; d_i is positive for *real* images and negative for *virtual* images; and f is positive for converging lenses and negative for diverging lenses.

In order to find the focal length of a diverging lens, we shall use a converging lens ahead of it to converge the rays before they reach the diverging lens. If a converging lens forms a real image at **I**, the introduction of the diverging lens between this lens and the real image will cause the image to be formed farther

away at **I'**. By taking the distance from the diverging lens to the position of **I** as the object distance d_o, and to the position of **I'** as the image distance d_i, the lens formula may be used to determine the focal length f of the diverging lens.

PROCEDURE: Mount the converging lens on the optical bench between the object box and the cardboard screen and adjust the lens and screen until a sharp image is formed. Determine at this point whether a reduced or enlarged image is preferable. This image locates **I** of Figure 38-1. Observe the edges of the image closely for color fringes while slowly moving the screen through the position of sharpest focus. Insert a diverging lens between the converging lens and the screen and again move the screen until a sharp image is formed. This is the position **I'**.

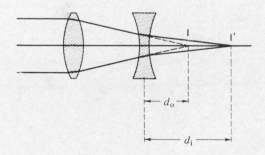

Figure 38-1

DATA

FIRST LENS				SECOND LENS			
TRIAL	d_o (cm)	d_i (cm)	f (cm)	TRIAL	d_o (cm)	d_i (cm)	f (cm)
1				1			
2				2			
3				3			
4				4			
	Average				*Average*		

Record the values of d_o and d_i in the data table to the nearest 0.01 cm and calculate the focal length. Be sure to use + and − signs correctly when recording these distances.

Make at least three additional determinations of f by varying d_o and d_i. Record all data as before and find the average focal length of the lens.

Substitute a second diverging lens and determine its focal length as before, finding the average of at least four trials.

QUESTIONS (Your answers should be complete statements.)

1. **a.** What variation in color of the image edge occurs when the screen is moved through the point of sharpest focus? **b.** Can you suggest a possible explanation?

a. _____
_____
_____

b. _____
_____
_____
_____

2. Why does the usual practice of assigning a negative value to the image distance d_i of a diverging lens not apply in this experiment?

_____
_____
_____
_____
_____
_____

3. What measurement was assigned a negative value in this experiment? Why?

_____
_____
_____

experiment **39**

Lens Magnification

PURPOSE: To determine experimentally the magnification of short-focal-length lenses commonly used as simple magnifiers.

APPARATUS: Three converging lenses of different focal lengths ranging from 5 cm to 15 cm; ring stand, with 2 iron rings, 2.5 cm and 5 cm O.D.; object screen; microscope slide 2.5 × 7.5 cm with 1 cm² of millimeter cross-section paper mounted; image screen; white Bristol board with millimeter scale; meterstick; lens holder; screen holder.

SUGGESTION: The object screens may be made up in advance of the laboratory period and saved for use year after year, or each student may be supplied with the raw materials from which to make the object screen. In either case, the object square of cross-section paper should be cut slightly larger than 1 cm² so the graduation lines at each edge of the object piece will be perpendicular to the edge.

INTRODUCTION: A converging lens of short focal length is frequently used to magnify small objects and may be in the form of a reading glass, a simple magnifier, or the eyepiece of a compound microscope or refracting telescope. The lens is held slightly less than one focal length away from the object and the eye is placed close to the lens on the side opposite the object. This is a practical application of the principle of Case 6 for converging lenses; the image is virtual, erect, enlarged, and appears to be on the same side of the lens as the object.

The linear magnification M of a lens is simply the ratio of the image size h_i to the object size h_o.

$$M = \frac{h_i}{h_o} \tag{1}$$

From $h_o/h_i = d_o/d_i$, it is apparent that the lens magnification may be expressed in terms of the image distance d_i and object distance d_o.

$$M = \frac{d_i}{d_o} \tag{2}$$

The normal eye can focus on objects as close as 25 cm; this distance is known as the *distance for most distinct vision*. Thus, if a simple magnifier is placed so that the image distance is 25 cm, the maximum detail of the object will be revealed by the image. Because the object is very near the principal focus, the magnification of a simple magnifier is *approximately* equal to the ratio of the distance for most distinct vision to the focal length f of the lens.

$$M = \frac{25 \text{ cm}}{f} \text{ (approx.)} \tag{3}$$

To arrive at a more precise expression for the magnification of a simple magnifier than the approximation given above, consider the lens equation:

$$\frac{1}{d_o} + \frac{1}{d_i} = \frac{1}{f} \tag{4}$$

Multiplying by d_i and rearranging terms, Equation 4 becomes

$$\frac{d_i}{d_o} = \frac{d_i}{f} - \frac{d_i}{d_i} = \frac{d_i}{f} - 1$$

Substituting in Equation 2,

$$M = \frac{d_i}{f} - 1 \tag{5}$$

Since the image formed at the distance for most distinct vision is virtual, $d_i = -25$ cm, and

$$M = \frac{25 \text{ cm}}{f} + 1 \tag{6}$$

where f is the focal length expressed in centimeters.

PROCEDURE: Determine the focal lengths of the three lenses to the nearest 0.01 cm by the method used in Experiment 37 and record each measurement in the data table. Magnification data will be taken for the three lenses in the order in which you have listed them in the data table. Take the necessary precautions to insure that the focal-length identity of each lens is retained.

249

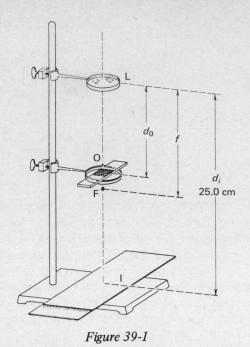

Figure 39-1

Arrange the support stand, lens support, and object support as shown in Figure 39-1. Arrange the image screen on the base of the stand so the metric scale is centered under the two ring supports.

Mount the first lens and adjust the lens support for a value of d_i of 25.0 cm measured from the lens plane to the image screen. Record d_i in the data table for all three trials, since this distance will remain constant for all lenses. Arrange the object screen below the lens so the object is centered on the principal axis of the lens.

With one eye close to the lens and sighting through the lens along the principal axis and the other eye

focused on the image screen, vary the object position until a sharp image of the aperture appears to fall on the scale of the image screen.

Determine whether a final adjustment of the object position is required by moving the eye laterally back and forth across the lens (parallax). Readjust the object position, if necessary, to eliminate any relative motion (parallax) between the virtual image and the lines of the metric scale as the eye moves.

Position the object screen and the image screen as necessary to locate one edge of the centimeter-square object on an appropriate mark on the metric scale.

Carefully read the image size h_i on the scale to the nearest 0.01 cm and record. Assume the cross-section graduations of the object to be accurate to 0.01 cm in recording the object size (one dimension). Measure the object distance d_o to the nearest 0.01 cm and record.

Repeat the procedure with the second lens and record the required data in the appropriate columns of the data table.

Repeat using the third lens and record the required data as before.

CALCULATIONS: From the tabulated data, compute the magnification of each lens by three methods indicated as Equations 1, 2, and 6. Determine the average value for the magnification of each lens. Record all results in the appropriate columns of the data table.

DIAGRAM: Using a well-sharpened pencil, straightedge, and compass, carefully construct a ray diagram for a simple magnifier. Show an object, an image, and all necessary construction lines. Label fully and attach to your report.

DATA

TRIAL	f (cm)	d_i (cm)	d_o (cm)	h_i (cm)	h_o (cm)	MAGNIFICATION			
						$\dfrac{d_i}{d_o}$	$\dfrac{h_i}{h_o}$	$\dfrac{25.0\ cm}{f} + 1$	Ave.
1									
2									
3									

The Compound Microscope

PURPOSE: To construct the lens system of a compound microscope and determine experimentally its magnification.

APPARATUS: Optical bench consisting of a meter-stick, 2 supports, light source, 3 screen holders, and 3 lens holders; 2 converging lenses, 5-cm focal length; object screen, black Bristol board with 4-mm-diam. aperture covered with wire gauze (see suggestion below); first-image screen, white Bristol board 10 × 12.5 cm with millimeter scale; second-image screen, white Bristol board 12.5 × 15 cm with 3.5-cm-diam. aperture, and metric scale (see suggestion below); steel metric rule graduated in 0.5 mm.

SUGGESTION: The object screens and second-image screens should be prepared in advance of the laboratory period. Screens constructed according to the following directions are quite satisfactory and may be retained for use year after year.

Object screen: Cut brass sheet, B and S No. 20, or iron sheet, B and S No. 28, into pieces 3 × 5 cm. Carefully drill a hole approximately 4 mm in diameter through the center of each sheet. (Use a No. 23 drill and dress with a flat file.) Mount the metal plate on a standard object screen made of black Bristol board with a triangular wire-gauze aperture to provide a small, round, wire-gauze aperture.

Second-image screen: The aperture location given below accommodates a lens system having a principal axis 5.5 cm or 7 cm above a meterstick optical bench and is suitable for 3.75-cm and 5-cm diameter lenses when mounted in their respective standard lens supports on a meterstick. If in doubt, determine the height of the lens center above the optical bench and adjust the aperture center location accordingly.

Cut white Bristol board into 12.5 × 16 cm rectangles and locate the aperture center 8 cm from either 12.5-cm edge and 7 cm from one 16-cm edge. Draw a line from edge to edge through the aperture center parallel to the two 16-cm sides. Draw a second line through the aperture center perpendicular to the first line extending it about 1 cm each way. Before cementing the paper scale, turn the screen so that the aperture center is at the proper height for your optical bench when measured from the *bottom* of the screen.

Cut a metric paper scale (printed for horizontal use) to slightly in excess of 15 cm. Locate the 7.5-cm graduation mark precisely on the aperture center with the millimeter graduations centered on the edge-to-edge line and bond the scale to the screen with a rubber-base cement. Trim the screen to 15 cm by the scale graduations. Cut out an aperture of approximately 3.5-cm diameter. (A 1⅜ in. Greenlee chassis punch is an excellent tool for this purpose.)

INTRODUCTION: The lens system of the compound microscope consists of two high quality, short focal-length converging lenses. One lens, the *objective,* is located slightly more than its focal length from the object **O** and produces a real, inverted, and enlarged image **I** in front of the second lens, the *eyepiece* or *ocular.* This real image becomes the *object* for the eyepiece located slightly less than its focal length away. Thus, the eyepiece is used as a simple magnifier to form a virtual, erect, and enlarged second image **I** '.

The linear magnification M of a lens is equal to the ratio of the image size, h_i, to the object size, h_o, and to the ratio of the image distance, d_i, to the object distance, d_o. Thus, the magnification M_o of the microscope objective is

$$M_o = \frac{h_i}{h_o} = \frac{d_i}{d_o} \qquad (1)$$

where h_i is the diameter of the first image **I**, h_o the diameter of the object aperture **O**, d_i the distance from the objective lens $\mathbf{L_o}$ to the first-image screen **I**, and d_o the distance from the objective lens $\mathbf{L_o}$ to the object screen **O**.

Similarly, the magnification M_e of the eyepiece is

$$M_e = \frac{h_i'}{h_i} = \frac{d_i'}{d_o'} \qquad (2)$$

where h_i' is the diameter of the second image **I** ', d_i' the distance from the eyepiece lens $\mathbf{L_e}$ to the second-image screen **I** ', and d_o' the distance from the eyepiece lens $\mathbf{L_e}$ to the first-image screen **I**.

The overall magnification M of the compound lens system is, of course, equal to the ratio of the second-image size to the object size.

$$M = \frac{h_i'}{h_o} \qquad (3)$$

From Equation 1,

$$h_i = M_o h_o$$

Substituting in Equation 2:

$$M_e = \frac{h_i'}{M_o h_o}$$

Solving for h_o:

$$h_o = \frac{h_i'}{M_o M_e}$$

Substituting in Equation 3:

$$M = M_o M_e \qquad (4)$$

In this experiment we shall determine experimentally the separate magnifications of the objective and eyepiece lenses using both size and distance ratios. We shall then determine the magnification of the lens system using both the size ratio and the product of the individual lens magnifications.

PROCEDURE: If the focal lengths of the two lenses are not known, they should be determined before proceeding with the experiment. Using one short focal-length lens as a simple magnifier and a steel metric rule graduated in 0.5 mm, carefully measure the diameter of the object-screen aperture, estimating to the nearest 0.01 cm. Record as h_o in the data table.

Set up the optical bench as shown in Figure 40-1. Locate near the right end of the bench one short focal-length lens that will serve as the eyepiece L_e. Adjust the position of the first-image screen I so that it is approximately one focal length away. Locate the second image I' approximately 25 cm from L_e.

Locate the remaining short focal-length lens (as the objective L_o) about 5 cm from I' and the object screen slightly more than a focal length away from L_o. The object-screen aperture and its luminous source, the two lenses, and the second image-screen aperture must be centered on a common principal axis PP'.

Illuminate the object (the laboratory should be darkened) and adjust the positions of the first-image screen I and the objective L_o to give a sharply defined real image, keeping the image distance roughly 5 times the object distance. In order to center the image on the first-image screen in front of the eyepiece lens, it may be necessary to shift the position of the object aperture slightly with respect to the principal axis. A final focus can be attained most readily by slight adjustments of the objective lens.

Shift the first-image screen I in its holder so that the image falls on the millimeter scale. (Be careful not to change its location on the optical bench.) Read the diameter of the image estimating to the nearest 0.01 cm and record as h_i in the data table. Similarly record the object distance d_o and the first-image distance d_i to the nearest 0.01 cm.

With one eye close to the eyepiece lens, view the back of the first-image screen and adjust the eyepiece slightly to bring it into sharp focus. Remove the screen I from its holder and reset screen I' if necessary to place it approximately 25 cm from L_e. Again with one eye close to the eyepiece and looking along the principal axis, view the virtual second image of the object.

Focus the other eye on the second-image screen I' and adjust the object screen slightly in its holder to superimpose the virtual image symmetrically about the aperture of the second-image screen. A little practice in this use of both eyes will develop skill in viewing the image superimposed on the metric scale of the screen. Adjust the position of the eyepiece slightly to yield the best definition of the wire-gauge image on the screen. With the image properly positioned on the metric scale, read the image diameter

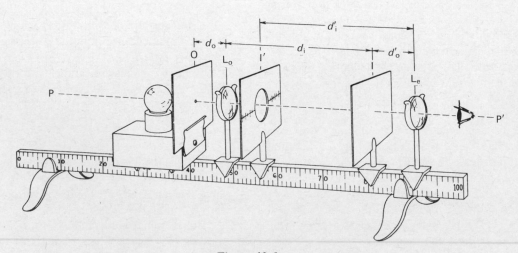

Figure 40-1

to the nearest 0.01 cm, and record as h_i'. Similarly record d_o' and d_i'.

As a second trial, increase the object distance d_o about 0.5 cm by moving the objective L_o 0.5 cm to the left and the object O 1 cm to the left, repeat the entire procedure, and record the required data.

If time permits, complete a third trial by increasing d_o as before. Record data as in previous trials.

CALCULATIONS

1. Magnification of the objective

Compute the magnification M_o of the objective lens for each trial from both size and distance data

by using Equation 1. Determine the average magnification for each trial and record the results in the data table.

2. Magnification of the eyepiece

Compute the magnification M_e of the eyepiece lens for each trial by using the appropriate data and Equation 2. Determine the average eyepiece magnification for each trial and record the results.

3. Magnification of the lens system

By using Equations 3 and 4, compute the overall magnification M of the compound lens system for each trial. Determine the average value M for each trial and record.

DATA

OBJECTIVE				EYEPIECE			M_o			M_e			M		
h_o	h_i	d_o	d_i	h_i'	d_o'	d_i'	$\dfrac{h_i}{h_o}$	$\dfrac{d_i}{d_o}$	Ave.	$\dfrac{h_i'}{h_i}$	$\dfrac{d_i'}{d_o'}$	Ave.	$\dfrac{h_i'}{h_o}$	$M_o M_e$	Ave.
(cm)	(cm)	(cm)	(cm)	(cm)	(cm)	(cm)									

QUESTIONS (Your answers should be complete statements. Problem solutions should be set down in the space provided below.)

1. Considering the focal length of the lens and the related object and image distances, the principle of which case for converging lenses is used **(a)** for the objective lens of a microscope **(b)** for the eyepiece lens?

a. _____

_____

b. _____

_____

2. Assuming that the focal length of the eyepiece, f_e, is very small compared with the length of the microscope tube, l, (the distance between objective and eyepiece lenses) and that the object to be magnified is very near to the principal focus of the objective lens of focal length f_o, show algebraically that the following expression for the total magnification is approximately correct:

$$\frac{l \times 25 \text{ cm}}{f_o \times f_e}$$

3. A converging lens of focal length 2.5 cm is used as an eyepiece lens to form a virtual image at the distance of most distinct vision. What is its magnification?

4. The lens of Problem 3 is used as the eyepiece of a compound microscope, the objective of which is a converging lens of 0.75 cm focal length. The real image is formed 12 cm from the objective. When the eye is held close to the eyepiece, the virtual image is viewed at the distance of most distinct vision. What is the magnification of the instrument?

experiment **41**

The Refracting Telescope

PURPOSE: To construct the lens system of a refracting telescope and determine experimentally its magnification.

APPARATUS: Optical bench consisting of a meterstick, 2 supports, 1 screen holder, and 3 lens holders; light box, with large-object screen; image screen, white Bristol board 10 X 12.5 cm; 1 long focal-length converging lens, f = 25 to 35 cm; 2 short focal-length converging lenses, f = 3 to 10 cm; 1 short focal-length diverging lens, f = 10 to 15 cm; telescope magnification scale, in centimeter divisions, mounted; measuring tape, 15 m.

SUGGESTION: 1. Suitable magnification scales may be made from 20-cm paper scales printed for horizontal use. Make the centimeter graduations heavy black lines and extend them to within 1.5 cm of the lower edge of the paper strip. Below these heavy lines print the numerals 1 cm high. Cement the paper scale to a suitable backing and mount on a ring stand with a utility clamp.

2. If time is short, the direct measurement of magnification with the magnification scale can be omitted from the procedure.

INTRODUCTION: Refracting telescopes are of three general types: (1) *celestial* or astronomical, (2) *terrestrial,* and (3) *Galilean* or opera glass. The essential elements of the lens system of the refracting telescope are the same as those of the microscope; an objective forms a real image of the object to be magnified, and an eyepiece, using this image as an object, forms an enlarged virtual image.

A telescope does not magnify objects in the sense that a microscope does. In a microscope, the image is actually larger than the object. In a telescope, however, the image is much smaller than the object, but since the image is much closer to the eye than the object is, the image *appears* to be larger than the object. Hence, the magnification of a telescope is an *apparent* magnification rather than a real one.

The astronomical telescope in its simplest form consists of a pair of converging lenses, an objective of long focal length f_o, and an eyepiece of short focal length f_e. When the object to be viewed is far away, a real first image is formed at the principal focus of the objective. The eyepiece, located approximately

a focal length f_e away, forms an enlarged second image. The apparent magnification of the astronomical telescope *for distant objects* is

$$M = \frac{f_o}{f_e} \qquad (1)$$

The telescope length l (separation of the lenses) for *distant objects* is

$$l = f_o + f_e \qquad (2)$$

When the telescope is focused on a nearby object (d_o being a measurable distance), the first image is formed beyond the principal focus and the tube length must be *increased.* Equations 1 and 2 would lead to erroneous results if applied to such a case. The tube length is the sum of the distances the first image is located from the objective, d_i, and from the eyepiece, d_o'. This first image serves as the object for the eyepiece lens.

$$l = d_i + d_o' \qquad (3)$$

The total magnification of the telescope is, of course, equal to the product of the magnification of the separate lenses and to the ratio of the size of the second image, h_i', to the apparent size of the object, h_o.

$$M = M_o M_e = \frac{h_i'}{h_o} \qquad (4)$$

The terrestrial telescope is similar to the astronomical version except for the inclusion of an inverting lens between the objective and the eyepiece to reinvert the real image. This enables the observer to view the virtual image in the same erect position as the object.

The Galilean telescope, or opera glass, consists of a conventional objective and a diverging (negative) eyepiece lens. The objective alone would form a real image of a distant object at its principal focus. The diverging eyepiece lens is placed ahead of this focal point so that its principal focus coincides with that of the objective. The real image then becomes a *virtual object* for the eyepiece and an enlarged virtual image is formed. Since this image is erect, the instrument may be used as a terrestrial telescope.

255

The apparent magnification of the Galilean telescope *for distant objects* is given by the expression

$$M = \frac{f_o}{f_e} \qquad (5)$$

Since f_e is negative for a diverging lens, the magnification is positive. The telescope length l for *distant objects* is the *algebraic* sum of the focal lengths of the two lenses (Equation 2).

PROCEDURE

1. Lens focal lengths

Determine the focal length of each of the three converging lenses by the method used in Experiment 37. Use the method of Experiment 38 to determine the focal length of the diverging lens. Devise a suitable means for maintaining the focal-length identity of each lens in use throughout the experiment.

2. Astronomical telescope

Construct a simple astronomical telescope on the optical bench using two converging lenses, a long focal-length objective, and a short focal-length eyepiece. Locate the eyepiece near the right end of the bench and determine, from the focal lengths of the lenses used, the approximate location of the objective. As before, focus as sharply as possible on a distant object and record the lens positions in the first data table. Compare the tube length l with the sum of the focal lengths and compute the magnification M from Equation 1.

3. Galilean telescope

Construct a Galilean telescope on the optical bench using the long focal-length converging lens as the objective and the diverging (negative) lens as the eyepiece. Mount the eyepiece lens near the right end of the bench and, with the objective lens located approximately a focal length f_o away, aim the telescope at a distant object through an open window. Considering the fact that the eyepiece is a negative lens, should the lens separation be increased or decreased to bring the object into focus? Establish a rough focus by moving the objective lens and then adjust the eyepiece for the sharpest image possible. Record the objective and eyepiece positions as L_o and L_e, respectively, in the data table. Compare the tube length l with the algebraic sum of the focal lengths. Compute the magnification M from Equation 5.

Mount an image screen on the optical bench approximately one focal length in front of the eyepiece and adjust its position as necessary to form a sharply focused first image of an illuminated object located a few meters in front of the objective (the laboratory should be darkened). Record the object distance d_o and the image distance d_i in the second data table.

Adjust the eyepiece position as necessary to focus on the back of the image screen; then remove the screen from its holder and adjust the eyepiece for sharpest detail of the virtual image of the illuminated object. Has the tube length l been increased or decreased as compared to that for the distant object? Taking the first image as the object for the eyepiece, record the object distance d_o' and the second-image distance d_i' (the distance of most distinct vision).

DATA   Distant Object

TELESCOPE	f_o (cm)	f_e (cm)	L_o (cm)	L_e (cm)	l		M
					$L_e - L_o$ (cm)	$f_o + f_e$ (cm)	
Astronomical							
Galilean							

DATA   Near Object

TRIAL	f_o (cm)	f_i (cm)	d_o (cm)	d_i (cm)	d_o' (cm)	d_i' (cm)	l $d_i + d_o'$ (cm)	M_o $\frac{d_i}{d_o}$	M_e $\frac{d_i'}{d_o'}$	M $M_o M_e$	$\frac{h_i'}{h_o}$
1											
2											

Compute the separate magnification of the objective and eyepiece, the total magnification of the telescope, and record as M_o, M_e, and M, respectively.

Replace the illuminated object with a magnification scale. Be careful to maintain the same object distance. Observe the scale through the telescope with one eye and directly with the other eye. Make slight adjustments of the eyepiece if necessary so that the scale seen through the lens and the scale seen by the unaided eye appear equally distant. Determine the magnification of the telescope by comparing the relative sizes of the scales as seen through the telescope and by the unaided eye. Record as the ratio of the second-image size d_i' to the object size d_o.

If time permits, increase the object distance as much as possible and collect data as you have previously done in this experiment.

OPTIONAL: Convert the astronomical telescope to a terrestrial instrument using a single inverting lens. Determine a position for the inverting lens that will leave the total magnification of the instrument unchanged. Plan a suitable table for recording data and results. Construct a ray diagram of the lens system, showing all significant positions and distances.

DIAGRAMS: On a separate sheet of paper, construct fully labeled ray diagrams of the astronomical and Galilean telescopes. Submit the diagrams with your report.

QUESTIONS (Your answers should be complete statements. Problem solutions should be set down in the space provided below.)

1. Compare the distances between the lenses of a refracting telescope when it is used for observing nearby and distant objects. Explain.

_____

_____

_____

_____

2. Two telescopes, one an astronomical and the other a Galilean, use identical objectives and a magnification of 3X for each. Show that the tube length of the astronomical telescope is twice that of the Galilean instrument.

experiment **42**

Color

PURPOSE: (1) To learn what determines the colors of transparent and opaque objects. (2) To learn what principle governs the combining of colored lights. (3) To learn what principle governs the combining of colored pigments.

APPARATUS: Glass slides: red, yellow, green blue; colored construction paper: red, orange, yellow, green, blue, violet; poster paints: red, yellow, green, blue; glass plates; glass rods.

SUGGESTION: A commercial color projection apparatus is ideal for this experiment. Good results may be obtained by using three slide projectors, or even three strong flashlights in a well-darkened room. Special color glass slides provide truer colors, but good results may be obtained by mounting several thicknesses of colored cellophane or spotlight gelatin between ordinary projection slide glasses.

PROCEDURE

1. Color of objects
a. Transparent objects. Look through the red, yellow, green, and blue glass slides, in turn, at a piece of white paper placed on your laboratory desk. How does the color of the white paper viewed through the slide compare with the color of the slide?

Observation: _____

_____

Now look through pairs of glass plates at the piece of white paper. Use the red and green plates, the red and blue plates, and the yellow and blue plates, for example.

Observation: _____

_____

_____

b. Opaque objects. In a darkened room, use a flashlight or a projector and the colored glass plates to shine beams of light of various colors on sheets of colored paper. In the table record the observed color of the various sheets of paper under different-colored beams of light.

2. Combining colors
Using a color apparatus, or three projectors, or three flashlights and colored slides in a well-darkened room, observe the colors produced by the overlapping of colored beams of light.

3. Combining pigments
Use a glass rod to mix a drop of each of the following poster paint colors on a glass plate and observe the color produced: yellow and blue; red and green; red and blue; blue and green; red, blue, and green. Record your observations.

DATA

COLOR OF INCIDENT LIGHT	COLOR OF OBJECT IN WHITE LIGHT					
	Red	*Orange*	*Yellow*	*Green*	*Blue*	*Violet*
Red						
Yellow						
Green						
Blue						

DATA

COLORS COMBINED	COLOR OBSERVED
Yellow and blue	
Red and green	
Red and blue	
Blue and green	
Red, blue, and green	

DATA

PIGMENTS MIXED	COLOR OBSERVED
Yellow and blue	
Red and green	
Red and blue	
Blue and green	
Red, blue, and green	

QUESTIONS   (Your answers should be complete statements.)

1. Upon what factors does the color of a transparent object depend?
_____
_____

2. What factors determine the color of an opaque object?
_____
_____

3. What determines the color observed when two beams of colored light are superposed?
_____
_____

4. What name is given to any two colored beams of light that form white light when they are superposed?
_____

5. What name is given to the three colors that form white light when superposed?
_____

6. What determines the color when two or more pigments are mixed?
_____
_____
_____
_____

7. What are the three primary pigments?
_____

8. What is the relationship between primary colors and primary pigments?
_____
_____

experiment **43**

Diffraction and Interference

PURPOSE: (1) To produce diffraction and interference patterns. (2) To study the wave nature of light.

APPARATUS: Straight filament clear glass electric lamp (showcase lamp will serve); lamp base and receptacle for vertical mounting of lamp; diffraction slits, single and double, of various widths and spacings; color filters of various colors (colored cellophane or spotlight gelatin will serve).

SUGGESTION: If diffraction slits are not available, satisfactory slits can be made by the students themselves. Clear glass microscope slides may be sprayed with black lacquer, then scored crosswise with a razor blade using a straightedge as a guide. With some practice using steady pressure, successful slits may be made. Several single slits and several double slits should be made on the slide so the most satisfactory ones can be used in the experiment. To make double slits, clamp two double-edged razor blades together. Strips of paper may be used as wedges for slits of varying separation.

A narrow slit 0.2 to 0.5 mm wide cut in a square of stiff black Bristol board and mounted in front of an ordinary frosted lamp will provide a suitable line source of light if a straight filament lamp is not available.

INTRODUCTION: According to Huygens' principle, every point on a light wave front may be considered a new source of light. In general, however, all parts of each new wavelet are cancelled by destructive interference except for those that are moving in the same direction as the original wave front. Thus the whole wave front appears to move as a unit.

If a series of wave fronts strike a barrier having two narrow slit openings, as shown in Figure 43-1, each opening acts as a new source and new wavelets travel out in phase with each other. In certain regions they will reinforce each other, producing bright bands. In alternate regions they will interfere, producing dark bands. White light, since it is a polychromatic source, yields indistinct bands.

PROCEDURE

1. Diffraction

Darken the laboratory and set up a line source of light in a vertical position. Hold a single slit close to your eye so that it is oriented vertically (parallel to the line source) and view the line source through it from a distance of one or two meters. Repeat using other single slits of different widths. Make sketches of the best diffraction patterns you observe through a narrow slit and a wide slit. Briefly describe the difference between the two patterns.

Observation: _____

_____

_____

_____

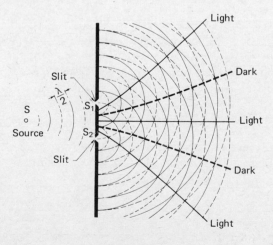

Figure 43-1

Narrow slit   Wide slit

2. Interference

Observe the line source through double slits. Compare the pattern seen through pairs of slits of different spacing. Sketch your best pattern observed through very closely spaced slits and your best pattern observed through the more widely spaced slits. Observe a single-slit pattern again and carefully note the similarities and differences.

Observation: _____

_____

_____

_____

Narrow spacing   Wide spacing

Examine a double-slit pattern carefully to see if color fringes are evident. Suggest an explanation for any color effects observed. Place a color filter in front of the white-light source. Record the result.

Observation: _____

_____

_____

Change to another color. Again record the result.

Observation: _____

_____

_____

Select two color filters from the end regions of the spectrum, red and blue for example, and observe the interference pattern with first one and then the other in front of the line source. Describe the changes you observe.

Observation: _____

_____

_____

Cover half the source with the red filter and the other half with the blue filter. From the pattern you observe, estimate the ratio of the wavelength of blue light to the wavelength of red light.

Observation: _____

_____

_____

QUESTIONS (Your answers should be complete statements.)

1. How does the diffraction pattern through a single slit change as a slit is made narrower?

_____

_____

2. How do the interference patterns compare when formed by two narrow slits very closely spaced and by two narrow slits more widely spaced?

_____

_____

_____

3. How do the interference patterns of red light and blue light compare when formed by the same pair of slits?

_____

_____

4. What do you think would happen to the interference pattern from a white-light line source if you were able to score many extremely narrow slits very close together, perhaps 2000-3000/cm, on your viewing plate?

_____

_____

_____

experiment **44**

Wavelength by Diffraction

PURPOSE: To measure the wavelength of light by means of a diffraction grating.

APPARATUS: Optical bench consisting of a meterstick, 2 supports, grating holder and support, metric scale and slit for meterstick mounting; bentpin riders for meterstick; Bunsen burner, with means of producing a sodium flame; diffraction grating, transmission replica, of the order of 4×10^3 lines/cm; incandescent light source, straight filament; sodium chloride; mercury vapor discharge tube and power supply if available.

SUGGESTION: If a flame-test rod (a glass tube with a platinum or nichrome wire sealed into one end) is available from the chemistry laboratory, attach a wad of asbestos fibers to the wire. Soak the asbestos in a sodium chloride brine and allow to dry overnight. To produce a sodium flame, place the wad of asbestos in the edge of the burner flame. Add sodium chloride solution as needed with a medicine dropper.

An asbestos collar that can be used repeatedly to produce a sodium flame can be formed to fit the Bunsen burner. Soak strips of soft asbestos mat or asbestos paper tape in a sodium chloride brine. Mold the soaked asbestos around the top of a burner barrel, forming a collar or barrel extension of approximately 3 cm, and allow to dry and harden. With the asbestos collar in place and the burner lit, adjust the gas-air mixture for best sodium flame. Add sodium chloride solution when needed, as suggested above.

INTRODUCTION: According to Huygens' principle, every point on a light wave front may be considered a new source of light. In general, all parts of each new wavelet are cancelled due to destructive interference except for that part traveling in the same direction as the original wave front.

When a diffraction grating of the transmission type is placed in the path of a plane wave front, only alternate parts of it pass through. The ruled lines are opaque to the light, and the uniform spacings between the lines, being transparent to the light, provide a large number of fine transmission slits very close together. The new wavelets originating at the slits inter-

fere in such a way that several new wave fronts are set up; one travels in the original direction and the others travel at various angles from this direction, depending on the wavelength.

If a narrow slit is illuminated by white (polychromatic) light and viewed through a transmission grating, a white image of the slit will be seen directly in line with the slit opening, and pairs of continuous spectra will be seen equally spaced on opposite sides of the slit opening. When the slit is illuminated by monochromatic light, successive pairs of slit images of decreasing intensity will be seen equally spaced on opposite sides of the slit opening. The first pair are known as the *first-order* images, the second pair as the *second-order* images, etc.

In Figure 44-1, **A** and **B** are parallel slits in a transmission grating uniformly separated by the distance d, known as the *grating constant.* A beam of monochromatic light from a distant slit incident normally on the grating gives rise to secondary wavelets simultaneously at each grating slit. A wave front of these wavelets travels along **MN** and, if converged, produces a direct image of the slit opening at **N**. Wave front **CB**, representing a given wave from **B** and the first preceding wave from **A**, travels along **MO** and, if converged, produces a *first-order* image of the slit opening at **O**. A given wave from **B** and the second preceding wave from **A** produce a wave front **BD** that yields a *second-order* image at **P**, etc. From the right triangle **ABC**, in which **AC** is equal to the wavelength λ of the incident light and the diffraction angle θ_1 is the angle of the diffracted wave front from the grating plane, it is evident that

$$\lambda = d \sin \theta_1 \tag{1}$$

Side **AD** of triangle **ABD** is equal to 2λ, as in the case of a second-order image,

$$\lambda = \frac{d \sin \theta_2}{2} \tag{2}$$

In the general case of n orders,

$$\lambda = \frac{d \sin \theta_n}{n} \tag{3}$$

The diffraction angle θ is determined experimen-

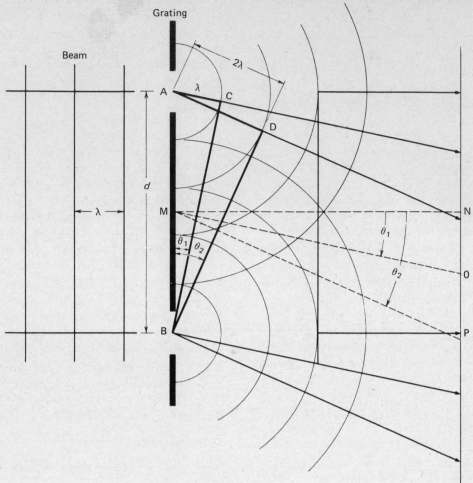

Figure 44-1

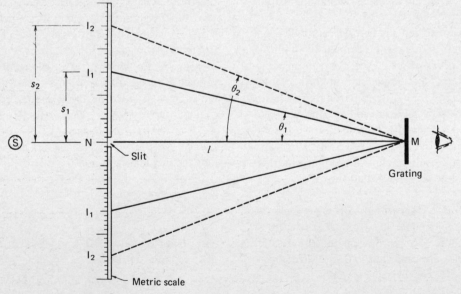

Figure 44-2

tally as shown in Figure 44-2, I_1 being a first-order slit image located on the metric scale. In the right triangle MNI_1,

$$\tan \theta_1 = \frac{NI_1}{MN} = \frac{s_1}{l} \qquad (4)$$

and

$$\theta_1 = \arctan \frac{s_1}{l} \qquad (5)$$

Knowing the order of image n observed, the diffraction angle θ_n, and the grating constant d, the wavelength λ can be computed from Equation 3.

PROCEDURE

1. Grating constant

Mount the scale and slit on one end of the optical bench and illuminate the slit with white light. Mount the grating near the opposite end of the optical bench and, with the eye close to the grating, observe the first-order spectra. Move the grating forward or backward as required to position the entire spectrum on the scale. Locate a rider on the scale at the point in each first-order spectrum where the yellow light is the purest yellow. Adjust the grating about its vertical axis to position these two corresponding regions (the two riders) equidistant from the slit. Read the distances s and l as precisely as possible, take the wavelength λ of this pure yellow region of the continuous spectrum as 5800 Å $(1 \text{ Å} = 10^{-8} \text{ cm})$, and compute the grating constant d from Equations 5 and 3. Record the required data in Data Table 1. If your instructor can provide the known number of lines per centimeter for your grating, enter the known value of d also.

2. Range of the visible spectrum

Examine a first-order continuous spectrum critical-ly under the best conditions of illumination attainable. Place riders on the scale at the extreme violet and extreme red ends of the spectrum. Read s and l and determine θ for each extreme. Using the known grating constant if available, compute the upper and lower limits of the visible spectrum. Complete Data Table 2.

3. Wavelength of sodium

Illuminate the slit with a sodium flame placed about 5 cm away and, if necessary, adjust the grating about its vertical axis as before. Carefully position a rider on a first-order image and, if possible, on a second-order image. Compute the wavelength of sodium light from each set of readings and record in Data Table 3. Substitute the white-light source for the sodium flame; be careful not to disturb the rider positions on the scale. Observe the location of the riders relative to the color regions of the continuous spectra.

4. Optional

Produce other bright-line spectra and measure the wavelengths of the prominent lines. Secure an unknown bright-line source from your instructor and attempt to identify it by comparing the wavelengths of the prominent lines with those of the characteristic spectra of the elements. Record all data in Table 3.

DATA Table 1

LIGHT SOURCE	λ (Å)	n	s (cm)	l (cm)	θ_n (°)	$\sin \theta_n$	d	
							experimental (cm)	actual (cm)

DATA Table 2

LIGHT SOURCE	COLOR extreme	n	s (cm)	l (cm)	θ_n (°)	$\sin \theta_n$	d (cm)	λ	
								experimental (Å)	actual (Å)

DATA Table 3

LIGHT SOURCE	n	s (cm)	l (cm)	θ_n (°)	$\sin \theta_n$	d (cm)	λ	
							experimental (Å)	actual (Å)

QUESTIONS (Your answers should be complete statements.)

1. Recognizing that θ cannot exceed $90°$, show that a coarse-ruled grating will yield a larger number of orders than a fine-ruled grating.

2. What would have been the effect on the measurements in this experiment of a grating with a smaller grating constant?

_____

_____

_____

3. Using Figure 44-1 as a basis, explain why the red end of the continuous spectrum was observed to be farther from the slit than the violet end when an incandescent lamp was used to illuminate the slit.

_____

_____

_____

_____

4. A single slit is illuminated by monochromatic light. Explain the fact that several orders of slit images may be seen with a grating but only one with a prism.

_____

_____

_____

5. In Procedure 3, to what region of the continuous spectrum does the sodium line correspond?

_____

_____

_____

6. Observe that the sodium spectrum in Color Plate VII of your text shows two narrow lines of 5980 Å and 5896 Å. Suggest a possible reason why you observed a single sodium line.

_____

_____

_____

experiment **45**

The Polarization of Light

PURPOSE: (1) To show some ways in which light may be polarized. (2) To illustrate several uses of polarized light.

APPARATUS: 2 Polaroid disks; piece of calcite (Iceland spar); piece of ferrotype plate or metal plate enameled on one surface; 12 glass plates, 5 cm square; cellophane strips mounted between 5-cm-square glass plates as shown in Figure 45-1 or cellulose tape on a square glass plate; U-shaped piece of transparent plastic; glass from broken molded bottle.

INTRODUCTION: Light waves that vibrate in only one plane are said to be polarized. There are several natural crystals, among them tourmaline and calcite, that possess the property of polarizing light that passes through them. Light may be partially polarized by reflection. Polaroid is a synthetic material that is used to polarize light. Through the use of polarized light and the means of detecting it, many scientific observations not possible with ordinary light may be made. Polarized light is used in identifying certain chemical compounds, in detecting strains in structural materials, and in determining the thickness of crystals and fibers. Polaroid is used in some sunglasses and in some types of reading lamps to reduce glare.

PROCEDURE

1. Production and detection of polarized light with Polaroid

Look through one of the Polaroid disks at one of the walls of your laboratory. Rotate the disk. Does the intensity of light vary?

_____ Do the same with the other disk. Do you get the same result? _____ How does the intensity of light coming through a single disk compare with that reaching your eye directly?

_____

_____

_____

_____

Figure 45-1

The light coming through a Polaroid disk is plane-polarized. That is, the light waves passing through are all vibrating in the same plane.

Now hold both disks together, and rotate one of them while you look through them at the wall. What effect do you observe?

_____

_____

_____

_____

How much do you have to turn one disk to go from maximum to minimum brightness?_____. When the Polaroid disks are placed so that a minimum of light passes through, the disks are said to be crossed. Explain why crossed polarizers transmit a minimum of light.

_____

_____

_____

_____

_____

267

2. Production of polarized light by crystals

Look through a transparent piece of calcite (Iceland spar) at the period at the end of this sentence. What do you see?

_____

Slowly turn the crystal. What movement do you observe?

_____

_____

Now look through a single rotated Polaroid disk at the images in the crystal. What happens?

_____

_____

_____

Explain. _____

_____

_____

3. Production of polarized light by reflection

Place a piece of ferrotype plate or a metal plate painted with black enamel on your laboratory desk. Find a position where the maximum amount of light from the window is reflected from the surface of the plate as "glare." Examine this glare through a single rotated Polaroid disk. Is the glare light polarized?

_____ How can you tell?

_____

_____

Examine the glare from a stack of 12 glass plates in a similar manner. What do you observe?

_____

_____

4. Elimination of glare by the use of Polaroid

In what plane is the glare reflected from a polished surface polarized?

_____

_____

_____

Hold the Polaroid disks, oriented so that their transmitting plane is at right angles to the plane in which the glare is polarized, one over each eye. Compare the amount of glare through the Polaroid disks with the amount you see without the Polaroid disks.

_____

_____

_____

What practical application does this observation have?

_____

_____

_____

_____

_____

_____

5. Use of polarized light to observe interference phenomena (Qualitative)

Cross the two Polaroid disks and place between them the glass slide containing the cellophane strips of varying thickness. Rotate the glass slide until you observe the brightest colors. How does the brightness of the color vary from the thin strips to the thick ones?

_____

_____

6. Use of polarized light to determine structural strains

Examine a small U-shaped piece of transparent plastic between crossed Polaroid disks. What do you observe?

_____

_____

Now pinch the open ends of the piece of plastic between your fingers. What happens?

_____

_____

How do the colors help you to detect the places where the strain is the greatest?

_____

_____

_____

Examine a piece of glass broken from a molded bottle between crossed polarizers. Are there strains in the glass?

_____

_____

experiment 46

Electrostatics

PURPOSE: To show certain properties of static electricity.

APPARATUS: Pith ball electroscope; ebonite or hard-rubber rods; cat's fur or wool pad; glass rod; silk pad; suspension support for hard-rubber rod; gold leaf electroscope; bare copper wire; silk thread; brass ball; demonstration capacitor.

INTRODUCTION: Whenever two dissimilar materials are rubbed together, static electricity is produced; one material acquires a positive charge and the other a negative charge. In most instances these charges are of negligible magnitude and go unnoticed. Sometimes, however, the accumulation of an electrostatic charge is quite significant, and its presence is readily detected.

In this experiment we shall produce charges, examine some of the properties of charged bodies, and verify the laws of electrostatics.

SUGGESTION: This experiment may be performed as a demonstration by the teacher or by a student. The most satisfactory results are obtained on clear, dry days.

PROCEDURE

1. Production of negative electricity

Rub an ebonite rod with a piece of cat's fur and bring it close to a pith ball electroscope as in Figure 46-1.

Result? _____

_____

Let the pith ball momentarily touch the ebonite rod.
Result? _____

_____

Explain the movement of the pith ball.

_____

_____

_____

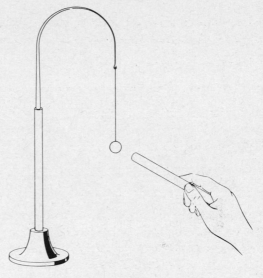

Figure 46-1

2. Production of positive electricity

Rub the glass rod with silk and repeat the procedure in step 1 with the pith ball.

Result? _____

_____

_____

Explain. _____

_____

How is the pith ball charged when it is repelled by the glass rod? _____

_____

If a charged ebonite rod were brought near such a charged pith ball, what would happen?

_____

_____

Explain. _____

Try it and see if your prediction is true.

Result? _____

_____

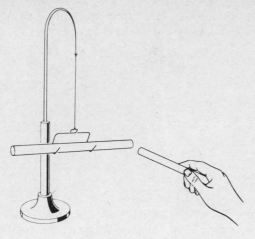

Figure 46-2

3. First law of electrostatics

Suspend a charged ebonite rod as in Figure 46-2. Bring a second charged ebonite rod near one end of the suspended rod.

Result? _____

_____

Try the other end.

Result? _____

_____

Bring a charged glass rod near one end of the suspended charged ebonite rod. What do you observe?

_____

_____

Try the other end.

Result? _____

_____

Is the charge the same at both ends of the suspended ebonite rod?

_____

_____

Is it the same charge that you produced on the second ebonite rod?

_____

_____

How can you determine this?

_____

_____

What conclusion do you draw with regard to the behavior of electric charges toward each other?

_____

_____

4. Charging an electroscope

a. By conduction. Charge an ebonite rod and scrape it against the knob of an electroscope.

Result? _____

_____

Explain. _____

_____

What kind of charge is on the electroscope?

_____

_____

Explain. _____

_____

The charge may be removed from the electroscope by touching the knob with the hand. Explain this action.

_____

_____

b. By induction. Bring a charged ebonite rod *near* the electroscope knob. What happens to the leaves of the electroscope?

_____

_____

With the ebonite rod still near, momentarily touch the knob of the electroscope with your finger. Explain what happens.

_____

_____

Remove the rod. Is the electroscope charged?

_____

What kind of charge does it have?

_____

Discharge the electroscope and repeat the procedure, using a glass rod charged by rubbing it with silk.

5. Conductors and insulators

Set up the apparatus as shown in Figure 46-3. Suspend a brass sphere from an electroscope stand (Figure 46-1) to serve as ball **B**. Make sure that the copper wire has good metal-to-metal contact with both ball **B** and electroscope knob **A**. See if you can charge the electroscope either by contact or by induction using the ball **B** the same way you would ordinarily use knob **A**.

Result? _____

_____

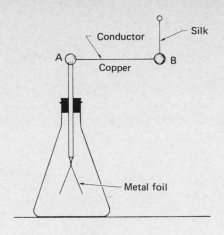

Conductor

Silk

A

Copper

B

Metal foil

Figure 46-3

Is copper a conductor?

_____

Replace the copper wire between **A** and **B** with a silk thread. Attempt to charge the electroscope using ball **B** as above.

Result? _____

Is silk a conductor?

_____

6. *Action of a capacitor*

Connect the knob of an electroscope to one plate of a demonstration capacitor by a short piece of copper wire. Charge this combination negatively. Bring

the second plate of the capacitor near the first. What happens to the leaves of the electroscope?

_____

Explain. _____

_____

Remove the second capacitor plate. Explain the results.

_____

_____

Bring the second plate near the first again. What must you do to cause the electroscope leaves to diverge the same amount as they did with the single capacitor plate?

_____

_____

Try it.

Result? _____

_____

How does a capacitor affect the amount of charge that must be placed on the electroscope knob to cause divergence of the electroscope leaves?

_____

_____

What is the function of a capacitor?

_____

_____

experiment 47

Electrochemical Cells

PURPOSE: (1) To study the reactions in a voltaic cell. (2) To study the reactions in a storage cell.

APPARATUS: Simple demonstration cell, consisting of some type of battery stand; 2 zinc electrodes; carbon electrode; copper electrode; d-c voltmeter, 0-3 v; d-c ammeter, 0-3 a; enameled pan; 2 lead electrodes; 2 dry cells; rheostat; knife switch, SPST; annunciator wire, 18 ga, for connections; dilute sulfuric acid, about 1 part acid to 14 parts water; amalgamating fluid; electric bell. See Appendix A for instructions in the use of meters.

Amalgamating fluid is made by reacting 200 g of mercury with a mixture of 175 mL of concentrated nitric acid and 625 mL of concentrated hydrochloric acid (hood). After the *poisonous fumes* have disappeared, the solution can be kept in a glass-stoppered bottle and used from year to year until the mercury is exhausted. CAUTION: *The solution is extremely corrosive.*

INTRODUCTION: There are two general types of electrochemical cells, the primary cell and the storage (secondary) cell. The essential difference is that the reacting materials of a storage cell are renewable.

Electrochemical reactions are oxidation-reduction reactions that occur spontaneously and thus can be used as a source of direct current. During the chemical action, electrons are removed from the cathode element, an *oxidation* process, and electrons are acquired by the anode element, a *reduction* process. In the storage cell this process is reversed to restore the electrodes by using electric energy from an external source.

PROCEDURE

1. Primary cell
a. The cathode. Place a strip of unamalgamated zinc in a tumbler one-third full of dilute sulfuric acid. CAUTION: *Dilute acid is very corrosive.* What action do you observe?

_____

_____

_____

_____

Since zinc is an element, composed of zinc only, what must have been the source of the gas bubbles?

_____

_____

The chemical formula for sulfuric acid is H_2SO_4. Zinc displaces hydrogen from the sulfuric acid. The zinc enters the solution as positively charged zinc ions, Zn^{++}. The hydrogen is released as bubbles of gas. Dip one end of a similar strip of zinc into a tumbler two-thirds full of amalgamating fluid for a few seconds. *(Caution)* Rinse with water and wipe the strip dry. What is the appearance of the amalgamated strip?

_____

_____

Dip it into the sulfuric acid solution and let it remain for two or three minutes. Do you observe any action?

_____

Remove the amalgamated strip from the acid, rinse it, and lay it in the enameled pan. Take care not to get any acid on your clothing or on the table.

b. The anode. Insert a strip of copper in the acid. Does the acid appear to act on the copper?

_____

Remove the copper strip and use in its place a carbon electrode. Is there any action of the acid on the carbon?

_____

_____

_____

2. A voltaic cell on open circuit
While the carbon rod is still in the acid solution, add the amalgamated zinc electrode. They must not touch each other. Is there any apparent action on open circuit when carbon is used with amalgamated zinc?

_____
_____

Repeat, using carbon and unamalgamated zinc. What action appears to be taking place?

_____
_____
_____

3. A voltaic cell on closed circuit

Rinse the copper and amalgamated zinc strips and place them in a battery stand. Connect their terminals to a voltmeter by means of short pieces of wire. Read the voltmeter when the elements are first dipped into the acid solution. Record the voltage.

_____ volts.

Repeat the experiment using the carbon rod and the amalgamated zinc strip. Record the voltage.

_____ volts. Where do the hydrogen bubbles appear to be liberated?

_____
_____

4. The lead storage cell

Sandpaper the lead strips until they are bright and clean. Clamp them in position in the demonstration cell and immerse them in the tumbler two-thirds full of dilute sulfuric acid. Does the voltmeter connected across the terminals show any difference in potential?

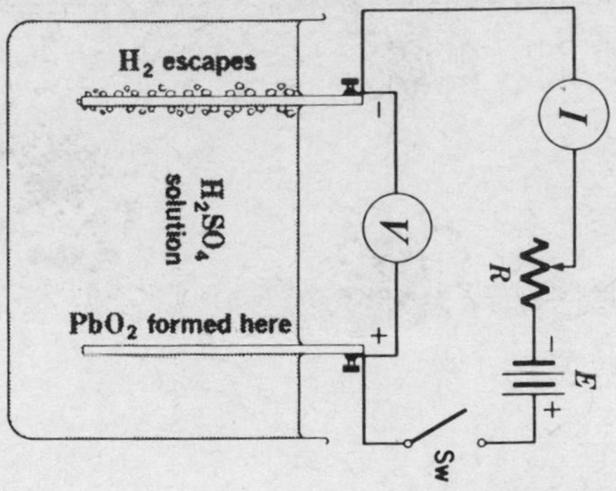

_____
_____
_____

Figure 47-1

Next, connect the lead strips in series with two dry cells, an ammeter, a rheostat, and a switch, as shown in Figure 47-1. With the switch closed, adjust the rheostat for about one ampere of current. Maintain this charging rate for approximately 5 minutes. Then lift the plates from the acid and examine them. Describe the changes that took place in the cell during charging.

_____
_____

What is the difference of potential between the electrodes now? _____ volts.

Connect the cell you have just charged with an electric bell, a small motor, or a voltmeter, and permit it to discharge. Record your observations.

_____
_____
_____

experiment **48**

Combinations of Cells: Internal Resistance

PURPOSE: (1) To learn how to group cells to supply proper current and potential difference for different loads. (2) To measure the internal resistance of a battery.

APPARATUS: Three No. 6 dry cells; d-c ammeter, 0-1/10 a or similar ranges; d-c voltmeter, 0-7.5 v; tubular rheostat, approximately 25 ohms; brass connectors, double; annunciator wire, No. 18, for connections; 2 momentary contact switches, SPST. See Appendix A for instructions in use of meters.

SUGGESTION: If the supply of dry cells is limited to no more than 3 per group, one or two groups may be asked to hook up the circuit for Part 3 and take measurements as a demonstration after each student has determined the circuit and drawn the circuit diagram. Sufficient ammeters will then be available for the demonstration circuit to make all current readings simultaneously.

Switch contacts and rheostat sliding contacts should be clean and bright. Dry cells should be fresh and as nearly identical as possible.

INTRODUCTION: A battery is composed of two or more cells connected either in series or in parallel. Cells are generally connected in series to provide a higher potential difference than that of a single cell. They are generally connected in parallel to increase the capacity for delivering continuous current to the external circuit. Only identical cells should be connected in parallel. When the laboratory supply is sufficient, the standard No. 6 dry cell should not be required to furnish more than 0.25 a of continuous current. *To conserve the life of the laboratory dry cells, the circuit should be opened when not actually taking meter readings.*

PROCEDURE

1. Cells in series

Connect 1 dry cell, an ammeter (10-a range), a voltmeter, a switch, and a rheostat in a circuit as shown in Figure 48-1. *Observe the polarity markings on d-c meters when connecting them in the circuit.* With the rheostat resistance R_L at the maximum, momentarily close the switch and note the meter deflections. The voltmeter should read about 1.5 v

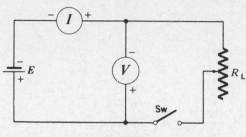

Figure 48-1

and the ammeter should show little noticeable deflection. Adjust the rheostat for a current of approximately 0.2 a, open the switch, and change the ammeter connection to the 1 a-range. Adjust the rheostat for precisely 0.2 a. Does the voltmeter reading change during the load adjustment? *Keep switch open except when taking readings.* The ammeter reads total current, I_T, in the circuit and the voltmeter reads the potential difference across the external circuit. Record both readings in the data table. Disconnect the negative lead of the voltmeter from the circuit and, *with switch closed*, momentarily touch it directly to the negative terminal of the dry cell. Record the voltage reading as V_1. *The detailed instructions concerning the circuit given above will not be repeated in the following paragraphs, but should be followed closely each time you perform the manipulation called for.*

Place a second dry cell in series with the one now in circuit by connecting the negative terminal of the first to the positive terminal of the second. The negative terminal of the second cell is then connected to the external circuit. See Figure 48-2. Close the switch and read both meters. How does the change in I_T compare with the change in V? Adjust R_L to give an I_T of 0.2 a. Does V change during this adjustment? Note the voltage across each cell as before. Remove

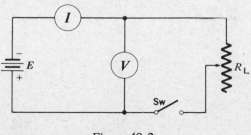

Figure 48-2

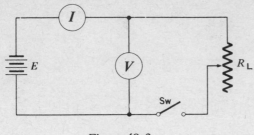

Figure 48-3

both voltmeter leads from the circuit this time. *Open switch.* Record I_T, V, V_1, and V_2. How does the sum of V_1 and V_2 compare with V?

Place a third dry cell in the battery in series with the other two. See Figure 48-3. Note changes in I_T and V. Are they what you expected? Adjust R_L to give an I_T of 0.2 a. Record I_T, V, V_1, V_2, and V_3 in the data table. How do the individual cell voltages compare with the battery voltage?

DATA Cells in Series

NUMBER OF CELLS	I_T (a)	V (v)	V_1 (v)	V_2 (v)	V_3 (v)
1					
2					
3					

2. Cells in parallel

Remove two of the cells, leaving the circuit as in Figure 48-1. Note the changes in I_T and V and quickly adjust R_L to give an I_T of 0.3 a. *Immediately open the switch.* When the open-circuit voltage reading is normal, record I_T and V.

Place a second cell in parallel with the one now in the circuit by connecting the negative terminals together and the positive terminals together as in Figure 48-4. Is there a change in either I_T or V? Should there be? If necessary, make an adjustment of R_L to give an I_T of 0.3 a, *open switch*, and record I_T and V. Remove the ammeter from the circuit and replace it with a brass connector to close the circuit. Determine the current in each of the two cells of the battery by inserting the ammeter first in position 1 and then in position 2 as shown in Figure 48-4. Record as I_1 and I_2 and return the ammeter to its original location in the circuit. How do the individual cell currents compare with the total current in the circuit?

Place a third cell in parallel in the battery as shown in Figure 48-5. Note any change in I_T or V. Adjust I_T to 0.3 a if necessary and record readings of I_T, V, I_1,

I_2, and I_3. How do the individual cell currents compare with the total current in the circuit?

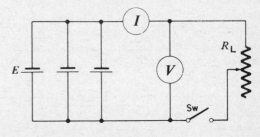

Figure 48-4

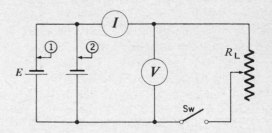

Figure 48-5

DATA Cells in Parallel

NUMBER OF CELLS	V_T (v)	I_T (a)	I_1 (a)	I_2 (a)	I_3 (a)
1					
2					
3					

3. Battery problem

Suppose an external load consisting of the rheostat R_L requires a current of 0.75 a and a potential difference across it of 3 v. Arrange a battery of No. 6 dry cells that will supply these requirements without any cell having a current in it in excess of 0.25 a. Connect the load and switch to the battery with the voltmeter to read the potential difference across the load and the ammeter to read the total current in the external circuit. Have maximum resistance in the circuit when the switch is closed. Adjust R_L for an I_T of 0.75 a. Remove the ammeter as before and use it to read the cell currents. Draw a diagram of your circuit showing an appropriate meter symbol in *each* location a meter reading was taken. Write in the current or voltage reading at each meter location.

4. Internal resistance

Make up a battery of three No. 6 dry cells connected in series. Connect the voltmeter across the battery and the ammeter (10-a range) in series with the rheostat as shown in Figure 48-6. The internal resistance of the battery is represented as a resistance r in series with the battery. Close Sw_1 and read the voltage across the battery. The voltmeter will draw a negligible current and we will assume that it reads the open circuit emf of the battery when Sw_2 is open. Close Sw_2 and adjust I_T to read 0.2-0.3 a, then immediately open Sw_2. Open Sw_1 and allow about one minute for the cells to recover.

With Sw_2 open, close Sw_1 and read the open-circuit emf of the battery. Record this emf as E in the data table, reading the meter to the nearest tenth of the smallest scale division. Close Sw_2 and read both meters to the nearest tenth of the smallest scale division. Record as I_T and V. The meter now reads

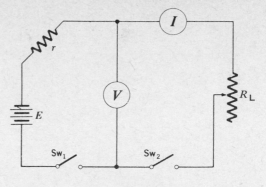

Figure 48-6

the potential difference across the battery terminals with the circuit current in the battery. How can you explain the difference in the voltmeter readings of E and V?

The circuit current in the internal resistance, r, of the battery develops a potential difference $I_T r$ that is in opposition to the emf of the battery E. The closed-circuit terminal potential difference V applied to the external circuit is the difference voltage. Thus

$$V = E - I_T r$$

Or

$$I_T r = E - V$$

Whence

$$r = \frac{E - V}{I_T}$$

Make the necessary computations to complete the data table. Assume the three cells composing the battery to be identical.

DATA Internal Resistance

NUMBER OF CELLS IN SERIES	E (v)	I_T (a)	V (v)	$E - V$ (v)	r battery (Ω)	r cell (Ω)

QUESTION (Your answer should be a complete statement.)

What difficulty would you encounter in attempting to determine the internal resistance of a battery consisting of three cells in parallel if you used the method described in Part 4?

_____

_____

_____

_____

_____

experiment **49**

Measurement of Resistance: Voltmeter—Ammeter Method

PURPOSE: (1) To measure the resistance of conductors by the voltmeter-ammeter method. (2) To determine the effect of length, diameter, and material on the resistance of a conductor.

APPARATUS: Battery, 3 to 6 v; d-c ammeter, 0-1/10 a; d-c voltmeter, 0-7.5 v; tubular rheostat; annunciator wire, 18 ga for connections; 3 nickel-silver resistance spools, 30 ga-200 cm, 28 ga-200 cm, 30 ga-160 cm (Constantan or German-silver spools may be used); 1 copper resistance spool, 30 ga-2000 cm; brass connectors, double; momentary contact switch, SPST. See Appendix A for instructions in the use of meters.

SUGGESTION: A convenient board for permanent use may be made as follows. Select a board from 25.4 to 30.5 cm wide and 38.1 cm long. Near one end, at **A** and **B**, fasten two universal binding posts about 7.5 cm apart. See Figure 49-1. At **C** and **D** fasten two universal binding posts. Attach a momentary contact switch to the board at **Sw** and connect its terminal at **A** and **C** by means of 14 ga insulated copper wire.

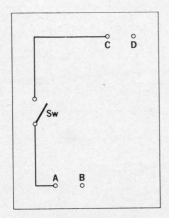

Figure 49-1

INTRODUCTION: Different substances offer different amounts of resistance to an electric current. In general, metals are good conductors, although even among the metals we find a wide range of conductivity. Silver and copper, for example, are much better conductors than iron, lead, nickel-silver (an alloy of copper and nickel), or nichrome (an alloy of nickel,

iron, chromium, and carbon used in electric heaters).

Physicists have found that four variables determine the resistance of a conductor to an electric current. These variables are: temperature, length, cross-sectional area, and the metal of which the conductor is made.

In this experiment we will observe the effects of length and cross-sectional area on the resistance of conductors of the same and different metals. By measuring the potential difference across the conductor specimen (resistance spool) and the current in the conductor, the resistance of the specimen can be calculated from Ohm's law.

The temperature of the specimen does not change appreciably if the current is kept small and of short duration. Therefore, the resistance is that of the conductor at room temperature. Knowing the resistance, length, and cross-sectional area of the conductor, the resistivity of the metal composing the conductor can be calculated.

NOTE: Tarnished metal surfaces make for poor electric contact. Assure that all metal-to-metal contact surfaces are clean and bright.

PROCEDURE: Connect the apparatus as shown in Figure 49-2. The voltmeter **V** is connected in *parallel* with the resistance spool R_x whose resistance is to be measured. The ammeter **A** (higher range) is connected

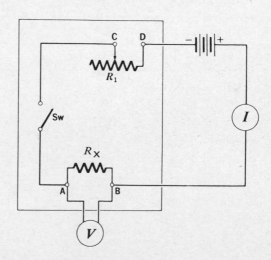

Figure 49-2

279

in *series* with the resistance spool, the battery, and the rheostat R_1. The rheostat serves as a variable resistance to limit the circuit current.

With the rheostat resistance R_1 in the circuit and the 200-cm spool of 30 ga nickel-silver wire connected across the terminals **AB** as R_x, gradually reduce the resistance R_1 until the ammeter reads approximately 0.2 a. Open the switch and change the ammeter to its lower range. Read both the voltmeter and the ammeter, estimating to the nearest tenth of the smallest scale division. Then open the switch immediately. Can you give two reasons for adjusting R_1 for the small current?

Substitute each of the other coils, in turn, for the coil just used, adjust the circuit current to a suitable value, and read the voltmeter and ammeter to the precision each instrument allows.

CALCULATIONS: The voltmeter gives the potential difference across the resistance spool, while the ammeter gives the current in the resistance spool. By Ohm's law,

$$R_x = \frac{V_x}{I}$$

calculate the resistance for each spool to the precision your measurements allow. The diameters and cross-sectional areas of wires are given in Appendix B, Table 21. Determine the resistivity of the metal composing each spool, compare with the accepted constants (Appendix B, Table 20), and determine your experimental error.

DATA

TRIAL	Metal	Gauge number	Length (cm)	Cross-sectional area (cm²)	V_x (v)	I (a)	R_x (Ω)
1							
2							
3							
4							

DATA

TRIAL	Resistivity experimental (Ω cm)	Resistivity accepted value (Ω cm)	Absolute error (Ω cm)	Relative error (%)
1				
2				
3				
4				

experiment **50**

Measurement of Resistance: Wheatstone Bridge Method

PURPOSE: To learn to use the Wheatstone bridge for precision measurements of resistance.

APPARATUS: Wheatstone bridge; No. 6 dry cell or other d-c power source; galvanometer; resistance box; 3 nickel-silver resistance spools, 30 ga-200 cm, 28 ga-200 cm, 30 ga-160 cm (Constantan or German-silver spools may be used); 1 copper resistance spool, 30 ga-2000 cm; annunciator wire, 18 ga, for connections; momentary contact switch, SPST; brass connectors, double; bare copper wire, 30 ga for galvanometer shunt. See Appendix A for instructions in the use of meters.

INTRODUCTION: The Wheatstone bridge provides a very precise means of measuring resistance. It is a simple *bridge* circuit consisting of a source of emf, a galvanometer, and a network of four resistors. By balancing the bridge and knowing three of the resistances, the fourth resistance can be calculated.

Referring to Figure 50-1, an unknown resistance R_x may be balanced against known resistances R_1, R_2, and R_3 by adjusting R_1, R_2, and R_3 until a galvanometer *bridged* across the parallel branches shows zero current. When the bridge is balanced, there can be no difference of potential between points **C** and **D**. Thus

$$V_{AD} = V_{AC} \text{ and } V_{DB} = V_{CB}$$

Then $I_2 R_x = I_1 R_1$ and $I_2 R_3 = I_1 R_2$

$$\frac{R_x}{R_3} = \frac{R_1}{R_2} \text{ or } R_x = R_3 \frac{R_1}{R_2}$$

In the laboratory form of the Wheatstone bridge, Figure 50-2, resistances R_1 and R_2 take the form of a uniform resistance wire; the position of contact **C** determines the lengths of R_1 and R_2. Since the resistance of the uniform wire is directly proportional to its length,

$$\frac{l_1}{l_2} = \frac{R_1}{R_2}$$

Therefore, $R_x = R_3 \dfrac{l_1}{l_2}$

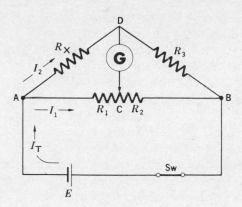

Figure 50-1

The Wheatstone bridge permits a more precise measurement of resistance than the voltmeter-ammeter method. However, it requires more careful work to ensure the precision of which it is capable. By using the same resistance spools measured previously by the voltmeter-ammeter method, a comparison of the relative precision of these two methods of measuring resistance can be made.

PROCEDURE: Set up the apparatus as shown in Figure 50-2. Make sure that all contact points are clean and bright. Use pieces of wire as short as possible for all connectors. One terminal of the galvanometer **G** is connected to the binding post at **D**; the other terminal of the galvanometer is connected to the slide contact **C** by a wire long enough to permit the contact key to touch any point of the wire **AC**. The resistance box R_3 is connected to the binding posts on the brass strips at one end of the Wheatstone bridge, and the unknown resistance R_x is connected to the binding posts at the other end of the bridge. A dry cell of 1.5 volts is connected in series with a momentary contact switch to the brass strips at the ends of the bridge which serve as terminals of the wire **AB**.

For the first trial use a 200-cm spool of 30 ga nickel-silver wire as R_x, whose resistance is to be measured. Place a low-resistance shunt across the galvanometer by winding several turns of 30 ga bare copper wire around the terminals. Why? Unplug some resistance from R_3, momentarily close the switch, and press the contact key near the 50-cm

281

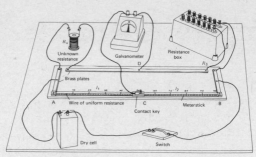

Figure 50-2

mark. If the galvanometer shows no deflection for several positions of the contact key, remove some of the shunting wire from the terminals. Allow the switch to remain closed for short periods only.

When the galvanometer shows some deflection, try moving the contact key to the right. Does the deflection increase or decrease? If the deflection increased, move the contact key to the left. Is there a region on the wire where the deflection reverses as the contact key is moved through it? Try to locate one, changing the resistance of R_3 if necessary.

If the balance region is located near either end of the slide wire, considerable error may be introduced. If l_1 is much shorter than l_2, then R_x must be smaller than R_3 since $R_x/R_3 = l_1/l_2$. Use this relation as a basis for determining what adjustment to make in R_3 to move the balance region between the 40-cm and 60-cm marks on the meterstick.

As the bridge is brought nearer the final balance, remove shunting turns from the galvanometer to in-

crease its sensitivity. Locate the final balance point, with all shunting turns removed, by holding the contact key down and sliding it back and forth to locate precisely the position of zero deflection on the galvanometer. Record the necessary data in the data table.

Replace the resistance spool just measured with the 200-cm spool of 28 ga nickel-silver wire. Balance the bridge as before and record the required data. In a similar manner measure the resistance of the 160-cm spool of 30 ga nickel-silver wire and that of the 2000-cm spool of 30 ga copper wire. Record the necessary data.

CALCULATIONS: Calculate the resistance of each spool to the precision your measurements will allow. Consult Appendix B, Table 21, for cross-sectional areas of the wires used. Determine the resistivity of the metal composing each spool. Compare with accepted constants (Appendix B, Table 20), and express your experimental error in each case.

DATA

TRIAL	Metal	Gauge number	Length (cm)	Cross-sectional area (cm^2)	l_1 (cm)	l_2 (cm)	R_3 (Ω)	R_x (Ω)
1								
2								
3								
4								

TRIAL	Resistivity experimental (Ω cm)		Resistivity accepted value (Ω cm)		Absolute error (Ω cm)		Relative error (%)	
1								
2								
3								
4								

experiment 51

Effect of Temperature on Resistance

PURPOSE: (1) To determine the temperature coefficient of resistance of a metallic conductor. (2) To study the effects of a change in temperature on the resistance of metallic and nonmetallic conductors.

APPARATUS: Wheatstone bridge; dry cell or other d-c power source; galvanometer; resistance box; momentary contact switch, SPST; annunciator wire, 18 ga, for connections; bare copper wire, 30 ga, for galvanometer shunt; temperature coil, copper, approximately 3 ohms; thermometer; magnifier; calorimeter; crushed ice; boiler or large beaker; burner; tripod; carbon lamp, 32 candle; tungsten lamp, 40 watts; lamp socket, standard base; fuse block, double, with 1-a fuses; split-line extension cord and plug; a-c milliammeter, 0-500 ma; a-c voltmeter, 0-150 v; cross-section paper.

INTRODUCTION: The resistance of a conductor depends on its composition, its length, its cross-sectional area, and its temperature. In the case of pure metals and most metallic alloys, resistance increases rapidly with a rise in temperature. Many nonmetals, on the other hand, show a decrease in resistance with a rise in temperature. Special alloys may have resistances that are practically independent of temperature.

The resistance of a conductor composed of a given material and at a constant temperature is equal to the product of a dimensional constant called resistivity, ρ (rho), and the ratio of the length l to the cross-sectional area A.

$$R = \rho \frac{l}{A} \text{ whence } \rho = \frac{RA}{l}$$

ρ has the dimension Ω cm.

The change in resistivity that occurs over a moderate temperature range defines a useful quantity characteristic of the substance known as the *temperature coefficient of resistivity*. The symbol for this coefficient is α (the Greek letter alpha). *Temperature coefficient of resistivity is the ratio of the change in resistivity due to a change in temperature of $1°$ C to the resistivity at $0°$ C.*

$$\alpha = \frac{\Delta\rho/\Delta T}{\rho_0} \tag{1}$$

The value of α depends on the temperature on which ρ_0 is based: conventionally $0°$ C. The change in resistivity, $\Delta\rho$, is expressed in terms of the resistivity at temperature T, ρ_T, and the resistivity at $0°$ C, ρ_0.

$\Delta\rho = \rho_T - \rho_0$. Similarly, $\Delta T = T - 0° = T$. Substituting these values for $\Delta\rho$ and ΔT, Equation 1 becomes

$$\alpha = \frac{\rho_T - \rho_0}{\rho_0 T} \tag{2}$$

Since it is the resistivity of a substance that changes with temperature, the resistance R of a given conductor changes accordingly. Thus R may be substituted for ρ in Equation 2.

$$\alpha = \frac{R_T - R_0}{R_0 T} \tag{3}$$

When R_T is the measured resistance in ohms at temperature T, R_0 the resistance in ohms at $0°$ C, and T the final temperature in $°$C, α is the *temperature coefficient of resistance* whose dimension depends only upon the unit of T.

PROCEDURE

1. Temperature coefficient of resistance
Set up the Wheatstone bridge apparatus as in Experiment 50, connect the temperature coil as R_x, and balance the bridge at room temperature. Immerse the coil in a calorimeter of ice water and balance the bridge when the coil temperature equals the temperature of the ice water. How can you tell when the coil temperature is constant? Record the bridge measurements and the temperature as precisely as possible. Use a magnifier to help you read the thermometer to the nearest $0.1°$. Immerse the coil in boiling water. Measure the resistance of the coil while it is submerged and record the temperature and the bridge measurements as before.
measurements as before.

On rectangular coordinate paper construct a graph of resistance as a function of temperature. Use the vertical axis for resistance and the horizontal axis for temperature. Locate $0°$ at the origin and extend the temperature scale to $100°$ C. Provide a suitable resistance scale on the vertical axis so that the graph yields resistance readings slightly above and below the two values found for R_x. (Observe that the origin *cannot* serve to locate zero resistance). Plot the two known points and join them with a straight line; for a pure metal the curve is known to be essentially linear.

By extrapolation (extending the curve beyond known data), read off the resistance at 0° C and at 100° C and record as R_0 and R_T. The final temperature T is recorded as 100° C. Compute the temperature coefficient of resistance and compare it with the accepted value for copper.

2. Resistance of cold lamp filaments

Measure the resistance of a carbon-filament lamp with the Wheatstone bridge; use two or three dry cells in series if necessary for satisfactory bridge performance. Record the required data. Repeat the measurement with a 40-watt tungsten lamp.

DATA

| MATERIAL | Temp. | Bridge measurements | | | | R_0 | R_T | T | α experimental | α accepted | Relative error |
| | | l_1 | l_2 | R_3 | R_x | | | | | | |
	(°C)	(cm)	(cm)	(Ω)	(Ω)	(Ω)	(Ω)	(°C)	(C°⁻¹)	(C°⁻¹)	(%)
Copper											

3. Resistance of hot lamp filaments

Arrange the circuit as shown in Figure 51-1. **CAUTION:** *Completely de-energize the circuit by removing the plug from the supply receptacle before manipulating the circuit components in any way.* Measure the resistance of the hot filaments of the carbon and tungsten filament lamps by the voltmeter-ammeter method. Record the required data in the table below.

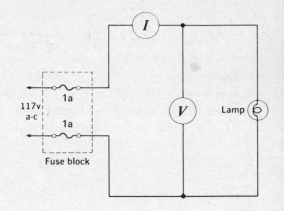

Figure 51-1

DATA

| MATERIAL | Cold filament | | | | Hot filament | | |
| | l_1 | l_2 | R_3 | R_x | Potential difference | Current | R |
	(cm)	(cm)	(Ω)	(Ω)	(v)	(a)	(Ω)
Carbon							
Tungsten							

QUESTIONS (Your answers should be complete statements. Problem solutions should be set down in the space provided below.)

1. Considering the change in resistance with temperature of the carbon and tungsten filaments, how do their temperature coefficients of resistance compare?

_____

_____

_____

2. The resistance of a certain tungsten wire at $0°$ C is 79.00 Ω and the temperature coefficient of resistance of tungsten is $0.0045/C°$. What is the resistance of the wire at $100.0°$ C?

3. How is the fact that all pure metals have an α the order of $0.004/C°$ related to the phenomenon of *superconductivity* of pure metals?

_____

_____

_____

_____

4. What temperature coefficient of resistance would be desirable for a wire used to make the resistance coils of a resistance box?

_____

_____

_____

_____

experiment **52**

Resistances in Series and Parallel

PURPOSE: (1) To measure the resistance of resistance elements joined in series. **(2)** To measure the equivalent resistance of resistance elements joined in parallel.

APPARATUS: The same as for Experiment 49 or 50, depending on the method used.

SUGGESTION: The instructor may wish to substitute resistance spools other than those used in the previous experiments. If equipment is limited, half the group can use the Wheatstone bridge method and the other half the voltmeter-ammeter method. A further comparison of the relative precision of the two methods in resistance measurements can be made.

INTRODUCTION: When resistances are connected in series, the *same* circuit current, I_T, is in each resistance. Each resistance is added to the other resistances in series and their combined resistance equals the sum of all the separate resistances. If R_1, R_2, R_3, etc., are individual resistances joined in series, the total resistance, R_T, is

$$R_T = R_1 + R_2 + R_3 + \text{etc.}$$

When two or more resistances are connected in parallel, more paths are provided for the electric current. The total current in the circuit is *larger* than the current in each separate path. Consequently, the equivalent resistance of the parallel circuit is *smaller* than the resistance of any separate path. If R_1, R_2, R_3, etc., are individual resistances joined in parallel, the reciprocal of the equivalent resistance R_{eq} is equal to the sum of the reciprocals of the resistances in parallel.

$$\frac{1}{R_{eq}} = \frac{1}{R_1} + \frac{1}{R_2} + \frac{1}{R_3} + \text{etc.}$$

Provisions are made in this experiment for determining the resistance of both series and parallel combinations, using the resistances of the separate spools as calculated from their known parameters. Knowing the kind of metal, length, and gauge number of each resistance spool, the resistance of the spool is

$$R = \rho \frac{l}{A}$$

where ρ is the resistivity constant of the metal in ohm centimeters, l is the length of wire in centimeters, A is its cross-sectional area in square centimeters, and R is the resistance of the spool in ohms.

PROCEDURE

1. Wheatstone bridge method

Set up the Wheatstone bridge as it was used in Ex-

DATA Table 1 Wheatstone Bridge Method

METAL	Length (cm)	Gauge	TYPE OF CIRCUIT	l_1 (cm)	l_2 (cm)	R_3 (Ω)	R_x (Ω)
1.							
2.							
1.							
2.							
3.							
4.							
3.							
4.							

periment 50. Insert the series combination of 200 cm of 30 ga nickel-silver and 200 cm of 28 ga nickel-silver as R_x and determine their combined resistance.

Join the same spools of wire in parallel and measure their equivalent resistance. Continue the experiment by measuring the combined resistance of the 160-cm spool of 30 ga nickel-silver wire joined in series with the 2000-cm spool of 30 ga copper wire. Join these spools of wire in parallel and measure the equivalent resistance.

Record all pertinent data and solve for R_x. Also record R_x in the Data Summary table of Part 3.

2. Voltmeter-ammeter method (Alternate method)

As an alternate experiment, the resistances may be found by the voltmeter-ammeter method in the same manner as in Experiment 49. Record all pertinent data and solve for R_x in each case. Also record R_x in the Data Summary table of Part 3.

3. Enter the data from either Part 1 or Part 2 in the Data Summary table. Record the resistivity constant for each spool using the resistivity tables in Appendix B. Calculate the resistance of each spool using the resistivity constant and the wire dimensions. Calculate the value of R_x for each series and parallel combination and compare these values with the corresponding experimental values of R_x. Express the experimental error in each instance as a relative error.

DATA Table 2   Voltmeter-ammeter Method

METAL	Length (cm)	Gauge	TYPE OF CIRCUIT	V_x (v)	I (a)	R_x (Ω)
1.						
2.						
1.						
2.						
3.						
4.						
3.						
4.						

DATA Summary

SPOOL NUMBER	TYPE OF CIRCUIT	Resistivity (Ω cm)	Separate resistances calculated (Ω)	R_x calculated (Ω)	R_x experimental (Ω)	Relative error (%)
1 / 2	series					
1 / 2	parallel					
3 / 4	series					
3 / 4	parallel					

288

experiment **53**

Simple Networks

PURPOSE: To study the relationships between potential difference, current strength, and resistance throughout a simple network.

APPARATUS: 3 d-c ammeters, 0-1 a; 4 d-c voltmeters, 0-3 v; 3 resistance boxes; 6 volt d-c power source; momentary contact switch; annunciator wire, 18 ga, for connections. See Appendix A for instructions in the use of meters.

SUGGESTION: Because the experiment calls for three ammeters, four voltmeters, and three resistance boxes, the instructor may wish to combine laboratory groups or assign it as a demonstration experiment.

INTRODUCTION: No matter how simple or how complicated an electric network is, Ohm's law expresses the relationships between resistance, potential difference, and current in each part of the circuit and over the entire circuit.

PROCEDURE: Set up the apparatus as shown in Figure 53-1. The ammeters A_1, A_2, and A_3, connected in series with each resistance, show the magnitude of current in each resistance. The voltmeters, V_1, V_2, and V_3, connected in parallel with each resistance, show the potential difference across each resistance. Voltmeter V shows the potential difference across the external circuit.

Set resistance boxes R_2 and R_3 at zero, but set R_1 at 10.0 ohms. Close the switch, read each of the meters, and record the values in the data table. You should be able to read to the nearest hundredth of an

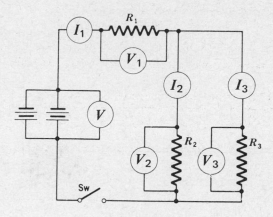

Figure 53-1

ampere and to the nearest hundredth of a volt. Also record the values of the three resistances. As a check on your setup, the reading of ammeter A_2 and ammeter A_3 should be the same. The reading of voltmeter V_2 and voltmeter V_3 should be zero. The reading of voltmeter V_1 should be the same as voltmeter V. If these values are not obtained, open the switch and check the wiring and the resistance boxes for loose connections or loose plugs.

Set the resistances in the three boxes as follows: R_1, 10.0 ohms; R_2, 10.0 ohms; R_3, 10.0 ohms. Close the switch and make all readings. Note that all three resistances have the same value.

Set the resistances in the three boxes as follows: R_1, 10.0 ohms; R_2, 20.0 ohms; R_3, 10.0 ohms. Close the switch and make all readings. In this trial one of the resistances in parallel has twice the resistance of the other.

DATA

TRIAL	V (v)	I_1 (a)	V_1 (v)	R_1 (Ω)	I_2 (a)	V_2 (v)	R_2 (Ω)	I_3 (a)	V_3 (v)	R_3 (Ω)	R_{eq} (Ω)	R_T (Ω)
1.												
2.												
3.												
4.												
5.												

Set the resistances in the three boxes as follows: R_1, 10.0 ohms; R_2, 5.0 ohms; R_3, 10.0 ohms. Close the switch and make all readings.

Set the resistances in the three boxes as follows: R_1, 10.0 ohms; R_2, 2.5 ohms; R_3, 10.0 ohms.

Close the switch and make all readings. In this case one of the resistances in parallel has four times the resistance of the other.

In each case calculate the equivalent resistance of R_2 and R_3 joined in parallel. Also calculate the total resistance of the entire circuit.

QUESTIONS (Your answers should be complete statements.)

What conclusions can you draw about:

1. the total current in the circuit and the current in the parallel branches?

_____

_____

2. the potential difference across each parallel branch?

_____

_____

3. the potential difference across the various parts of a circuit and across the entire circuit?

_____

_____

_____

4. resistance and current in two parallel branches?

_____

_____

5. the relationship between the equivalent resistance of two parallel branches, the potential drop across the branches, and the total current in the branches?

_____

_____

_____

6. the relationship between the potential difference across a circuit, the total resistance of the circuit, and the current in the circuit?

_____

_____

_____

experiment 54

Electric Equivalent of Heat

PURPOSE: To determine the number of calories per joule of electric energy.

APPARATUS: Stopwatch; d-c voltmeter, 0-7.5/ 15 v; d-c ammeter, 0-10 a; tubular rheostat; knife switch, SPST; electric calorimeter with a 2.5 to 5.0 ohm heating coil; thermometer; magnifier; platform balance; set of masses; 6-volt or 12-volt storage battery, or other low voltage d-c source capable of delivering approximately 3 a of continuous current; annunciator wire, 18 ga, for connections. See Appendix A for instructions in the proper use of meters.

INTRODUCTION: Electric energy is converted to heat energy in the resistance of a conductor. In this experiment we will use an electrically heated coil to warm a known mass of water a measured number of Celsius degrees. By observing the time required to heat the water, the current in the heating coil, and the potential difference across its terminals, we can calculate the number of calories per joule of electric energy, or the electric equivalent of heat. Since 1 joule of electric energy = 1 watt s and 1 watt = 1 volt ampere, it is apparent that the electric energy converted to heat energy in the resistance coil is

$$W = VIt$$

All work done by a current in a resistance appears as heat. Thus, the electric energy expended in the resistance is directly proportional to the heat energy that appears.

$$W = JQ$$

Where W is electric energy in joules and Q is the quantity of heat produced in calories, J is the proportionality constant which we shall call the *electric equivalent of heat,* having the dimensions joules/ calorie. Solving this equation for Q, we have a general expression for Joule's law.

$$Q = W/J \qquad \text{(Joule's law)}$$

PROCEDURE: Set up the apparatus as shown in Figure 54-1. A 6-v or 12-v storage battery may be used to furnish the electric energy. Adjust the rheostat for a current of about 2 amperes and immediately open the switch.

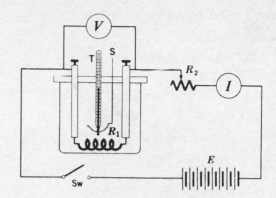

Figure 54-1

The heating coil usually has a resistance of 2.5 or 5.0 ohms, the latter value requiring a 12-volt source for most satisfactory operation. If the heating coil you are to use has different current and voltage requirements, your instructor will provide the information.

Determine the mass of the calorimeter cup. Then fill the calorimeter cup about three-fourths full of water that is about 10 degrees below room temperature. Find the mass of the calorimeter cup and water and seat the cup in its outer jacket. Place the cover on the calorimeter, stir the water thoroughly, and determine its temperature accurately. Use the magnifier to help you read the thermometer to the nearest 0.1°. Observe the time to the nearest second or start the stopwatch just as you close the switch. Immediately read the voltmeter and ammeter as accurately as possible. Keep the current as nearly constant as possible by slight adjustments of the rheostat.

Take both voltmeter and ammeter readings at one-minute intervals and record their final average values in the data table. Stir the water occasionally. Continue the heating until the water is about 10 Celsius degrees above room temperature. Open the switch and record the time to the nearest 0.1 second. Stir the water thoroughly and read the thermometer accurately to the nearest 0.1° when it reaches its highest temperature. Immediately lift the heating unit out of the water.

Take data from a second trial if time permits. Record all pertinent data and make the necessary computations.

DATA

	TRIAL 1	TRIAL 2
1. Mass of calorimeter cup	_____g	_____g
2. Specific heat of calorimeter	_____cal/g C°	_____cal/g C°
3. Mass of calorimeter cup and water	_____g	_____g
4. Voltmeter readings, final average	_____v	_____v
5. Ammeter readings, final average	_____a	_____a
6. Temperature of water and calorimeter, initial	_____°C	_____°C
7. Temperature of water and calorimeter, final	_____°C	_____°C
8. Mass of water heated	_____g	_____g
9. Temperature change of water and calorimeter cup	_____C°	_____C°
10. Heat gained by water	_____cal	_____cal
11. Heat gained by calorimeter cup	_____cal	_____cal
12. Total heat gained, Q	_____cal	_____cal
13. Total time of heat, t	_____s	_____s
14. Electric energy input, W	_____j	_____j
15. Electric equivalent of heat, J (experimental)	_____j/cal	_____j/cal
16. Electric equivalent of heat, J (accepted value)	_____j/cal	_____j/cal
17. Absolute error	_____j/cal	_____j/cal
18. Relative error	_____%	_____%

CALCULATION: Derive an equation from which the *heat* developed in the resistance of an electric circuit can be calculated directly from the *resistance* of the circuit, the *current* in the circuit, and the *time* the current is maintained.

experiment **55**

Electrochemical Equivalent of Copper

PURPOSE: To determine experimentally the electrochemical equivalent of copper.

APPARATUS: Copper cathode, 7.5 × 10 cm (see suggestion below); 6-v storage battery; knife switch, DPST; d-c ammeter, 0-3 a; tubular rheostat, 25 ohm; triple-beam balance, 0.01 g sensitivity; stopwatch or watch with sweep second hand; demonstration cell; copper wire, bare, 14 ga; annunciator wire, 18 ga, for connections; fine sandpaper; copper plating solution (see suggestion below); 1 beaker each of distilled water, alcohol, and acetone for use by the class as dipping baths.

SUGGESTION: The copper plating solution should be made up in advance by dissolving 125 g of $CuSO_4$ · $5H_2O$ in 900 mL of distilled water. When dissolved, *slowly* add (while stirring) 35 mL of concentrated H_2SO_4 and 50 mL of ethyl alcohol.

The copper cathode should be cut from copper sheet so as to be shaped into a cylinder. A strip should be left extending beyond the top of the cylinder to accomodate the electrode clamp of the cell. The detail of a cathode blank most suitable for the particular electrode clamps to be used can best be determined by the instructor.

INTRODUCTION: The electrodeposition of copper is an electrolytic process: an oxidation-reduction chemical reaction. In this experiment a careful determination will be made of the mass of copper deposited by the passage of a known quantity of electric charge through the electroplating cell.

Michael Faraday first observed that the mass of an element deposited during electrolysis is directly proportional to the quantity of charge that passes and to the chemical equivalent (atomic weight/valence) of the ion. A charge of 96,500 coulombs (1 faraday) deposits the chemical equivalent of any element in grams. Such quantities of elements are said to be *electrochemically equivalent.* The electrochemical equivalent, z, of an element is the mass of the element, in grams, deposited by 1 coulomb of electricity.

$$z = \frac{m}{Q} \tag{1}$$

Where m is the mass in grams of an element deposited and Q is the quantity of electricity in coulombs passed through the cell, z is the electrochemical equivalent of the element in g/c.

Since the quantity of electric charge, Q, is determined by the product of the current in the circuit in amperes and the time in seconds,

$$z = \frac{m}{It} \tag{2}$$

PROCEDURE: Clean the copper cathode with steel wool or fine sandpaper until it has a smooth polished surface. Shape it into a cylinder suitable for clamping into the cell to be used. *Handle between the folds of a clean towel to avoid finger contact.* Why? Deter-

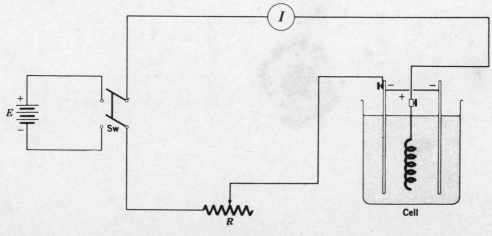

Figure 55-1

mine the mass of the cathode to the nearest 0.01 g and record in the data table. Clean a section of heavy copper wire and form a spiral anode of suitable length by winding the wire around a lead pencil. Then carefully assemble the cell (do not add the electrolyte until you are ready to put the cell in operation).

Arrange the circuit as shown in Figure 55-1. Be certain that the cylinder is connected as the cathode and the spiral as the anode. Estimate as accurately as you can the cathode area to be submerged in electrolyte and compute an appropriate current magnitude to be used on the basis of about 0.02 a per cm² of cathode area. Carefully mark this reading on the glass face of the ammeter to aid in monitoring the current during the timed operation of the cell.

With the rheostat resistance all in the circuit, add the electrolytic solution to the predetermined level and *close the switch just long enough to quickly adjust the rheostat to give approximately the current reading indexed.* Open the switch immediately and prepare to start a timed operation of 20 to 30 minutes duration.

Start the timed operation by closing the switch and quickly adjust the rheostat for the precise current reading. Record the initial time (if stopwatch is not the timing device) and monitor the circuit to maintain the current reading indexed on the ammeter.

At the end of the timed operation open the circuit, record the time, remove the cathode from the cell, and carefully dip it in distilled water, then in alcohol, and finally in acetone. When dry, determine the mass of the cathode to the nearest 0.01 g and record.

CALCULATIONS: From the data collected, compute the experimental value of the electrochemical equivalent of copper. Enter the accepted value from Appendix B, Table 19, and compute your relative error.

DATA

1. Time, initial _____

2. Time, final _____

3. Elapsed time _____ s

4. Average current _____ a

5. Quantity of electricity passed _____ c

6. Mass of cathode, initial _____ g

7. Mass of cathode, final _____ g

8. Mass of copper deposited _____ g

9. z for copper (experimental) _____ g/c

10. z for copper (theoretical) _____ g/c

11. Absolute error _____ g/c

12. Relative error _____ %

experiment 56

Magnetic Field about a Conductor

PURPOSE: To study the effect of the magnetic field that is set up in vertical and horizontal conductors by currents in them.

APPARATUS: Galvanoscope, with binding posts for a single turn, a few turns, and many turns of wire; annunciator wire, 18 ga, for connections; dry cell; d-c ammeter, 0-1 a; rheostat, approximately 25 ohms; momentary contact switch, SPST; 1 large compass; Ampère's law stand; 4 small compasses.

SUGGESTION: A galvanoscope can be improvised by wrapping a single turn, a few turns, and many turns of insulated wire into a coil large enough to accommodate the large compass.

For best results, all apparatus should be isolated from local magnetic fields, such as those created by d-c power supplies. For that reason, dry cells are recommended as the source of d-c current.

INTRODUCTION: The Danish physicist Hans Christian Oersted (1777-1851) was the first to show that a current in a conductor produces a magnetic field about the conductor, proving that there is a relation between electricity and magnetism. A magnetic needle placed near a conductor carrying an electric current is deflected. In this experiment we shall study the magnitude and direction of these deflections.

PROCEDURE

1. Horizontal conductors

Place the large compass inside the galvanoscope

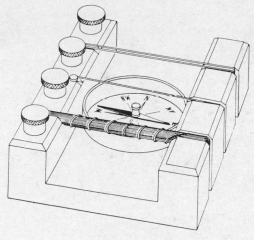

Figure 56-1

coil of many turns. Turn the galvanoscope until the turns of wire lie in the North-and-South plane as indicated by the compass needle. Next turn the compass around until its N-pole is directly above the zero index of the compass card. Connect a dry cell that is in series with a rheostat, ammeter, and switch to the binding posts serving the coil of many turns in such a manner that electron flow will be from *south to north* through the loop segments *above* the needle. *With all the resistance of the rheostat in the circuit,* close the switch and adjust the current to a magnitude that just produces the maximum deflection of the compass needle. Record the current, the direction in which the N-pole of the compass needle is deflected, and the number of degrees of deflection. *By rheostat adjustments, maintain this same magnitude of current for all galvanoscope tests in Part 1.*

DATA   Horizontal Conductor

COIL	Current (a)	Electron flow	Deflection direction	Deflection (°)
Many turns		S to N		
Many turns		N to S		
Few turns		S to N		
Few turns		N to S		
Single turn		S to N		
Single turn		N to S		

Reverse the direction of the electron flow and adjust the rheostat if necessary to supply the same current as before. Note the direction and magnitude of the deflection of the needle and record.

Keeping the galvanoscope in the same position, move the compass until it is inside the coil of a few turns. Connect the supply circuit to the proper binding posts so the electron flow will be from south to north above the needle. Adjust the rheostat to give the same current previously recorded and observe the direction and magnitude of deflection. Reverse the direction of electron flow, and again observe and record the readings.

Repeat the experiment using the coil of one turn, with the electrons first flowing from south to north above the needle, and then from north to south.

2. Vertical conductor

Arrange the 4 small compasses on the Ampère's law stand as shown in Figure 56-2. Connect the terminals to the supply circuit so that the electrons flow upward. Adjust the rheostat to supply the *least*

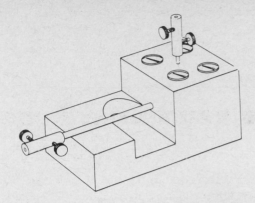

Figure 56-2

current that will yield conclusive deflections of the compass needles. Note the position taken by the needles. Reverse the direction of the electron flow. Observe the directions indicated by the N-poles of the compass needles, and make sketches in the labeled squares to show them for each case. Do not leave the switch closed any longer than is required to make your observations.

Vertical conductor

No current   Electrons flowing downward   Electrons flowing upward

QUESTIONS (Your answers should be complete statements.)

1. State the rule that enables you to predict the direction in which the N-pole of a compass will be deflected if it is placed beneath a conductor through which electrons are flowing.

_____

_____

2. The flow of electrons through a conductor is from south to north. In which direction will the N-pole of a compass needle placed over the conductor be deflected?

_____

3. State the rule that enables you to predict the direction in which the magnitude lines of flux circle a vertical conductor through which electrons are flowing.

_____

_____

_____

4. A compass is placed to the east of a vertical conductor. In which direction must electrons flow through the conductor to cause the N-pole of the compass to point south?

_____

Galvanometer Constants

PURPOSE: To determine the resistance, current sensitivity, and voltage sensitivity of a galvanometer.

APPARATUS: Wheatstone bridge, slide-wire form; 4 resistance boxes, 1 of the order of 100 ohms, 2 of 1000 ohms, 1 of 10,000 ohms; galvanometer; tubular rheostat, approximately 200 ohms for meter resistance of the order of 100 ohms, approximately 500 ohms for meter resistance of the order of 40 ohms; knife switch, SPST; contact key; annunciator wire, 18 ga, for connections; 2 new No. 6 dry cells; d-c voltmeter, 0-3 v.

SUGGESTION: Part 1 should be performed by each laboratory group. Part 2, however, may be performed as a demonstration due to the number and variety of resistance boxes required.

INTRODUCTION: Due to the resistance of a conductor, there is a fall of potential between two points on a conductor carrying a current. If a circuit is connected across two such points, a current proportional to the IR drop between these points will be established in the circuit; the difference of potential is used as a source of emf.

A galvanometer connected in the slide circuit between two points on a length of resistance wire, as shown in Figure 57-1, enables us to observe the rela-

tion between the current in the slide circuit and the distance between the contact points on the resistance wire. We shall assume that the deflection of the galvanometer is directly proportional to the magnitude of current in it and, since its resistance remains constant, to the voltage applied across the slide circuit.

The sensitivity of a galvanometer may be expressed in several ways. Collectively, these expressions are known as the galvanometer constants. The most commonly used constants are *current sensitivity* and *voltage sensitivity*. Current sensitivity k is defined as the current required to produce a deflection of one scale division and is expressed in *microamperes per scale division*. Voltage sensitivity is defined as the potential difference across the terminals that produces a deflection of one scale division. Voltage sensitivity may be derived from the current sensitivity and resistance of the galvanometer according to Ohm's law.

In the circuit of Figure 57-2, we shall assume that the internal resistance of new dry cells is negligible and that R_3 is very large compared to R_2 so that the current in the galvanometer is negligible compared to that in R_1 and R_2. The battery current in R_1 and R_2 is

$$I = \frac{E}{R_1 + R_2}$$

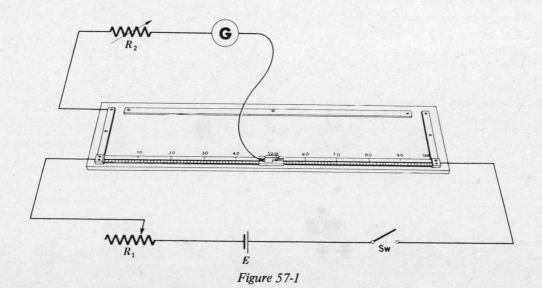

Figure 57-1

The potential difference across R_2 is

$$V_2 = IR_2$$

Substituting the value of I

$$V_2 = \frac{ER_2}{R_1 + R_2}$$

The current in the galvanometer, I_G, is

$$I_G = \frac{V_2}{R_3 + R_G}$$

where R_G is the galvanometer resistance. If the current I_G causes a pointer deflection s, then the current sensitivity k is

$$k = \frac{I_G}{s}$$

Substituting

$$k = \frac{1}{s} \times \frac{ER_2}{(R_1 + R_2)(R_3 + R_G)}$$

PROCEDURE

1. Galvanometer resistance

Connect the circuit as shown in Figure 57-1. The battery should consist of at least two dry cells connected in *parallel*. The resistance box, 111 ohms, is connected as R_2.

Set R_2 at zero resistance and adjust the rheostat R_1 so that all resistance is in the circuit. Close the switch and readjust R_1 for a convenient galvanometer deflection less than midscale when the slider contacts the resistance wire at midpoint, the 50-cm mark. Record the deflection and the initial slide position. *Keep the knife switch open at all times except when actually taking a reading.*

Move the slider to the 100-cm mark. The length of resistance wire across which the galvanometer is connected is now doubled. Thus, the voltage drop is doubled, and the potential difference placed across the galvanometer circuit, the current in the galvanometer, and the galvanometer deflection are all doubled. Record the deflection and the final slide position.

Adjust the resistance of R_2 to return the galvanometer deflection to its initial reading. According to Ohm's law, if V is doubled, R must be doubled in order to maintain I constant. The original resistance in the slide circuit was that of the galvanometer itself. Thus, the value of R_2 must equal the galvanometer resistance R_G.

Repeat the entire procedure several times, each time selecting new initial slider positions and adjusting R_1 as necessary, and then double the slider setting, adjusting R_2 to return the galvanometer to the initial deflection. Record three trials that are in close agreement and average the resistance of R_2 to give an average value of galvanometer resistance R_G.

2. Current sensitivity

Connect the circuit as shown in Figure 57-2. R_1 and R_2 are resistance boxes of the order of 1000 ohms each; R_3 is a resistance box of the order of 10,000 ohms. The battery should consist of at least two new dry cells in *parallel*. The contact key **K** is closed only to take occasional readings of E to be sure there is no variation during the experiment. *Keep the switch **Sw** open at all times when not taking galvanometer readings.* Set R_1 at $30\overline{0}$ ohms and leave constant for all trials. For the initial trial, set R_2 at 500 ohms and R_3 at $800\overline{0}$ ohms. Momentarily close the knife switch observing whether the galvanometer deflection is a convenient readable value. If not, make other initial settings of resistances, but keep $R_1 + R_2$ fairly

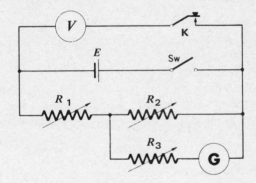

Figure 57-2

DATA Galvanometer Resistance

TRIAL	Original slider position (cm)	Original deflection relative	Final slider position (cm)	Final deflection relative	R_G (Ω)
1					
2					
3					
Average					

large and R_3 at least 2 or 3 thousand ohms larger than R_2. Record R_1, R_2, R_3, and the galvanometer deflection s.

Make at least four trials with different combinations of R_1, R_2, and R_3 and record the pertinent data required.

Using the expression for the current sensitivity k derived in the Introduction, solve for k for each trial. The galvanometer resistance R_G is the average value determined for your instrument in Part 1.

3. Voltage sensitivity

Using the average value of the galvanometer resistance R_G and the average value of the current sensitivity k, determine the voltage sensitivity of your galvanometer.

Assuming enough significant digits in your experimental results, calculate to the nearest 0.1 ohm the amount of resistance required in series with your galvanometer in order for a potential difference of 1 volt to produce a deflection of one scale division.

DATA Current Sensitivity

TRIAL	R_1 (Ω)	R_2 (Ω)	R_3 (Ω)	s relative	k (μa/div)
1					
2					
3					
4					
5					
6					
Average					

experiment **58**

Electromagnetic Induction

PURPOSE: **(1)** To study some of the phenomena of electromagnetic induction. **(2)** To determine the factors that influence the magnitude and direction of induced currents. **(3)** To recognize the principle of the electric generator.

APPARATUS: Pair of bar magnets, or a large horse-shoe magnet; compact coil of approximately 100 turns wound on brass or plastic spool through which the bar magnet will pass; insulated copper wire, 22 ga and 28 ga; test tubes, one 200 mm X 25 mm, one 150 mm X 18 mm for making electromagnets for Part 2 (student-type primary and secondary coil set with iron core may be used for Part 2); twine; galvanometer, zero center; contact key, or push button; dry cell; tubular rheostat, about 10 ohms; iron rod suitable as a core.

SUGGESTION: Suitable coils of wire for Parts 1 and 3 may be made up and tied with twine to make them permanent. The coils for Part 2 may be made as follows: Wrap 80 turns of 28 ga insulated copper wire in a single layer around a large test tube, 200 mm X 25 mm. Wrap forty turns of 22 ga wire in a single layer around a regular size tube, 150 mm X 18 mm. The free ends of the coils may be secured by rubber bands. The wrapped smaller test tube will slip inside the larger one for the experiment.

INTRODUCTION: After Oersted discovered that electricity and magnetism were related, Michael Faraday in England and Joseph Henry in the United States both began investigating the use of magnets in the generation of electricity. Working independently, both found at nearly the same time that an emf can be induced across a conductor that is moving through a magnetic field in such a manner that there is relative motion between the conductor and the magnetic flux. Faraday is usually given credit for the pioneer work that led to the invention of the electric generator, while Henry pioneered in developing the electromagnet and the principles of self-induction.

PROCEDURE

1. Induction with a permanent magnet
Connect the ends of a compact coil to a sensitive

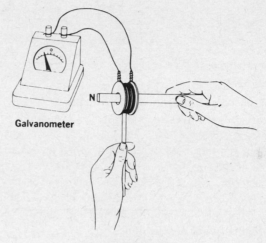

Galvanometer

Figure 58-1

galvanomter and then thrust the coil over the N-pole of a magnet, as shown in Figure 58-1.

Result? _____

_____

Remove the coil quickly. Repeat both motions more slowly.

Result? _____

_____

Repeat the experiment, but thrust the coil down over the S-pole of the magnet and then remove it quickly.

Holding the coil stationary, thrust one pole of the magnet into the coil, remove it quickly, and then try the other pole. Repeat both motions more slowly.

Result? _____

_____

2. Induction with an electromagnet
Attach the terminals of a large coil of about 80 turns of fine insulated wire, about 28 ga, to a galvanometer, as shown in Figure 58-2. Connect the terminals of a small coil of about 40 turns of insulated 22 ga copper wire in series with a contact key, a dry cell, and a rheostat. Slip this coil inside the large coil, adjust the rheostat as necessary to provide an

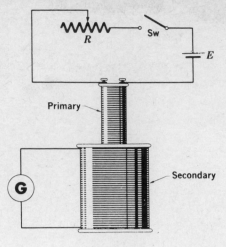

Figure 58-2

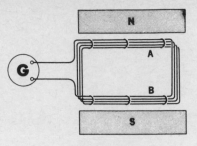

Figure 58-3

appropriate deflection, and observe the galvanometer: 1. when the circuit is closed; 2. when the circuit remains closed for a few seconds; 3. when the circuit is interrupted suddenly; 4. when the magnitude of the current is varied; 5. when the direction of electron flow is reversed by changing the battery connections; 6. when an iron rod is placed inside the small coil and the circuit is opened and closed. Record all of your observations.

3. The generator principle

Wind about 20 turns of 28 ga insulated copper wire into a coil like that shown in Figure 58-3. The oblong coil should be of such a size that it can be rotated between the poles of the magnet that you are using. Tie the separate turns together with twine to make a compact coil, and leave at least 46 cm at each end of the loop so it can be easily attached to the galvanometer. Hold the end of the coil between the thumb and finger so that the coil is between the poles of a horseshoe magnet or a V-magnet formed by two bar magnets. Give the coil a sudden twist so that its upper half **A** will move about 60° past the N-pole of the magnet. Note the direction in which the galvanometer needle is deflected. Continue to turn the coil until that part of the loop **B** is nearly adjacent to the N-pole. Note the deflection of the needle. See whether you can find a position for the loop in which the turning of its coils will cause no deflection of the needle. Rotate the loop in the opposite direction and observe the results. Record all observations.

experiment 59

The Electric Motor

PURPOSE: To study the construction and operation of an electric motor.

APPARATUS: Demonstration motor (St. Louis type is satisfactory); dry cell or storage cell; compass; 2 dual range d-c ammeters, 0-3/30 a; annunciator wire, 18 ga, for connections.

INTRODUCTION: A d-c motor consists of three parts: **(1)** the field magnet, which sets up a stationary magnetic field; **(2)** the armature, which is free to turn on its axis when attracted and repelled by the stationary magnetic field of the field magnet; and **(3)** the commutator, which acts as a current reverser, and the brushes, by means of which the current enters the armature. When the commutator changes the direction of the current, the poles of the armature also change polarity. In order to keep the armature turning, the current must change direction in the armature at such a time that the poles of the armature will be continuously repelled and attracted by the poles of the field magnet. That means that the N-pole of the armature is always repelled by the N-pole of the field magnet and attracted to the S-pole of the field magnet. It means, too, that at the same time, the S-pole of the armature is repelled by the S-pole and attracted by the N-pole of the field magnet. The polarity of the armature is reversed at just the right time to keep the rotation continuous.

PROCEDURE

1. The commutator and the armature

Remove the bar magnets or electromagnet from the demonstration motor and connect the armature to the cell. Use a small compass to test the polarity of the armature in different positions as you turn it slowly through a complete revolution. At what position of the armature does its polarity change? What causes this change in polarity?

Observation: _____

_____

In Figure 59-1 indicate the polarity of the armature at 30° intervals of its rotation.

Reverse the dry cell connections to the armature. Test the polarity of the armature now throughout a complete revolution. How does the polarity compare with that found previously?

Observation: _____

_____

In Figure 59-2 indicate the polarity of the armature at 30° intervals of its rotation. Restore the armature and dry cell connections to their original arrangement.

2. Magnetic field furnished by permanent magnets

Place the permanent magnets in their holders with the N-pole of one magnet to the left of the armature and the S-pole of the other magnet to the right of the armature. Give the armature a gentle push to start it rotating. In Figure 59-1 mark the polarity of the field magnets and the direction of rotation of the armature.

Reverse the connections between the dry cell and the armature. In Figure 59-2 mark the polarity of the field magnets and the direction of rotation of the armature.

Reverse the polarity of the field magnets, making the pole to the left of the armature an S-pole and that to the right of the armature an N-pole.

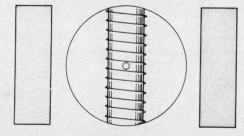

Figure 59-1

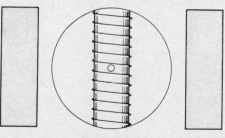

Figure 59-2

Observation: _____

_____

Reverse the armature connections once again.

Observation: _____

_____

What keeps the armature rotating when the poles of the armature and the field are all in a straight line?

_____

_____

3. The series-wound motor

Replace the bar magnets with the electromagnet, and connect the cell in such a manner that the armature and field are in series, as in Figure 59-3. Test the polarity of the field magnet and the polarity of the armature as the armature makes a complete revolution.

Observation: _____

_____

Permit the motor to run freely and note the direction of rotation of the armature. Reverse the connections to the dry cell. What effect does this have on the direction of rotation of the motor?

_____

_____

Reverse the connections to the field magnet only. What effect does this have on the direction of rotation of the motor?

_____

_____

In what other way can such a motor be reversed?

_____

_____

Connect an ammeter in series (high range first) with the dry cell and motor. Prevent the armature from rotating, and read the ammeter.

Armature stationary _____

Now permit the armature to rotate and observe the ammeter readings as the armature comes up to speed.

Ammeter reading at full speed _____

Explain. _____

_____

4. The shunt-wound motor

Connect the cell with the motor so that the field magnet and the armature are connected in parallel. See Figure 59-4. Test the polarity of the field magnet and the polarity of the armature as the armature makes a complete revolution.

Observation: _____

_____

Insert an ammeter in each branch of this circuit so that it is possible to measure the current in the field coil and in the armature separately. Hold the armature to prevent it from rotating, and read the ammeters.

Field coil _____

Armature _____

Now let the motor come up to speed. Read the ammeters again.

Field coil _____

Armature _____

Explain these observations. _____

_____

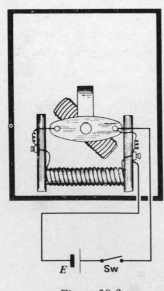

Figure 59-3

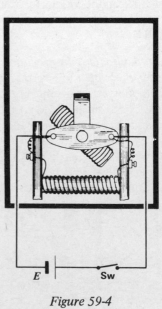

Figure 59-4

experiment 60

Capacitance in a-c Circuits

PURPOSE: (1) To observe the effects of capacitance in a-c circuits. (2) To determine the reactance of capacitors.

APPARATUS: Knife switch, DPST; 4 dry cells or other d-c power source; d-c milliammeter, low range (a galvanometer shunted with fine wire will serve); d-c voltmeter, 0-7.5 v; 6-v lamp, No. 40 miniature screw base, 150 ma; lamp base, miniature screw; 2 test leads with alligator clips; capacitors (25 v), 1-25 μf, 2-50 μf; 6- volt filament transformer, or other 6-vac source; a-c milliammeter, 0-200 ma; a-c voltmeter, 0-7.5 v; annunciator wire, 18 ga, for connections.

INTRODUCTION: A *capacitor* is a combination of conducting plates separated by a dielectric and is used in electric circuits to store electric charge. The ratio of the charge on either plate to the potential difference between the plates is called *capacitance* and is a constant for any fixed capacitor. It is ordinarily expressed in microfarads. The difference in the effect of capacitance in a-c and d-c circuits will be observed in this experiment.

A good quality capacitor offers essentially pure reactance to an alternating current and thus the capacitive reactance can be determined directly from the current in the capacitor circuit and the potential difference across the capacitor. This voltage may be assumed to lag the circuit current by 90°.

PROCEDURE

1. Capacitors in d-c circuits

Make up a 6-volt battery with standard dry cells to serve as a d-c source. Arrange a No. 40 pilot lamp, a 25 μf capacitor, and a d-c milliammeter in series and connect to the battery through a DPST knife switch, as shown in Figure 60-1. Attach short test leads with alligator clips on the free ends to a d-c voltmeter. While observing the milliammeter, close the switch. Was there any initial movement of the milliammeter pointer? _____ Describe it. _____

_____

_____

_____

Does the lamp light up? _____

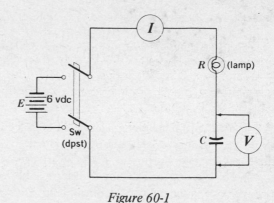

Figure 60-1

Giving attention to the polarity of the voltmeter terminals, clip the voltmeter across the lamp and then across the capacitor. Result?

_____

_____

Explain the two voltmeter readings and the milliammeter reading.

_____

_____

_____

_____

With the voltmeter clipped across the capacitor, open the switch. Explain the action of the voltmeter.

_____

_____

What is the discharge path of the capacitor when the switch is open?

_____

Charge and discharge the capacitor several times, observing closely the rate at which the meter pointer falls to zero. Can you detect any change in rate?

_____

If a 20,000 ohm per volt d-c voltmeter is available, place it across the capacitor and observe the discharge rate.

305

Replace the 25 µf capacitor with a 50 µf capacitor and repeat the measurements and observations. Place a second 50 µf capacitor in *parallel* with the one in the circuit. What is the total capacitance now in the circuit?

Observe the discharge rate on the voltmeter. (This may not be very successful unless a 20,000 ohm per volt voltmeter can be used.) As the meter pointer approaches zero during the discharge cycle, observe carefully. Can you suggest the type of curve that would result from a graph of V_C as a function of time during the discharge of C?

2. Capacitors in a-c circuits

Replace the d-c milliammeter and the d-c voltmeter with a-c instruments. Replace the battery circuit with a 6-vac source. The circuit should be arranged as shown in Figure 60-2. The lamp will serve as both a resistance and visual indicator in the circuit. The resistance of the filament will change, however, with the filament temperature.

With the two 50 µf capacitors in parallel, measure the circuit current I, the potential difference V applied across the series combination of R and C, the voltage V_R across the lamp, and the voltage V_C across the capacitor. Read each value to the degree of precision your instruments will allow and record in the data table along with the total capacitance used. How do the voltages across the lamp and the capacitor compare with the applied voltage?

Replace one of the 50 µf capacitors with a 25 µf capacitor, connecting it in parallel with the remaining 50 µf capacitor. Repeat all measurements and record. Next, record all measurements with 50 µf capacitance in the circuit, then with 25 µf in the circuit.

What would be the total capacitance in the circuit if you connected a 50 µf and a 25 µf capacitor in series?

From the data you have already collected, predict the magnitude of circuit current and the potential drop across the series capacitors. Try this series combination in the circuit. Result?

After measuring V_C, predict how the voltage V_C is divided between the two capacitors in series. Measure the potential drop across each. Do the measured voltages agree with your prediction? _____

Explain. _____

_____

_____

Do not record these data in the data table.

CALCULATIONS

1. From the circuit current I and the potential difference across the lamp V_R, calculate the resistance of the lamp filament, R, for each set of observations and record the values of R in the data table.

2. Similarly, calculate the values of the capacitive reactance X_C and record in the data table. A good quality capacitor acts as an essentially pure reactance and thus the potential difference V_C measured across it may be considered to be a reactance voltage.

3. Capacitive reactance produces a lagging voltage and is plotted in a negative direction, producing a negative phase angle. Knowing capacitive reactance and the series resistance, the phase angle ϕ is an angle whose tangent is $-X_C/R$.

$$\phi = \arctan \frac{-X_C}{R}$$

Determine the phase angle ϕ in each case and record.

4. Since R, X_C, and ϕ are known, the magnitude of the impedance Z of each circuit may now be found

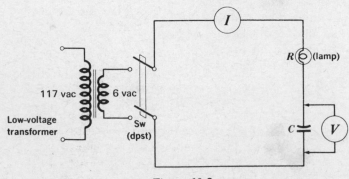

Figure 60-2

by any one of several methods. Record these magnitudes in the data table.

5. Using a straightedge and a protractor, construct voltage vector diagrams for each set of data. Choose a scale that will allow the four diagrams to be arranged on one page. Identify each by the capacitance value used and show the impedance magnitude and phase angle as found graphically.

DATA

C (μf)	I (ma)	V (v)	V_R (v)	V_C (v)	R (Ω)	X_C (Ω)	Z (Ω)	ϕ ($^\circ$)

QUESTIONS (Your answers should be complete statements.)

1. Compare the performance of a capacitor in d-c and a-c circuits.

_____

_____

_____

_____

_____

_____

_____

2. How does capacitive reactance vary with capacitance and with frequency?

_____

_____

_____

_____

_____

3. How do you explain the voltages measured across each capacitor when the 25 μf and 50 μf capacitors were connected in series?

_____

_____

_____

_____

_____

4. Explain the fact that you found the lamp filament to have a different resistance for each different value of capacitance placed in the series circuit.

_____

_____

_____

_____

_____

experiment **61**

Inductance in a-c Circuits

PURPOSE: (1) To observe the effects of inductance in a-c circuits. (2) To determine the reactance of inductors.

APPARATUS: Storage battery, 6 volt; knife switch, DPDT; primary and secondary coil set with iron core, student type; lamp, 6-volt carbon filament; lamp base with socket; d-c ammeter, 0.3 a; d-c milliammeter, 0-100 ma; d-c voltmeter, 0-7.5 v; 2 test leads with alligator clips; 6-volt filament transformer, or other 6-vac source; tubular rheostat, about 10 ohms; a-c ammeter, 0-3 a; a-c milliammeter, 0-50 ma; a-c voltmeter, 0-7.5 v; annunicator wire, 18 ga.

INTRODUCTION: An inductor is simply a coil of wire in its usual form. Because the wire has resistance, it offers resistive opposition to current in both d-c and a-c circuits. In a-c circuits there is the additional effect of inductance, an inertia-like property opposing any change in current. The effects of inductance will be observed in this experiment.

The inductance of a coil may be varied by varying the amount of iron in the core; by withdrawing the iron core the inductance is decreased and by inserting the iron core it is increased. Because an inductor offers both resistance and inductive reactance to an alternating current, the current does not lag the voltage by the full 90°. If we know the d-c resistance of the coil, and we measure the voltage across it and the current in the inductor circuit, we can find the impedance of the circuit. Knowing both the impedance magnitude and the phase angle, the inductive reactance and the inductance of the coil can be computed.

PROCEDURE

1. Inductor in a d-c circuit

Arrange the circuit as shown in Figure 61-1. Be careful to observe the proper polarity in connecting the d-c ammeter and voltmeter. *Do not connect the transformer to the a-c line at this time.* Use the primary coil of a small induction coil set as the inductor *L*. Connect test leads to the voltmeter and clip it across the coil.

Throw the switch to the d-c source and observe the lamp while inserting and withdrawing the iron core of the coil.

Result? _____

_____

Can you determine the resistance of the coil with this circuit?

_____

_____

If the voltage reading across the coil is too low to read directly, determine it indirectly by using the more accurate midscale region of the meter.

2. Inductor in an a-c circuit

Before connecting the circuit to the a-c source, replace the d-c meters with a-c instruments, using an a-c ammeter, 0-3 a range. Throw the switch to the a-c source and adjust the rheostat to provide the same voltage as the battery. Observe the lamp intensity while inserting and withdrawing the iron core.

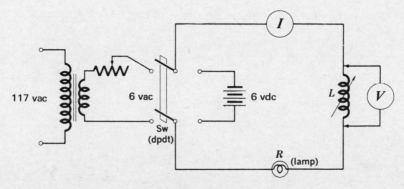

Figure 61-1

Result? _____

_____

Read the circuit current and the potential difference
across the coil as the inductance is varied. How do
you explain the meter readings?

_____

_____

_____

3. Inductive reactance

Replace the primary coil with the larger secondary
coil and remove the lamp from the circuit entirely.
Determine the resistance R_L of the coil by replacing
the a-c meters with a d-c voltmeter and a d-c milliammeter, 0-100 ma. De-energize the a-c source completely and switch to the d-c source. Read the meters
as accurately as possible, compute the resistance of
the inductor, and record as R_L in the data table.

Replace the d-c milliammeter with an a-c milliammeter, 0-50 ma, and the d-c voltmeter with the a-c
voltmeter. Place the iron core in the secondary coil
and switch to the a-c source. Adjust the rheostat for
a convenient current reading and record I and V_L,
reading as accurately as possible.

CALCULATIONS

1. Knowing the circuit current I and the potential
difference V_L across the circuit, calculate the circuit
impedance and record.

2. The power factor in an a-c circuit is defined as
the ratio of the circuit resistance to the circuit impedance. This ratio is the cosine of the phase angle ϕ

$$pf = \frac{R}{Z} = \cos\phi$$

Therefore, the phase angle is an angle whose cosine
equals the power factor

$$\phi = \arccos\frac{R}{Z}$$

Determine the phase angle ϕ and record in the
data table.

3. Using a separate sheet of unlined paper, a
straightedge, and a protractor, construct the impedance vector diagram. Find the magnitude of X_L
graphically and record. Attach this sheet to your
laboratory report.

4. Inductive reactance is directly proportional to
both the frequency and the inductance and is expressed as $X_L = 2\pi fL$.

Assume the frequency of your a-c source to be 60
hz and calculate the inductance L of your coil. Record this value in the data table.

DATA

I (ma)	V_L (v)	R_L (Ω)	Z (Ω)	ϕ ($°$)	X_L (Ω)	L (h)

QUESTIONS   (Your answers should be complete statements.)

1. Explain the difference in the effect of an inductor in d-c and a-c circuits.

_____

_____

_____

_____

2. What would be the effect on the current in the a-c circuit of Part 3 if the frequency of the source were
doubled?

_____

_____

_____

_____

3. How could the impedance diagram be converted to a voltage diagram?

_____

_____

experiment **62**

Series Resonance

PURPOSE: To observe the condition of electric resonance in a series circuit containing inductance, capacitance, and resistance.

APPARATUS: Capacitor decade box, 0.01 μf to 1.1 μf in 0.01 μf steps; 3 inductors, filter chokes ranging from 8 to 30 h; lamp, 117 v, clear glass 7 to 25 watts; lamp base with socket; plugs and split line for 117-v receptacle; a-c milliammeter, 0-50/300 ma (determined by lamp used); a-c voltmeter, 0-600 v, with insulated test leads; a-c voltmeter, 0-150 v; annunciator wire, 18 ga, for connections.

SUGGESTION: Because of the equipment requirements and the danger of electric shock from exposed connections to the 117-vac service, it is recommended that the instructor perform this experiment as a demonstration.

INTRODUCTION: A practical inductor offers both resistance and inductive reactance to an alternating current. We may consider the resistance and reactance to act in series. Thus, the voltages appearing across an inductance and a capacitance in series in an a-c circuit are of opposite polarity. If X_L is larger than X_C, the load is inductive and the potential difference across the circuit leads the current. However, if X_C is the larger reactance, the load is capacitive and the circuit voltage lags the current. In general, the impedance Z of the circuit has a magnitude and a phase angle ϕ that can be expressed as

$$Z = \sqrt{R^2 + (X_L - X_C)^2}$$

and

$$\phi = \arctan (X_L - X_C)/R$$

Figure 62-1 shows that over a range of low frequencies the load of an L, R, C series circuit is capacitive and over a range of high frequencies the load is inductive. At some intermediate frequency the inductive and capacitive reactances are equal and the reactance of the circuit ($X_L - X_C$) equals zero; this is the condition of *series resonance*. The impedance is equal to the resistance, the circuit current is maximum, and the voltage across the circuit is in phase with the circuit current.

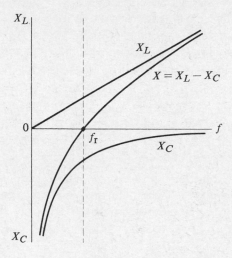

Figure 62-1

For a particular combination of L and C, there is one resonance frequency f_r. At this frequency

$$X_L = X_C, \; 2\pi f_r L = \frac{1}{2\pi f_r C}, \; f_r{}^2 = \frac{1}{4\pi^2 LC}, \; f_r = \frac{1}{2\pi\sqrt{LC}}$$

Where L is in henrys and C is in farads, f_r is expressed in hertz.

In this experiment we shall supply a signal voltage at a fixed frequency, 60 hz, to a series circuit consisting of a fixed inductor, an indicator lamp, and a variable capacitor. See Figure 62-2. We will select the capacitance that allows the maximum (resonant) current in the circuit and, by solving for L, we will be able to determine the inductance of the coil.

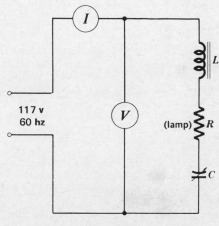

Figure 62-2

PROCEDURE: Mark each inductor for identification purposes. Filter chokes commonly range from about 7 henrys to nearly 30 henrys. Assuming a frequency of 60 hz, compute the limiting values of capacitance necessary to produce resonance over this range of inductance. By using a capacitance decade box of suitable range in which the smallest capacitance is 0.01 μf, you will be able to find the desired value of capacitance to the nearest 0.01 μf.

Connect one inductor, the indicator lamp, the capacitance decade box, and a milliammeter of suitable range (if available) in series. Connect the voltmeter across the entire load. When the circuit components are arranged for maximum accessibility and all exposed connections are secure, plug the circuit into the 117-vac receptacle.

CAUTION: *Dangerous electric shock is possible from the exposed circuit connection at this voltage. A standard rubber-covered plug should be used and removed from the receptacle before any change is made in the circuit.*

Determine the rough setting of the decade box that provides the highest luminous intensity of the lamp. Then, by observing the meter deflection, find the resonating capacitance to the nearest 0.01 μf. Record this capacitance C, the resonant current I, and the applied voltage V in the data table. Using insulated probes, momentarily connect a voltmeter,

600-v range, across the inductor (*CAUTION*) and record the potential difference as V_L. Also record V_R and V_C.

Unplug the circuit before making any circuit changes. What function does the voltmeter connected across the circuit serve when the plug is removed from the receptacle? Short out the inductor and observe the effect on the circuit. Remove the short from the inductor. Now short out the capacitor and observe the effect on the circuit.

Results? ────────────────────

────────────────────────────

────────────────────────────

In a similar manner test at least two other inductors, recording the necessary data in the table.

CALCULATIONS

1. The impedance of a series L, R, and C circuit is minimum at resonance and is equal to R_T, which is composed of the resistance of the lamp filament and the inherent resistance of the inductor turns. Compute the impedance of each circuit and record. From the data recorded, determine the approximate resistance of each inductor.

2. Assuming the frequency of the applied voltage to be $\overline{60}$ hz, compute the inductance of each inductor used.

DATA

INDUCTOR USED	C (f)	I (ma)	V (v)	V_L (v)	V_R (v)	V_C (v)	$Z = R_T$ (Ω)	R_L (Ω)	L (h)

QUESTIONS (Your answers should be complete statements.)

1. How do you explain the voltages recorded across different components of the resonant circuit?

──

──

──

──

──

2. What would be the effect on the resonant current if the lamp were removed from the circuit?

_____

_____

_____

3. Since the capacitance in the circuit is not continuously variable, the precise point of resonance may not be obtainable using the procedure of this experiment. Assuming that the precise resonance point had been obtained, should V_L and V_C be expected to read precisely the same? Explain.

_____

_____

_____

_____

experiment 63

Thermionic Emission

PURPOSE: To determine the relation between the electric emission of a vacuum tube and the cathode temperature as controlled by the filament voltage.

APPARATUS: Diode, type 6H6, or triode, type 6J5; octal socket, mounted; d-c milliammeter, 0-50 ma; d-c voltmeter, 0-7.5 v; rheostat, 50 ohms, 25 watt; knife switch, SPST; contact key; "A" battery, 12-v storage battery or 6 dry cells; "B" battery, 22.5-v and 45-v terminals (Burgess type 5308, or equivalent); annunciator wire, 18 ga, for connections; cross-section paper.

INTRODUCTION: The conductivity of metals is the result of the movements of free electrons within the material. Free electrons move about inside the conductor with a speed that increases with temperature. Attractive forces at the surface of the material normally restrain the free electrons and keep them within the material.

If an electron is to escape from the surface of a conductor, it must do the work necessary to overcome the surface forces. The energy for this escape must come from the electron's kinetic energy, which results from its motion. When an electron's kinetic energy exceeds the work it must perform to overcome the surface forces, it can escape into the space beyond the surface. At high temperatures the average kinetic energy of the free electrons is large, and an appreciable number are able to escape from the surface of the material. Thus the number of electrons escaping from the surface of a material is related to the nature of the material (surface forces) and its absolute temperature. The escaping of electrons

from the surface of a hot body is called *thermionic emission.*

Electron emission in practically all receiving-type vacuum tubes is derived from cathodes coated with a mixture of barium and strontium oxides over which is formed a surface layer of metallic barium and strontium. Such emitters may be heated to their operating temperature either indirectly by radiation from an incandescent tungsten filament or directly by the conduction of filament current.

An electron-emitting cathode in a vacuum tube is surrounded by an electron cloud that constitutes a negative space charge. If the cathode is surrounded by a plate or anode, as in a diode, electrons from the space charge are attracted to the plate when a positive plate potential is applied. This movement of electrons constitutes a plate current and is conveniently measured by a milliammeter in the plate-cathode circuit. In this experiment we shall hold the plate voltage constant and measure the change in plate current as the temperature of the cathode filament is varied. The variation in temperature will be accomplished by varying the potential difference across the filament.

PROCEDURE: On separate paper set up a data table, using the headings shown at the end of the procedure. Include this data sheet with your report of this experiment.

One section of a 6H6 twin diode or a 6J5 triode may be used. The triode can be operated as a diode by connecting the grid directly to the plate. The socket connection diagrams (bottom views) for both tube types are given in Figure 63-1. If another tube type is to be used, you should have modifying in-

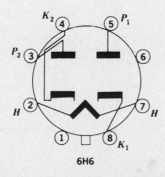

6H6

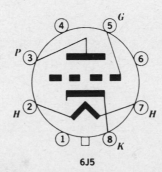

6J5

Figure 63-1

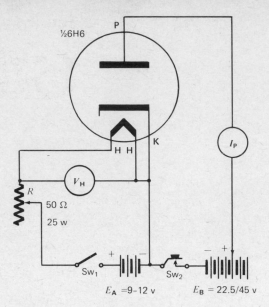

Figure 63-2

structions from your instructor before proceeding.

Connect the vacuum tube in the test circuit as shown in Figure 63-2. Be careful to follow the proper socket diagram for pin connections. Return the plate to the 22.5-v terminal of the "B" battery and record this voltage as your initial value of E_P. When the circuit connections are completed, place all the resistance of the rheostat R in the filament circuit, leave the switch Sw_1 open, and request that your instructor inspect your circuit before you proceed further.

Close the contact key Sw_2 when milliammeter readings are required. Does the milliammeter show any current in the plate-cathode circuit while the cathode-heater circuit is open? The contact key Sw_2 is placed in the plate circuit to protect the tube from excessive plate current when the heater voltage is increased beyond the rated value of approximately 6 volts. When taking plate current readings above this

heater voltage, close the plate circuit only long enough to get a steady milliammeter reading. Close the heater switch and read the initial voltage across the filament. Did you expect it to be zero with maximum R in the circuit? Explain the voltmeter reading.

Adjust the rheostat for the nearest even half volt across the filament. Record this voltage as your initial heater voltage reading V_H in the proper E_P column of the data table. Record also the milliammeter reading for the plate current I_P. Increase the heater voltage in half-volt increments, allowing sufficient time between adjustments to permit the filament to reach a constant temperature. When the first indication of plate current appears (Sw_2 must be closed), be sure that the milliammeter pointer is steady before recording data. Record data for filament voltages to 7.5 v, opening the heater switch after the final reading.

Return the plate to the 45-v terminal on the "B" battery and repeat the procedure, recording V_H and I_P as before.

DATA

TUBE TYPE			
E_P = _____ v		E_P _____ v	
V_H (v)	I_P (ma)	V_H (v)	I_P (ma)

DATA REDUCTION: Prepare a graph of plate current as a function of heater voltage for each value of plate voltage used. Plot V_H as abscissas and I_P as ordinates and construct smooth curves, both on the same sheet. Attach this graph, properly labeled, to your regular report.

QUESTION (Your answer should be a complete statement.)

Explain why your two curves had separated (assumed different slopes) by the time the design voltage of the heater, approximately 6 v, was reached.

_____

_____

_____

_____

_____

_____

_____

experiment 64

Vacuum Diode Characteristics

PURPOSE: To determine the change in plate current of a diode with increases in plate voltage.

APPARATUS: Diode, type 6H6, or triode, type 6J5, with grid connected to the plate; octal socket, mounted; d-c milliammeter, 0-15 ma; d-c voltmeter, 0-7.5 v; d-c voltmeter, 0-150 v, 20,000 ohms/volt or VTVM; "A" battery, 12-v storage battery or 6 dry cells in series; "B" battery, 135 v (3 Burgess type 5308, or equivalent); rheostat, 50 ohms, 25 watts; potentiometer, 4000 ohms, 10 watts; knife switch, SPST; contact key; 4 resistors, 5 watts, 10,000 ohms, 20,000 ohms, 40,000 ohms, and 80,000 ohms; annunciator wire, 18 ga; cross-section paper.

INTRODUCTION: When the plate of a diode is made positive with respect to the cathode, space-charge electrons are attracted to the plate and the tube *conducts*. Emission from an oxide-coated cathode is quite abundant; at normal plate voltages, electrons are supplied to the space charge by the emitting cathode as rapidly as they are removed by the plate. When a full space charge is present, the plate current depends upon the plate voltage. The modern diode would probably be damaged by the excessive plate voltage before this voltage could be raised enough to cause the total electron emission to be in transit to the plate.

In this experiment the heater temperature of a diode will be maintained at the normal level and the positive voltage applied to the plate will be varied. By measuring the plate current, I_P, through a range of plate voltages, V_P, you will be able to plot a characteristic curve of diode plate current as a function of plate voltage. Different values of plate-load resistance can be introduced and a family of characteristic curves can be plotted.

PROCEDURE: Arrange a data table, using a heading similar to the one that follows. Provide for 14 lines of data. Include this data sheet with your report of this experiment.

Arrange the diode circuit as shown in Figure 64-1, using one section of a 6H6 twin diode or a 6J5 triode connected as a diode, *but with the negative terminal of the milliammeter connected directly to the diode plate* ($R_L = 0 \ \Omega$). Refer to the tube-base diagrams of Figure 63-1, Experiment 63, for proper pin connections. The potentiometer R_2 is connected across the plate supply battery E_B through the contact key Sw_2 to conserve the "B" battery. Plate voltage adjustments and plate current readings are made with the contact key closed; at other times Sw_2 should be left open.

Adjust R_2 for an initial plate voltage V_P of 0 v. Close the knife switch Sw_1, adjust the rheostat R_1

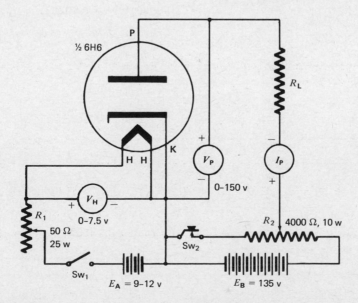

Figure 64-1

for a heater voltage V_H of 6 v, and allow the tube to warm up to normal operating temperature. Take plate current readings at plate voltage intervals of 5 v from 0 v to 20 v. Record V_P and I_P in the appropriate column in the data table. Open the heater circuit (Sw_1) while preparing the circuit for the next series of readings and between all successive series of readings.

Place a resistance R_L of 10,000 ohms in the plate circuit by inserting the resistor between the diode plate and the milliammeter. Take plate current read-ings at plate voltage intervals of 10 v from 0 v to 120 v and record in the data table. Repeat the readings for an R_L of 20,000 ohms, of 40,000 ohms, and of 80,000 ohms.

DATA REDUCTION: Prepare a family of charac-teristic diode curves of plate current as a function of plate voltage on a sheet of rectangular coordinate paper. Plot I_P as ordinates and V_P as abscissas for each value of R_L. Attach the graph, properly labeled, to your regular report.

DATA

TUBE TYPE:								HEATER VOLTAGE:	v
$R_L = 0\ \Omega$		$R_L = 10,000\ \Omega$		$R_L = 20,000\ \Omega$		$R_L = 40,000\ \Omega$		$R_L = 80,000\ \Omega$	
V_P (v)	I_P (ma)	V_P (v)	I_P (ma)	V_P (v)	I_P (ma)	V_P (v)	I_P (ma)	V_P (v)	I_P (ma)

QUESTIONS (Your answers should be complete statements.)

1. What is the source of the energy that is delivered to the diode (energy input) during its operation in a circuit?

2. How is this energy first expended in the tube and what is the energy transformation?

3. What is the evidence that the plate is heated, other than the proximity of the plate to the cathode heater, and what is the energy transformation?

4. What could cause the plate to be warmed to a red heat during the tube operation?

5. Why was the plate voltage limited to a low value when making plate-current readings with a minimum of resistance in the plate circuit (no load resistance added)?

6. From the diode characteristic curves, under what circumstance does the plate current appear to be directly proportional to the plate voltage?

experiment 65

Vacuum Triode Amplifier

PURPOSE: To study factors that influence the voltage gain of a vacuum triode amplifier.

APPARATUS: Power supply, 6.3 vac at 0.3 a, 180 vdc at 10 ma; 6J5 triode; a-c/d-c voltmeter, VTVM multi-range; oscilloscope; audio generator; octal socket, mounted; capacitor, electrolytic, 25 μf, 25 v; capacitors, paper, 400 v, two 0.002 μf, one 0.05 μf; resistors, carbon, ½ watt, one 1800 ohms, one 10,000 ohms, one 15,000 ohms, one 22,000 ohms, one 47,000 ohms, three 100,000 ohms, one 1,000,000 ohms; leads with insulated alligator clips for connections.

SUGGESTION: Because of the apparatus required for this experiment, it is suggested that it be performed as a demonstration. The instructor may prefer to have each student study the experiment procedure in advance of the demonstration and prepare a suitable data table in which to record all pertinent measurements and calculation results. The data table should be a part of the student's report of the experiment.

INTRODUCTION: The primary consideration in the use of the triode as a voltage amplifier is the voltage gain developed across the circuit: that is, the ratio of the alternating output voltage developed across the plate circuit to the alternating input voltage applied to the grid. If the input signal is small, the tube operation is essentially linear and the output

signal is a faithful, amplified reproduction of the input. This is an essential characteristic of an amplifier at audio frequencies.

In this experiment we shall determine the voltage gain of the amplifier and recognize the influence that different circuit components have on the gain and on the character of the output signal.

PROCEDURE: Arrange the amplifier circuit as shown in Figure 65-1. A metallic cold-water pipe provides a good ground connection. Supply 6.3 vac across the heater and 180 vdc to the plate circuit. **CAUTION:** *De-energize the plate circuit before making any circuit changes.* Connect an audio signal generator across the input circuit and an oscilloscope across the output circuit.

With heater and plate power on, measure the following d-c voltages *with respect to ground* (d-c voltmeter): *a.* d-c plate supply voltage, *b.* voltage at the plate of the tube, *c.* cathode voltage, and *d.* grid voltage. What is the control-grid bias? What is the bias-voltage polarity with respect to the cathode? Verify both the polarity and magnitude of the bias voltage by measuring directly with the d-c voltmeter. How do you account for the difference between the plate supply voltage and the voltage at the plate of the tube? Measure the potential drop across R_L.

Observation: _____

_____

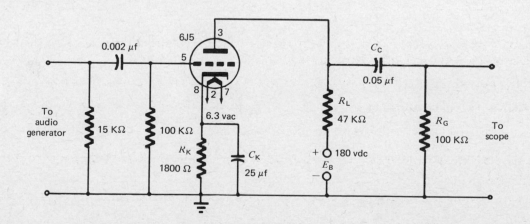

Figure 65-1

_____

_____

_____

Apply a signal voltage of 1000 hz from the audio generator to the amplifier input circuit. Adjust the input signal to 0.50 v, measuring the a-c voltage at the generator terminals (a-c voltmeter). Adjust the oscilloscope to obtain an oscillogram of the output signal of no more than two wavelengths. What is the appearance of the output wave form? Is there any evidence of amplitude distortion? How can you determine this? Measure the a-c voltage at the output terminals (scope terminals). What is the voltage gain of the amplifier?

Observation: _____

_____

_____

_____

With the a-c voltmeter across the signal generator terminals, increase the input signal until a definite indication of wave form distortion appears on the scope. Describe. The signal input voltage is an rms value. It corresponds to a sine wave of voltage having what peak or maximum value? Considering the d-c grid bias, to what can you attribute the distortion?

Observation: _____

_____

_____

_____

Remove the cathode bypass capacitor C_K from the cathode circuit by disconnecting the ungrounded lead. (*CAUTION*) What change is observed in the output wave form of the scope? What is the effect on voltage gain? Can you suggest an explanation based on the change in the path of the a-c component of the plate

current? Measure the d-c voltage between grid and cathode (d-c voltmeter). Compare this voltage with the bias voltage previously measured.

Observation: _____

_____

_____

_____

Return the input signal to 0.50 v and replace C_K. Replace the 47,000-ohm R_L with a 22,000-ohm resistor. **CAUTION**: *De-energize the plate circuit before making any circuit changes.* Measure the a-c output voltage as before and determine the gain. How has it changed? Change R_L to 10,000 ohms (*CAUTION*) and determine the gain. What conclusion can you reach regarding the influence of R_L on the voltage gain of the amplifier?

Observation: _____

_____

_____

_____

Determine the effect of C_C and R_G on the output voltage. Replace R_G with a 10,000-ohm resistor (*CAUTION*). Result? Next, replace C_C with a 0.002 μf capacitor. Result? Considering C_C and R_G as a voltage divider in parallel with R_L for the a-c component of V_L, explain the changes in the a-c signal output observed. Now replace R_G with a 1-megohm resistor. Result? Is the change in gain what you expected? Can you suggest an explanation?

Observation: _____

_____

_____

_____

_____

QUESTIONS (Your answers should be complete statements.)

1. Why is the a-c output voltage measured at the oscilloscope terminals rather than at the plate of the triode?

_____

_____

_____

_____

2. a. Why is the grid-to-cathode voltage reduced when the cathode capacitor C_K is removed? **b.** Would this same reduction in bias occur with the a-c input signal removed?

_____

_____

_____

_____

_____

_____

3. What causes the portion of the output wave form corresponding to the positive peak of the input signal on the grid to become flattened (distorted)?

_____

_____

_____

_____

4. What causes the opposite peak of the output wave form to become flattened?

_____

_____

_____

5. Suggest a possible use for the performance described in Questions 3 and 4.

_____

_____

_____

experiment 66

Diode Characteristics of the P-N Junction

PURPOSE: (1) To compare the relationships of current, voltage, and resistance in an ohmic resistance circuit and in a semiconductor diode. (2) To observe the directional resistance in the P-N junction.

APPARATUS: N-P-N power transistor, RCA 2N1490; d-c milliammeter, 0-1 ma; d-c microammeter (optional); d-c voltmeter, VTVM with 0-1 vdc range; No. 6 dry cell, 1.5 v; rheostats, 10 KΩ and 100 KΩ, ½-watt molded composition TV control potentiometers will do; resistor, 1 KΩ, wirewound; knife switch, SPST; connecting leads.

SUGGESTION: Due to the type of apparatus required for this experiment, it is suggested that it be performed as a demonstration. The instructor may prefer to have one laboratory group prepare the demonstration. Each student should study the experiment procedure in advance and prepare a suitable data table in which to record all pertinent measurements.

NOTE: A rheostat has a fixed terminal at one end of the resistance element and a terminal on the movable contact. The usual laboratory "rheostat" is actually a potentiometer with fixed terminals at both ends of the resistance element and a terminal on the movable contact. A rheostat cannot be used as a potentiometer, but a potentiometer can be used as a rheostat by connecting only one end-terminal and the movable-contact terminal into the circuit.

If a small control potentiometer is to be used as the rheostat R_1 of Procedure Part 2, it is important that the student determine which rotation of the shaft (clockwise or counterclockwise) places *maximum* resistance into the circuit. This is determined by which one of the two end terminals is used. The middle terminal is for the movable-contact connection.

The rheostat R_1 acts as the current-limiting resistor required to protect the junction diode. If rheostat R_1 were mistakenly adjusted to minimum instead of maximum resistance before applying power to the circuit, the diode would be damaged by the excessive circuit current when the switch is closed.

INTRODUCTION: A junction transistor consists of two P-N junctions back-to-back with a thin P-type or N-type region separating the junctions. The N-P-N transistor used in this experiment is one in which the two junctions are separated by P-type material. See Figure 66-1.

The N-type semiconductor crystal is an electron-rich material. It is characterized by equal numbers of free electrons and bound positive charges. The *negative* charge carriers, the free electrons, are the *majority* carriers mainly responsible for its conductivity. Its *minority* carriers are positive *holes* into which electrons can fall.

The P-type semiconductor crystal is a hole-rich material. It is characterized by equal numbers of free positive holes and bound negative charges. The *positive* charge carriers, the positive holes, are the *majority* carriers mainly responsible for its conductivity. Its *minority* carriers are negative electrons.

By connecting only the emitter and base terminals of the transistor into the test circuit, the transistor performs the functions of a P-N junction diode. If

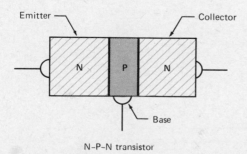

N-P-N transistor

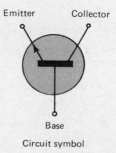

Circuit symbol

Figure 66-1

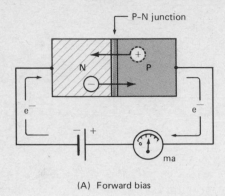

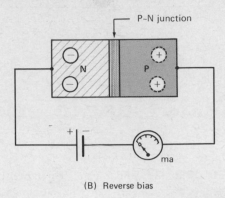

(A) Forward bias

(B) Reverse bias

Figure 66-2

the P-type base is charged positively and the N-type emitter is charged negatively by impressing a very small potential difference across the diode (forward bias), free electrons are repelled across the junction into the P-crystal. Simultaneously positive holes cross into the N-crystal. An electron current is established in the external circuit, as shown in Figure 66-2(A).

If the battery connections are reversed (reverse bias), as in Figure 66-2(B), the free electrons of the N-crystal and the free holes of the P-crystal are attracted away from the P-N junction and the junction region is depleted of charge carriers. In this condition the junction has much higher resistance than the P- and N-regions on either side of the junction. Consequently, charge conduction across the P-N junction and the net electron current in the external circuit are essentially zero.

A sensitive microammeter in the external circuit may register a feeble electron current. This negligible current is the result of minority-carrier conduction across the junction of the reverse-biased diode.

When a small potential difference is applied across the junction in the forward sense, the junction permits unidirectional electron flow with ease in the external circuit—the diode characteristic. Thus, the P-N junction is the rectifying element of semiconductor crystals.

PROCEDURE

1. Ohmic resistance

Arrange the circuit as shown in Figure 66-3. Recheck the meter polarities to assure that the milliammeter and the VTVM are connected properly. Use the 0-1 vdc VTVM scale across R_2. *Leave the switch open at all times except when adjusting the circuit and taking meter readings.*

Set the rheostat R_1 for maximum resistance and close the switch. Adjust the rheostat for a potential difference of 0.30 v across R_2 and read the milliammeter for the current in R_2, *estimating the last significant figure.* Open the switch and record the voltage V_2 and the current I_2 in a suitable data table.

Repeat the potential difference adjustment, increasing the potential difference across R_2 in 0.10-v steps to 0.60 v. Record both V_2 and I_2 for each step. Open the switch after the final readings are taken.

2. The P-N junction diode, forward-biased

Arrange the circuit as shown in Figure 66-4 and leave the switch in the open position. Observe the correct polarities of the d-c meters and of the base and emitter connections of the transistor. Use the 0-1 vdc VTVM scale across the emitter-base junction. Recall that this P-N junction performs as a semicon-

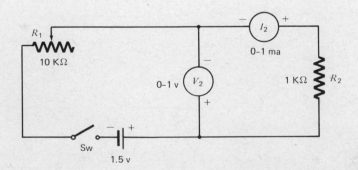

Figure 66-3

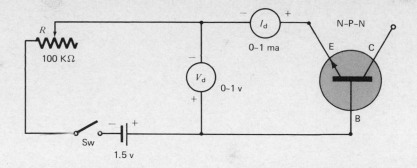

Figure 66-4

ductor diode when the collector section of the transistor is not connected into the circuit. How can you determine that the junction diode is forward-biased in this circuit?

Set the rheostat R for maximum resistance. CAUTION: *See the NOTE inserted earlier in this experiment.* Close the switch and adjust the rheostat for a potential difference of 0.40 v across the diode. Read the milliammeter for the diode current, *estimating the last significant figure.* Record the diode voltage V_d and the diode current I_d in your data table.

Repeat the potential difference adjustment, increasing the potential difference across the diode in 0.04-v steps to 0.60 v. Record both V_d and I_d for each step. Open the switch after the final readings are taken.

3. The P-N junction diode, reverse-biased

Arrange the circuit as shown in Figure 66-5 by reversing the battery connections to make the transistor base positively charged and the emitter negatively charged. Note that the milliammeter and voltmeter connections must also be reversed to ob-

serve their proper polarity. How can you determine that the junction diode is reverse-biased in this circuit?

Close the switch and gradually adjust the rheostat R for minimum resistance while observing the milliammeter for an indication of diode current. Result? Open the switch.

OPTIONAL: If a microammeter is available, substitute it for the milliammeter and repeat the above procedure. Result?

GRAPH: Plan the vertical and horizontal axes of a full-page graph to accommodate the data collected in both Parts 1 and 2. Using the data collected in Procedure 1, construct a graph of the current in R_2 as a function of the potential difference across R_2. Plot the values of V_2 as abscissas and the values of I_2 as ordinates. Label this graph "resistance."

On the same graph, plot the data collected in Procedure 2. Plot the diode current I_d as a function of the potential difference V_d. Label the graph "junction diode."

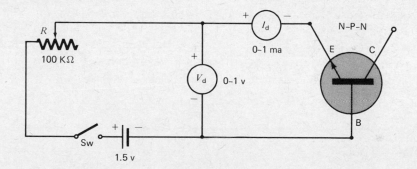

Figure 66-5

QUESTIONS (Your answers should be complete statements.)

1. **a.** Describe your graph of Part 1, the resistance circuit. **b.** How do you interpret this graph?

_____

_____

_____

_____

2. Calculate the ratio V_2/I_2 for the values of V_2 and I_2 obtained in each set of readouts recorded in your data table. Do the results support your interpretation in Question 1b?

_____

_____

_____

_____

3. **a.** Describe your graph of Part 2, the junction-diode circuit. **b.** How do you interpret this graph?

_____

_____

_____

_____

_____

_____

_____

_____

4. Explain the absence of an appreciable diode current when the P-N junction is reverse-biased.

_____

_____

_____

_____

_____

5. What characteristic of the P-N junction accounts for its performance as a diode?

_____

_____

_____

6. The electric current inside a P-N junction diode is described in terms of both positive holes and negative electrons. How can you explain the fact that the current in the external circuit consists of electrons only?

_____

_____

_____

_____

experiment **67**

Junction Transistor Characteristics

PURPOSE: (1) To graph characteristic curves for a common-base transistor circuit. (2) To determine the power gain and current gain of a common-base circuit. (3) To determine the current gain of a common-emitter circuit.

APPARATUS: N-P-N transistor, RCA 2N1490 or Motorola 2N3713-3716; 2 d-c milliammeters, 0-5 ma, 0-50/500 ma; 2 d-c voltmeters, 0-3 v, 0-15 v; 2 batteries, 1.5 v, 12 v; 2 rheostats, 100 ohm (2 w), 1000 ohm (2 w); 2 knife switches, SPST; connecting leads.

INTRODUCTION: Transistor circuits are of three types depending on which transistor element is *common* to the bias supplies for the other two elements. These circuits are called *common-emitter, common-base,* and *common-collector.* In N-P-N transistor circuits the N-type emitter is forward-biased: negative with respect to the P-type base. The N-type collector is reverse-biased positively. See Figures 67-1 and 67-2. In P-N-P transistor circuits the polarities of the bias voltages are reversed.

A small signal applied to the input circuit of a transistor can be amplified because the magnitude of collector current in its output circuit is controlled by the current in its input circuit. The performance characteristic of a transistor in a specific circuit configuration is expressed in terms of a current ratio.

A common-base configuration is shown in Figure 67-1. The collector current I_C is independent of the collector-to-base voltage V_{CB} but is dependent on the magnitude of the emitter current I_E. Variations in I_E produce variations in I_C. At a constant magnitude of V_{CB}, the ratio of the change in I_C to

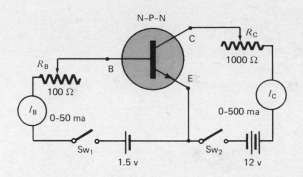

Figure 67-2

the change in I_E expresses the *current gain of the common-base circuit.* This ratio is called the alpha (α) characteristic of the common-base circuit.

$$\alpha = \frac{\Delta I_C}{\Delta I_E} \ (V_{CB} \text{ constant})$$

The alpha characteristic, the forward current gain, of a common-base circuit is always slightly less than unity. Typical values of α range from 0.95 to 0.99. Although the collector current is slightly smaller than the emitter current, a power gain is realized because of the high impedance of the output circuit.

A common-emitter configuration is shown in Figure 67-2. Base currents are very small compared to emitter and collector currents. In the common-emitter circuit small variations in base current I_B produce large variations in collector current I_C. At a constant magnitude of collector-to-emitter voltage V_{CE}, the ratio of the change in I_C to the change in I_B expresses the *current gain of the common-emitter cir-*

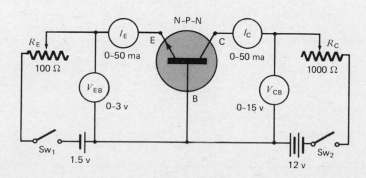

Figure 67-1

cuit. This ratio is called the beta (β) characteristic of the common-emitter circuit.

$$\beta = \frac{\Delta I_C}{\Delta I_B} \quad (V_{CE} \text{ constant})$$

Typical values of β range from 20 to 200.

PROCEDURE

1. Common-base circuit

Arrange the common-base circuit as shown in Figure 67-1. Before proceeding further, check meter, battery, and transistor connections to assure correct polarities.

With the switches open, set both rheostats for maximum resistance. Close both switches and adjust the emitter rheostat R_E for an emitter current I_E of 10.0 ma. Check the collector rheostat R_C setting to ascertain that the potential difference V_{CB} is its minimum value, 0 v or very nearly so. With I_E at 10.0 ma, record V_{CB} and I_C in the appropriate columns of the data table, *estimating the last significant figure in the meter readouts* (and in all subsequent meter readouts).

Adjust R_E as necessary to hold I_E constant at 10.0 ma and increase V_{CB} to 2.0 v. Record V_{CB} and I_C. In a similar manner maintain I_E constant at 10.0 ma and increase V_{CB} in 2.0-v steps to 12.0 v, recording I_C and V_{CB} for each 2-v step.

Repeat the procedure for I_E values of 20.0 ma, 30.0 ma, 40.0 ma, and 50.0 ma. Adjust R_E as required to hold I_E constant during the V_{CB} 2-v steps for each I_E value. Record the I_C and V_{CE} readouts for each V_{CE} step in each I_E value. In the step in which I_E is 30.0 ma and V_{CB} is 12.0 v (or as

nearly 12.0 v as your battery will allow), also record V_{EB} in the space provided at the bottom of the data table.

2. Common-emitter circuit

Arrange the circuit as shown in Figure 67-2. Again re-check the circuit for correct polarities of meter, battery, and transistor connections before proceeding.

With the switches open, set the collector rheostat R_C for minimum resistance and the base rheostat R_B for maximum resistance. Close both switches and adjust the base rheostat R_B for a collector current I_C of 400.0 ma. Record I_B and I_C, estimating the last significant figure for each readout. Leaving R_C as set originally, adjust R_B for a collector current I_C of 500.0 ma and record I_B and I_C in the data table. By leaving the collector rheostat R_C unchanged, V_{CE} may be assumed to remain constant.

DATA Common-emitter Circuit

I_B (ma)	I_C (ma)	ΔI_B (ma)	ΔI_C (ma)	β

GRAPH: Using your data for the common-base circuit, Part 1, construct a full-page graph of collector current I_C as ordinates vs. collector-to-base voltage V_{CB} as abscissas. Plot the set of data for each value of I_E as a separate curve on the graph to give a family of common-base output characteristics. Label each curve with its value of I_E.

DATA Common-base Circuit

V_{CB} (v)	I_C				
	I_E = 10.0 ma (ma)	I_E = 20.0 ma (ma)	I_E = 30.0 ma (ma)	I_E = 40.0 ma (ma)	I_E = 50.0 ma (ma)
V_{EB} (at I_E = 30.0 ma and V_{CB} = 12.0 v)					v

CALCULATIONS

1. Determine the forward current gain, alpha, of the common-base configuration from your family of output characteristics. Select a constant collector-base voltage V_{CB} (suggestion: 6.0 v), and determine at this constant voltage the change in collector current, ΔI_C, caused by a change in emitter current, ΔI_E, of 20.0 ma. To do this, select the points on your graph where the selected constant voltage line intercepts the 10.0-ma and 30.0-ma curves. Transfer the vertical distance between these points to the I_C axis and determine the change in I_C from the ma scale.

Verify these values of ΔI_C and ΔI_E by determining them independently from your data table. Select the same constant V_{CB} voltage line of data and determine the change in I_C between the values posted on that line in the 10.0-ma and 30.0-ma columns. Calculate your common-base alpha factor.

2. Determine the power gain for the common-base circuit from the data recorded for an I_E of 30.0 ma and a V_{CB} of 12.0 v.

3. Determine the forward current gain, beta, of the common-emitter circuits.

QUESTIONS (Your answers should be complete statements.)

Considering your graph of collector current vs. collector voltage for different values of emitter current in the common-base circuit:

1. How is the collector current affected by the collector voltage?

_____

_____

_____

2. How is the collector current related to the emitter current?

_____

_____

_____

experiment **68**

Radioactivity

PURPOSE: (1) To study the effect of radioactive materials on an electroscope and on a Geiger tube. (2) To study the absorptive effect of air, cardboard, aluminum, and lead on beta radiation.

APPARATUS: Simple electroscope; wool pad; hard-rubber rod; stopwatch, or watch with second hand; Geiger tube and associated counting apparatus; various radioactive samples; 20 cardboard sheets, $1\overline{0}$ cm square, 1.0 mm thick; 15 aluminum sheets of the same size; 15 lead sheets of the same size.

INTRODUCTION: The nuclei of the atoms of radioactive materials break down spontaneously with the resultant emission of particles and rays: alpha particles, beta particles, and gamma rays. Radiation can be detected by an electroscope and by a Geiger tube. While alpha particles ionize gas molecules in the air and discharge an electroscope, their penetrating power is not great enough to affect a Geiger tube. Beta particles and gamma rays are detected by the Geiger tube.

In this experiment the radioactivity of several materials will be determined. The penetrating power of beta particles given off from radioactive materials and the effect of cosmic rays on a Geiger tube will also be observed.

PROCEDURE

1. Effect of radioactive materials on an electroscope

Charge an electroscope by induction using the wool pad and hard-rubber rod. Determine the rate of discharge of the electroscope by observing how much the leaves collapse during a fifteen-minute period. Now recharge the electroscope and place a radioactive sample below the leaves of the electroscope. Observe the rate of discharge of the electroscope during a fifteen-minute period. (Other parts of the experiment may be performed in the intervals between these observations.) Record your observations.

Observation: _____

_____

_____

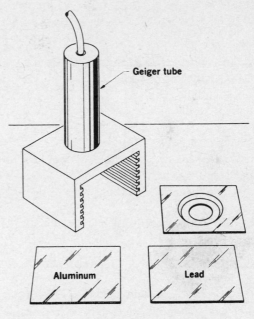

Figure 68-1

2. Effect of radioactive materials on a Geiger tube

a. Background count. Set the Geiger counter apparatus in operation. Note the frequency of clicks when there are no radioactive materials near the tube. In accurate work this background count must be subtracted from all other measurements.

Observation: _____

_____

_____

_____

b. Intensity of radiation. Place a radioactive sample at such a distance from the Geiger tube that you obtain the maximum count reading that the apparatus can measure. Record this reading.

_____ Repeat this procedure with the other radioactive samples.

Observation: _____

_____

_____

331

DATA

Distance	Count	Distance	Count	Distance	Count

3. Absorptive effect of air on beta particles

Place a radioactive sample 5.0 cm from the Geiger tube. Determine the count. Now place the sample 10.0 cm from the tube. Again determine the count. Continue to move the sample away from the tube in 5.0-cm intervals up to a distance of 60.0 cm. Make a count reading for each position and record the measurements in the data table. Do not forget to subtract the background count in each case if it is significant.

GRAPH: Plot a curve of these data, using the distances as abscissas and the counts as ordinates.

4. Absorptive effect of other materials on beta radiation

Place a radioactive sample close to the Geiger tube so as to obtain the maximum reading of which the counter is capable. Record this count in the data table. Now place one sheet of cardboard between the sample and the tube. Make a count reading. Continue to place additional sheets of cardboard between the sample and the counter tube, making a count reading after the addition of each sheet. Use a total of 20 sheets of cardboard.

Repeat the experiment but use sheets of aluminum instead of cardboard. Make readings when 1, 2, 3, 4, 5, 7, 10, 12, and 15 sheets of aluminum are placed between the counter and the radioactive sample.

Repeat the experiment, using sheets of lead this time. Make readings when 1, 2, 3, 4, 5, 7, 10, 12, and 15 sheets of lead are used.

GRAPH: Plot curves of these data on the same sheet of graph paper, using the number of sheets of various materials as abscissas and the counts as ordinates. Use different colored pencils to draw the graph lines so that the curves may be identified.

DATA

CARDBOARD				ALUMINUM		LEAD	
No. sheets	Count	No. sheets	Count	No. sheets	Count	No. sheets	Count
0		11		0		0	
1		12		1		1	
2		13		2		2	
3		14		3		3	
4		15		4		4	
5		16		5		5	
6		17		7		7	
7		18		10		10	
8		19		12		12	
9		20		15		15	
10							

Which is the most effective material for absorbing beta radiation?

_____   _____

_____   _____

_____   _____

QUESTIONS   (Your answers should be complete statements.)

1. What is the source of background radiation?

_____

_____

_____

2. a. How far can beta particles travel through the air without being absorbed? b. What type of radiation from the radioactive sample still reaches the tube?

_____

_____

_____

_____

3. What is the most effective material for absorbing beta radiation?

_____

_____

_____

4. In order to absorb beta radiation effectively, what must be the relative thickness of cardboard, aluminum, and lead?

_____

_____

_____

_____

experiment **69**

Half-Life

PURPOSE: To measure the half-life of a radioactive element.

APPARATUS: Geiger tube and associated counting apparatus; radioactive isotope; sample holder; clock or watch with second hand.

INTRODUCTION: The *half-life* of a radioactive element is the length of time during which half a given number of atoms of the element will decay. In this experiment the activity of a radioisotope will be measured with a Geiger tube over a period of several days. The resulting data will be plotted on a graph and the half-life determined by inspection. Half-life does not depend on the number of atoms in the sample. Consequently, the size of the radioactive sample is not important. It is important, however, to obtain a sample with a half-life of the order of magnitude of a few days (rather than a few seconds or several years).

PROCEDURE: Familiarize yourself with the operation of the Geiger tube and its associated counting apparatus. Set the apparatus in operation and note the frequency of clicks per minute when there is no radioactive material near the tube. This is the background count. Record it in the data table.

Place the radioactive sample in a holder and position it near the Geiger tube. Note the exact time and record it. Mark the position of the tube and sample so that they can be duplicated for future readings. Measure the count for exactly ten minutes, divide by ten, and record.

At the same time the next day, make another count for exactly ten minutes, divide by ten, and record it. Repeat this procedure for about one week.

DATA

Date and time	Count (min^{-1})	Background count (min^{-1})	Corrected count (min^{-1})

GRAPH: Plot a graph of your data, using elapsed time as abscissas and the corrected count/minute as ordinates. Read the half-life from the graph. If necessary, extend the graph to obtain this reading. Compare it with the accepted value of the half-life furnished by your instructor.

QUESTIONS   (Your answers should be complete statements.)

1. Why is it important to maintain the same relative position of Geiger tube and sample in this experiment?

_____

_____

_____

_____

2. Are the clicks of the counting apparatus uniform during the ten-minute counts? Does the rate vary in different directions? Explain.

_____

_____

_____

_____

_____

3. Do you think temperature affects the results? Elaborate.

_____

_____

_____

_____

4. Does the sensitivity of the counting apparatus affect the results? Explain.

_____

_____

_____

_____

experiment 70

Simulated Nuclear Collisions

PURPOSE: (1) To simulate the relationship between the kinetic energy of a nuclear particle and its stopping distance in a detection device. (2) To show that energy and momentum are conserved in nuclear collisions.

APPARATUS: Ring stand, tall, or table support; masonite or plywood, about 30 cm × 40 cm; manila folders; nickels; masking tape.

INTRODUCTION: In a nuclear collision, all or part of the kinetic energy of the incident particle is imparted to a target particle. In particle detection devices such as the cloud or bubble chamber, these energies are proportional to the distances that the particles travel in the device before coming to rest. If the masses of the particles are known, their kinetic energies and their momenta can then be calculated from these distances.

In this experiment nickels will be used to simulate incident and target nuclear particles with equal masses. Manila folders will act as the detection device for the measurement of distances. Kinetic energy will be imparted to the incident nickel by sliding it down an incline. The collisions, both in one and two dimensions, will then be analyzed by means of vector diagrams.

PROCEDURE

1. Energy measurements

Set up the nuclear collision simulator as shown in Figure 70-1. The slope of the inclined path should be about 70°. The masonite or plywood backing is used to make the inclined path as straight and smooth as possible. The curvature at the bottom of the incline should be sharp enough to serve as a good reference for distance measurements, but not so sharp that the nickel will jump when it passes over it. A little practice is required in order to adjust this part of the simulator properly.

Release a nickel near the top of the incline and note how far it slides on the "detector" (manila folders). Mark the initial and final positions of the nickel. Repeat this procedure with several nickels until you have two nickels that slide the same distance when released from the same height. *Be sure to*

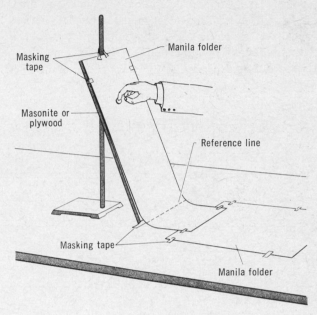

Figure 70-1

use the same sides of the nickels throughout the experiment. You will also find that worn nickels slide better than new ones.

When you have selected a pair of nickels for your final trials, make a series of measurements of the relationship between release height (measured along the incline from the center of curvature at the bottom) and stopping distance on the "detection" paper (also measured from the reference line). Make three determinations for each trial and record the average in the data table.

DATA

TRIAL	Release height (cm)	Stopping distance (cm)
1		
2		
3		

337

2. One-dimensional collisions

Place one of the selected nickels on the "detection" paper a few cm from the reference line. Mark its position by drawing a line around it. Release the other nickel from a previously measured height directly in line with the target nickel. Practice this collision until the incident nickel stops upon impact and the target nickel moves away in the same direction that the incident nickel had before impact.

After the target nickel has come to rest, mark its position and measure its distance from its starting point. Make two more determinations and record the average measurements under Trial 1 in the data table. Conduct two more trials, using different release heights and different positions for the target nickel. Record the results.

Add the second and third distances for each trial and compare that sum with the stopping distance of the nickel in Part 1 that was released from the same height. Record the difference in the data table as the deviation.

3. Two-dimensional collisions

Place and mark the position of a target nickel as before. Release the incident nickel along a line that will strike the target slightly off-center. Both nickels will now move away from the impact in different directions. Mark the positions of the nickels after they have come to rest. Some practice is needed to obtain a collision in which both nickels stay on the "detection" paper during the entire event. When you have obtained a satisfactory trial, draw the lines shown in Figure 70-2.

DATA

TRIAL	Release height (cm)	Distance of target from reference (cm)	Stopping distance of target (cm)	Deviation (cm)
1				
2				
3				

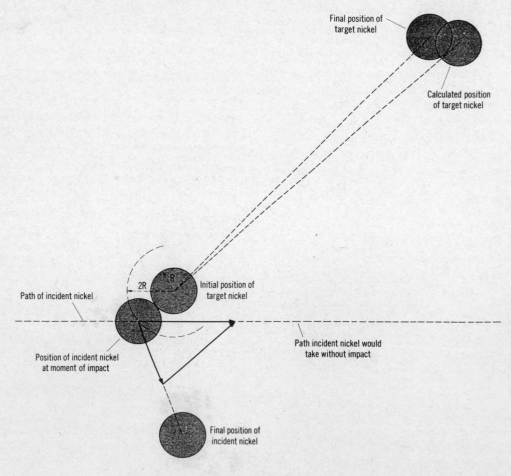

Figure 70-2

To make a vector analysis of the collision, start with the line joining the position of the incident nickel at the moment of impact and the final position of the incident nickel. (The diagram shows how the impact position is found.) Draw a vector along this line equal in magnitude to the square root of this distance. Draw a second vector along the line that the incident nickel would have taken if it had not collided with a target. This vector should be equal in magnitude to the square root of the distance it would have traveled from the point of impact. This distance can be obtained from the data table for Part 1. Now connect these two vectors with a third vector. This vector represents the momentum of the target nickel.

Square the magnitude of the final vector. Starting from the center of the position of the target nickel, draw a line with this magnitude that is parallel to the third vector. The end of this line represents the calculated position of the center of the target nickel after collision. Compare this line with that drawn to the actual position of the target nickel. Record the magnitude and angular differences on your diagram.

GRAPH: Plot a graph of the data in the data table for Part 1, using stopping distances as abscissas and release heights as ordinates.

QUESTIONS   (Your answers should be complete statements.)

1. What is the relationship between the kinetic energies of the incident nickels and their stopping distances in this experiment?

_____

_____

2. In the one-dimensional collisions, how is the stopping distance of the target nickel related to the kinetic energy of the incident nickel?

_____

_____

_____

_____

3. Why does the incident nickel stop at the moment of impact in a one-dimensional collision?

_____

_____

_____

_____

4. Why is the square root of the distance used in making the vector analysis of the two-dimensional collision?

_____

_____

_____

_____

_____

_____

Use of Electric Instruments

A. Introduction.

Meters used for electric measurements are delicate instruments and must be handled with care. The greater the precision of the instrument, the more fragile it is and the more easily it is damaged. Ordinary commercial-grade meters are satisfactory for most laboratory experiments. Laboratory-grade meters may be required for experiments in which a high order of precision is essential.

Recall that the heating effect in an electric circuit increases as the *square* of the current. For this reason, excessive meter currents must be avoided so that the meter movement will not quickly burn out. If a circuit that contains a meter is closed and the meter pointer moves off scale, an excessive meter current is indicated. *The switch must be opened immediately.*

If a meter that is to be used in an electric circuit is a multirange instrument, a meter-protection procedure should be followed. First connect the highest meter range into the circuit. If a readout is not possible, open the circuit and connect the next highest range. Repeat this procedure until a meter readout is possible. Then connect the meter range that displays the readout in the middle region of the calibrated scale.

Meters used in a-c circuits are constructed differently from those used in d-c circuits. *These meters are not interchangeable between the two kinds of circuits.* Multiple-purpose meters, known as *multimeters,* contain several instrument circuits in a single enclosure. Multimeters provide the means for measuring different electric quantities in a circuit. They may be designed to provide both a-c and d-c instrument capabilities.

B. The Voltmeter.

A meter designed to give readings in volts is used to measure the difference in potential between two points in an electric circuit. Thus a *voltmeter is always connected in parallel with the part of a circuit across which the potential difference is to be measured.* Suppose the potential difference across a 1.5-v dry cell is to be measured. A d-c voltmeter with a range of 0 to 3 volts is more suitable than one with a higher range. For a commercial lighting circuit, an a-c voltmeter with a range of 0 to 250 volts provides a midscale readout across the circuit. Assume you have a multirange voltmeter with ranges of 0 to 3 v, 0 to 15 v, 0 to 30 v, and 0 to 150 v, and you have no idea of the potential difference across the circuit in which the meter is to be used. To protect the meter, begin with the highest range in the circuit and then adjust to a range that provides an approximately midscale readout.

Because a voltmeter is connected in parallel with a circuit, it acts to *load* the circuit. The range of the meter together with its built-in resistance determines its sensitivity in *ohms-per-volt.* If the meter has a 0 to 3-volt range and is rated at 1000 ohms-per-volt, it has a loading effect of 3000 ohms when placed across a circuit. In practice, the loading effect should be held as low as possible (the meter resistance should be high compared with the circuit resistance). The meter resistance should be at least 10 times the resistance of the circuit across which it is connected, in order to avoid an excessive change in the circuit constants. The higher the ohms-per-volt rating of the meter, the lower will be its loading effect on a circuit.

C. The Ammeter.

A commercial-grade ammeter may have a movement that consists of a coil pivoted between the poles of a permanent magnet. Because the coil resistance is very low, a shunt is connected across the meter terminals to protect the coil from excessive current. The instrument may have different shunts to provide different ranges.

An ammeter is connected in series in a circuit. If the approximate current magnitude in a circuit is not known, precautions should be taken when connecting an ammeter in the circuit to assure that the current does not exceed the range of the instrument. A rheostat can be connected in series with the meter to reduce the current in the meter. This resistance can then be removed gradually as it is determined that the meter range is greater than the magnitude of current in the circuit.

Suppose an ammeter with different shunts is available for use in the circuit. One shunt provides the meter with a range of 0 to 5 a and the other shunt gives a range of 0 to 25 a. Start with the 25-a range in the circuit. If the current readout is less than 5 a, change to the 5-a range to secure the advantage of a midscale readout. *Never connect an ammeter in parallel with a circuit component or another instrument.*

D. Galvanometers.

A galvanometer is used for detecting feeble electric currents, for determining their directional sense, and for indicating their relative magnitudes. Zero-centered galvanometers are used in Wheatstone-bridge measurements and for testing induced currents. A galvanometer movement is not protected by either a high resistance in series or a low resistance shunt in parallel. Thus, it may be used safely *with very small currents only.* Your instructor may direct that a resistance coil or a shunt be used with the instrument.

E. Rheostats and Resistance Coils.

A rheostat can be used in a circuit to introduce a variable resistance for the control of current, to control the voltage across the load, or to protect certain instruments. It may be calibrated to serve as a measuring instrument.

Although a rheostat, resistance coil, and resistance box (set of resistance coils) are only slightly affected by changes in temperature, excessive heating must be avoided. The maximum current or the power dissipation for such a resistance element is usually given. The terms "rheostat" and "resistance box" are sometimes used interchangeably. However, in this laboratory manual the term "resistance box" designates a calibrated measuring instrument, and the term "rheostat" designates any variable resistance inserted into a circuit to control current. Resistance boxes are designed for use with *small* currents, as in Wheatstone-bridge circuits, and should not be used as current-limiting resistances in general circuit applications where rheostats would be appropriate.

Tables

CONTENTS

Table 1 PREFIXES OF THE METRIC SYSTEM

Factor	Prefix	Symbol
10^{12}	tera	T
10^{9}	giga	G
10^{6}	mega	M
10^{3}	kilo	k
10^{2}	hecto	h
10	deka	da
10^{-1}	deci	d
10^{-2}	centi	c
10^{-3}	milli	m
10^{-6}	micro	μ
10^{-9}	nano	n
10^{-12}	pico	p
10^{-15}	femto	f
10^{-18}	atto	a

Table 2 GREEK ALPHABET

Greek letter	Greek name	English equivalent	Greek letter	Greek name	English equivalent
A α	alpha	ä	N ν	nu	n
B β	beta	b	Ξ ξ	xi	ks
Γ γ	gamma	g	O o	omicron	o
Δ δ	delta	d	Π π	pi	p
E ϵ	epsilon	e	P ρ	rho	r
Z ζ	zeta	z	Σ σ	sigma	s
H η	eta	ā	T τ	tau	t
Θ θ	theta	th	Y υ	upsilon	ü, ōō
I ι	iota	ē	Φ ϕ	phi	f
K κ	kappa	k	X χ	chi	h
Λ λ	lambda	l	Ψ ψ	psi	ps
M μ	mu	m	Ω ω	omega	ō

Table 3 SELECTED PHYSICAL QUANTITIES AND MEASUREMENT UNITS

Physical quantity	Quantity symbol	Measurement unit	Unit symbol	Unit dimensions
		Fundamental Units		
length	l	meter	m	m
mass	m	kilogram	kg	kg
time	t	second	s	s
electric charge	Q	coulomb	c	c
temperature	T	degree Kelvin	°K	°K
luminous intensity	I	candle	cd	cd
		Derived Units		
acceleration	a	meter per second per second	m/s^2	m/s^2
area	A	square meter	m^2	m^2
capacitance	C	farad	f	c^2 s^2/kg m^2
density	D	kilogram per cubic meter	kg/m^3	kg/m^3
electric current	I	ampere	a	c/s
electric field intensity	$\mathscr{E}$	newton per coulomb	n/c	kg m/c s^2
electric resistance	R	ohm	Ω	kg m^2/c^2 s
emf	E	volt	v	kg m^2/c s^2
energy	E	joule	j	kg m^2/s^2
force	F	newton	n	kg m/s^2
frequency	f	hertz	hz	s^{-1}
heat	Q	joule	j	kg m^2/s^2
illumination	E	lumen per square meter	lm/m^2	cd/m^2
inductance	L	henry	h	kg m^2/c^2

(Cont. on next page)

Table 3 SELECTED PHYSICAL QUANTITIES AND MEASUREMENT UNITS (Cont'd)

Physical quantity	Quantity symbol	Measurement unit	Unit symbol	Unit dimensions
luminous flux	Φ	lumen	lm	cd
magnetic flux	Φ	weber	wb	$kg\ m^2/c\ s$
magnetic flux density	B	weber per square meter	wb/m^2	$kg/c\ s$
potential difference	V	volt	v	$kg\ m^2/c\ s^2$
power	P	watt	w	$kg\ m^2/s^3$
pressure	p	newton per square meter	n/m^2	$kg/m\ s^2$
velocity	v	meter per second	m/s	m/s
volume	V	cubic meter	m^3	m^3
work	W	joule	j	$kg\ m^2/s^2$

Table 4 PHYSICAL CONSTANTS

Quantity	Symbol	Value
atmospheric pressure, normal	atm	$1.01325 \times 10^5\ n/m^2$
atomic mass unit, unified	u	$1.6605655 \times 10^{-27}\ kg$
Avogadro number	N_A	$6.022094 \times 10^{23}/mole$
charge to mass ratio for electron	e/m_e	$1.7588047 \times 10^{11}\ c/kg$
electron rest mass	m_e	$9.109534 \times 10^{-31}\ kg$
		$5.4858026 \times 10^{-4}\ u$
electron volt	ev	$1.60210 \times 10^{-19}\ j$
electrostatic constant	k	$8.987 \times 10^9\ n\ m^2/c^2$
elementary charge	e	$1.6021892 \times 10^{-19}\ c$
faraday	f	$9.648456 \times 10^4\ c/mole$
gas constant, universal	R	$6.236 \times 10^4\ mm\ cm^3/mole\ {}^\circ K$
		$8.20568 \times 10^{-2}\ L\ atm/mole\ {}^\circ K$
		$8.3143 \times 10^0\ j/mole\ {}^\circ K$
gravitational acceleration, standard	g	$9.80665 \times 10^0\ m/s^2$
mechanical equivalent of heat	J	$4.1868 \times 10^0\ j/cal$
molar volume of ideal gas at STP	V_m	$2.241383 \times 10^1\ L/mole$
neutron rest mass	m_n	$1.6749543 \times 10^{-27}\ kg$
		$1.008665012 \times 10^0\ u$
Planck's constant	h	$6.626176 \times 10^{-34}\ j\ s$
proton rest mass	m_p	$1.6726485 \times 10^{-27}\ kg$
		$1.007276470 \times 10^0\ u$
speed of light in a vacuum	c	$2.99792458 \times 10^8\ m/s$
speed of sound in air at STP	v	$3.3145 \times 10^2\ m/s$
universal gravitational constant	G	$6.6720 \times 10^{-11}\ n\ m^2/kg^2$

Table 5   CONVERSION FACTORS

Length

$1 \text{ m} = 10^{-3} \text{ km} = 10^2 \text{ cm} = 10^3 \text{ mm} = 10^6 \text{ } \mu\text{m} = 10^9 \text{ nm} = 10^{10} \text{ Å}$

$1 \text{ } \mu = 1 \text{ } \mu\text{m} = 10^{-6} \text{ m} = 10^{-4} \text{ cm} = 10^{-3} \text{ mm} = 10^3 \text{ m}\mu = 10^3 \text{ nm} = 10^4 \text{ Å}$

$1 \text{ m}\mu = 1 \text{ nm} = 10^{-9} \text{ m} = 10^{-7} \text{ cm} = 10^{-6} \text{ mm} = 10 \text{ Å}$

$1 \text{ Å} = 10^{-10} \text{ m} = 10^{-8} \text{ cm} = 10^{-4} \text{ } \mu = 10^{-1} \text{ m}\mu = 10^{-1} \text{ nm}$

Area

$1 \text{ m}^2 = 10^{-6} \text{ km}^2 = 10^4 \text{ cm}^2 = 10^6 \text{ mm}^2$

Volume

$1 \text{ m}^3 = 10^{-9} \text{ km}^3 = 10^3 \text{ L} = 10^6 \text{ cm}^3$

$1 \text{ L} = 10^3 \text{ mL} = 10^3 \text{ cm}^3 = 10^{-3} \text{ m}^3$

Angular

$1° = 1.74 \times 10^{-2} \text{ radian} = 2.78 \times 10^{-3} \text{ revolution}$

$1 \text{ radian} = 57.3° = 1.59 \times 10^{-1} \text{ revolution}$

$1 \text{ revolution} = 360° = 6.28 \text{ radians}$

Mass

$1 \text{ kg} = 10^3 \text{ g} = 10^6 \text{ mg} = 6.02 \times 10^{26} \text{ } u$

$1 \text{ g} = 10^{-3} \text{ kg} = 10^3 \text{ mg} = 6.02 \times 10^{23} \text{ } u$

$1 \text{ } u = 1.66 \times 10^{-24} \text{ g} = 1.66 \times 10^{-21} \text{ mg} = 1.66 \times 10^{-27} \text{ kg}$

Time

$1 \text{ hr} = 60 \text{ min} = 3.6 \times 10^3 \text{ s}$

$1 \text{ min} = 60 \text{ s} = 1.67 \times 10^{-2} \text{ hr}$

$1 \text{ s} = 1.67 \times 10^{-2} \text{ min} = 2.78 \times 10^{-4} \text{ hr}$

Velocity

$1 \text{ km/hr} = 10^3 \text{ m/hr} = 16.7 \text{ m/min} = 2.78 \times 10^{-1} \text{ m/s}$

$1 \text{ m/min} = 10^2 \text{ cm/min} = 1.67 \times 10^{-2} \text{ m/s} = 1.67 \text{ cm/s}$

$1 \text{ m/s} = 10^{-3} \text{ km/s} = 3.6 \text{ km/hr} = 10^2 \text{ cm/s}$

Acceleration

$1 \text{ cm/s}^2 = 10^{-2} \text{ m/s}^2 = 10^{-5} \text{ km/s}^2$

$1 \text{ m/s}^2 = 10^2 \text{ cm/s}^2 = 10^{-3} \text{ km/s}^2$

$1 \text{ km/hr/s} = 10^3 \text{ m/hr/s} = 2.78 \times 10^{-1} \text{ m/s}^2 = 2.78 \times 10^1 \text{ cm/s}^2 = 2.78 \times 10^2 \text{ mm/s}^2$

Force

$1 \text{ n} = 10^5 \text{ dynes}$

$1 \text{ dyne} = 10^{-5} \text{ n}$

Pressure

$1 \text{ atm} = 760.00 \text{ mm Hg} = 1.013 \times 10^5 \text{ n/m}^2 = 1.013 \times 10^6 \text{ dynes/cm}^2$

$1 \text{ n/m}^2 = 10 \text{ dynes/cm}^2 = 9.87 \times 10^{-6} \text{ atm}$

Energy

$1 \text{ j} = 10^7 \text{ ergs} = 2.39 \times 10^{-1} \text{ cal} = 2.39 \times 10^{-4} \text{ kcal} = 2.78 \times 10^{-7} \text{ kw hr} = 6.25 \times 10^{18} \text{ ev}$

$1 \text{ cal} = 10^{-3} \text{ kcal} = 4.19 \text{ j} = 1.16 \times 10^{-6} \text{ kw hr}$

$1 \text{ kcal} = 10^3 \text{ cal} = 4.19 \times 10^3 \text{ j} = 1.16 \times 10^{-3} \text{ kw hr}$

$1 \text{ ev} = 10^{-6} \text{ Mev} = 1.60 \times 10^{-12} \text{ erg} = 1.60 \times 10^{-19} \text{ j}$

$1 \text{ kw hr} = 10^3 \text{ w hr} = 3.6 \times 10^3 \text{ kw s} = 3.6 \times 10^6 \text{ w s} = 8.6 \times 10^5 \text{ cal}$

$1 \text{ w s} = 2.78 \times 10^{-4} \text{ w hr} = 2.78 \times 10^{-7} \text{ kw hr}$

Mass-Energy

$1 \text{ j} = 1.11 \times 10^{-17} \text{ kg} = 1.11 \times 10^{-14} \text{ g} = 6.69 \times 10^9 \text{ } u$

$1 \text{ ev} = 1.07 \times 10^{-9} \text{ } u = 1.78 \times 10^{-33} \text{ g}$

$1 u = 1.49 \times 10^{-3} \text{ erg} = 1.49 \times 10^{-10} \text{ j} = 931 \text{ Mev} = 9.31 \times 10^8 \text{ ev}$

$1 \text{ kg} = 9.00 \times 10^{16} \text{ j} = 9.00 \times 10^{23} \text{ ergs}$

Table 6 NATURAL TRIGONOMETRIC FUNCTIONS

Angle (°)	Sine	Cosine	Tan-gent	Angle (°)	Sine	Cosine	Tan-gent
0.0	0.000	1.000	0.000				
0.5	0.009	1.000	0.009	23.0	0.391	0.921	0.424
1.0	0.017	1.000	0.017	23.5	0.399	0.917	0.435
1.5	0.026	1.000	0.026	24.0	0.407	0.914	0.445
2.0	0.035	0.999	0.035	24.5	0.415	0.910	0.456
2.5	0.044	0.999	0.044	25.0	0.423	0.906	0.466
3.0	0.052	0.999	0.052	25.5	0.431	0.903	0.477
3.5	0.061	0.998	0.061	26.0	0.438	0.899	0.488
4.0	0.070	0.998	0.070	26.5	0.446	0.895	0.499
4.5	0.078	0.997	0.079	27.0	0.454	0.891	0.510
5.0	0.087	0.996	0.087	27.5	0.462	0.887	0.521
5.5	0.096	0.995	0.096	28.0	0.470	0.883	0.532
6.0	0.104	0.995	0.105	28.5	0.477	0.879	0.543
6.5	0.113	0.994	0.114	29.0	0.485	0.875	0.554
7.0	0.122	0.992	0.123	29.5	0.492	0.870	0.566
7.5	0.131	0.991	0.132	30.0	0.500	0.866	0.577
8.0	0.139	0.990	0.141	30.5	0.508	0.862	0.589
8.5	0.148	0.989	0.149	31.0	0.515	0.857	0.601
9.0	0.156	0.988	0.158	31.5	0.522	0.853	0.613
9.5	0.165	0.986	0.167	32.0	0.530	0.848	0.625
10.0	0.174	0.985	0.176	32.5	0.537	0.843	0.637
10.5	0.182	0.983	0.185	33.0	0.545	0.839	0.649
11.0	0.191	0.982	0.194	33.5	0.552	0.834	0.662
11.5	0.199	0.980	0.204	34.0	0.559	0.829	0.674
12.0	0.208	0.978	0.213	34.5	0.566	0.824	0.687
12.5	0.216	0.976	0.222	35.0	0.574	0.819	0.700
13.0	0.225	0.974	0.231	35.5	0.581	0.814	0.713
13.5	0.233	0.972	0.240	36.0	0.588	0.809	0.726
14.0	0.242	0.970	0.249	36.5	0.595	0.804	0.740
14.5	0.250	0.968	0.259	37.0	0.602	0.799	0.754
15.0	0.259	0.966	0.268	37.5	0.609	0.793	0.767
15.5	0.267	0.964	0.277	38.0	0.616	0.788	0.781
16.0	0.276	0.961	0.287	38.5	0.622	0.783	0.795
16.5	0.284	0.959	0.296	39.0	0.629	0.777	0.810
17.0	0.292	0.956	0.306	39.5	0.636	0.772	0.824
17.5	0.301	0.954	0.315	40.0	0.643	0.766	0.839
18.0	0.309	0.951	0.325	40.5	0.649	0.760	0.854
18.5	0.317	0.948	0.335	41.0	0.656	0.755	0.869
19.0	0.326	0.946	0.344	41.5	0.663	0.749	0.885
19.5	0.334	0.943	0.354	42.0	0.669	0.743	0.900
20.0	0.342	0.940	0.364	42.5	0.676	0.737	0.916
20.5	0.350	0.937	0.374	43.0	0.682	0.731	0.932
21.0	0.358	0.934	0.384	43.5	0.688	0.725	0.949
21.5	0.366	0.930	0.394	44.0	0.695	0.719	0.966
22.0	0.375	0.927	0.404	44.5	0.701	0.713	0.983
22.5	0.383	0.924	0.414	45.0	0.707	0.707	1.000

Table 6 NATURAL TRIGONOMETRIC FUNCTIONS (cont'd)

Angle (°)	Sine	Cosine	Tangent	Angle (°)	Sine	Cosine	Tangent
45.5	0.713	0.701	1.018	68.0	0.927	0.375	2.475
46.0	0.719	0.695	1.036	68.5	0.930	0.366	2.539
46.5	0.725	0.688	1.054	69.0	0.934	0.358	2.605
47.0	0.731	0.682	1.072	69.5	0.937	0.350	2.675
47.5	0.737	0.676	1.091	70.0	0.940	0.342	2.747
48.0	0.743	0.669	1.111	70.5	0.943	0.334	2.824
48.5	0.749	0.663	1.130	71.0	0.946	0.326	2.904
49.0	0.755	0.656	1.150	71.5	0.948	0.317	2.983
49.5	0.760	0.649	1.171	72.0	0.951	0.309	3.078
50.0	0.766	0.643	1.192	72.5	0.954	0.301	3.172
50.5	0.772	0.636	1.213	73.0	0.956	0.292	3.271
51.0	0.777	0.629	1.235	73.5	0.959	0.284	3.376
51.5	0.783	0.622	1.257	74.0	0.961	0.276	3.487
52.0	0.788	0.616	1.280	74.5	0.964	0.267	3.606
52.5	0.793	0.609	1.303	75.0	0.966	0.259	3.732
53.0	0.799	0.602	1.327	75.5	0.968	0.250	3.867
53.5	0.804	0.595	1.351	76.0	0.970	0.242	4.011
54.0	0.809	0.588	1.376	76.5	0.972	0.233	4.165
54.5	0.814	0.581	1.402	77.0	0.974	0.225	4.331
55.0	0.819	0.574	1.428	77.5	0.976	0.216	4.511
55.5	0.824	0.566	1.455	78.0	0.978	0.208	4.705
56.0	0.829	0.559	1.483	78.5	0.980	0.199	4.915
56.5	0.834	0.552	1.511	79.0	0.982	0.191	5.145
57.0	0.839	0.545	1.540	79.5	0.983	0.182	5.396
57.5	0.843	0.537	1.570	80.0	0.985	0.174	5.671
58.0	0.848	0.530	1.600	80.5	0.986	0.165	5.976
58.5	0.853	0.522	1.632	81.0	0.988	0.156	6.314
59.0	0.857	0.515	1.664	81.5	0.989	0.148	6.691
59.5	0.862	0.508	1.698	82.0	0.990	0.139	7.115
60.0	0.866	0.500	1.732	82.5	0.991	0.131	7.596
60.5	0.870	0.492	1.767	83.0	0.992	0.122	8.144
61.0	0.875	0.485	1.804	83.5	0.994	0.113	8.777
61.5	0.879	0.477	1.842	84.0	0.994	0.104	9.514
62.0	0.883	0.470	1.881	84.5	0.995	0.096	10.38
62.5	0.887	0.462	1.921	85.0	0.996	0.087	11.43
63.0	0.891	0.454	1.963	85.5	0.997	0.078	12.71
63.5	0.895	0.446	2.006	86.0	0.998	0.070	14.30
64.0	0.899	0.438	2.050	86.5	0.998	0.061	16.35
64.5	0.903	0.431	2.097	87.0	0.999	0.052	19.08
65.0	0.906	0.423	2.145	87.5	0.999	0.044	22.90
65.5	0.910	0.415	2.194	88.0	0.999	0.035	28.64
66.0	0.914	0.407	2.246	88.5	1.000	0.026	38.19
66.5	0.917	0.399	2.300	89.0	1.000	0.017	57.29
67.0	0.921	0.391	2.356	89.5	1.000	0.009	114.1
67.5	0.924	0.383	2.414	90.0	1.000	0.000	. . .

Table 7   TENSILE STRENGTH OF METALS

Metal	Tensile strength (n/m^2)
aluminum wire	2.4×10^8
copper wire, hard drawn	4.8×10^8
iron wire, annealed	3.8×10^8
iron wire, hard drawn	6.9×10^8
lead, cast or drawn	2.1×10^8
platinum wire	3.5×10^8
silver wire	2.9×10^8
steel (minimum)	2.8×10^8
steel wire (maximum)	$32 \ \times 10^8$

Table 8   YOUNG'S MODULUS

Metal	Elastic modulus (n/m^2)
aluminum, 99.3%, rolled	6.96×10^{10}
brass	9.02×10^{10}
copper, wire, hard drawn	11.6×10^{10}
gold, pure, hard drawn	7.85×10^{10}
iron, cast	$9.1 \ \times 10^{10}$
iron, wrought	$19.3 \ \times 10^{10}$
lead, rolled	1.57×10^{10}
platinum, pure, drawn	$16.7 \ \times 10^{10}$
silver, hard drawn	7.75×10^{10}
steel, 0.38% C, annealed	$20.0 \ \times 10^{10}$
tungsten, drawn	$35.5 \ \times 10^{10}$

Table 9   RELATIVE DENSITY AND VOLUME OF WATER

The mass of one cm^3 of water at 4°C is taken as unity.
The values given are numerically equal to the absolute density in g/mL.

T (°C)	D (g/cm^3)	V (cm^3/g)	T (°C)	D (g/cm^3)	V (cm^3/g)
−10	0.99815	1.00186	45	0.99025	1.00985
−5	0.99930	1.00070	50	0.98807	1.01207
0	0.99987	1.00013	55	0.98573	1.01448
+1	0.99993	1.00007	60	0.98324	1.01705
2	0.99997	1.00003	65	0.98059	1.01979
3	0.99999	1.00001	70	0.97781	1.02270
4	1.00000	1.00000	75	0.97489	1.02576
5	0.99999	1.00001	80	0.97183	1.02899
+10	0.99973	1.00027	85	0.96865	1.03237
15	0.99913	1.00087	90	0.96534	1.03590
20	0.99823	1.00177	95	0.96192	1.03959
25	0.99707	1.00294	100	0.95838	1.04343
30	0.99567	1.00435	110	0.9510	1.0515
35	0.99406	1.00598	120	0.9434	1.0601
40	0.99224	1.00782	150	0.9173	1.0902

Table 10 SURFACE TENSION OF VARIOUS LIQUIDS

Liquid	In contact with	Temp. (°C)	Surface tension (n/m)
carbon disulfide	vapor	20	3.233×10^{-2}
carbon tetrachloride	vapor	20	2.695×10^{-2}
ethyl alcohol	air	0	2.405×10^{-2}
ethyl alcohol	vapor	20	2.275×10^{-2}
water	air	20	7.275×10^{-2}

Table 11 MASS DENSITY OF GASES

Gas	(T = 0°C; p = 760 mm Hg) Formula	Density (g/L)
acetylene	C_2H_2	1.17910
air, dry, CO_2 free		1.29284
ammonia	NH_3	0.77126
argon	Ar	1.78364
chlorine	Cl_2	3.214
carbon dioxide	CO_2	1.9769
carbon monoxide	CO	1.25004
ethane	C_2H_6	1.3562
helium	He	0.17846
hydrogen	H_2	0.08988
hydrogen chloride	HCl	1.6392
methane	CH_4	0.7168
neon	Ne	0.89990
nitrogen	N_2	1.25036
oxygen	O_2	1.42896
sulfur dioxide	SO_2	2.9262

Table 12 EQUILIBRIUM VAPOR PRESSURE OF WATER

Temp. (°C)	Pressure (mm Hg)	Temp. (°C)	Pressure (mm Hg)	Temp. (°C)	Pressure (mm Hg)
0	4.6	25	23.8	90	525.8
5	6.5	26	25.2	95	633.9
10	9.2	27	26.7	96	657.6
15	12.8	28	28.3	97	682.1
16	13.6	29	30.0	98	707.3
17	14.5	30	31.8	99	733.2
18	15.5	35	42.2	100	760.0
19	16.5	40	55.3	101	787.5
20	17.5	50	92.5	103	845.1
21	18.7	60	149.4	105	906.1
22	19.8	70	233.7	110	1074.6
23	21.1	80	355.1	120	1489.1
24	22.4	85	433.6	150	3570.5

Table 13 HEAT CONSTANTS

Material	Specific heat (cal/g C°)	Melting point (°C)	Boiling point (°C)	Heat of fusion (cal/g)	Heat of vaporization (cal/g)
alcohol, ethyl	0.581 (25°)	−115	78.5	24.9	204
aluminum	0.214 (20°)	660.2	2467	94	2520
	0.217 (0–100°)				
	0.220 (20–100°)				
	0.225 (100°)				
ammonia, liquid	1.047 (−60°)	−77.7	−33.35	108.1	327.1
liquid	1.125 (20°)				
gas	0.523 (20°)				
brass (40% Zn)	0.0917	900			
copper	0.0924	1083	2595	49.0	1150
glass, crown	0.161				
iron	0.1075	1535	3000	7.89	1600
lead	0.0305	327.5	1744	5.47	207
mercury	0.0333	−38.87	356.58	2.82	70.613
platinum	0.0317	1769	3827 ± 100	27.2	
silver	0.0562	960.8	2212	26.0	565
tungsten	0.0322	3410 ± 10	5927	43	
water	1.00		100.00		538.7
ice	0.530	0.00		79.71	
steam	0.481				
zinc	0.0922	419.4	907	23.0	420

Table 14 COEFFICIENT OF LINEAR EXPANSION

(Increase in length per unit length per Celsius degree)

Material	Coefficient ($\Delta l/l$ C°)	Temperature (°C)	Material	Coefficient ($\Delta l/l$ C°)	Temperature (°C)
aluminum	23.8×10^{-6}	20–100	invar (nickel steel)	0.9×10^{-6}	20
brass	19.30×10^{-6}	0–100	lead	29.40×10^{-6}	18–100
copper	16.8×10^{-6}	25–100	magnesium	26.08×10^{-6}	18–100
glass, tube	8.33×10^{-6}	0–100	platinum	8.99×10^{-6}	40
crown	8.97×10^{-6}	0–100	rubber, hard	$8\bar{0} \times 10^{-6}$	20–60
Pyrex	3.3×10^{-6}	20–300	quartz, fused	0.546×10^{-6}	0–800
gold	14.3×10^{-6}	16–100	silver	18.8×10^{-6}	20
ice	50.7×10^{-6}	−10–0	tin	26.92×10^{-6}	18–100
iron, soft	12.10×10^{-6}	40	zinc	26.28×10^{-6}	10–100
steel	10.5×10^{-6}	0–100			

The coefficient of cubical expansion may be taken as three times the linear coefficient.

Table 15 COEFFICIENT OF VOLUME EXPANSION

(Increase in volume per unit volume per C° at 20° C)

Liquid	Coefficient ($\Delta V/V$ C°)
acetone	14.87×10^{-4}
alcohol, ethyl	11.2×10^{-4}
benzene	12.37×10^{-4}
carbon disulfide	12.18×10^{-4}
carbon tetrachloride	12.36×10^{-4}
chloroform	12.73×10^{-4}
ether	16.56×10^{-4}
glycerol	5.05×10^{-4}
mercury	1.82×10^{-4}
petroleum	9.55×10^{-4}
turpentine	9.73×10^{-4}
water	2.07×10^{-4}

Table 16 HEAT OF VAPORIZATION OF SATURATED STEAM

Temp. (°C)	Pressure (mm Hg)	Heat of vaporization (cal/g)
95	634.0	541.9
96	657.7	541.2
97	682.1	540.6
98	707.3	539.9
99	733.3	539.3
100	760.0	538.7
101	787.5	538.1
102	815.9	537.4
103	845.1	536.8
104	875.1	536.2
105	906.1	535.6
106	937.9	534.9

Table 17 SPEED OF SOUND

Substance	Density (g/L)	Velocity (m/s)	$\Delta v/\Delta t$ (m/s C°)
GASES (STP)			
air, dry	1.293	331.45	0.59
carbon dioxide	1.977	259	0.4
helium	0.178	965	0.8
hydrogen	0.0899	1284	2.2
nitrogen	1.251	334	0.6
oxygen	1.429	316	0.56
LIQUIDS (25°C)	(g/cm³)		
acetone	0.79	1174	
alcohol, ethyl	0.79	1207	
carbon tetrachloride	1.595	926	
glycerol	1.26	1904	
kerosene	0.81	1324	
water, distilled	0.998	1497	
water, sea	1.025	1531	
SOLIDS (thin rods)			
aluminum	2.7	5000	
brass	8.6	3480	
brick	1.8	3650	
copper	8.93	3810	
cork	0.25	500	
glass, crown	2.24	4540	
iron	7.85	5200	
lucite	1.18	1840	
maple (along grain)	0.69	4110	
pine (along grain)	0.43	3320	
steel	7.85	5200	

Table 18 INDEX OF REFRACTION

(λ = 5893 Å; Temperature = 20°C except as noted)

Material	Refractive index
air, dry (STP)	1.00029
alcohol, ethyl	1.360
benzene	1.501
calcite	1.6583
	1.4864
canada balsam	1.530
carbon dioxide (STP)	1.00045
carbon disulfide	1.625
carbon tetrachloride	1.459
diamond	2.4195
glass, crown	1.5172
flint	1.6270
glycerol	1.475
ice	1.310
lucite	1.50
quartz	1.544
	1.553
quartz, fused	1.45845
sapphire (Al_2O_3)	1.7686
	1.7604
water, distilled	1.333
water vapor (STP)	1.00025

Table 19 ELECTROCHEMICAL EQUIVALENTS

Element	g-at wt (g)	Valence (+ ionic charge)	z (g/c)
aluminum	27.0	3	0.0000932
cadmium	112	2	0.0005824
calcium	40.1	2	0.0002077
chlorine	35.5	1	0.0003674
chromium	52.0	6	0.0000898
chromium	52.0	3	0.0001797
copper	63.5	2	0.0003294
copper	63.5	1	0.0006558
gold	197	3	0.0006812
gold	197	1	0.0020435
hydrogen	1.01	1	0.0000104
lead	207	4	0.0005368
lead	207	2	0.0006150
magnesium	24.3	2	0.0001260
nickel	58.7	2	0.0003041
oxygen	16.0	2	0.0000829
potassium	39.1	1	0.0004051
silver	108	1	0.0011179
sodium	23.0	1	0.0002383
tin	119	4	0.0003075
tin	119	2	0.0006150
zinc	65.4	2	0.0003388

Table 20 RESISTIVITY

(Temperature = 20° C)

Material	Resistivity (Ω cm)	Melting point (°C)
advance	48×10^{-6}	1190
aluminum	2.824×10^{-6}	660
brass	7.00×10^{-6}	900
climax	87×10^{-6}	1250
constantan (Cu 60, Ni 40)	49×10^{-6}	1190
copper	1.724×10^{-6}	1083
german silver (Cu 55, Zn 25, Ni 20)	33×10^{-6}	1100
gold	2.44×10^{-6}	1063
iron	10×10^{-6}	1535
magnesium	4.6×10^{-6}	651
manganin (Cu 84, Mn 12, Ni 4)	44×10^{-6}	910
mercury	95.783×10^{-6}	−39
monel metal	42×10^{-6}	1300
nichrome	115×10^{-6}	1500
nickel	7.8×10^{-6}	1452
nickel silver (Cu 57, Ni 43)	49×10^{-6}	1190
platinum	10×10^{-6}	1769
silver	1.59×10^{-6}	961
tungsten	5.6×10^{-6}	3410

Table 21 PROPERTIES OF COPPER WIRE

American Wire Gauge (B&S)—for any metal (Temperature, 20°C)			for copper only	
Gauge number	Diameter	Cross section	Resistance	
	(mm)	(mm^2)	(Ω/km)	(m/Ω)
0000	11.68	107.2	0.1608	6219
000	10.40	85.03	0.2028	4932
00	9.266	67.43	0.2557	3911
0	8.252	53.48	0.3224	3102
1	7.348	42.41	0.4066	2460
2	6.544	33.63	0.5027	1951
3	5.827	26.67	0.6465	1547
4	5.189	21.15	0.8152	1227
5	4.621	16.77	1.028	972.9
6	4.115	13.30	1.296	771.5
7	3.665	10.55	1.634	611.8
8	3.264	8.366	2.061	485.2
9	2.906	6.634	2.599	384.8
10	2.588	5.261	3.277	305.1
11	2.305	4.172	4.132	242.0
12	2.053	3.309	5.211	191.9
13	1.828	2.624	6.571	152.2
14	1.628	2.081	8.258	120.7
15	1.450	1.650	10.45	95.71
16	1.291	1.309	13.17	75.90
17	1.150	1.038	16.61	60.20
18	1.024	0.8231	20.95	47.74
19	0.9116	0.6527	26.42	37.86
20	0.8118	0.5176	33.31	30.02
21	0.7230	0.4105	42.00	23.81
22	0.6438	0.3255	52.96	18.88
23	0.5733	0.2582	66.79	14.97
24	0.5106	0.2047	84.21	11.87
25	0.4547	0.1624	106.2	9.415
26	0.4049	0.1288	133.9	7.486
27	0.3606	0.1021	168.9	5.922
28	0.3211	0.08098	212.9	4.697
29	0.2859	0.06422	268.5	3.725
30	0.2546	0.05093	338.6	2.954
31	0.2268	0.04039	426.9	2.342
32	0.2019	0.03203	538.3	1.858
33	0.1798	0.02540	678.8	1.473
34	0.1601	0.02014	856.0	1.168
35	0.1426	0.01597	1079	0.9265
36	0.1270	0.01267	1361	0.7347
37	0.1131	0.01005	1716	0.5827
38	0.1007	0.007967	2164	0.4621
39	0.08969	0.006318	2729	0.3664
40	0.07987	0.005010	3441	0.2906

Table 22 THE CHEMICAL ELEMENTS

Name of element	Symbol	Atomic number	Atomic weight	Name of element	Symbol	Atomic number	Atomic weight
actinium	Ac	89	[227]	lawrencium	Lr	103	[257]
aluminum	Al	13	26.9815	lead	Pb	82	207.2
americium	Am	95	[243]	lithium	Li	3	6.941
antimony	Sb	51	121.75	lutetium	Lu	71	174.97
argon	Ar	18	39.948	magnesium	Mg	12	24.305
arsenic	As	33	74.9216	manganese	Mn	25	54.9380
astatine	At	85	[210]	mendelevium	Md	101	[256]
barium	Ba	56	137.34	mercury	Hg	80	200.59
berkelium	Bk	97	[247]	molybdenum	Mo	42	95.94
beryllium	Be	4	9.01218	neodymium	Nd	60	144.24
bismuth	Bi	83	208.9806	neon	Ne	10	20.179
boron	B	5	10.81	neptunium	Np	93	237.0482
bromine	Br	35	79.904	nickel	Ni	28	58.71
cadmium	Cd	48	112.40	niobium	Nb	41	92.9064
calcium	Ca	20	40.08	nitrogen	N	7	14.0067
californium	Cf	98	[249]	nobelium	No	102	[254]
carbon	C	6	12.011	osmium	Os	76	190.2
cerium	Ce	58	140.12	oxygen	O	8	15.9994
cesium	Cs	55	132.9055	palladium	Pd	46	106.4
chlorine	Cl	17	35.453	phosphorus	P	15	30.9738
chromium	Cr	24	51.996	platinum	Pt	78	195.09
cobalt	Co	27	58.9332	plutonium	Pu	94	[244]
copper	Cu	29	63.546	polonium	Po	84	[210]
curium	Cm	96	[245]	potassium	K	19	39.102
dysprosium	Dy	66	162.50	praseodymium	Pr	59	140.097
einsteinium	Es	99	[254]	promethium	Pm	61	[147]
erbium	Er	68	167.26	protactinium	Pa	91	231.0359
europium	Eu	63	151.96	radium	Ra	88	226.0254
fermium	Fm	100	[255]	radon	Rn	86	[222]
fluorine	F	9	18.9984	rhenium	Re	75	186.2
francium	Fr	87	[223]	rhodium	Rh	45	102.9055
gadolinium	Gd	64	157.25	rubidium	Rb	37	85.4678
gallium	Ga	31	69.72	ruthenium	Ru	44	101.07
germanium	Ge	32	72.59	rutherfordium	Rf	104	[261]
gold	Au	79	196.9665	samarium	Sm	62	150.4
hafnium	Hf	72	178.49	scandium	Sc	21	44.9559
hahnium	Ha	105	[260]	selenium	Se	34	78.96
helium	He	2	4.00260	silicon	Si	14	28.086
holmium	Ho	67	164.9303	silver	Ag	47	107.868
hydrogen	H	1	1.0080	sodium	Na	11	22.9898
indium	In	49	114.82	strontium	Sr	38	87.62
iodine	I	53	126.9045	sulfur	S	16	32.06
iridium	Ir	77	192.22	tantalum	Ta	73	180.9479
iron	Fe	26	55.847	technetium	Tc	43	98.9062
krypton	Kr	36	83.80	tellurium	Te	52	127.60
kurchatovium	Ku	104	[261]	terbium	Tb	65	158.9254
lanthanum	La	57	138.9005	thallium	Tl	81	204.37

Table 22   THE CHEMICAL ELEMENTS (cont'd)

Name of element	Sym-bol	Atomic number	Atomic weight	Name of element	Sym-bol	Atomic number	Atomic weight
thorium	Th	90	232.0381	vanadium	V	23	50.9414
thulium	Tm	69	168.9342	xenon	Xe	54	131.30
tin	Sn	50	118.69	ytterbium	Yb	70	173.04
titanium	Ti	22	47.90	yttrium	Y	39	88.9059
tungsten	W	74	183.85	zinc	Zn	30	65.37
uranium	U	92	238.029	zirconium	Zr	40	91.22

A value given in brackets denotes the mass number of the isotope of longest known half-life. The atomic weights of most of these elements are believed to have no error greater than ±1 of the last digit given.

Table 23   MASSES OF SOME NUCLIDES

Element	Symbol	Atomic mass* (u)**	Element	Symbol	Atomic mass* (u)**
hydrogen	$^{1}_{1}H$	1.007825	sodium	$^{23}_{11}Na$	22.9898
deuterium	$^{2}_{1}H$	2.0140	magnesium	$^{24}_{12}Mg$	23.98504
helium	$^{3}_{2}He$	3.01603		$^{25}_{12}Mg$	24.98584
	$^{4}_{2}He$	4.00260		$^{26}_{12}Mg$	25.98259
lithium	$^{6}_{3}Li$	6.01512	sulfur	$^{32}_{16}S$	31.97207
	$^{7}_{3}Li$	7.01600	chlorine	$^{35}_{17}Cl$	34.96885
beryllium	$^{6}_{4}Be$	6.0197		$^{37}_{17}Cl$	36.96590
	$^{8}_{4}Be$	8.0053	potassium	$^{39}_{19}K$	38.96371
	$^{9}_{4}Be$	9.01218		$^{41}_{19}K$	40.96184
boron	$^{10}_{5}B$	10.0129	krypton	$^{95}_{36}Kr$	94.9
	$^{11}_{5}B$	11.00931	molybdenum	$^{100}_{42}Mo$	99.9076
carbon	$^{12}_{6}C$	12.00000	silver	$^{107}_{47}Ag$	106.90509
	$^{13}_{6}C$	13.00335		$^{109}_{47}Ag$	108.9047
nitrogen	$^{12}_{7}N$	12.0188	tellurium	$^{137}_{52}Te$	136.91
	$^{14}_{7}N$	14.00307	barium	$^{138}_{56}Ba$	137.9050
	$^{15}_{7}N$	15.00011	lead	$^{214}_{82}Pb$	213.9982
oxygen	$^{16}_{8}O$	15.99491	bismuth	$^{214}_{83}Bi$	213.9972
	$^{17}_{8}O$	16.99914	polonium	$^{218}_{84}Po$	218.0089
	$^{18}_{8}O$	17.99916	radon	$^{222}_{86}Rn$	222.0175
fluorine	$^{19}_{9}F$	18.99840	radium	$^{228}_{88}Ra$	228.0303
neon	$^{20}_{10}Ne$	19.99244	thorium	$^{232}_{90}Th$	232.0382
	$^{22}_{10}Ne$	21.99138	uranium	$^{235}_{92}U$	235.0439
				$^{238}_{92}U$	238.0508
			plutonium	$^{239}_{94}Pu$	239.0522

*Atomic mass of neutral atom is given.

**1 atomic mass unit (u) = $1.6605655 \times 10^{-27}$ kg.

Table 24 FOUR-PLACE LOGARITHMS

n	0	1	2	3	4	5	6	7	8	9
10	0000	0043	0086	0128	0170	0212	0253	0294	0334	0374
11	0414	0453	0492	0531	0569	0607	0645	0682	0719	0755
12	0792	0828	0864	0899	0934	0969	1004	1038	1072	1106
13	1139	1173	1206	1239	1271	1303	1335	1367	1399	1430
14	1461	1492	1523	1553	1584	1614	1644	1673	1703	1732
15	1761	1790	1818	1847	1875	1903	1931	1959	1987	2014
16	2041	2068	2095	2122	2148	2175	2201	2227	2253	2279
17	2304	2330	2355	2380	2405	2430	2455.	2480	2504	2529
18	2553	2577	2601	2625	2648	2672	2695	2718	2742	2765
19	2788	2810	2833	2856	2878	2900	2923	2945	2967	2989
20	3010	3032	3054	3075	3096	3118	3139	3160	3181	3201
21	3222	3243	3263	3284	3304	3324	3345	3365	3385	3404
22	3424	3444	3464	3483	3502	3522	3541	3560	3579	3598
23	3617	3636	3655	3674	3692	3711	3729	3747	3766	3784
24	3802	3820	3838	3856	3874	3892	3909	3927	3945	3962
25	3979	3997	4014	4031	4048	4065	4082	4099	4116	4133
26	4150	4166	4183	4200	4216	4232	4249	4265	4281	4298
27	4314	4330	4346	4362	4378	4393	4409	4425	4440	4456
28	4472	4487	4502	4518	4533	4548	4564	4579	4594	4609
29	4624	4639	4654	4669	4683	4698	4713	4728	4742	4757
30	4771	4786	4800	4814	4829	4843	4857	4871	4886	4900
31	4914	4928	4942	4955	4969	4983	4997	5011	5024	5038
32	5051	5065	5079	5092	5105	5119	5132	5145	5159	5172
33	5185	5198	5211	5224	5237	5250	5263	5276	5289	5302
34	5315	5328	5340	5353	5366	5378	5391	5403	5416	5428
35	5441	5453	5465	5478	5490	5502	5514	5527	5539	5551
36	5563	5575	5587	5599	5611	5623	5635	5647	5658	5670
37	5682	5694	5705	5717	5729	5740	5752	5763	5775	5786
38	5798	5809	5821	5832	5843	5855	5866	5877	5888	5899
39	5911	5922	5933	5944	5955	5966	5977	5988	5999	6010
40	6021	6031	6042	6053	6064	6075	6085	6096	6107	6117
41	6128	6138	6149	6160	6170	6180	6191	6201	6212	6222
42	6232	6243	6253	6263	6274	6284	6294	6304	6314	6325
43	6335	6345	6355	6365	6375	6385	6395	6405	6415	6425
44	6435	6444	6454	6464	6474	6484	6493	6503	6513	6522
45	6532	6542	6551	6561	6571	6580	6590	6599	6609	6618
46	6628	6637	6646	6656	6665	6675	6684	6693	6702	6712
47	6721	6730	6739	6749	6758	6767	6776	6785	6794	6803
48	6812	6821	6830	6839	6848	6857	6866	6875	6884	6893
49	6902	6911	6920	6928	6937	6946	6955	6964	6972	6981
50	6990	6998	7007	7016	7024	7033	7042	7050	7059	7067
51	7076	7084	7093	7101	7110	7118	7126	7135	7143	7152
52	7160	7168	7177	7185	7193	7202	7210	7218	7226	7235
53	7243	7251	7259	7267	7275	7284	7292	7300	7308	7316
54	7324	7332	7340	7348	7356	7364	7372	7380	7388	7396

Table 24 FOUR-PLACE LOGARITHMS (cont'd)

n	0	1	2	3	4	5	6	7	8	9
55	7404	7412	7419	7427	7435	7443	7451	7459	7466	7474
56	7482	7490	7497	5505	7513	7520	7528	7536	7543	7551
57	7559	7566	7574	7582	7589	7597	7604	7612	7619	7627
58	7634	7642	7649	7657	7664	7672	7679	7686	7694	7701
59	7709	7716	7723	7731	7738	7745	7752	7760	7767	7774
60	7782	7789	7796	7803	7810	7818	7825	7832	7839	7846
61	7853	7860	7868	7875	7882	7889	7896	7903	7910	7917
62	7924	7931	7938	7945	7952	7959	7966	7973	7980	7987
63	7993	8000	8007	8014	8021	8028	8035	8041	8048	8055
64	8062	8069	8075	8082	8089	8096	8102	8109	8116	8122
65	8129	8136	8142	8149	8156	8162	8169	8176	8182	8189
66	8195	8202	8209	8215	8222	8228	8235	8241	8248	8254
67	8261	8267	8274	8280	8287	8293	8299	8306	8312	8319
68	8325	8331	8338	8344	8351	8357	8363	8370	8376	8382
69	8388	8395	8401	8407	8414	8420	8426	8432	8439	8445
70	8451	8457	8463	8470	8476	8482	8488	8494	8500	8506
71	8513	8519	8525	8531	8537	8543	8549	8555	8561	8567
72	8573	8579	8585	8591	8597	8603	8609	8615	8621	8627
73	8633	8639	8645	8651	8657	8663	8669	8675	8681	8686
74	8692	8698	8704	8710	8716	8722	8727	8733	8739	8745
75	8751	8756	8762	8768	8774	8779	8785	8791	8797	8802
76	8808	8814	8820	8825	8831	8837	8842	8848	8854	8859
77	8865	8871	8876	8882	8887	8893	8899	8904	8910	8915
78	8921	8927	8932	8938	8943	8949	8954	8960	8965	8971
79	8976	8982	8987	8993	8998	9004	9009	9015	9020	9025
80	9031	9036	9042	9047	9053	9058	9063	9069	9074	9079
81	9085	9090	9096	9101	9106	9112	9117	9122	9128	9133
82	9138	9143	9149	9154	9159	9165	9170	9175	9180	9186
83	9191	9196	9201	9206	9212	9217	9222	9227	9232	9238
84	9243	9248	9253	9258	9263	9269	9274	9279	9284	9289
85	9294	9299	9304	9309	9315	9320	9325	9330	9335	9340
86	9345	9350	9355	9360	9365	9370	9375	9380	9385	9390
87	9395	9400	9405	9410	9415	9420	9425	9430	9435	9440
88	9445	9450	9455	9460	9465	9469	9474	9479	9484	9489
89	9494	9499	9504	9509	9513	9518	9523	9528	9533	9538
90	9542	9547	9552	9557	9562	9566	9571	9576	9581	9586
91	9590	9595	9600	9605	9609	9614	9619	9624	9628	9633
92	9638	9643	9647	9652	9657	9661	9666	9671	9675	9680
93	9685	9689	9694	9699	9703	9708	9713	9717	9722	9727
94	9731	9736	9741	9745	9750	9754	9759	9763	9768	9773
95	9777	9782	9786	9791	9795	9800	9805	9809	9814	9818
96	9823	9827	9832	9836	9841	9845	9850	9854	9859	9863
97	9868	9872	9877	9881	9886	9890	9894	9899	9903	9908
98	9912	9917	9921	9926	9930	9934	9939	9943	9948	9952
99	9956	9961	9965	9969	9974	9978	9983	9987	9991	9996

Equipment and Supplies

Quantities listed are for *12 stations*. For a smaller number of stations the quantities should be reduced accordingly. The *Equipment* list is subdivided for Mechanics, Heat, Sound, Light, Electricity and Electronics, and Atomic and Nuclear Physics. *Supplies* listed cover the complete range of experiments. Equipment needed in more than one section is listed in each section in which it is used. If this list is used for drawing up an order for equipment, please bear in mind that there is some duplication of standard items such as balances, beakers, metersticks, etc. Items marked with an asterisk (*) are new additions.

EQUIPMENT LIST

Mechanics: Experiments 1–18

12	Acceleration board, Packard's
6	Air table
12	Balance, 0.01-g sensitivity
12	Balance, inertia
12	Balance, platform, with set of masses, 1-1000 g
12	Balance, triple beam
36	Balance, spring, 5-n and 20-n capacity
24	Beaker, 100 mL
12	Block, wood, rectangular
12	Car, metal (Hall's car)
24	Cart, dynamics
1 roll	*Cellulose tape
48	Clamp, C, 100-g to 150-g mass
12	Compass, pencil
12	Composition of forces apparatus
12	Crane boom, simple
12	Cylinder, numbered, of brass or aluminum
12	Dry cell, No. 6, or other d-c power source
12 yd	Fishline, nylon, 27 lb test
12	Glass tube, 15 cm × 1.0 cm o.d.
12	Hooke's law apparatus
12	Inclined plane board and table support
6	*Instant camera with stand
12	J-tube apparatus
12	Level, spirit, for Packard's acceleration board
6	*Magnifying lens with scale
1 roll	Masking tape
12	Meterstick
60	Meterstick clamp
12	Meterstick support, knife edge
1 lb	Nails, small
1 box	Paper clips
12	Pendulum bob, metal
12	Pendulum bob, wood

12	Pendulum clamp
12	Protractor
6 sets	Puck, with light, for air table
24	Pulley, single sheave
24	Pulley, 2 or 3 sheaves
12	Pulley, single sheave, with table clamp
12	Ring stand
12	Rubber stopper, No. 6, 1-hole
12	Ruler, metric, 15-cm or 30-cm length
1	*Scale, bathroom
24	Solids, various, with masses less than 1 kg
1	Stopwatch 10-s sweep
1 ball	String
6	Stroboscope
12	Switch, knife, SPST
12	Thermometer, Celsius − 10° to 110°
1 spool	Thread, No. 8
12	Timer, recording with accessories
1 ball	Twine
12	Vernier caliper, metric
60	Weight hanger
12	Weights, slotted, set
2 lb	Wire, annunciator, No. 18

Heat: Experiments 19–27

12	Asbestos board, 30 cm × 30 cm
12	Balance, platform, with masses, or triple beam
1	*Barometer
12	Beaker, 100 mL
12	Beaker, 600 mL
24	Block, metal, assortment of lead, aluminum, brass, and copper
12	*Box, asbestos lined
12	Burner and tubing
12	Calorimeter
12	*Can, small, shiny

12	Charles' law tube
24	Clamp, buret
12	Coefficient of linear expansion apparatus
12	*Dish, large (such as ripple tank)
8 ft	Glass tubing, 6 mm
12	Hydrometer jar
12	*J-tube apparatus
12	Magnifier
12	*Medicine dropper
12	Meterstick
4	Pan, large metal
12	*Pipet, 1 mL
12	Ring, iron
12	Ring stand, tall, or table support
24	Rod for expansion apparatus, assortment of aluminum, brass, copper, and steel
12 ft	Rubber tubing, 3/16 in i.d.
30 ft	Rubber tubing, 1/4 in i.d.
12	Steam boiler, with chimney
12	Stirring rod
24	*Stopper, cork, to fit cardboard tube
12	Test tube, 125 mm × 15 mm
12	Thermometer, Celsius − 1° to 101° in 0.2° div.
12	Tripod for steam boiler
12	Towel
12	*Tube, cardboard, 1 m × 1 cm
1 ball	Twine
12	Water trap
12	Wire gauze

Waves and Sound: Experiments 28–31

6 sets	Coil spring: Slinky and heavy metal coil matched to give approximately equal amplitudes of reflected and transmitted pulses
2 pkg	Corks, student assortment of 100
6	Glass, flat, shaped like a prism or lens, for ripple tank
12	Glass tube, 40 cm × 4 cm i.d.
12	Hydrometer jar
12	Meterstick
4	Paintbrush, 1 in
18	Paraffin blocks or separators
6	Protractor
6	Ripple tank, with attachments to produce linear waves and waves from a point source
12 ft	Rubber hose, 2.0 cm o.d.
1	Sheet of metal, thin, bent in the shape of concave and convex mirrors, and other irregular shapes, for ripple tank
1	Stopwatch, 10-s sweep
6	Stroboscope, hand
12	Thermometer, Celsius − 10° to 110°
24	Tuning fork, assortment of C, E, G, and C′ forks, concert pitch (Physical pitch forks may be used)

12	Tuning fork hammer
1	Vibrograph
12	Vibrograph glass plate or strip of paper
6	Wooden rod, 2.0 cm o.d.

Light: Experiments 32–45

12	Bristol board, white, at least 12.5 × 15 cm
12	Bunsen burner, with hose
12	Calcite (Iceland spar) crystal, approx. 2 cm long
12	Candle, or small illuminated object
12 pkg	Cellophane sheets, for thickness plates
12	China-marking pencil
12	Cobalt glass filter
12 sets	Color filters, various colors
12	*Compass, pencil
1 pkg	Construction paper, containing red, orange, yellow, green, blue, and violet
1 pkg	*Cross-section paper, mm
12	Diffraction grating, transmission replica, about 4×10^3 lines/cm
12	Diffraction slits, single and double, of various widths and spacings
1 ream	Drawing paper
12	Evaporating dish, size 00
12	Ferrotype plate, 5 × 5 cm
12	*Galvanometer (for photoelectric photometer only)
12	Glass bottle, molded
12	Glass plate, 7 × 7 × 0.9 cm
1 gro	Glass plate, 5 × 5 cm
12	Glass prism, equilateral faces, 7.5 cm long and 8 mm thick
1 set	Glass slides, including red, yellow, green, and blue, to fit color apparatus
30	Glass stirring rod
12	Grating holder and support for meterstick
12	Image screen, Bristol board with metric scale
6	Image screen, 25-cm square
1 pkg	Index cards, white
12	Lamp, clear glass, straight filament
12	Lamp, new 40 watt
36	Lamps, assorted incandescent, including 25 w, 40 w, 60 w
12	Lamp socket, standard base, with extension cord and plug
24	Lens, converging, 5-cm focal length, 3.75-cm diam
12	Lens, converging, 10-cm focal length, 3.75-cm diam
12	Lens, converging, 15-cm focal length, 3.75-cm diam
12	Lens, converging, 25 to 35-cm focal length, 3.75-cm diam
12	Lens, diverging, 10-cm focal length,

	3.75-cm diam
12	Lens, diverging, 15-cm focal length, 3.75-cm diam
24	Lens holder, for 3.75-cm diam lens
12	Magnifier
1	Mercury vapor discharge tube and power supply
12	Meter, galvanometer, zero-center
12	Meterstick
24	Meterstick supports
12	Metric scale and slit, for meterstick mounting
36	Metric paper scale, 20 cm, for horizontal use
12	Metric rule, steel, graduated in 0.5 mm
12	Microscope, 16 mm (10X) and 32 mm (4X) objectives (Borrow from Biology Dept.)
12	Microscope objective lens, 32 mm (4X) (Needed only if 16 mm (10X) objective is not divisible)
½ gro	Microscope slides 2.5 X 7.5 cm
12	Mirror, plane, rectangular
12	Mirror, spherical, 4.0 cm, concave and convex, 25-cm focal length
12	Object box, with electric lamp, extension cord and plug
12	Object screen
12	Object screen, black Bristol board with triangular wire-gauze aperture
12	Photometer, Joly or Bunsen, or *photoelectric
12	Photoelastic specimens, U-shaped transparent plastic
1 box	Pins, large, straight
12 pr	Polaroid disks, 4-cm diam, or 5-cm square
1 set	Poster paints, containing red, yellow, green, and blue
12	Protractor
12	Ring stand, rectangular base, with 2.5-cm ring and 5-cm ring
1 box	Rubber bands
12	Ruler, metric
36	Screen holder
1	Tape measure, metric
12	Vernier caliper, metric
2 lb	Wire, copper, annunciator, No. 18
12	Wooden block, rectangular, to support plane mirror

Electricity and Electronics: Experiments 46-67

12	Ampere's law stand
1	*Audio generator
12	Balance, platform, accurate to 0.1 g
12	Balance, triple beam, 0.01 g sensitivity
12 sets	Balance masses, brass, in wood block, 1 g to 1 kg

12	Ball, brass, drilled, 2.54-cm diam
36	Battery, "B", 22.5-v and 45-v terminals (Burgess 5308 or equivalent)
12	Battery, "A", 12 v (Burgess 732 or equivalent)
12	Battery, storage, 12 v, tapped for 6-v service
3	*Beaker, 600 mL
12	Boiler, or large beaker
12	Burner, with tripod
12	*Calorimeter
12	Calorimeter, electric, 2-5 ohm heating coil
12	Capacitor, 25 microfarads, 25 v
24	Capacitor, 50 microfarads, 25 v
1	Capacitor, demonstration, for gold-leaf electroscope
2	*Capacitor, paper, 0.002 μf, 400 v
1	*Capacitor, paper, 0.05 μf, 400 v
1	Capacitor decade box, 0.01 microfarad to 1.1 microfarad in 0.01 microfarad steps
24	Coil, for induction, on brass spool to accommodate 19 X 6 mm bar magnet
12	Coil set, primary and secondary, student type
48	Compass, 1-cm diam
12	Compass, 5-cm diam
6 doz	Connector, brass, double
12	Contact key, or push-button switch
4 ft²	Copper sheet
6 pkg	Cross-section paper, mm
12	Demonstration cell, student form
12	Diode, type 6H6
48	Dry cell, standard No. 6
12	Electric bell, 1-3 v
12	Electrode, carbon, flat, 12.5 X 2 cm
12	Electrode, copper, flat, 12.5 X 2 cm
24	Electrode, lead, flat 12.5 X 2 cm
24	Electrode, zinc, flat, 12.5 X 2 cm
1	Electroscope, gold leaf, demonstration type
12	Electroscope, pith-ball
12	Enameled pan
12	Exciting pad, fur or wool
12	Exciting pad, silk
12	Extension cord, split line, and plug
3	Filter chokes ranging from 8 h to 30 h
24	Flexible leads, short, with insulated alligator clips
12	Friction rod, ebonite or hard rubber
12	Friction rod, glass
24	Fuse, 1 a, standard screw base
12	Fuse block, double, for standard screw base
12	Galvanoscope, 3 windings of 1, 25, and 100 times
12	Lamp, tungsten, 40 watt
12	Lamp, 6 v, No. 40 miniature screw base
12	Lamp, 6 v, carbon, standard base

1	Lamp, 117 v, clear glass, 7–25 watts
12	Lamp base, miniature screw
12	Lamp base, standard
12 pr	Magnets, bar, 19 × 6 mm cross section
12	Magnet, horseshoe, with keeper
12	Magnet core, iron, 10 cm long, 8 mm diam
12	Magnifier, 3 to 10X
12	Meter, a-c ammeter, 0-3 a
12	Meter, a-c milliammeter, 0-50/200/500 ma
12	Meter, a-c voltmeter, 0-7.5 v
12	Meter, a-c voltmeter, 0-150/300/600 v
1	Meter, a-c/d-c VTVM, multirange
12	Meter, d-c ammeter, 0-1/3/30 a
1	*Meter, d-c milliammeter, 0-1 ma
12	Meter, d-c milliammeter, 0-15/50/150 ma
12	Meter, d-c voltmeter, 0-3/7.5/15 v
12	Meter, d-c voltmeter, 0-150 v, 20,000 ohms/volt
12	Meter, galvanometer, zero-center
12	Motor, St. Louis, with 2 bar magnets and electromagnet
12	Octal socket, mounted
1	*Oscilloscope
12	Potentiometer, 4000 ohms, 10 watts
12	Power supply, variable d-c
1	Power supply, 6.3 vac at 0.3 a, 180 vdc at 10 ma
12	Resistance box, plug type, of the order of 100 ohms
2	Resistance box, plug type, of the order of 1000 ohms
1	Resistance box, plug type, of the order of 10,000 ohms
12 sets	Resistance spools, each set consisting of the following spools:
	30 ga – 200 cm – nickel silver
	28 ga – 200 cm – nickel silver
	30 ga – 160 cm – nickel silver
	30 ga – 2000 cm – copper
	(Constantan or German silver may be used instead of nickel silver)
1	*Resistor, 1000 ohms, wirewound
1	*Resistor, 1800 ohms, ½ watt
1	*Resistor, 10,000 ohms, ½ watt
1	*Resistor, 15,000 ohms, ½ watt
1	*Resistor, 22,000 ohms, ½ watt
1	*Resistor, 47,000 ohms, ½ watt
3	*Resistor, 100,000 ohms, ½ watt
1	*Resistor, 1,000,000 ohms, ½ watt
12	Resistor, 10,000 ohms, 5 watts
12	Resistor, 20,000 ohms, 5 watts
12	Resistor, 40,000 ohms, 5 watts
12	Resistor, 80,000 ohms, 5 watts
12	Rheostat, 10 ohms, 25 watts
12	Rheostat, 25 ohms, 25 watts
12	Rheostat, 50 ohms, 25 watts
1	Rheostat, 200 ohms (for galvanometers of the order of 100-ohms resistance), or 500 ohms (for galvanometers of the order of 50-ohms resistance)
1	*Rheostat, 100 ohms, 2 watts
1	*Rheostat, 1000 ohms, 2 watts
1	*Rheostat, 10,000 ohms, ½ watt
1	*Rheostat, 100,000 ohms, ½ watt
1 pkg	Sandpaper, fine grit
12	Stopwatch, 10-s sweep
12	Switch, knife, DPDT
12	Switch, knife, DPST
24	Switch, knife, SPST
12	Temperature coil, copper, approx. 3 ohms
1 pr	Test leads, 1000-v insulation
24	Test lead, with alligator clips
12 pr	Test lead, with pointed probes
12	Test tube, 200 mm × 25 mm
12	Test tube, 150 mm × 18 mm
12	Thermometer, Celsius, − 10° to 110°
1 spool	Thread, silk
12	Transformer, 6-v filament
1	*Transistor, N-P-N (RCA 2N1490 or equivalent)
12	Triode, type 6J5
1 lb	Twine, cotton
12	Wheatstone bridge, slide-wire form
2 lb	Wire, annunciator, No. 18
1 spool	Wire, copper, bare, No. 14
1 spool	Wire, copper, bare, No. 30
1 spool	Wire, copper, insulated, No. 22
2 lb	Wire, copper, insulated, No. 28

Atomic and Nuclear Physics: Experiments 68–70

1	Electroscope
1	Geiger tube and associated counting apparatus
1	Hard-rubber rod
1 roll	Masking tape
12	Manila folder
12	Masonite or plywood, about 30 cm × 40 cm
1 set	Radioactive samples, various
1	Radioactivity sample holder
12	Ring stand, tall, or table support
12	Ruler, metric, 15 cm or 30 cm
1	Stopwatch
20	Sheet, aluminum, 10 cm square, 1.0 mm thick
15	Sheet, cardboard, 10 cm square, 1.0 mm thick
15	Sheet, lead, 10 cm square, 1.0 mm thick
1	Uranium, metal or compound sample
1	*Wool pad

SUPPLIES

1 lb	Acetamide crystals	4 oz	Lycopodium powder
6 lb	Acid, hydrochloric, tech	16 lb	Mercury, tech
7 lb	Acid, nitric, tech	1 lb	Naphthalene crystals
18 lb	Acid, sulfuric, tech	1 oz	Oleic acid
1 qt	Alcohol, ethyl, denatured	1 pt	Rubber cement
12 kg	*Buckshot	4 oz	*Talcum powder, fine
3 lb	Copper sulfate, tech	1 pt	Whiting suspended in alcohol
5 gal	Distilled water ice cubes, as needed		

appendix **D**

Mathematics Refresher

1. Introduction.

The topics selected for this Mathematics Refresher are those which sometimes trouble physics students. You may want to study this section before working on certain types of physics problems. The presentation here is not so detailed as that given in mathematics textbooks, but there is sufficient review to help you perform certain types of mathematical operations.

The following references are given for your convenience in reviewing these topics:

Section 2.3 defines *significant figures* and gives rules for their notation.

Section 2.4 explains the *scientific notation* system.

Section 2.7 describes the *orderly procedure* you should use *in problem solving*, and the proper method of handling units in computations.

2. Conversion of a fraction to a decimal.

Divide the numerator by the denominator, carrying the answer to the required number of significant figures.

Example

Convert $\frac{45}{85}$ to a decimal.

Solution

Dividing 45 by 85, we find the equivalent decimal to be 0.53, rounded to two significant figures.

$$
\begin{array}{r}
0.529 \\
85\overline{)45.000} \\
42\ 5 \\
\hline
2\ 50 \\
1\ 70 \\
\hline
800 \\
765 \\
\hline
\end{array}
$$

3. Calculation of percentage.

Uncertainty always exists in measurements of physical phenomena. Uncertainty exists because measuring instruments have limited precision. The instruments you use in laboratory experiments generally have less precision than those used by the physicists who obtained the "best known values" you find in tables. *The precision of any measurement is limited to the measurement detail which the instrument used is capable of providing.* In physics, an error is defined as the difference between experimentally obtained data and the accepted values for these data. In experimental work, the *relative error* (percentage error) is usually more significant than the *absolute error* (the actual difference between an observed value and its accepted value). Hence, as a physics student you must be able to calculate percentages and percentage errors, and convert fractions to percentages and percentages to decimals.

Example

What percentage of 19 is 13?

Solution
We divide 13 by 19, and multiply the quotient by 100%. A multiplication by 100% does not change the value of the quotient, since 100% actually has a value of 1. When we multiply by 100%, we multiply the number by 100, and affix the % sign to the product: $\frac{13}{19} \times 100\% = 68\%$ rounded to two significant figures.

4. Calculation of relative error.

$$\text{Relative Error} = \frac{\text{Absolute Error}}{\text{Accepted Value}} \times 100\%$$

where the *absolute error* is the difference between the *observed value* and the *accepted value*.

Example
In a laboratory experiment carried out at 20.0°C, a student found the speed of sound in air to be 329.8 m/s. The accepted value at this temperature is 343.5 m/s. What was the relative error?

Solution
$$\text{Absolute Error} = 343.5 \text{ m/s} - 329.8 \text{ m/s}$$
$$= 13.7 \text{ m/s}$$
$$\text{Relative Error} = \frac{13.7 \text{ m/s}}{343.5 \text{ m/s}} \times 100\% = 3.99\%$$

5. Conversion of fractions to percentages.

To convert a fraction to a percentage, divide the numerator by the denominator and multiply the quotient by 100%.

Example
Express $\frac{11}{13}$ as a percentage.

Solution
$\frac{11}{13} \times 100\% = 85\%$, rounded to two significant figures.

6. Conversion of percentages to decimals.

To convert a percentage to a decimal, move the decimal point two places to the left, and remove the percent sign.

Example
Convert 62.5% to a decimal.

Solution
If we express 62.5% as a fraction, it becomes 62.5/100. If we actually perform the indicated division, we obtain 0.625 as the decimal equivalent. Observe that the only changes have been to move the decimal point two places to the left, and remove the percent sign.

7. Proportions.

Many physics problems involving temperature, pressure, and volume relationships of gases may be solved by using proportions.

Example
Solve the proportion $\frac{x}{225 \text{ mL}} = \frac{273°}{298°}$ for x.

Solution
Multiply both sides of the equation by 225 mL, the denominator of x, giving
$x = \frac{225 \text{ mL} \times 273°}{298°}$. Solving, $x = 206$ mL.

A26

8. Fractional Equations.

The equations for certain problems involving lenses, mirrors, and electric resistances produce fractional equations where the unknown is in the denominator. To solve such equations, clear them of fractions by multiplying each term by the lowest common denominator. Then isolate the unknown and complete the solution.

Example

Solve $\dfrac{1}{d_o} + \dfrac{1}{d_i} = \dfrac{1}{f}$ for f.

Solution

The lowest common denominator of d_o, d_i, and f is $d_o d_i f$. Multiplying the fractional equation by this product, we obtain

$$\frac{d_o d_i f}{d_o} + \frac{d_o d_i f}{d_i} = \frac{d_o d_i f}{f} \qquad \text{or} \qquad d_i f + d_o f = d_o d_i$$

Thus, $f(d_o + d_i) = d_o d_i \qquad$ and $\qquad f = \dfrac{d_o d_i}{d_o + d_i}$

9. Equations.

When a known equation is employed in solving a problem and the unknown quantity is not the one usually isolated, the equation should be solved algebraically to isolate the unknown quantity of the particular problem. Then the values (with units) of the known quantities can be substituted and the indicated operations performed.

Example

From the equation for potential energy, $E_p = mgh$, we are to calculate h.

Solution

Before substituting known values for E_p, m, and g, the unknown term h is isolated and expressed in terms of E_p, m, and g. This is accomplished by dividing both sides of the basic equation by mg.

$$\frac{E_p}{mg} = \frac{mgh}{mg} \qquad \text{or} \qquad h = \frac{E_p}{mg}$$

If E_p is given in joules, m in kilograms, and g in meters/second^2, the unit of h is

$$h = \frac{\text{j}}{\text{kg m/s}^2} = \frac{\text{kg m}^2/\text{s}^2}{\text{kg m/s}^2} = \text{m} \qquad \text{Thus } h \text{ is expressed in meters.}$$

10. Laws of exponents.

Operations involving exponents may be expressed in general fashion as $a^m \times a^n = a^{m+n}$; $a^m \div a^n = a^{m-n}$; $(a^m)^n = a^{mn}$; $\sqrt[n]{a^m} = a^{m/n}$. For example:

$$x^2 \times x^3 = x^5 \quad 10^5 \div 10^{-3} = 10^8 \qquad (t^2)^3 = t^6 \quad \sqrt[4]{4^2} = 4^{2/4} = 4^{1/2} = 2$$

11. Quadratic formula.

The two roots of the quadratic equation $ax^2 + bx + c = 0$ in which a does not equal zero are given by the quadratic formula

$$x = \frac{-b \pm \sqrt{b^2 - 4ac}}{2a}$$

12. Triangles.

In physics some facts about triangles are used to solve problems about forces and velocities.

1. *30°—60°—90° right triangle.* It is useful to remember that the hypotenuse of such a triangle is twice as long as the side opposite the 30° angle. The length of the side opposite the 60° angle is $l\sqrt{3}$, where l is the length of the side opposite the 30° angle.

2. *45°—45°—90° right triangle.* The sides opposite the 45° angles are equal. The length of the hypotenuse is $l\sqrt{2}$, where l is the length of a side.

3. *Trigonometric functions.* Trigonometric functions are ratios of the lengths of sides of a right triangle and depend on the magnitude of one of its acute angles. Using right triangle **ABC**, below, we define the following trigonometric functions of $\angle$**A**:

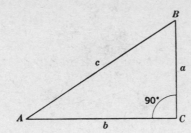

$$\text{sine } \angle \mathbf{A} = \frac{\mathbf{a}}{\mathbf{c}}$$

$$\text{cosine } \angle \mathbf{A} = \frac{\mathbf{b}}{\mathbf{c}}$$

$$\text{tangent } \angle \mathbf{A} = \frac{\mathbf{a}}{\mathbf{b}}$$

These functions are usually abbreviated as sin **A**, cos **A**, and tan **A**. Appendix B, Table 6, gives values of trigonometric functions.

Example
In a right triangle one side is 25.3 and the hypotenuse is 37.6. Find the angle between these two sides.

Solution
Using the designations in the triangle shown above, $b = 25.3$ and $c = 37.6$. You are to find $\angle A$. Hence you will use the trigonometric function $\cos A = b/c$,

or $\cos A = 25.3/37.6 = 0.673$. From Appendix B, Table 6, the cosine of 47.5° is 0.676 and the cosine of 48.0° is 0.669. The required angle is $3/7 \times 0.5°$, or 0.2°, greater than 47.5°. Thus $\angle A = 47.7°$.

Example
In a right triangle, one angle is 23.8° and the adjacent side (not the hypotenuse) is 43.2. Find the other side.

Solution
Again using the designations in the above triangle, $\angle A = 23.8°$ and $b = 43.2$. The function involving these values and the unknown side, a, is $\tan A = a/b$. Solving for a: $a = b \tan A$. From Appendix B, Table 6, $\tan 23.8° = 0.441$. Thus $a = 43.2 \times 0.441 = 19.1$.

4. *Sine law and cosine law.* For any triangle **ABC**, below, the sine law and the cosine law enable us to calculate the magnitudes of the remaining sides and angles if the magnitudes of one side and of any other two parts are given.

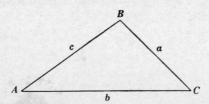

Sine law: $\dfrac{\mathbf{a}}{\sin \mathbf{A}} = \dfrac{\mathbf{b}}{\sin \mathbf{B}} = \dfrac{\mathbf{c}}{\sin \mathbf{C}}$

Cosine law: $\mathbf{a} = \sqrt{\mathbf{b}^2 + \mathbf{c}^2 - 2\mathbf{bc} \cos \mathbf{A}}$

$\mathbf{b} = \sqrt{\mathbf{c}^2 + \mathbf{a}^2 - 2\mathbf{ca} \cos \mathbf{B}}$

$\mathbf{c} = \sqrt{\mathbf{a}^2 + \mathbf{b}^2 - 2\mathbf{ab} \cos \mathbf{C}}$

13. Circles.

The circumference of a circle is $c = \pi d$, where d is the diameter.
The area of a circle is $A = \pi r^2$, where r is the radius.

14. Cylinders.

The volume of a circular cylinder is $V = \pi r^2 h$, where r is the radius of the base and h is the height.

15. Spheres.

The surface area of a sphere is $A = 4\pi r^2$, where r is the radius.
The volume of a sphere is $V = \frac{4}{3}\pi r^3$, where r is the radius.

16. Logarithms.

The common logarithm of a number is the exponent or the power to which 10 must be raised in order to obtain the given number. A logarithm is composed of two parts: the *characteristic*, or integral part; and the *mantissa*, or decimal part. The characteristic of the logarithm *of any whole or mixed number* is one less than the number of digits to the left of its decimal point. The characteristic of the logarithm *of a decimal fraction* is always negative and is numerically one greater than the number of zeros immediately to the right of the decimal point. Mantissas are always positive and are read from tables such as Appendix B, Table 24. Proportional parts are used when numbers having four significant figures are involved. In determining the mantissa, the decimal point in the original number is ignored since its position is indicated by the characteristic.

Logarithms are exponents and follow the laws of exponents:
Logarithm of a product = sum of the logarithms of the factors
Logarithm of a quotient = logarithm of the dividend minus logarithm of the divisor
To find the number whose logarithm is given, determine the digits in the number from the table of mantissas. The characteristic indicates the position of the decimal point.

Example
Find the logarithm of 35.76.

Solution
There are two digits to the left of the decimal point. Therefore the characteristic of the logarithm of 35.76 is one less than two, or 1. To find the mantissa, ignore the decimal point and look up 3576 in Appendix B, Table 24. Read down the *n* column to 35. Follow this row across to the 7 column, where you will find 5527. This is the mantissa of 3570. Similarly, the mantissa for 3580 is 5539. To calculate the mantissa for 3576, take 6/10 of the difference between 5527 and 5539, or 7, and add it to 5527. Thus, the required mantissa is 5534, and the complete logarithm of 35.76 is 1.5534.

Example
Find the logarithm of 0.4692.

Solution
There are no zeros immediately to the right of the decimal point, hence the characteristic of the logarithm of 0.4692 is -1. However, only the characteristic is negative; the mantissa is positive and is found from Appendix B, Table 24, to be 6714. The complete logarithm of 0.4692 may be written as $\overline{1}.6714$, or $0.6714 - 1$, or $9.6714 - 10$.

Example
Find the logarithm of (1) 357,600,000   (2) 0.0000003576

Solution
(1) $357,600,000 = 3.576 \times 10^8$ log = 8.5534
(2) $0.0000003576 = 3.576 \times 10^{-7}$ log = $\overline{7}.5534$, or $0.5534 - 7$, or $3.5534 - 10$